GIOVANNA SCIRÈ NEPI

TREASURES
OF VENETIAN PAINTING
THE GALLERIE DELL'ACCADEMIA

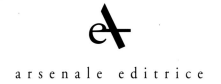

arsenale editrice

Designer
Alberto Prandi

Research Assistant
Roberto Fontanari

Photo Credits
Osvaldo Böhm, Venice
Photographic Archive of the Museo Correr, Venice
Photographic Archive of the Soprintendenza ai Beni Artistici e Storici, Venice
Reale Fotografia Giacomelli, Venice
Francesco Turio Böhm, Venice

Particular thanks go to Filippo Pedrocco
also to Rosa Bagarotto, Alfeo Micheletto, Luigi Sante Savio, Paolo Spezzani, Dino Zanella

This volume has been produced with the collaboration of the
Ente Autonomo Fiere di Verona.

This volume has been typesetted with Bauer Bodoni
designed in 1926

Printing by
EBS Editoriale Bortolazzi-Stei, Verona

First published in September 1991 by
Arsenale Editrice srl
San Marco 4708
I-30124 Venice
Italy

First reprint January 2006

Copyright © 1991 Arsenale Editrice

English translation © 1991 The Vendome Press and Thames and Hudson

ISBN 88-7743-103-2

TABLE OF CONTENTS

LIST OF ARTISTS
BY PAGE

LIST OF WORKS IN SEQUENCE

Please note that these listings are by page, rather than plate number. Then, above all for works of the 14th. and 15th. centuries, and occasionally for later paintings, the support rather than the technique is mentioned as quite often the pictorial medium used is hypothetical. Measurements are given first by height, then by width. Only the latest restorations are mentioned. When there is no mention, the date of the last restoration is unknown.

To Augusto

PLAN OF THE
MUSEUM TODAY

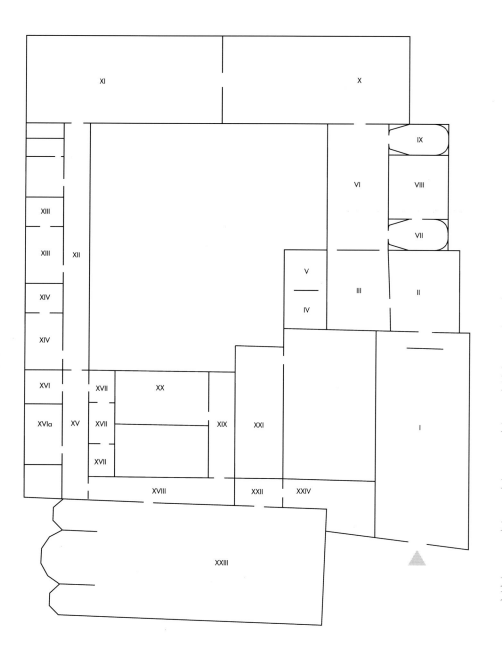

I   Works of the 14th. and early 15th. centuries
II   Large altarpieces of the second half of the 15th. century
III   Connecting wing. Revolving installation
IV   Andrea Mantegna
        Piero della Francesca
        Cosmè Tura
        Hans Memling
        Jacopo Bellini
        Giovanni Bellini
V   Giovanni Bellini
        Giorgione
VI   Paris Bordon
        Titian
        Veronese
        Tintoretto
VII   Lorenzo Lotto
        Giovanni Gerolamo Savoldo
VIII   Girolamo Romani called Romanino
        Palma il Vecchio
IX   Video Room
X   Titian
        Veronese
        Tintoretto
XI   Bonifacio De' Pitati
        Tintoretto
        Bernardo Strozzi
        Giambattista Tiepolo
XII   Marco Ricci
        Francesco Zuccarelli
        Giuseppe Zais
XIII   Titian
        Portraits of Tintoretto
        Jacopo da Ponte called Bassano
XIV   Paintings of 17th. century
XV   Francesco Solimena
        Giovan Antonio Pellegrini
        Giambattista Pittoni
        Giambattista Tiepolo
        Giandomenico Tiepolo
        Gian Antonio Guardi
XVI   Giambattista Tiepolo
        Sebastiano Ricci
XVIa   Vittore Ghislandi called Fra' Galgario
        Giambattista Piazzetta
        Alessandro Longhi
XVII   Canaletto
        Bernardo Bellotto
        Francesco Guardi
        Michele Marieschi
        Giambattista Tiepolo
        Pietro Longhi
        Rosalba Carriera
XVIII   Examples of academicians
        Vitrine with models by Antonio Canova
XIX   Giovanni Agostino da Lodi
        Antonello de Saliba
        Benedetto Cincani called Montagna
        Jacopo Parisati called da Montagnana
XX   Miracle of the Cross Cycle from the Scuola di San Giovanni Evangelista
XXI   The St. Ursula Cycle by Vittore Carpaccio from the homonymous School
XXII   Neoclassical atmosphere
XXIII   The former Church of the Carità
        Work of the Venetian School of 15th. century
XXIV   Already the sala dell'Albergo of the Scuola della Carità
        Antonio Vivarini
        Giovanni D'Alemagna
        Titian
        Reliquiary and portrait of Cardinal Bessarione

A MUSEUM FOR VENETIAN ART

The Gallerie dell'Accademia, the most important collection of paintings in Venice and the Veneto, is also the region's premier museum, born of political necessity as the protector of last resort for the Venetian patrimony of historic art works. Apart from the few pictures assembled over the centuries in the Palazzo Ducale, the Signoria had no repository of paintings comparable to the Statuario Pubblico, the sculpture collection given by the Grimani family in 1593 and exhibited in the Libreria Marciana (now the Archaeological Museum).

When the Venetian Republic collapsed in 1797, as a consequence of the Napoleonic wars, its government departments were suppressed, and its religious houses secularized, by the first provisional administration and its Austrian successor. The process continued apace with the annexation of Venice by the Kingdom of Italy, following the Treaty of Pressburg, signed on December 26, 1805, and by means of successive decrees issued in 1806, 1808, and 1810. Art works from Venetian institutions, if not sold outright or even destroyed for market reasons, were shipped off to the Accademia di Brera in Milan, or used to adorn various viceregal palaces. Some—a very small part of the whole—entered the Accademia di Venezia, an art school established by a decree dated February 12, 1807. Its principal mission was strictly educational, which led to the organization of a school broken up in various faculties and to the creation of an art gallery "for the convenience of students of painting."

In addition, the Accademia had to move, from its original home in the Fonteghetto della Farina at San Marco, to a complex of buildings comprising the Convent of the Lateran Canons, designed by Andrea Palladio in 1561, the Church of Santa Maria della Carità, rebuilt between 1441 and 1452 by Bartolommeo Bon, and the Scuola Grande of Santa Maria della Carità, established in 1260 and the oldest of the Great Confraternities of Venice. Finding these premises ill suited to their functions, the Academicians proposed instead that they be installed in the Convent of Santi Giovanni e Paolo and the adjoining Scuola Grande di San Marco, in the Misericordia complex, or in the Church and Monastery of Santa Caterina. This, however, was not to be.

The task of reconstruction fell to the architect Giannantonio Selva, beginning in 1811. Selva gutted the Church of the Carità and partitioned it vertically as well as horizontally, walling up the Gothic windows and cutting skylights in the roof, so as to create five great rooms on the lower floor for the school and two on the upper floor for exhibition purposes. He then cut a passage through the ground-floor wall of the *sala dell'albergo*, the business center of the old scuola, which created a corridor connecting the various facilities and a short flight of stairs.

The Scuola della Carità underwent fewer alterations, thanks to a major reconstruction carried out during the previous century by Giorgio Massari and Bernardino Macaruzzi. In 1766, the ground-floor entrance hall had been completely rebuilt, at the same time that work was begun on the façade and a new front doorway cut at its center. The old stairs, no longer functional, gave way to a divided flight designed by Macaruzzi and leading to the *sala capitolare* , or "chapter hall" (Room I).

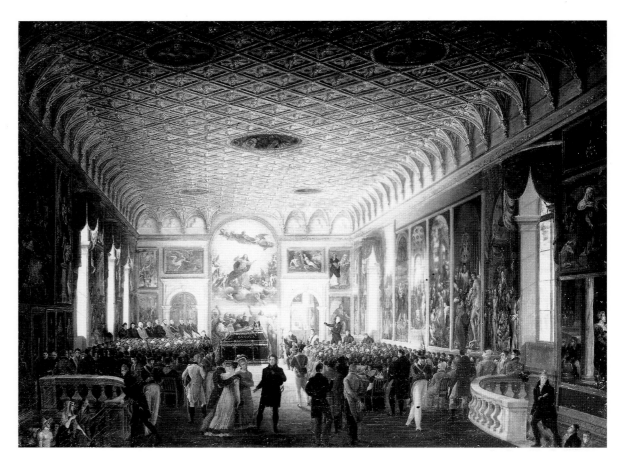

The façade joining church and scuola, as well as providing entrance to the latter, still stands, in red Verona marble embellished with three formerly polychromed statues: Marco Zuliani's *Madonna and Child with Worshipers* (1345), *Saint Christopher*, and *Saint Leonard* (both 1378). Outside in the courtyard can be found the 14th-century doorway, untouched but also unusable and therefore walled up. Above there remains a lunette in polychrome stone bearing the device of the Carità, commemorating the plague of 1348.

The diamond-coffered ceiling and acanthus-leaf cornice of the *sala capitolare* remain in place, complete with the head of an eight-winged angel at the center of each cell. From this unusual bit of iconography came the legend that Ulisse Aliotti, the Scuola's *Guardian Grande* in 1461 and thus probably the sponsor of the work, wanted to be remembered in such guise. Executed between 1461 and 1484 by Marco Cozzi, a member of the confraternity, the ceiling originally held five plaques in high relief devoted to the *Madonna della Misericordia* and symbols of the other *Scuole Grandi*. All were

removed and dispersed in 1814. They have been supplanted, at the center, by a *God the Father*, attributed to Pier Maria Pennacchi and formerly in the Venetian Oratory of San Girolamo, and, elsewhere, by images of four Prophets by Domenico Campagnola (but also attributed to Stefano dell'Arzere) from the Scuola della Madonna in Padua. In his *Notatori* Pietro Gradenigo recorded that on March 30, 1756, the ceiling was entirely gilded in fine gold "at great expense." Restoration during the last several years has now recaptured the original coloring of the blue background as well as the figures in the surrounding vaults. The *sala dell'albergo* also retains its gilded polychrome ceiling, made of paste and carved wood, with a *God the Father* at the center (probably moved there in the late 15th century from an earlier ceiling, destroyed by fire, in the *sala capitolare*) and images of the four Evangelists in the corners.

The modifications to the convent, a structure already much altered following a fire in 1630, were not at first substantial. Selva treated the architecture with respect, but provided more generous exhibition space by

walling up the arcades of the Ionic loggia and leaving open only half-lunettes for light. He then repartitioned the top floor into an engraving/etching atelier and accommodations for teachers.

The Accademia's original collection of painting and sculpture had accumulated from gifts and *pièces de réception*. Now came the works adorning the new premises, particularly the Scuola and the church, and those plaster casts from the antique or from original clay models assembled by a passionate collector, *abate* Filippo Farsetti, and not sold by his great-nephew Anton Francesco to Tsar Paul I of Russia. These had been acquired for the Accademia by the Austrian administration in 1805.

Meanwhile, the Accademia's collection had suffered from the dilatory habits of its first curator, Pietro Edwards. The English-born Edwards had moved to Venice for religious as well as political reasons and had attended the Accademia, eventually becoming its president. Responsible for the public painting collection from 1778 until the fall of the Republic, he determined to become the faithful servant of each successive administration, which, despite his protestations of honor and integrity, placed him in an ambivalent position that could only compromise the interests of the Gallerie. As a result, major works left Venice for Milan, causing important series and ensembles to be broken up between the two cities. Nevertheless, when Ferrarese Count Leopoldo Cicognara became president of the Accademia he set about vigorously to recover the most significant of the dispersed works, now the property of the State, and to restore them to place. Meanwhile, in January 1812, Edwards compiled the first catalogue of the Gallerie's holdings, which came to some two hundred entries. In the same year the Gallerie acquired from the Viceroy, Eugène de Beauharnais, through the Grimani brothers, Bonifacio Pitati's *Parable of the Rich Man.* In 1815-16, for reasons of conservation, Cicognara arranged for three great paintings by Giovanni Bellini, Carpaccio, and Basaiti to enter the Gallerie from the Church of San Giobbe, followed by Titian's great *Assumption* from the Frari. Thanks to the active assistance of the Italian Neoclassical sculptor Antonio Canova, many works of art carried off by Napoleon to Paris were returned to Venice. As a consequence, the Gallerie received Paris Bordon's *Presenting the Ring to the Doge,* Tintoretto's *Saint Mark Freeing the Slave* from the Scuola di San Marco (which in the meantime had been suppressed), and, from San Zaccaria, Paolo Veronese's *Feast in the House of Levi* and *Madonna and Child Enthroned.*

These capital acquisitions may have consoled Cicognara for the daily attrition of Venice's privately owned artistic legacy, which he attempted to protect by promoting laws that, as elsewhere in Italy, would control the export of art works. But such legislation, even when finally enacted in 1817, took little or no account of the inexhaustible liquidity and resourcefulness of the art market. On August 10, 1817, the Gallerie opened to the public for a brief period, and with great success. The appearance of Room I is rendered with almost photographic

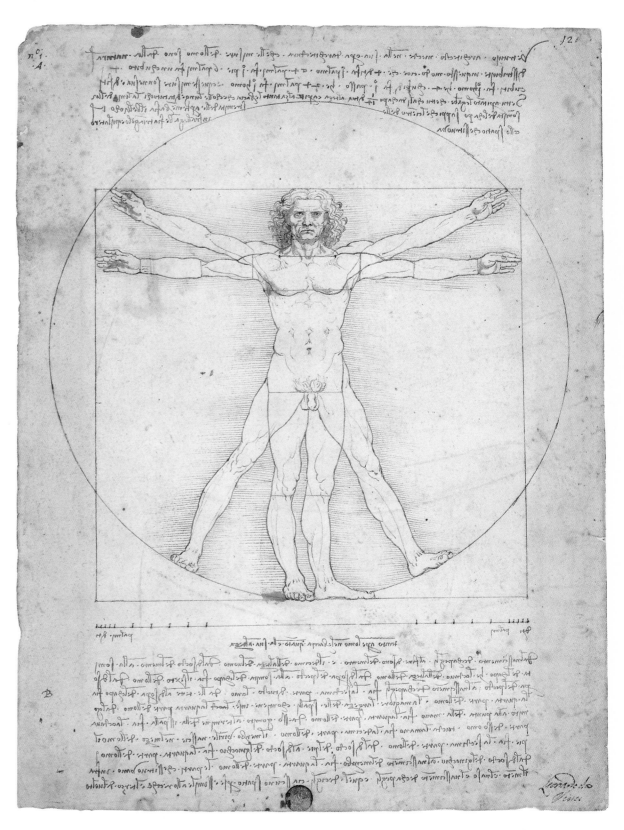

precision in a painting by Giuseppe Borsato, executed in 1822 for the Canova commemoration (fig. 1).

In 1822, *abate* Luigi Celotti, predatory collector and opportunistic dealer, arranged for the Gallerie to frustrate the aims of the Brera and acquire the distinguished collection of drawings assembled by Giuseppe Bossi. A man of enlightened culture and friendly with the aristocracy no less than with the

intelligentsia, and himself a painter, Bossi had served as secretary of the Accademia di Brera from 1801 to 1807. He worked to rebuild that institution in keeping with policies both ethical and civic (set by Parini), paying particular attention to its picture collection. Bossi enriched the Brera with many paintings from securalized religious foundations, and thereby saved them from removal beyond the Alps. He also obtained not a

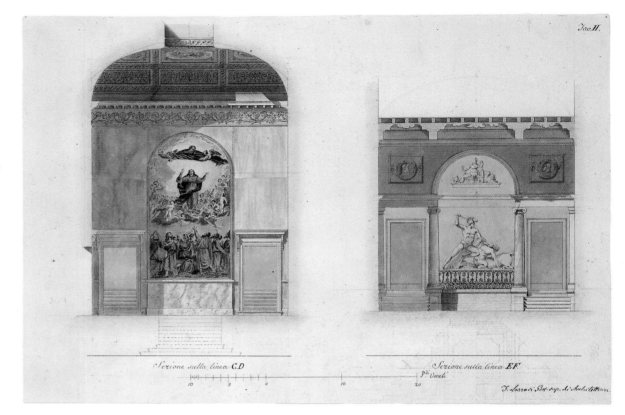

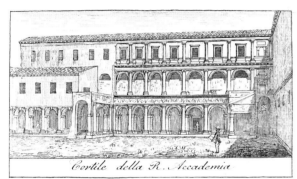

Cortile della R. Accademia

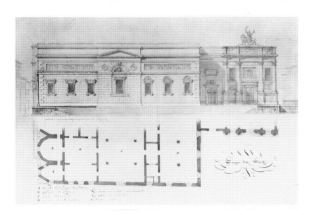

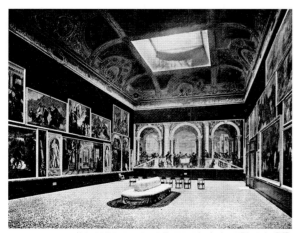

few masterpieces, such as Raphael's *Marriage of the Virgin*. His own outstanding collection of some 3,000 drawings included not only sheets by Leonardo and his circle (among them the Renaissance master's *Vitruvian Man* [fig. 2] and preliminary sketches for his *Battle of Anghiari*) but also 16th- and 17th-century works of the Bolognese, Roman, Tuscan, Ligurian, and Lombard schools, not to mention drawings from Germany, France, and Flanders. In 1824, again through Celotti, Venice's Gallerie acquired another large body of drawings, this time some 602 sheets by the Italian architect Giacomo Quarenghi, long active in Russia at the court of Empress Catherine II. Through drawings, therefore, students in Venice could gain a less provincial sense of the figurative arts, embracing all of Italian and European culture, than would have been had from the painting collections, limited as these almost entirely were to the art of Venice itself. Indeed, the Gallerie made a serious attempt throughout the 19th century to overcome their geographical limitations. By the end of this period, however, the Gallerie's role as a teaching institution had so diminished that the broadening effort did not receive the respect it merited.

The Gallerie's collections now began to be enhanced as well by private gifts. The year 1816 brought the Girolamo Molin bequest, which included triptychs by Alberegno and Jacobello del Fiore, Lorenzo Veneziano's *Annunciation*, and Giambono's *Coronation of the Virgin in Paradise*. The younger brother of Antonio Canova contributed two large plasters for the master's *Theseus* and *Hercules*. In 1833, Felicita Renier made a will that became effective in 1850, endowing the Gallerie with such masterpieces as Piero della Francesca's *Saint Jerome with a Donor*, Giovanni Bellini's *Madonna and Child between Two Saints* and *Madonna and Child between Saint Catherine and the Magadalene*, and the *Pietà* of Cima da Conegliano. Then, in 1838, Girolamo Contarini made the Gallerie the beneficiary of his splendid collection of no fewer than 188 paintings, among them the *Madonna of the Saplings*, *Madonna and Standing Child Blessing*, and a suite of *Allegories*, all by Giovanni Bellini, together with six scenes of Venetian life by Pietro Longhi. By its very size, however, this increase in holdings made the chronic problem of inadequate space even more acute. Only in 1819, after the death of Selva, did the

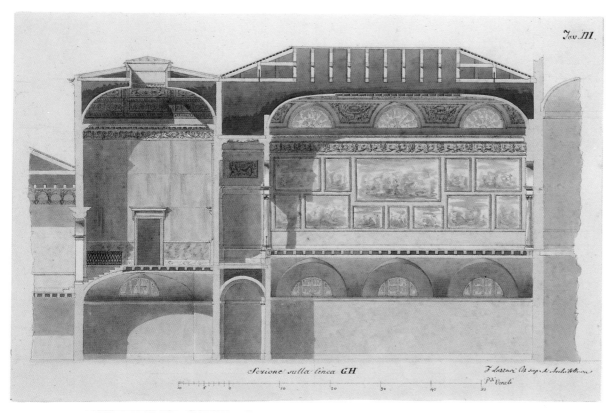

additional floor he had planned come into being, built by his pupil Francesco Lazzari.

In 1835, Lazzari wrote at length of his accomplishments, both real and projected, as well as of his regret at having to tamper with the Palladian structure (fig. 3). Work on the new exhibition halls adjoining the convent to the south had begun in 1820 and finished in 1828. Room I opened right away, and when Room II opened in 1834, it displayed on the end wall, as it does today, Veronese's *Feast in the House of Levi* (fig. 5). Between the two great galleries—now lit from above, since the lateral windows had been walled up one by one over the years—Lazzari placed four large columns of Greek marble brought from the Scuola Grande di Santa Maria della Misericordia. From 1821 to about 1823, the architect oversaw the layout of the little circular entrance to the *sala dell'albergo*, which he decorated with sculptures and bas-reliefs by two Canovians, De Martini and Rinaldi. In 1829, he initiated the reconstruction of the convent, leaving the façade untouched, but demolishing the corner arches of Palladio's courtyard, while adding one more bay to the six left intact. Lazzari also reclaimed the Ionic

colonnade (see fig. 3), formerly walled up to create more hanging space, so that both it and the Doric portico could be glassed in, the better to reduce humidity and thus improve the conservation of the art works. Between 1824 and 1830 the architect reworked the façade, replacing the emblems of the Carità with those of the Accademia and piercing the niches to make windows. Before all this could be undertaken, many sketches were made— today preserved in the Museo Correr (fig. 4)—and prolonged discussions held between the Accademia and the government about whether to crown the façade with a Minerva or a lion. The dispute ended with the choice of Antonio Giaccarelli's *Minerva Seated on the Adriatic Lion* (fig. 9), later moved to the Public Gardens. Fortunately, a number of projects that would have hidden the side of the Church of the Carità and its little Gothic façade behind a new, modern front never progressed beyond the planning stage.

In these same years Lazzari busied himself promoting further renovations, inspired by his friend Quarenghi, at the Scuola della Carità, all of which would have allowed a more logical progression through the galleries (fig. 6) and provided an appropriate setting for the

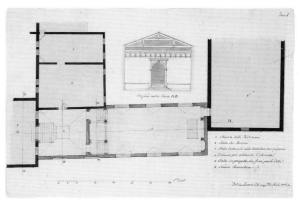

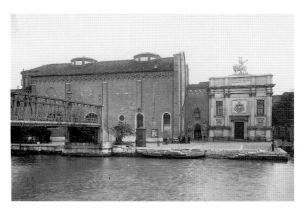

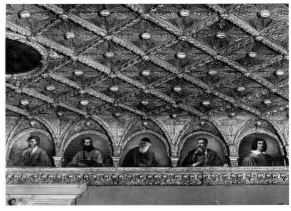

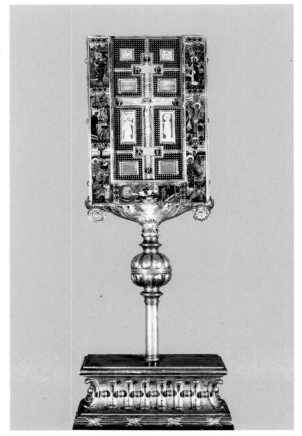

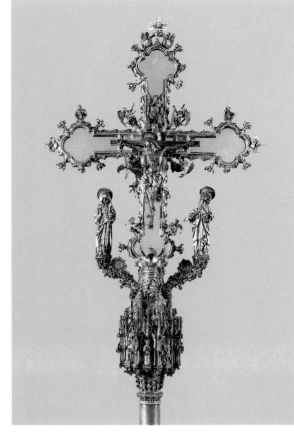

Assumption and the *Theseus* (figs. 7, 8). The government, unsympathetic to yet more large expenditures, refused the lot.

In the lunettes above the cornice of Room I were placed portraits of Venice's most important artists (fig. 10), all executed by the Accademia's own painters and students. Removed for safekeeping during World War II, the portraits have remained in storage ever since. One may assume that within the same period as the work on the lunettes the plans drawn up by Combatti in 1846-47 were implemented, resulting in a subdivision of the *sala*'s great space so as to provide the Gallerie with an entrance independent of the Accademia.

As already noted, the Contarini collection entered the Accademia in 1838. To house it, certain alterations, completed in 1841, had to be effected in areas corresponding to the present Room XXI, where the *Saint Ursula Cycle* is exhibited, and in the adjoining corridor (Room XIX).

Finally, a connecting wing was approved on February 1, 1845, which within two years brought into being the so-called *nuovissime* ("newest") galleries. Haste, however, left them in need of

restoration as early as 1856 and, despite the good offices of President Pietro Selvatico, not ready to reopen until 1859. In 1856, Emperor Franz Josef, although resistant to more comprehensive proposals, did allow the Gallerie to acquire certain key items from the Galleria Manfrin, including Nicolò di Pietro's *Madonna and Child*, Andrea Mantegna's *Saint George*, and Giorgione's *Old Woman*.

Over the next few years the Accademia underwent its most profound changes, in the wake of Venice's incorporation into the new, independent Kingdom of Italy. The institution received a fresh charter by royal decrees dated September 8, 1878, and November 9, 1879. Then, on March 30, 1882, following a short period under the President of the Fellows of the Accademia, the Gallerie were finally emancipated from both the school and the Accademia. Still, interference from without abated only when the Cultural Ministry made Adolfo Venturi and Giulio Cantalamessa responsible for reorganizing the collections, but even then the Gallerie did not gain true autonomy until March 1906. In 1886, a radical restructuring got under way with

Giacomo Franco's new setting for Titian's *Assumption* in Room II. Cantalamessa renewed the process in 1895, for the purpose of "bringing into proximity works that belong together because they come from related schools, because their artists have influenced each other, because they share certain ideals, because they are contemporaries...." Moreover, the new director intended "to reorder the Museum so as to highlight its rare and precious homogeneity...," and at the same time "not to lose sight of the concept of historic continuity, but rather to stress it as much as possible." The revisions proved radical indeed, despite the immovability of certain paintings, such as Titian's *Assumption* and Veronese's *Feast in the House of Levi*, the sheer size of yet other works, and the limitations of the available space. Eliminating contemporary painting, relocating plaster casts to the school as instructional materials, and giving the Archaeological Museum several bronzes and terra-cottas, which eventually wound up in the Galleria Franchetti at the Ca' d'Oro, Cantalamessa found it possible to attempt, for the first time, some kind of chronological arrangement.

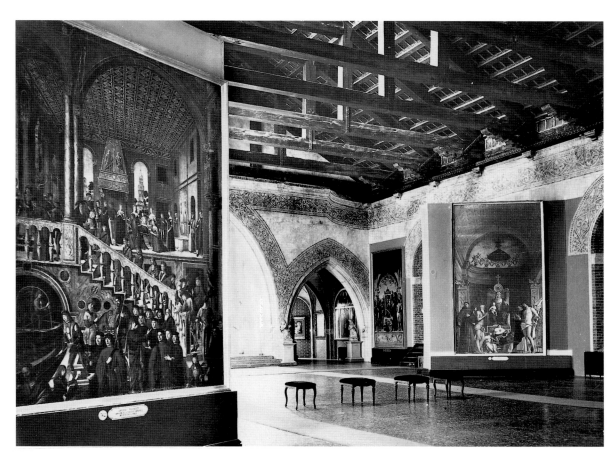

13. The Church of the Carità as reconstructed by Gino Fogolari.

14. The room designed by Fogolari for Carpaccio's *Saint Ursula Cycle*.

Fifteenth-century paintings, which, simply because of their dimenions, had been hung next to Veronese's *Feast in the House of Levi*, could now be moved into two of the rooms in the church and arranged by period, giving effect to a policy that remained undisturbed until the most recent round of reorganization. The polygonal space created for the *Saint Ursula Cycle* did not so much reproduce the original setting (the exact character of which no one knew for sure, in any event) as suggest the continuous nature of the pictorial narrative. Encouraged by a certain segment of public opinion, Cantalamessa decided to return Titian's *Presentation of the Virgin in the Temple* to the *sala dell'albergo*, whence it had been moved in 1828. The director reasoned, with some justice, that the picture should be seen under the same low lighting for which the artist had painted it. Cantalamessa also replaced the room's 18th-century benches with a 16th-century piece acquired for the purpose. By such means did the Gallerie more and more assume the characteristics of a true art gallery rather than a run-of-the-mill museum, even while preserving as well as emphasizing their inherent quality as a uniquely Venetian institution.

Meanwhile, the collections could only be enhanced by such accessions as Cosmè Tura's *Madonna*, Crivelli's *Saints Peter and Paul*, the *Holy Family* of Palma Vecchio, Veronese's *Hercules and Ceres*, and two youthful works by Giovanni Battista Tiepolo.

In 1906, Gino Fogolari succeeded Cantalamessa, with whom he had worked closely as supervisor. Always a vigorous leader, Fogolari reigned over the Gallerie until his death early in 1941. Instead of rebuilding, he concentrated on vastly increasing the Gallerie's patrimony of paintings and graphics. Among many shrewd acquisitions, some of the most significant were Pier Maria Pennacchi's *Dormition of the Virgin*, the organ shutters from the Church of Santa Maria dei Miracoli, Romanino's *Deposition*, Luca Giordano's *Crucifixion of Saint Peter*, the *Feast in the House of Simon* by Bernardo Strozzi, the *Portrait of Count Giovanni Battista Vailetti* by Fra Galgario, Paolo Veneziano's *Madonna*, and a sketch by Tiepolo for the *Exaltation of the Holy Cross*.

World War I checked the growth of the

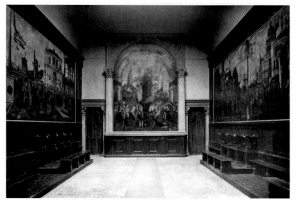

Gallerie's collections; indeed, it required consigning some 200 objects to the Convent of San Salvi in Florence for safekeeping. After 1918, Titian's *Assumption* was returned to its original location on the high altar of the Basilica of Santa Maria dei Frari. By way of compensation, however, the Gallerie recovered a number of art works carried off to Austria between 1816 and 1838. The most significant of these were a 14th/15th-century Veneto-Byzantine reliquary, given to the Scuola Grande della Carità by Cardinal Bessarion in 1472 (fig. 11), and the rock-crystal-and-silver cross once in the Scuola di San Teodoro (fig. 12), both of which had found their way to Vienna through the nefarious dealings of Celotti.

15. Room V as reconstructed by Fogolari.

16. A room devoted to 18th-century easel paintings as laid out by Fogolari.

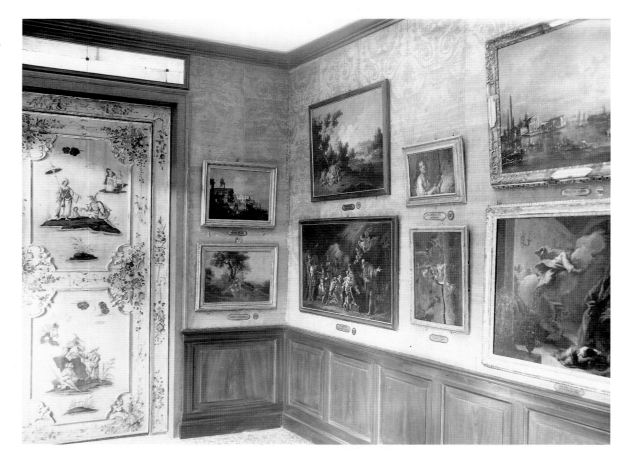

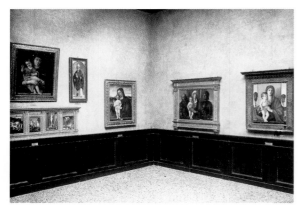

Between 1921 and 1923, Fogolari reorganized the Gallerie anew, at the same time that, aided by architect Aldo Scolari, he also restored the great interior space of the church, with its apsidal chapels, beamed ceiling, and Gothic side windows. This gallery would now house the *Miracles of the Cross Cycle* (fig. 13), while, somewhat more arbitrarily, the canvases of the *Saint Ursula Cycle* went into the small gallery where they remain today (Room XXI; fig. 14). This represented a step backward from Cantalamessa's perceptive setting, a situation in no way helped by intrusively alien choirstalls and settles scarcely less suitable than imitations. The small galleries set aside for 18th-century easel paintings (Room XVII) were given a

period "feeling" with reproduction fabrics and a door that, while historically authentic, looked out of context (fig. 16).

In 1912, Fogolari obtained 18th-century doorways, painted by Pietro Scalvini and Saverio Gandini, probably for some palazzo in Brescia, and placed them in the Palladian corridor, where they remain. Rustic *boiseries*, reflecting a widespread taste of the time, ran beneath the collection along the lower part of the gallery walls (fig. 15). The "new order," no less than Cantalamessa's, banned 19th-century art works, almost all of which Fogolari consigned to the Galleria d'Arte Moderna in the Ca' Pesaro, while dispatching foreign paintings to the Ca' d'Oro. In 1932, Room VII (in the "newest" wing, picturesquely hung in green velvet) became the setting for Giorgione's *Tempest*, acquired the year before, as well as for a fragment of a *Nude* from the Fondaco dei Tedeschi, now in the Galleria Franchetti at the Ca' d'Oro.

When Vittorio Moschini became director in 1941, he immediately acknowledged the need for more up-to-date museological practices, such as had already wrought profound changes in

many European and American museums. An uncommonly intuitive and cultivated man, Moschini proved well qualified to introduce an intelligent program of modernization. During the war years, he, together with the architect Carlo Scarpa, worked out a carefully considered plan of reorganization, designed to prune the collections and create a more logical progress through the galleries. The plan entailed the construction of a large new building, on an expropriated site towards the Zattere. Connected to the 18th-century structures by an overpass, it would have housed the collections' historic core.

At the end of the war, however, the urgent need to rebuild other Italian museums precluded so vast an undertaking. At the same time, to reinstall as before those items now redeemed from wartime storage did not seem practicable. Moreover, a violent explosion had caused great damage to the Gallerie, making it necessary to launch a major restoration and reconstruction program, all of which marked "the end of a museological paradigm that, almost without exception, had obdurately resisted change from the

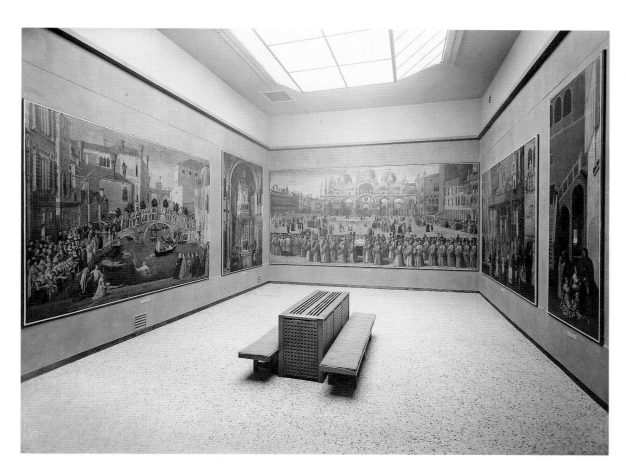

17. The gallery devoted to the *Miracle of the Cross Cycle* as arranged by Carlo Scarpa.

18. The same room in its definitive setting by Carlo Scarpa.

reign of King Umberto to the fall of the monarchy."

The Moschini regime had to overcome such obstacles as inadequate space, the need to air-condition the museum's entire monumental complex, the pressure to reopen the Gallerie as soon as possible, and, of course, the lack of funds. In letter after unanswered letter asking Scarpa to hasten the work, or to deliver drawings, Moschini nonetheless implored: "I urge on you simplicity . . . and economy."

The first phase, begun in 1945, was completed in 1948, at which time carpets and paneling, gloomy styles and color schemes gave way to plastered surfaces with unusual textures and clear, neutral tones. In a letter to the Cultural Ministry, Moschini wrote:

We have given much thought to the freshly plastered walls and even more to their coloring. For the walls, we have alternated smooth surfaces with rougher ones made with coarser sand. So too with the colors; we avoided glue-based paints, because of their density, in favor of fluid casein colors or those thickened with oil and gesso and finished with powdered talc. Even the mode of applying the colors was important for producing lively surfaces. Because sponges leave regular tracks, we generally avoided them and, for the sake of fluid colors, had them sprayed on irregularly, or slathered on by hand, or yet glazed by means of rags.

The paintings, rigorously selected and placed at suitable distances from one another, would no longer appear in frames not appropriate to them, hang on temporary panels, or be encapsulated in "corridors of circular emptiness." Rather, they would greet the viewer at eye level in stylistically as well as chronologically coherent groups, except in a few instances, where a complex arrangement, spatial limitation, or the size of individual works dictated otherwise.

One key objective was to remedy the illogical transition from the Primitives in Room I to the late-16th-century works in Room II, by replacing the latter with several important 15th-century paintings. The large Titians, Tintorettos, and Veroneses appeared together in Rooms X and XI (reopened in September 1946), along with the works of Padovanino, Ricci, and Pittoni

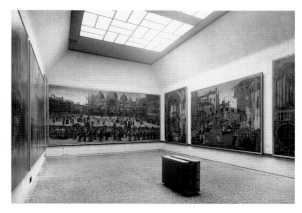

positioned somewhat apart. Room XI especially, its walls covered in coarse gray fabric, contained masterpieces from the 17th and 18th centuries that, owing to their size, proved hard to relocate; thus, they shared gallery space—albeit segregated by partitions covered in the same fabric—with the 16th-century paintings. Beyond this provisional compromise, Scarpa never succeeded in moving towards a more definitive solution to the problem of how to exhibit what were some very important works. Under an ivory ceiling, the walls of Room X received a coat of light-gray paint, as well as a thin guardrail of black iron, a feature that would subsequently be extended to all the Gallerie's exhibition spaces. However, in 1955-56,

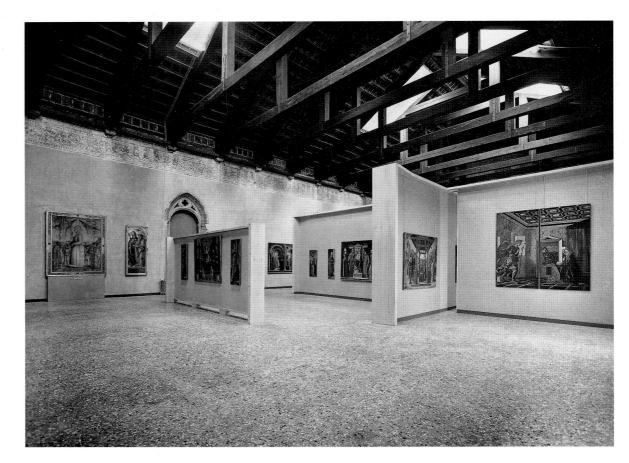

after the plaster crumbled because of defective construction, the resurfaced walls were washed in the present dark gray.

At first, it proved impossible to introduce a heating system in this area. Eventually, to avoid sacrificing precious wall space, Scarpa resigned himself to the inevitable and reinstalled the prewar central-heating system, painting its ancient radiators black and foregoing any attempt to disguise them.

In 1947, the canvases of the *Miracles of the Cross* were brought from the Church of the Carità to a space built for them in 1940, at the side of the corridor leading to the *Saint Ursula* room. This allowed two rooms reserved for two very similar painting cycles to be connected by a small gallery affording a view of the Palladian convent. The arrangement constituted a first step towards the reordering that followed in 1959-60. Now Scarpa did away with the freestanding exhibition panels, reconfigured the ceiling, refashioned the skylight for more evenly dispersed illumination (figs. 17, 18), replastered the walls with a rough, clear surface designed to set off without

competing with the paintings' own colors, and posed the collection on a dark iron band that reinforced the overall sense of continuity. In this second phase too, Scarpa decided not to mask the radiators with gratings, inasmuch as it seemed better to leave them in full view.

In that same year, Scarpa also rearranged the *Saint Ursula* room according to carefully thought-out principles of consistency, eliminating the old blend of authentic and fake period décor. He lowered the big canvases, which had been difficult to see at 6 feet above the floor, and supported as well as framed them with a strip of pale oak sumptuously contoured in gold, against walls of warm ivory. Slightly recessed within their mounts and lit from a new lateral source, each altarpiece occupied a separate space protected left and right by a pair of scumbled wood screens. In 1959, Scarpa repainted the ceiling the same dark gray as the color in Room X, which replaced his first scheme, that one scarcely warmer than bare walls.

Early in the summer of 1947, he managed to reopen Rooms VII, VIII, and IX, after having given them a slightly

trapezoidal shape by means of false walls. There he hung major works by Lotto, Savoldo, Romanino, Palma Vecchio, Bonifacio, and Veronese. The three spaces, reserved for lesser 18th-century works, now flowed into each other, becoming a sort of articulated gallery on their own. "The mosaic floor is uniformly dark gray and the skirting in light gray; the walls are glazed in a delicate shade of clear/opaque ivory, while a single gauzy scrim diffuses illumination from the skylight," wrote Moschini to the Cultural Ministry on July 17.

In what is now Room XVIa, "with its rougher and more aggressively colored plaster," Scarpa placed Piazzetta's *Fortune-teller* and works by Alessandro Longhi. Other 18th-century paintings found their way to the adjoining corridor, "these also widely spaced, even at the cost of keeping lesser works off the walls and in reserve where scholars may inspect them." At about the same time, Scarpa began (but briefly ceased) to reorder and simplify the rooms dedicated to the late 16th and 17th centuries.

In the spring of 1948, during the Biennale, Moschini quietly reopened the

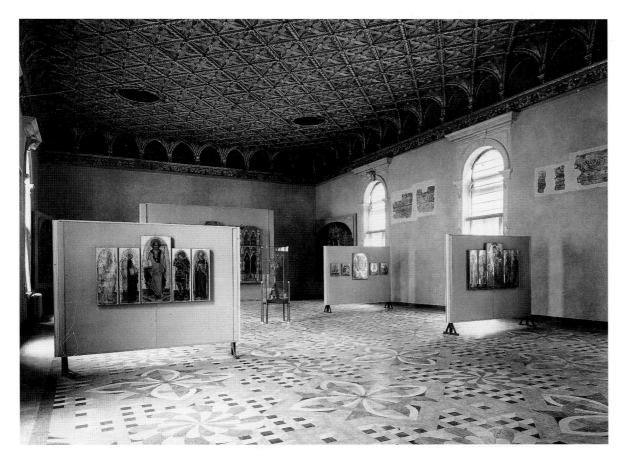

restored Church of the Carità. The walls had been scrubbed clean of their pseudo-historical décor, and the 14th-century paintings systematically displayed on large panels, as well as lit by four new skylights. After much reflection, larch, lightly but warmly glazed and faced with jute, was finally chosen as the wood against which to show the pictures. The combination of materials was "the same used for the Giovanni Bellini exhibition in the Palazzo Ducale" (fig. 19). Scarpa had treated the huge space, albeit cut in half, with proper respect for its remaining architectural values; thus, he did the preparatory work almost as if for a temporary exhibition. His intention was to create an access through the church and the *sala dell'albergo* so that Selva's 19th-century doorway, with its little flight of stairs connecting the Scuola and the convent, could be closed off. In this way, the triptych by Antoni Vivarini and Giovanni d'Alemagna might have been restored to its original position. In the end, the picture was simply put back whence it came, on the one available wall.

On September 10, 1949, Scarpa presented "a large-scale plan for the fitting-out and systematic arrangement of Rooms I, II, III, IV, V, VI, and IX, with attached estimate of costs." In 1950, work began on the first, or Primitives, room, which, for reasons of obvious urgency, had been under study since 1948. Scarpa reopened the windows, bricked up in the 19th century to gain display space. He also removed the green fabric and wood dado from the walls and replaced them with clear plaster (a process that uncovered some fragments of late-14th-century wall decoration). To disguise the awkward proportions of the room that once housed Titian's *Assumption*, Scarpa introduced a large room divider. Here he hung Lorenzo Veneziano's polyptych, flanking it with a pair of large paintings placed on screens, or freestanding walls, of scumbled wood. When it came to the windows, he lavished much care on their frames, using iron on the outside and wood within.

After framing the gold-ground panels in lightly glazed chestnut, Scarpa set them on an iron-rail base and against panels covered with sand-colored fustian. The smaller paintings he displayed like jewels in glass cases, and for the *Cross of Saint Theodore* he designed a fine reliquary made of iron, glass, and an antique porphyry fragment found in the Gallerie's storerooms (fig. 20).

Here Scarpa had to contend with two brooding, even overwhelming presences: the sumptuous 15th-century carved-wood ceiling and the polychrome marble floor, installed by Bernardino Macaruzzi in the 18th century. Nevertheless, "each several element of the museological display shows . . . an architectural talent undeniably sure in its touch. The materials used—wood, iron, and glass— are meaningfully and appropriately employed, and their interaction is so arranged as to please the eye."

Meanwhile, as part of the second project for 1951, Scarpa built a new flight of stairs (using materials salvaged from an old, excessively cumbersome stairway leading from Room II to Room III, against which stood a velvet-covered settle). He resurfaced the *faux* coffered ceiling in dark-green plaster, replaced the polychrome-marble pavement with a dark-gray Venetian-style terrazzo floor, and repainted the walls ivory-white. To compensate for the small size of Cima da Conegliano's *Incredulity of Saint Thomas*

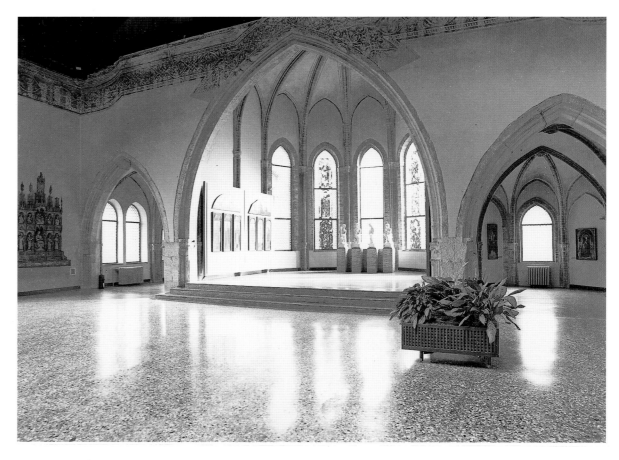

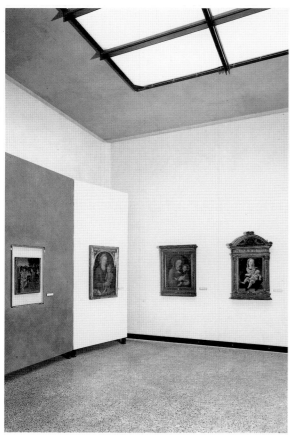

and *Madonna of the Orange Tree*, relative to adjacent works, Scarpa backed them with large panels covered in orange-pink velvet. This arrangement must also have given the room a touch of color carried over from the exceptionally rich palette and decoration of the neighboring Primitives room.

Moschini had long deplored the constricted entrance, with its banal glass doors. Hoping to replace it with a seemly and functional entrance, he had repeatedly invited Scarpa to prepare sketches and a full proposal. He even hoped to claim for the Gallerie the entire ground-floor hall of the Scuola, which would have provided a noble entrance indeed. As a practical matter, however, it proved impossible to obtain more than a small additional area from the Accademia. In 1950, the crumbling terra-cotta floor tiles were replaced, but not until the fall of 1952 did Scarpa submit his design for a revolving door. When completed at the end of 1953 in oak, glass, and iron, the entrance had a sales counter, in the same russet oak as the floor, and behind that a grating for the display of announcements, which in turn concealed a cloakroom.

For Rooms IV and V, both small and intended to house cabinet-size masterpieces of the 15th and early 16th centuries, the redesign proved particularly difficult. In the 1920s, the spaces had been seriously overcrowded with art works and lit by two windows curtained in red damask. Shortly before the war, the Gallerie had planned to remove Giorgione's *Tempest* from such busy surroundings for more appropriate display elsewhere. Towards this end, two skylights were opened so that a few little masterworks could be exhibited on the ornamental walls. When the museum reopened after the war, the *Tempest* hung provisionally in one of these galleries. Plans for a further rearrangement got under way in 1951, and on November 26 Moschini wrote to Scarpa: "My inclination is to cut only two narrow openings between the two rooms, so that such a mixed bag of paintings as hangs on their walls should not all be in view from the same spot. For the same reason, I'd like to see the doorway into Room II closed off. I hope we shall return to this matter." Four years later Scarpa acted on the suggestion when he redesigned the rooms, closing off the two windows and creating a single space with a divider down the middle, properly placed in relation to the doorways and the pre-existing skylights, with the latter now filtered by a silk scrim. The floor was relaid *alla veneziana* in a light, warm color, and an iron protective

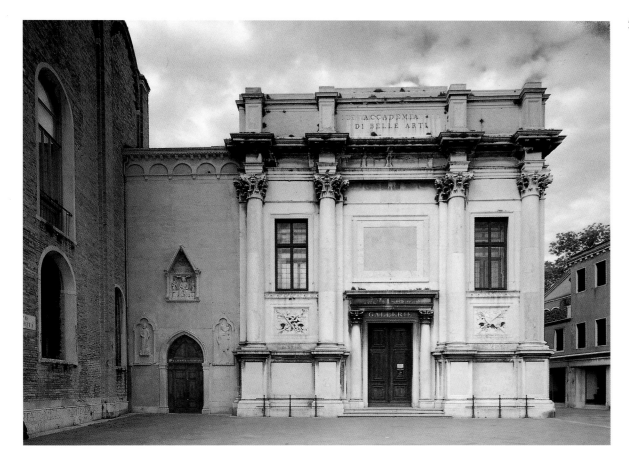

railing attached to walls surfaced in clear, porous plaster. Those paintings with antique frames were hung directly against the walls, while the others appeared on scumbled wood panels faced in neutral-colored fabric (fig. 21). The *Tempest* alone, after endless search for a contemporary frame and careful consideration of other expedients, took pride of place upon a background of antique brown velvet.

One space left almost unchanged from its prewar configuration was the poorly proportioned Room VI, always the ugly duckling of the Gallerie. Moschini and Scarpa had wanted to drop the ceiling and create a row of three rooms analogous to the adjoining Rooms VII, VIII, and IX. But when funds finally became available in 1959, they allowed for nothing but fresh plaster on the walls and a more intelligent arrangement of the paintings. Not even the projected flight of steps to Room X could be provided. In the same year, the long-awaited mounting for Piazzetta's *Fortune-teller* finally came about, followed, a year later, as we have seen, by the completion of improvements to the room housing the *Miracles of the*

Cross Cycle as well as to its adjacent corridor. Meanwhile, Room III received new wood casements.

Thus ended the contribution made by Carlo Scarpa to the Gallerie's reordering—"always the goal," as Moschini wrote, "of your work at the Museums."

The solutions devised by Scarpa were, and remain, distinguished by their compelling elegance and logic. Nonetheless, materials, however carefully chosen and applied, do wear out; new works enter the collections; fresh laws come into being (for example, Decree No. 818, of 1984, on fire prevention); and, above all, new objectives must be met. Inevitably, Scarpa's solutions have been, and will be, subject to these processes of change. Museologists deplore recent trends towards modification, substitution, and removal, all of which compromise or distort the stylistic integrity of the exemplary work done in the 1950s. Some deterioration, needless to say, is inevitable by the very nature of things. Moreover, there is no denying that Italian museums, during the immediate postwar period, oriented themselves towards a limited, privileged

audience of connoisseurs. Traveling students—still less tourists—had little or no place in their scheme of things. Now, however, it is precisely the new, broader appeal of museums that compels us to wonder whether older styles of presentation, or indeed whole institutions designed to conserve and exhibit art—places never built to accommodate such daily throngs of visitors—can be expected to survive. Given present realities, Scarpa's work may seem wanting in forethought (understandably so, given the limited space at his disposal), but it still stands as an unsurpassed exercise in museology. For this very reason, one may hope that his structure will be preserved, altered as little as possible, and, in the course of time, fully restored.

In 1961-77, and even subsequently, after Francesco Valcanover became director, top priority went to the development of services, beginning with the most basic needs but eventually embracing anti-theft and fire-control systems, the climatization of the Drawings Collection (now assembled on the top floor in suitable steel cabinets), an organized reserve system, and small but well-equipped conservation laboratories. In the church, across from the apses, was installed a temporary-exhibition space dedicated to Gino Fogolari. In time, the need for more adaptable facilities for such purposes has required the addition of movable partitions not, like Scarpa's, fixed to the floor, as well as a more open or spacious way of arranging exhibitions (fig. 22). In the 1980s, long-foreseen wear and tear made it necessary to rehabilitate Room XI, with solutions already devised by Scarpa for the twin gallery (Room X), which had suffered scarcely at all.

The postwar years saw a halt in the flood of accessions. In 1949, Guido Cagnola generously donated a Canaletto sketchbook filled with landscape studies and Venetian scenes, providing an invaluable aid to understanding the artist's creative processes. Then, in the 1970s, acquisitions resumed, with Francesco Guardi's *Fire at the Oil Deposit at San Marcuola* and Montagna's little *Saint Peter Blessing with Donor*. In 1979, the Gallerie acquired from Count Nani Mocenigo the large *Family of the Procurator Luigi Pisani* by Alessandro Longhi. Two years

later they exercised the right of preemption to acquire Strozzi's *Portrait of a Procurator* from the Palazzo Barbaro Curtis.

The year 1983 brought Jacopo Bassano's *Adoration of the Shepherds*, formerly in the Giusti del Giardino collection. In 1987 came two *putti* holding scrolls, as well as the personified *Justice* and *Patience* executed by Giorgio Vasari in 1542 for the ceiling of a room in the Palazzo Corner on the Grand Canal. In 1983, following the death of Rodolfo Siviero, former chief of the agency for recovering property forcibly taken to Germany during World War II (and later to other countries), Valcanover boldly asserted rights to at least thirty works that, thanks to tardy handling, had languished for decades in the storerooms of the Palazzo Pitti in Florence. While only part of the claim, seven paintings did return in 1988, including an episode from Giannantonio Guardi's *Gerusalemme Liberata*, long missing from the Gallerie, in addition to two small *Mythological Tales* by Sebastiano Ricci and two *Capriccios* attributed to Canaletto.

Also in 1988, following an exhibition

based on the restored works of Paolo Veronese, the Gallerie moved the master's ceiling paintings into Room VI, freeing Room IX for small meetings and slide shows. Gradually, the lighting system was upgraded to prevailing standards, and a series of "defenders" installed to provide a satisfactory degree of control over temperature and humidity.

As always, the Gallerie suffer from a built-in, frustrating lack of space, which not only makes it difficult to meet all the demands placed upon the museum, but also impedes a chronlogical layout and precludes the display of certain masterworks, particularly from the 17th century—a period abundantly represented in the reserve collection but, in the public galleries, confined to small Room XIV.

The problem could be resolved by moving the Accademia elsewhere, since it has no activities in common with the Gallerie. Only thus could the enlarged Gallerie assume their proper place among the great museums of Europe. Meanwhile, however, they still function as the indispensable magnet for students of Venetian art.

MASTERPIECES IN THE MUSEUM

Active, 1333-58; d. before September 1362
Enthroned Madonna and Child with Two Donors
Panel, 57 x 36"; with original frame, 63 x 42" (cat.
no. 786)
Last restored 1986 (special conservation)

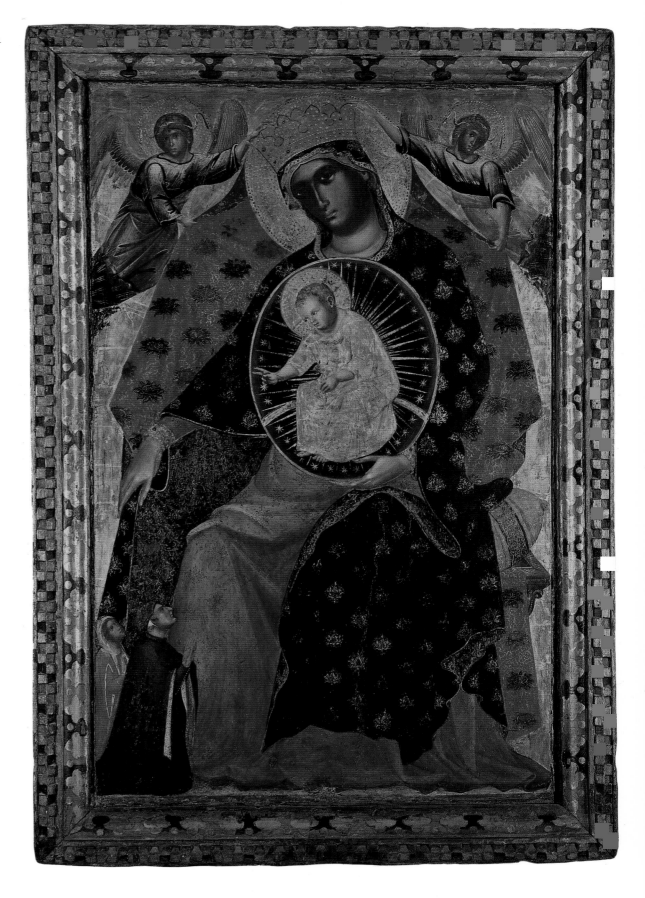

Acquired in 1913 from the Venetian antiquarian Salvadori, the picture retains the original dentillated, two-color frame as well as the old cruciform stretcher, but the figures have lost their glazing and the Virgin's clothing some of its color. Also gone is the inscription at the bottom. Since the publication of the 1928 catalogue that identified Paolo Veneziano as the author of this work, the attribution has

come to be accepted unconditionally. Thanks to stylistic affinities with a 1321 altar front by Dignano, we can date Paolo's altarpiece a bit later, perhaps in the second half of the 1320s.

The Madonna holding the Christ Child framed within an oval shield or gloriole represents a Syrian iconographic variation on the *Platytera*, while the Child's welcoming gesture to a pair of tiny donors—so specific in

their features that they must be portraits— offers an unexpected echo of the *Madonna della Misericordia*. The monumentality of the Virgin, "dark-faced as a Coptic or Cretan icon," the harmonious assimilation of Eastern and Western elements, the touching humanity of the patrons, and the rich, sumptuous colors suggest that here may be the artist's masterpiece.

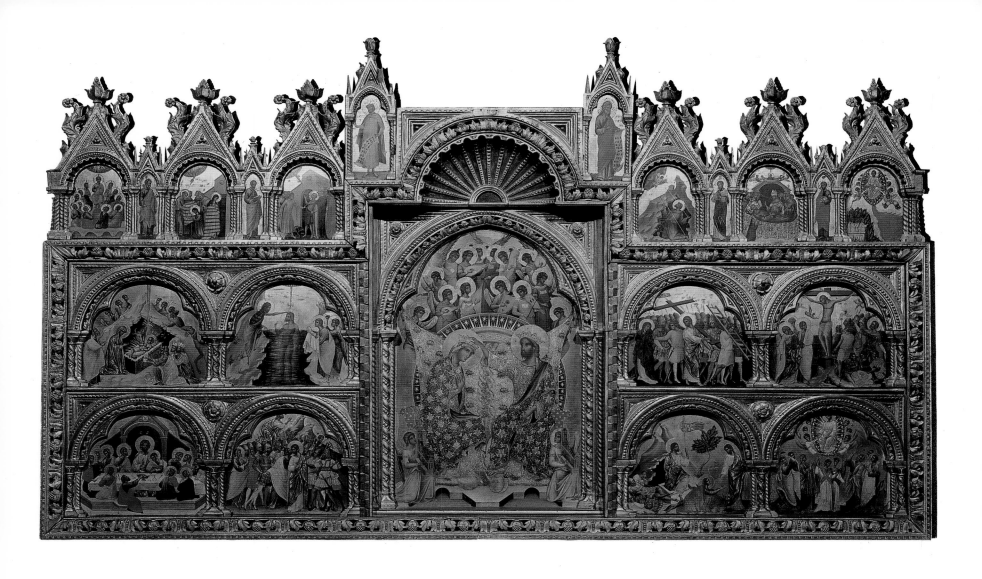

PAOLO VENEZIANO 2

Active, 1333-58; d. before September 1362
Coronation of the Virgin, with Scenes from the Life of Christ
Polyptych: *Coronation of the Virgin* (center);
Adoration of the Magi, Baptism of Christ, Last Supper, Prayer in the Garden of Gethsemane, and *Taking of Christ* (left); *Road to Calvary, Meeting with the Virgin, Crucifixion, Resurrection, Noli me Tangere,* and *Ascension* (right); *Pentecost, Saint Matthew, Vesting of Saint Clare, Saint John, Saint Francis Returning His Clothing to His Father; Saint Francis in Ecstasy, Saint Mark, Death of Saint Francis, Saint Luke,* and *Christ in Judgment* (top center); and *Isaiah* and *Daniel* (top center).
Panels: center, 39 x 25"; side, left and right, 16 x 38" each; top, six largest, 10 x 8" each; top, four smallest, 9 x 3" each; top, two tallest, 12 x 6" each. (Cat. no. 21).
Last restored 1951

This polyptych comes from the Venetian Church of Saint Clare, a provenance confirmed by the Franciscan subjects in the upper tier of panels, particularly the *Death of Saint Francis,* where the little nun is probably the donor. The polyptych came to the Gallerie in 1812, as a result of secularization, but only after the central panel had been sent by mistake to the Brera in 1808, making it necessary to substitute a *Coronation* by Stefano da Sant'Agnese. This remained in place until 1950, when the entire complex was assembled in its original form.

The work can be dated around 1350, by virtue of its involvement not only with the contemporary process of introducing everyday themes into a Byzantine context—a process already present in Washington's 1324 *Coronation of the Virgin* (National Gallery, Washington D.C.)—but also with the recomplication of the process through a reactionary emphasis on decorative effects and Byzantanism in general. The latter characteristic has in turn caused some to speculate that Paolo may have visited Constantinople and been stylistically influenced by the experience.

The polyptych presents a striking contrast between the small lateral scenes and the large central figures with their remarkable arabesque grace.

The differences, however, do not justify an assumption that they result from different hands, inasmuch as the quality of composition remains unfailingly high. The artist simply alternated the courtly, refined language of Byzantium—its iconic fixity well suited to an event transcending time and space—with a decidedly Occidental, relatively down-to-earth idiom for the unfolding narratives of the "histories." Consistent throughout, however, is the glory brought to both composition and stylistic diversity by the vitreous richness of the artist's color.

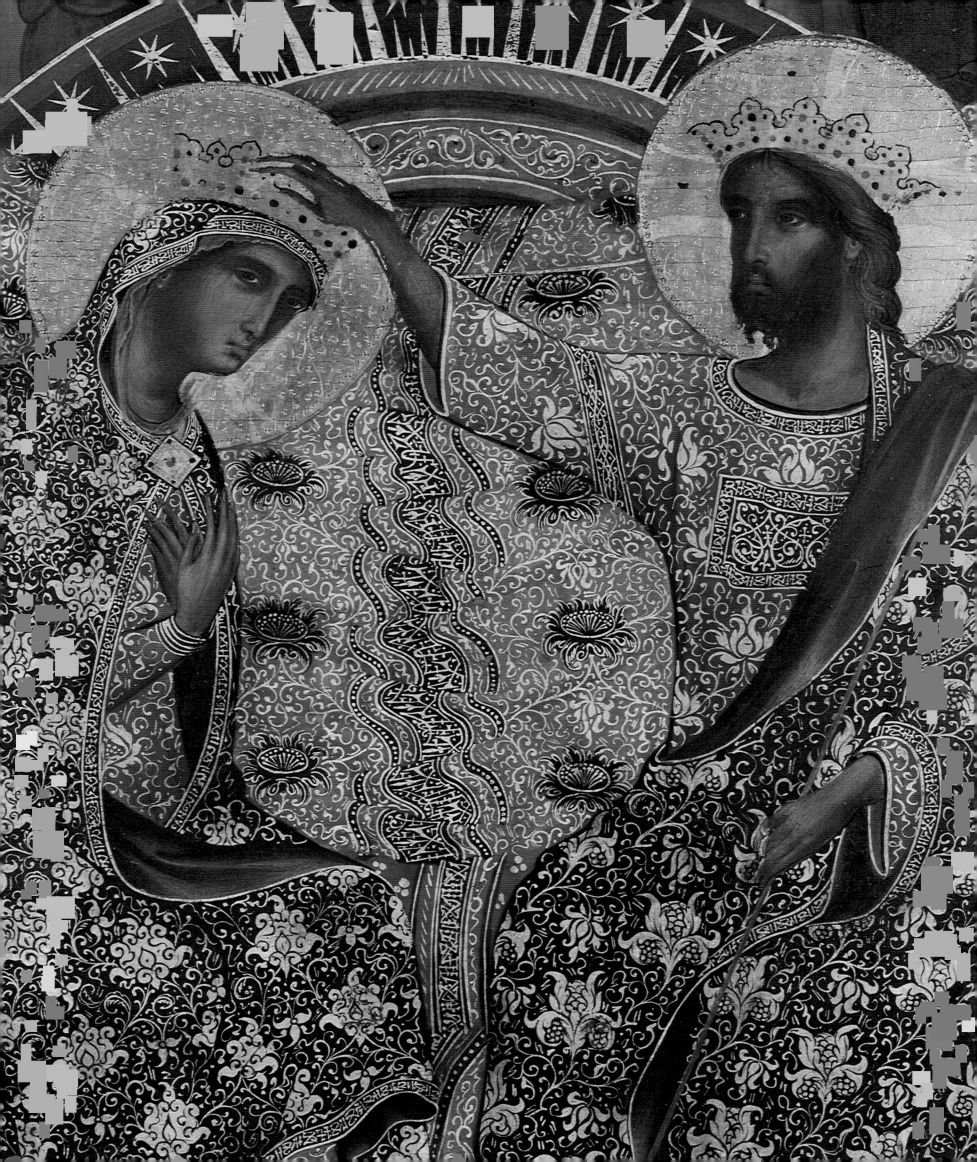

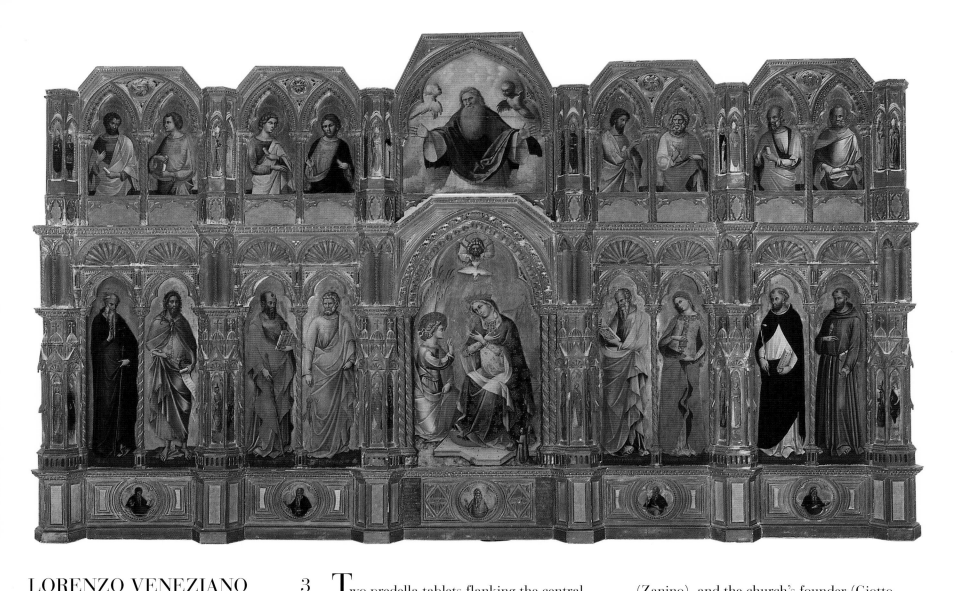

LORENZO VENEZIANO   3

Mentioned, 1356-72
Polyptych: The Annunciation, with Saints
Lower tier, center compartment: *Annunciation*;
lateral compartments on the left: *Saints Anthony
Abbot, John the Baptist, Paul, and Peter*; lateral
compartments on the right: *Saints John the
Evangelist, Mary Magdalene, Dominic, and
Francis.*
Upper tier, central compartment: *The Eternal
Father Blessing*; lateral compartments left and
right: *Prophets* (half-length figures).
Predella, lateral compartments: *Saints Saba,
Macarius, Paul, Hilary,* and *Theodore*
(cinquefoils containing holy hermits).
Pilasters separating compartments: 36 *Saints*
with their names inscribed alongside.
Lower tier: central compartment, 70 x 30";
lateral compartments, 48 x 24" each. Upper tier:
central compartment (altered), 33 x 33"; lateral
compartments, 27 x 12" each. Pilaster figures:
14 x 2" each. (cat. no. 10)
Last restored 1990-91 (major conservation)

Two predella tablets flanking the central
panel bear the following inscription, as
transcribed by Cicogna in 1824, before the
retouching of 1829 (today's variant readings in
parentheses): MCCCLVII / HEC TABELLA / F͞CA FUIT
7 … C (F͞CA FUIT & HIC) / AFFISSA P̄ / LAURĒ CIUS
/ PICTORES / 7 ҪANINUS SC / ULTORES I͞TPE / RĒGIS
V̄EN VI / RI D͞NI F͞RIS (K͞RIS) / ҪOTI D̄ ABBA / TIB’ D̄
F͞LOT P’ / OIS 7 FU … (IOIS & FUNTO) / MON … TI
(MONIS ISTI) // HANC TUIS / … S AGNE /
TRIUNPHAT͞O / ORBIS … / DOMINICUS / LION EGO /
NUNC SUPPLEX (NUNC SU͞PPLX) / ARTE PRE /
POLITAM / DONO TA / BELLAM. On the left tablet,
reflectographic analysis has revealed a small
worshiper, possibly a portrait of the donor. The
date MCCCLVIII (1358), also confirmed
reflectographically, appears on the step,
towards the left, leading to the throne in the
central compartment. Acquired in 1812,
following secularization, but not exhibited
until 1829, the polyptych came from the
destroyed Church of Sant'Antonio di Castello.
It had been commissioned for 300 gold ducats
by Dominico Lion, an adjunct member of the
Venetian Senate in 1356-57, who is portrayed
kneeling before the Virgin in the central
compartment. Besides the date on which work
began (1337), the epigraph gives the names of
the artist (Lorenzo), the frame carver

(Zanino), and the church's founder (Giotto
degli Abbati). It also includes the donor's
dedication.

This great complex, also known as the *Lion
Polyptych*, was scrambled and damaged in the
19th century while being transported. From
the upper tier it lost the central compartment,
now replaced by a *God the Father*, probably
from the hand of Benedetto Diana. Moreover,
ten of the little pilaster *Saints* are not original
but, instead, the results of repainting
undertaken during the 1829 restoration, which
also reworked the frame even while preserving
the overall structure of the original. Executed,
as the inscriptions declare, in 1357-58, the
work evinces a lingering Byzantinism inherited
from Paolo Veneziano, at the same time that it
shows the artist already moving towards an
exquisitely elegant Gothicism in the figures of
the Saints. Liberated from hieratic frontality,
the *Annunciation* abounds in closely observed
naturalism, learned, probably, from Bolognese
contemporaries. Finally, however, the two
antithetical cultures find resolution in the
general opulence and extended variety of the
artist's palette. Under the edges of the frame
there are, perhaps not accidentally, trial
strokes of pure color and a few fresh bits of
charcoal sketching.

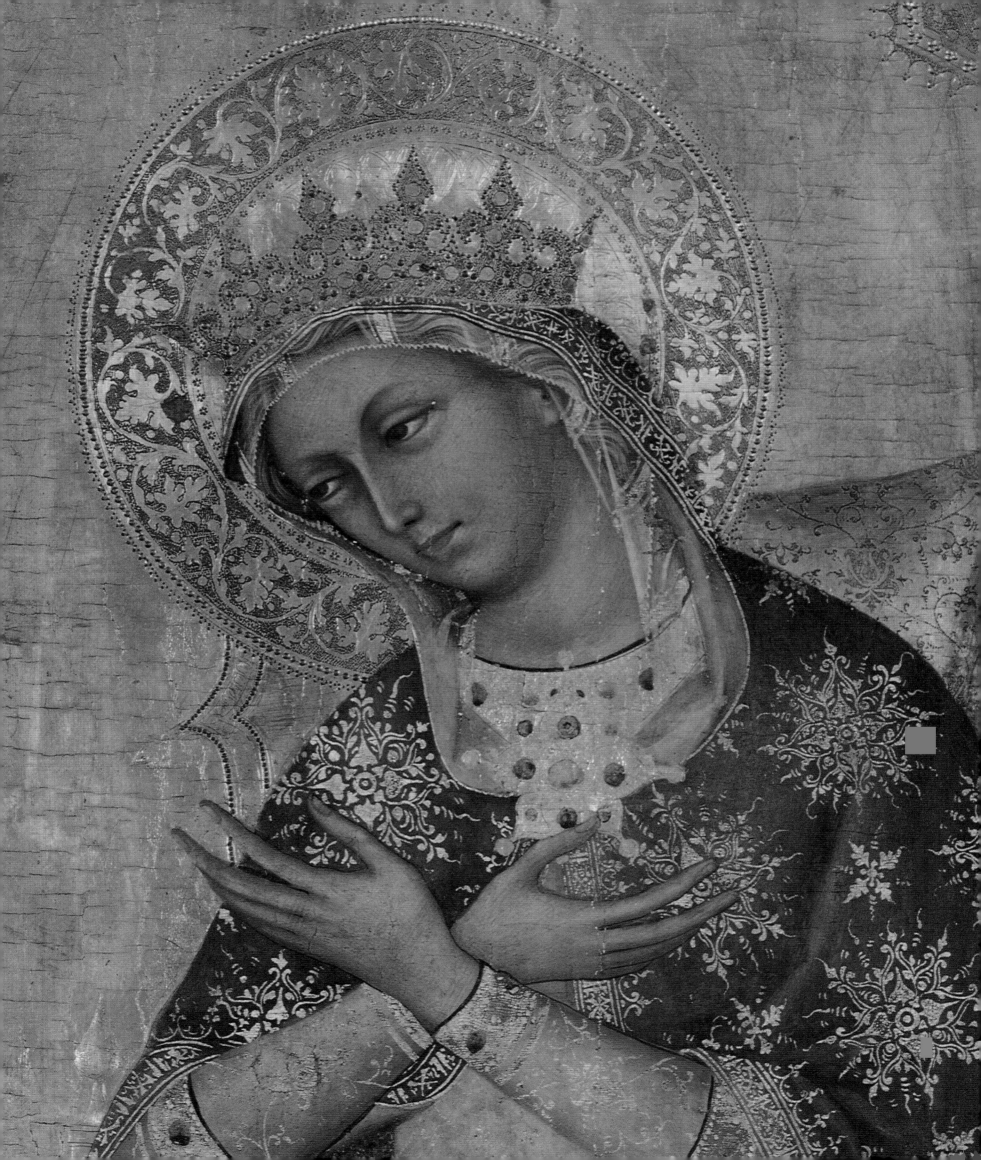

Mentioned, 1356-72
*Polyptych: The Annunciation, with Saints John
the Baptist and Gregory, James and Stephen*
Five panels: center, 44 x 22"; lateral, 38 x 10" each
(cat. no. 9)
Last restored 1979

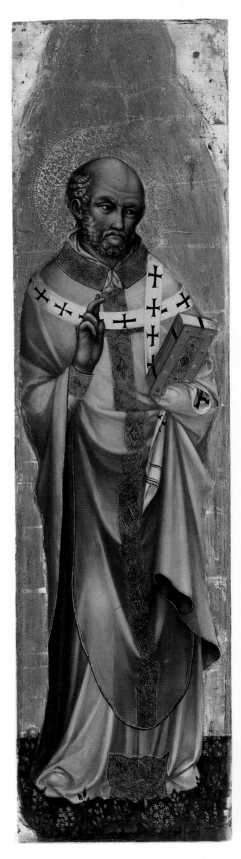
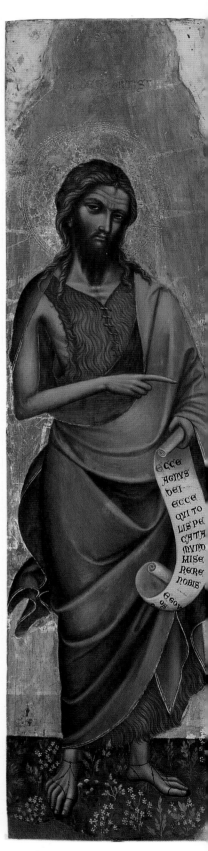

This polyptych came to the Gallerie in 1816
through a bequest from Girolamo Molin. The
date (1371) and signature have been inscribed
on the base of the throne: MCCC.LXXI.LAURECI. /
PINSIT. The gold ground is quite worn on the
surface of a work whose original destination is
not known. The solidity of the central figures
suggests Emilian influence, but the luminary
sensibility, the coloristic and decorative
richness, and the presence of a fresh, flowering
meadow (possibly one of the earliest of its
kind) foreshadow the International Gothic,
which would soon dominate the figurative arts
throughout Europe.

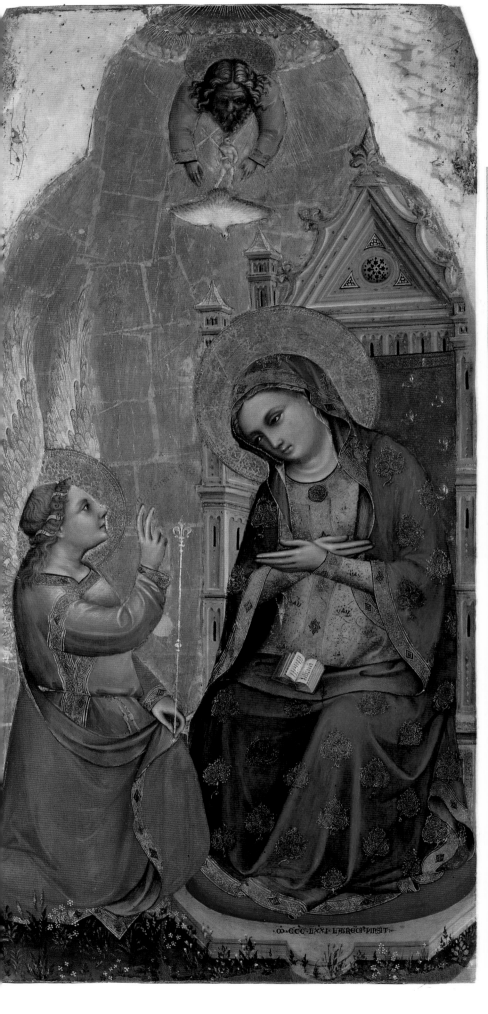

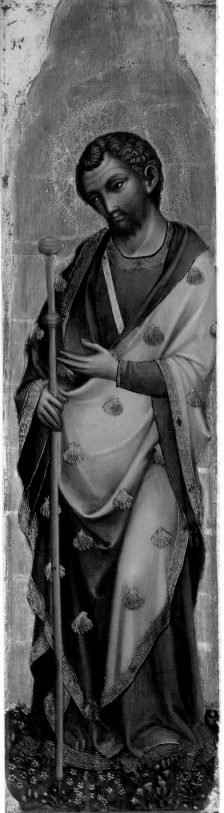

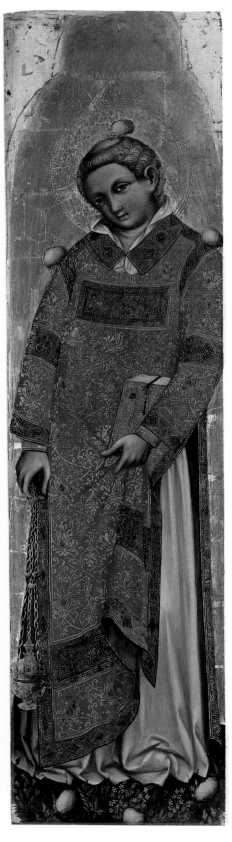

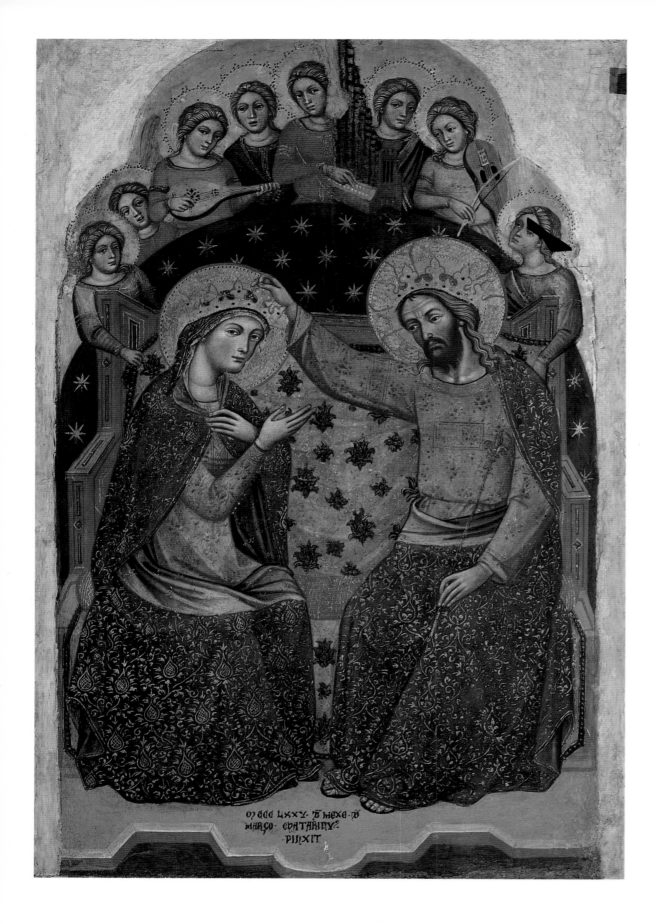

CATARINO

Venice, 1362-82 (mentioned)
Coronation of the Virgin
Panel, 36 x 23" (cat. no. 16)
Last restored 1948

5

Dated 1375 and signed at the center of the bottom step: MCCCLXXV. Ø MEXE Ø /MARÇO. CHATARINUS. / PINXIT.

Count Vincenzo Galli acquired the painting for the Gallerie in 1877. Though of unknown origin, it is believed to have been the central section of a polyptych. The iconography may derive from Paolo Veneziano (see ill. no. 1), as well as the rich and sumptuous color, but everything has undergone a kind of popularization, albeit carried out with deft skill. As for the angels, they found their source in Lorenzo Veneziano and his Veronese contemporaries.

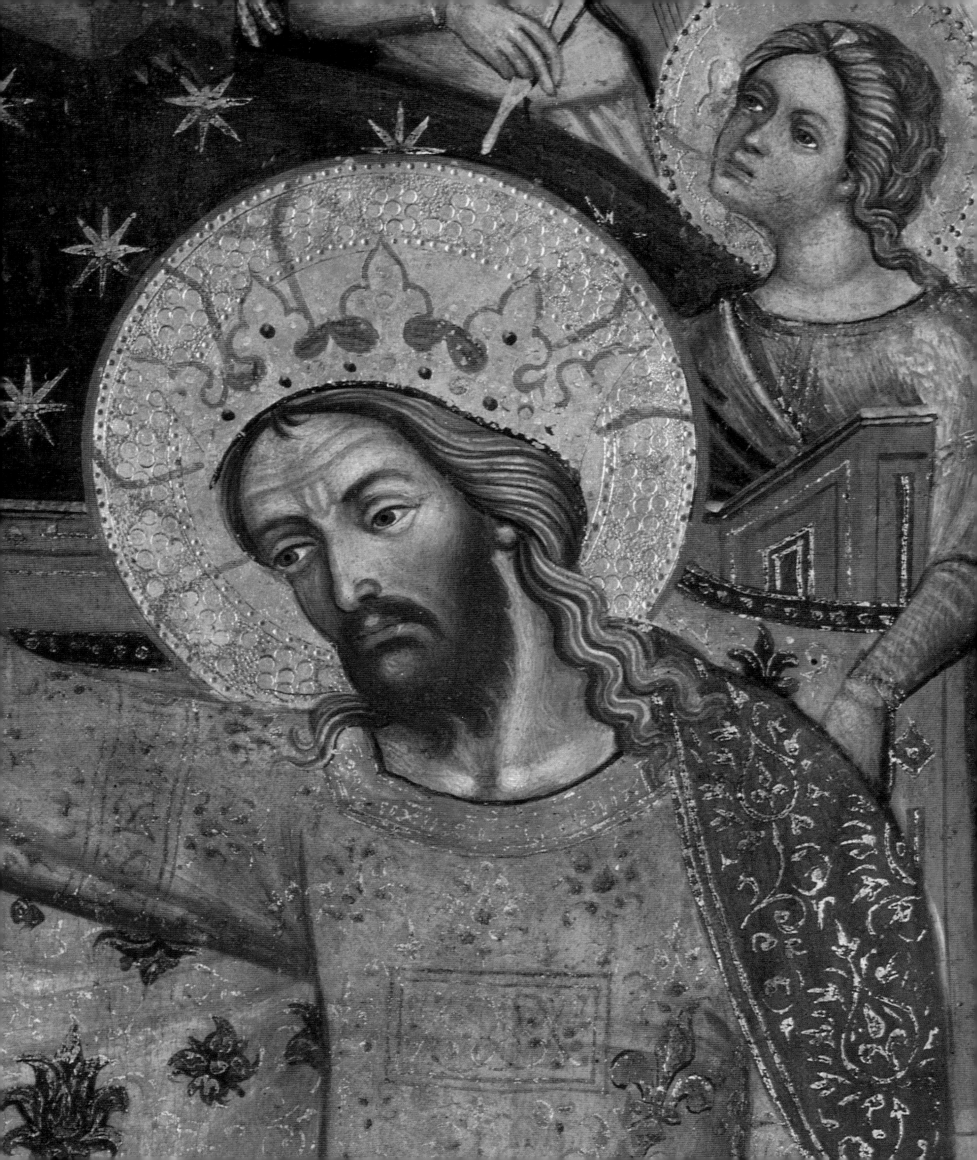

d. before July 14, 1397
Polyptych of the Apocalypse
Five paintings on gold ground: central panel 38 x 25",
side panels 18 x 13" each (cat. no. 1000)
Last restored 1952

The five panels narrate one of the visions described by Saint John in Revelations, for which references are given in Roman numerals. In the center is God the Father in Glory with the Lamb, between the symbols of the four Evangelists, with "six wings . . . and full of eyes," adored by twenty-four elders; at the sides, *The Harvest of the World*, as described in Rev. 14:5-16:1: "Thrust in thy sharp sickle and gather the clusters of the vine of the earth; for her grapes are fully ripe"; *Babylon* (17), or "the great whore . . .the beast that carrieth her . . . which hath seven heads and ten horns" (16:2-17:8); *Riding of the Kings* (19): "...and behold a white horse; and he that sat upon him [bore] on his head . . . many crowns . . . and the armies which were in heaven followed him upon white horses . . . ." (18:18-19:21); and *Last Judgment* (20): "And I saw a great white throne, and him that sat on it . . . . And I saw the dead, small and great, stand before God; and another book was opened . . . ." (20:11-22:5). Inscribed on the book open in Christ's hands: CHI NO / N È SCRI / TI. SU / QUESTO / LIBRO // SERA DA / NADI. ("Whosoever is not writ herein shall be damned").

After secularization in 1810, these paintings remained "in trust" at Torcello's Church of San Giovanni Evangelista, where they had always hung. Gradually, however, the building fell into ruin and had to be demolished, whereupon Vienna acquired the *Vision* and *Judgment* panels. In 1919, *Judgment* returned as war reparation and went on exhibition at the Torcello Museum until 1948. Now both *Vision* and *Judgment* were reunited with the other parts of the painting, which had been in reserve at the Museo Correr since 1840. In 1951, the entire cycle entered the Gallerie.

The complex allegory serves its didactic purpose with admirable clarity, at the same time that the iconography borrowed from Giusto de' Menabuoi appears to be typically Venetian, thanks to the chromatic sensibility and expressive vigor with which it has been treated. A *terminus a quo* for dating the cycle is 1343, the year that Torcello's San Giovanni Evangelista was rebuilt following a fire. The paintings must in fact have been executed during the second half of the 14th century.

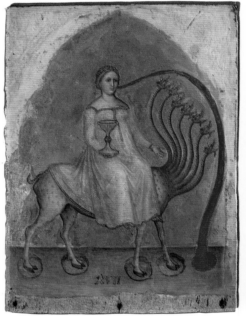
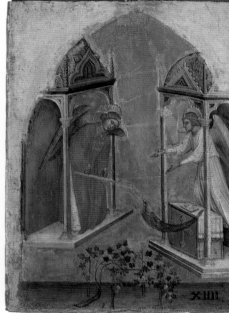

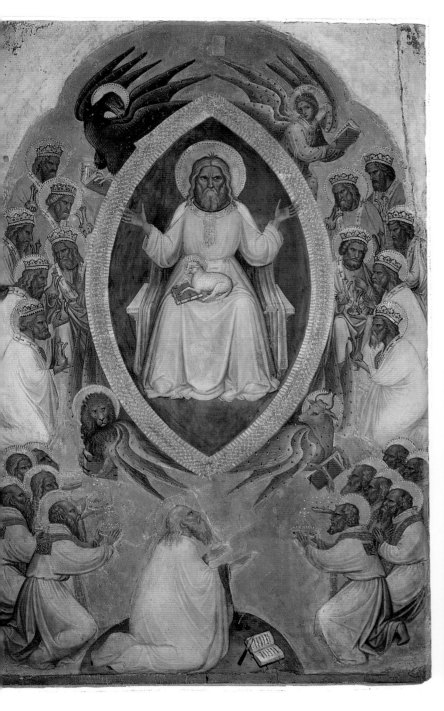

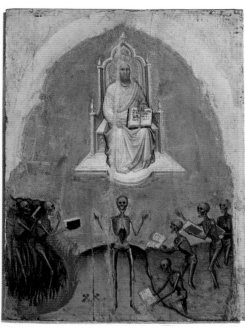

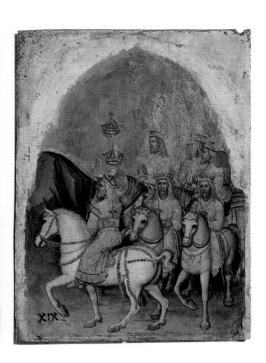

Recorded in Venice, 1394-1427
Madonna and Child Enthroned with the Donor
Vulcanio Belgarzone di Zara
Panel, 43 x 26" (cat. no. 19)
Last restored 1949

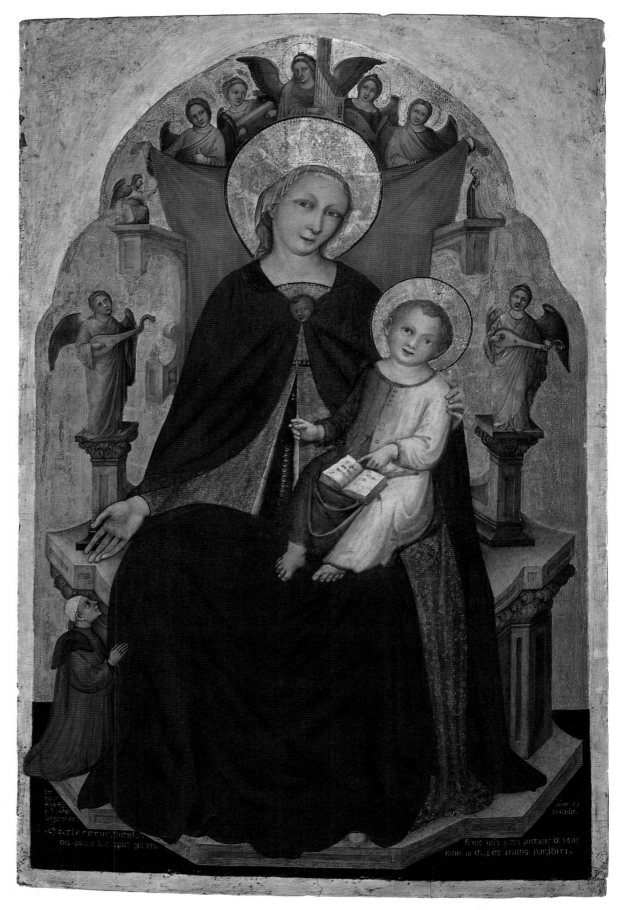

This panel has been inscribed, under the throne's footstool, with the date (1394), the name of the donor, the artist's signature, and his address "at the head of the bridge of Pardise": HOC / OPUS / FECIT FIEI / DNS VULCIA / BELGARCONE / CIVIS.YA / DRIENSIS / MCCCLXXXXIIII.NICHOLA. / FILIUS MRI PETRI PICTORIS DE VENE / CIIS PINXIT HOC OPUS QUI MO / RATUR IN CHAPITE PONTIS PARADIXIS.

Acquired from the Manfrin collection in 1856, the *Madonna and Child Enthroned* is the earliest known work by Nicolò di Pietro, and it is sufficiently coherent and mature to raise questions that have yet to receive adequate answers. Where, for instance, was he trained? And what were his earlier paintings like? Thus, albeit important, his role in helping Venetian painting make the transition from the 14th century to the 15th has never been fully clarified.

Compared to the abstract tendencies of Paolo Veneziano, the coloristic refinement of Lorenzo, or the decorativeness of Jacobello, Nicolò stands apart for his new urge towards color and volume. More than the Bohemian painters, whom he is often said to have emulated, Nicolò appeared to take a keen interest in the culture all about him, from the works of Altichiero and Avanzo to the Trevisan frescoes of Tommaso da Modena, the activities of Vitale da Bologna, and contemporary Bolognese artists in general. Thus, it is no accident that we find Nicolò's signature on a *Crucifixion* dated 1409 and painted for the Church of Sant'Agostino in Verrucchio, a work now in the Pinacoteca in Bologna. Indeed, an Emilian spirit reigns throughout the serene good-naturedness of the Virgin and the witty grace of the angel musicians, all symptoms of a warm, humane naturalism.

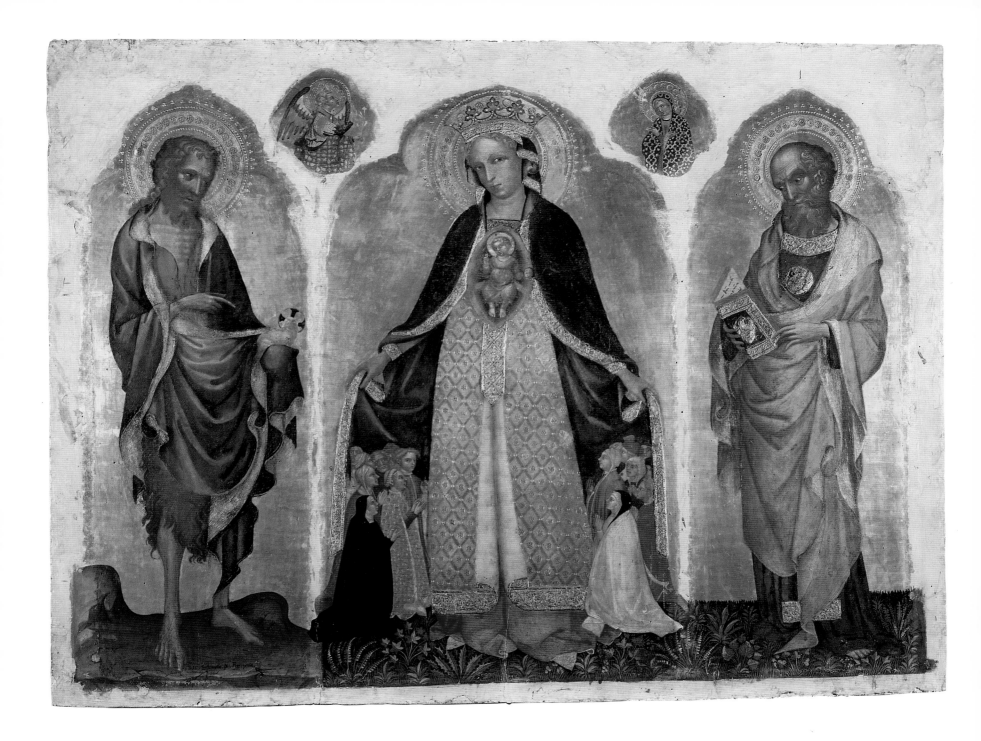

JACOBELLO DEL FIORE   8

Venice, 1400-39 (mentioned)
*Our Lady of Mercy, with Saints John the Baptist
and John the Evangelist*
Panel with gilt-plaster ornaments, 34 x 45" (cat. no. 13)
Last restored 1987

The Gallerie received this panel of unknown provenance from Girolamo Molin in 1816. It has been inscribed, at bottom center, with a date and an apocryphal signature: 1436 JACHOMELLO DE FLOR PENSE.

This could have been copied from an old inscription on the original frame, now lost. In any event, the date is certainly wrong, since it bears no relation to the work's stylistic qualities. Although the Madonna *Platytera* or *Misericordia* theme harks back to Paolo Veneziano (see ill. no. 1), the artist would seem to have undergone greater influence from Gentile da Fabriano and Michelino da Besozzo. Jacobello had already experimented with a variation on the theme in the Montegranaro triptych of 1407, now in a Swiss private collection. By comparison with that work, the

one seen here exhibits a more subtle and finished elegance, less iconic rigidity, and a more portrait-like characterization of the tiny donors kneeling in flower-spangled grass.

The panel should probably be dated between 1415 and the early 1420s, given its stylistic nearness to the *Walking Lion* in the Palazzo Ducale, a work signed and dated 1415, and its obvious chronological priority relative to Jacobello's opulent *Justice* triptych of 1421 (see ill. no. 9). It seems possible that the date in the original inscription should have been read as 1416.

Once the 18th-century frame had been removed, it brought to light, along the panel's lower edge, not only brief passages of paint unaffected by either light or varnish but also a few trial brushstrokes.

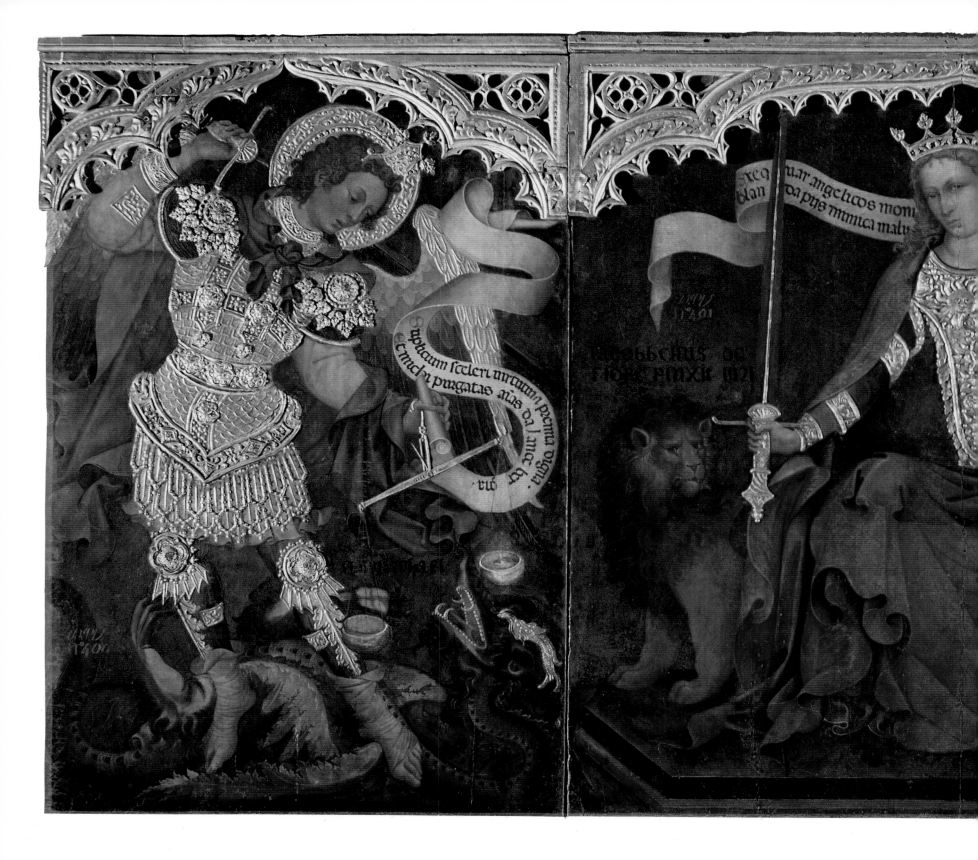

JACOBELLO DEL FIORE 9

Venice, 1400-39 (mentioned)
Justice between the Archangels Michael and Gabriel
Triptych: central panel 83 x 78"; partial left panel (Archangel Michael) 8 x 77"; right panel (Archangel Gabriel) 83 x 65"; decorated with gilded plaster (cat. no. 15).
Last restored 1946

Originally at the Palazzo Ducale, in the chamber of the Magistrato del Proprio, who presided over both civil and criminal courts, the painting was assigned to the Gallerie in 1884.

To the left of Justice, above the lion, appears this inscription: JACOBELLUS DE / FLORE PINXIT, 1421 ("Painted by Jacobello del Fiore, 1421"). Although not original, the signature and date nonetheless correspond fairly well with what sources tell us.

The decorative canopy above has been partly reworked and regilded, in addition to bits of retouching and alteration on the painted surface.

In the central panel, between two lions symbolic of Divine Wisdom, sits Justice with a sword in her right hand and a pair of scales in her left. For the Archangel Michael, who brandishes scales while simultaneously engaged in dragon-slaying, the closest iconographic precedent is a mosaic in the

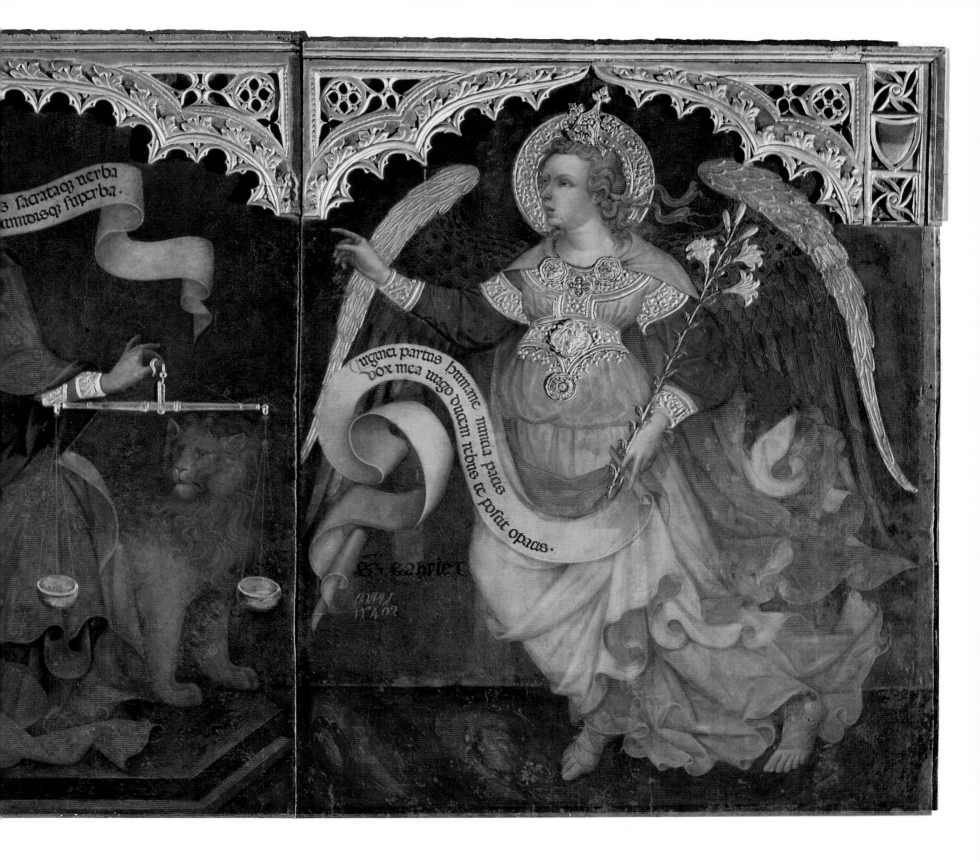

baptistery at San Marco. According to the Latin inscription on the unfurled scrolls, the Annunciatory Angel solicits the Virgin to perform humanitarian acts even in the face of humanity's dark behavior.

The warrior Archangel Michael, defender of the Church, does double duty, weighing and judging human souls at the same time that he also dispatches the dragon symbolic of Satan. Here he beseeches the Virgin to allot reward and punishment as deserved. The words

behind Justice: "I shall obey the admonitions of the angels and the words of Holy Writ, dealing gently with the devout, angrily with the wicked, and proudly with the vainglorious."

In Northern European art, the statement is usually put in the mouth of Christ the Judge. In the present instance, however, Justice would seem to be identified with Venice, even more than in the almost-contemporary relief along the western façade of the Palazzo Ducale,

where the Venice/Justice and Peace/Virgin coupling reflects ideals deemed fundamental to the Venetian State.

In this triptych—an important commission, complex in its symbology—Jacobello interpreted the courtly Gothic spirit in perfect accord with a decorative idiom that, like the period's architecture and sculpture, may be called "flamboyant." It would offer an important model for Michele Giambono and Michele di Matteo.

Active in Bologna, 1410-69
Polyptych
The whole comprises two tiered sequences separated
by a band measuring 9 x 90" and supported by a
predella measuring 13 x 50". Each sequence consists
of five panels, the central one of the upper tier
measuring 45 x 26" and the lower 57 x 25". The four
side panels above measure 45 x 34" each, and below
57 x 33" each. (Cat. no. 24)
Last restored 1979

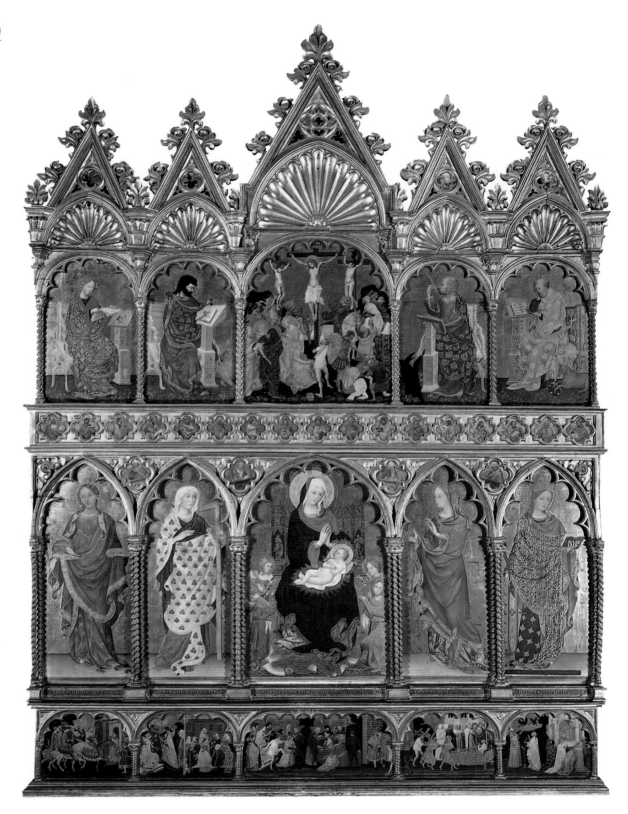

At the center below appears the *Madonna Enthroned Adoring the Child, with Four Angels*, flanked by *Saints Lucy and Helena* on the left and, on the right, *Mary Magdalene and Catherine of Alexandria*. Four rosettes depicting *Doctors of the Church* occupy the spandrels—the triangular spaces between the four arches. The upper sequence displays a *Crucifixion* at the center flanked by *Matthew and Mark* on the right and *John and Luke* on the left. The predella presents five episodes from the Invention of the Cross: *Saint Helena Arrives in Jerusalem and Summons the Jews, Who Take Counsel; Judas Does Not Wish to Reveal the Whereabouts of the Cross, but, When Lowered into a Well, Discloses the Cross and then Digs for It; The True Cross Manifests Itself in the Healing of a Boy; Adoration of the Cross, as Devils Take Flight*. Inscribed at the feet of Saint Catherine: *Michael Mathei da Bononia F.* ("Michele di Matteo from Bologna Painted This").

The painting comes from the Church of Sant'Elena, where it hung above an altar dedicated to the patron Saint and presented by Alessandro Borromei in 1518. The frame, though restored in 1829, is the original. Michele di Matteo painted this, his masterpiece, after 1427, for an altar which until that year had borne a wooden cross. The painting was probably commissioned by the Bolognese Prior, Fra Bernardo de' Schappi. Its sinuous rhythms, understated elegance, and refined palette confirm that Michele's vocabulary had been enriched by contact with the sumptuous culture of the Venetian High Gothic, specifically through the work of Jacobello del Fiore, Nicolò di Pietro, and even Lorenzo Veneziano. The polyptych gave High Gothic one of its most evocative achievements, especially in the delectable freshness of the little narrative scenes on the predella.

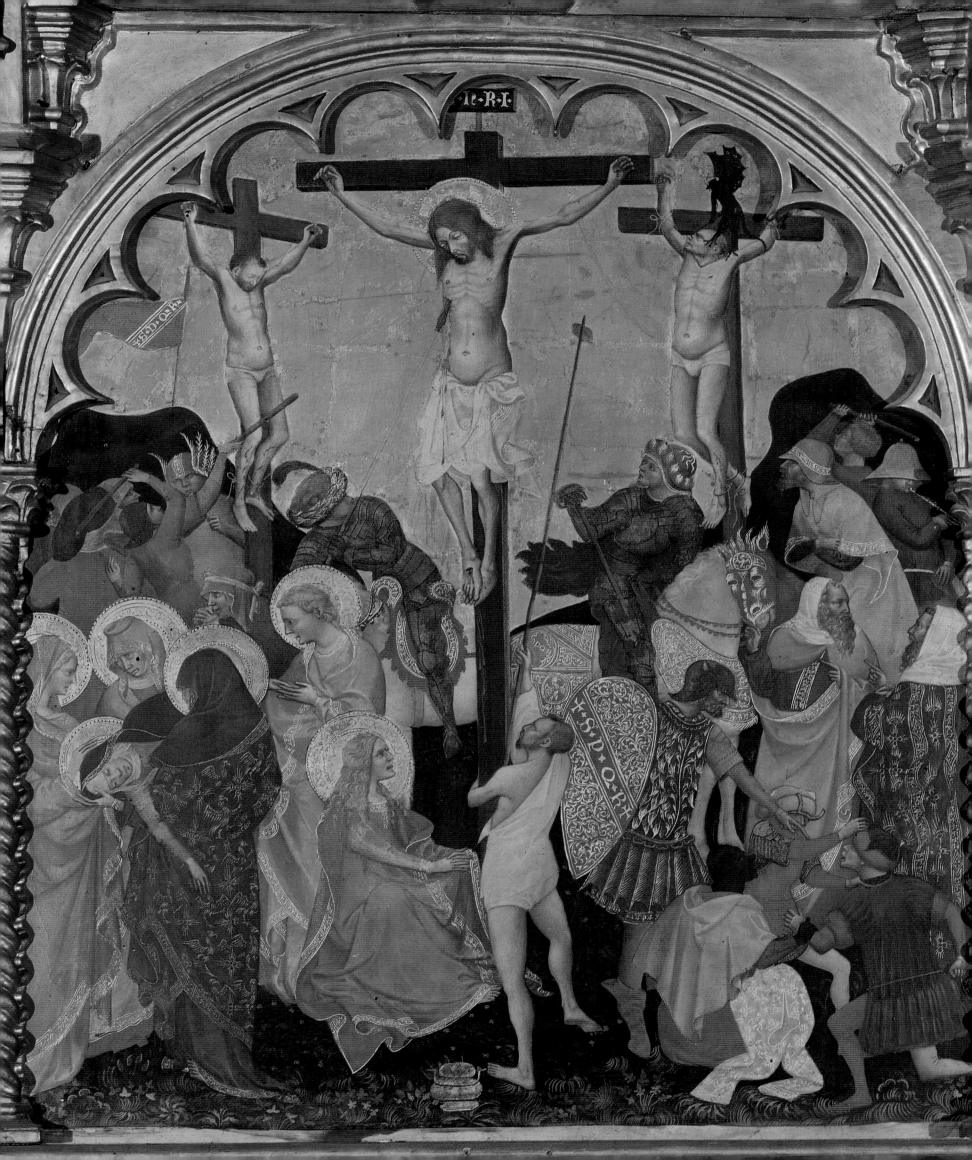

Mentioned, November 10, 1420—April 20, 1462
Coronation of the Virgin in Paradise, Surrounded by the Hierarchies of Angels, Saints, the Four Doctors of the Church, and the Evangelists
Panel decorated in gilt plaster, 92 x 70" (cat. no. 33)
Last restored 1949

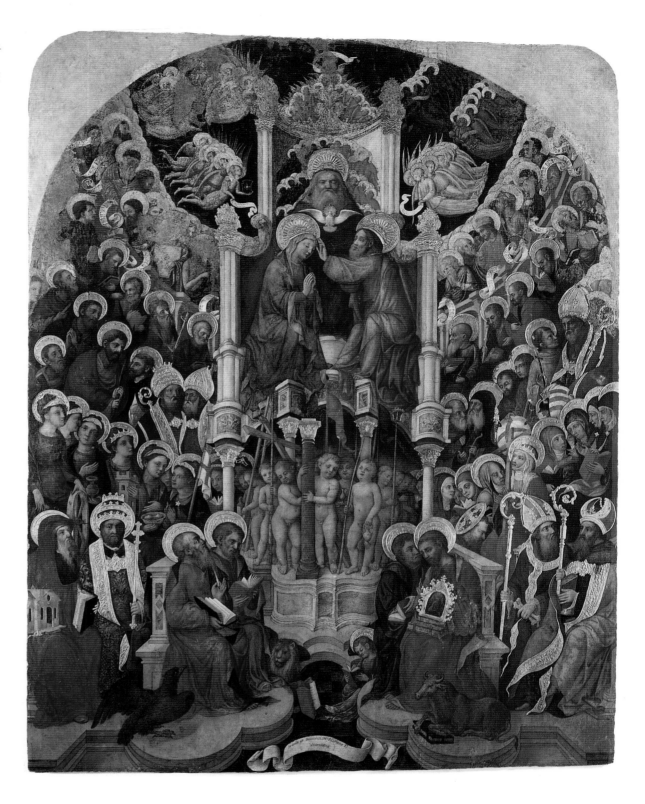

An apocryphal signature and date have been inscribed at the lower center: IOANES ET ANTONIUS DE MURIANO F. / MCCCCXXXX. Acquired in 1816 through a bequest from Girolamo Molin, this panel is probably the one commissioned for the Church of Sant'Agnese by Giovanni Dotto in 1447 for a fee of 130 ducats. The agreement specified that Giambono make the picture identical in all respects with the painting by Antonio Vivarini and Giovanni d'Alemagna in the Church of San Pantalon, an altarpiece delivered in 1448 and still in existence.

The original frame for the *Coronation*, ordered by Giambono from Francesco Moranzone, has been lost. The painting itself, which seems to have been damaged by fire, was covered with an arbitrary coat of repainting throughout the upper zone, from the arch down to the last row of Saints, until it was removed during the 1949 restoration.

What survives, incomplete as it is, shows clearly that, even while following his client's instructions almost to the T, Giambono succeeded in making his artistic personality felt, through precious, decorative touches and a refined elegance.

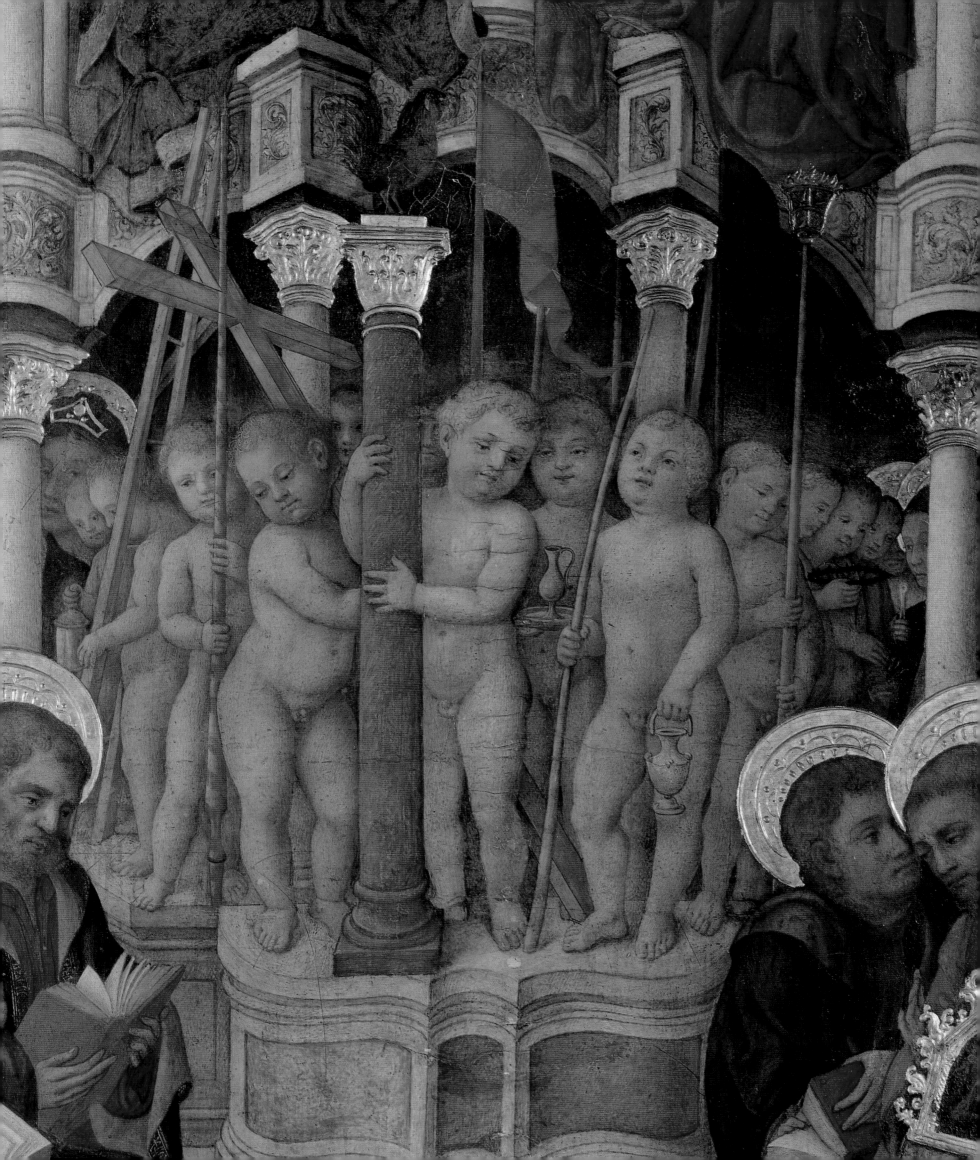

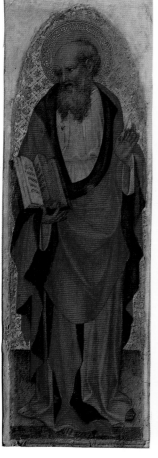 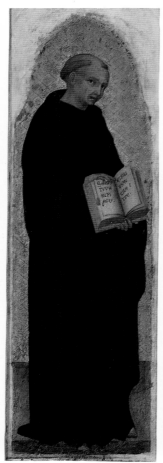 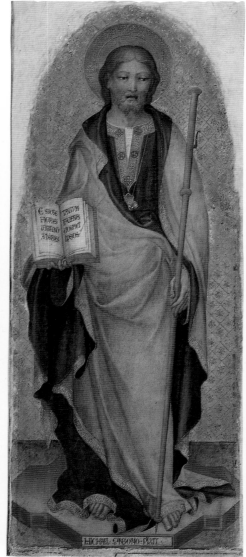 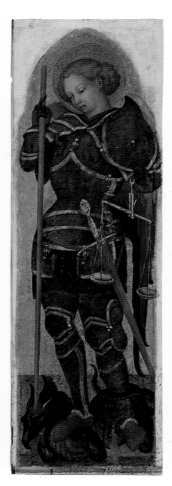 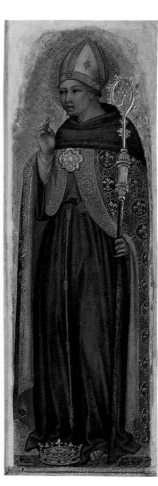

MICHELE GIAMBONO   12

November 10, 1420—April 20, 1462
Polyptych: Saint James the Greater between Saint John the Evangelist, the Venerable Filippo Benizi, the Archangel Michael, and Saint Louis of Toulouse
Five-panel polyptych: center panel, 44 x 18"; side panels, 35 x 12" (cat. no. 3)
Last restored 1948; conservation 1979

The central panel, at its lower edge, has been inscribed thus: MICHAEL / ÇIAMBONO PIXIT. The Gallerie acquired the polyptych in 1812 from the suppressed Scuola del Cristo on the Giudecca, but it must have been in the island's Church of San Giacomo that the painting first hung. The patron Saint occupies the central panel, identified by his staff and his Gospel, open to 1:22, while on his left Filippo Benizi, founder of the Servites (unhaloed because not canonized until 1671) holds the Book of Psalms turned to the verse *Servus Tuus sum ego* ("I am thy servant").

This is a later work, from around 1450, in which, despite the sumptuous ground of engraved gold, the artist softened his insistent linearism, enough at least to suggest that he had come to know, if not to understand, the innovations of the Tuscans then active in Venice, especially Andrea del Castagno, who was working on his frescoes for the San Tarasio Chapel at San Zaccaria.

At the Albertina in Vienna, there is a drawing with studies that seem related to Giambono's figures for Saint Philip and Saint Michael.

Mentioned, 1424—d. after January 7, 1470, and
before November 25, 1471
Madonna and Child
Panel, 28 x 21" (cat. no. 835)
Last restored 1950

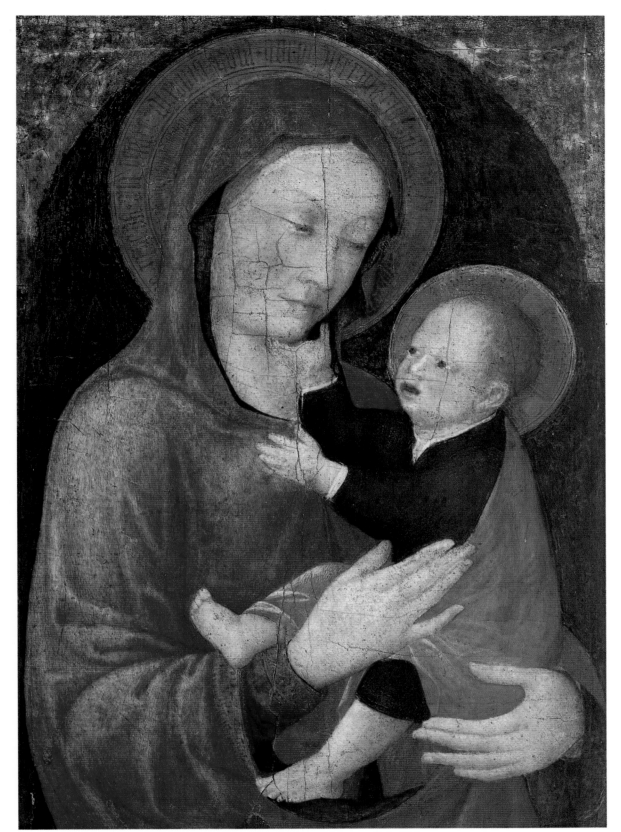

Acquired in 1920 from the Paduan parish of
Legarno, this panel is inscribed in Gothic
characters, on the Virgin's aureole, with a brief
antiphonal verse: REGINA. CELI. LETARE.
ALLELUIA. QUIA. QUEM. MERUISTI. PORTARE.
ALLELUIA ("Rejoice, O Queen of Heaven,
Alleluia, for Him whom Thou wast found
worthy to bear, Alleluia"). The original
surface has suffered abrasions and been
reworked in several places, particularly on the
faces as well as on the Christ Child's garment
and limbs. Moreover, the ground still bears the
imprint or outline of what must have been the
original frame. Nevertheless, here is the work
of an artist who constituted one of the key
figures in the complex process of renewal that
occurred in Venetian painting between the
1440s and the 1460s. And however poor its
state of preservation, the painting reflects
Jacopo's bold departure from the hieratic
frontality of Byzantine tradition, allowing
Mother and Child to turn towards one another,
rather than pose full face, and thus engage in a
tender dialogue, albeit one remote from Gothic
precedent. All together, these qualities make it
possible to date the panel after the Brera's
Madonna and Child, which Jacopo painted in
1448.

Mentioned, 1424—d. after January 7, 1470, and
before November 25, 1471
Madonna and Child with Cherubim
Panel, 38 x 26" (cat. no. 582)
Last restored 1979

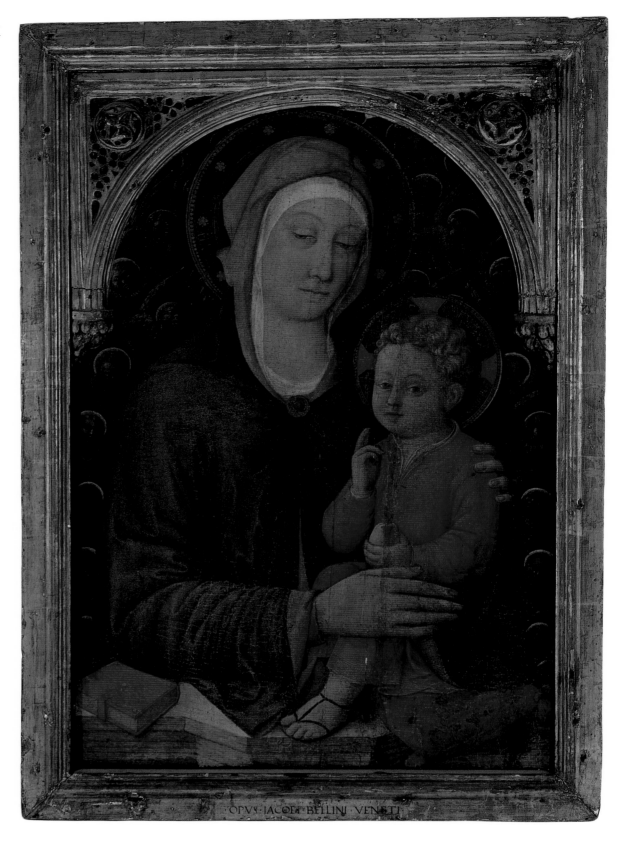

This panel may once have hung in the Palazzo Ducale (Paoletti, 1903), but at the end of the 18th century it belonged to the Paduan *abate* Foscarini, who sold it to the engraver Sasso.

By 1928 the Gallerie had come into possession of the work, but from what source is not known. An inscription on the original frame reads: OPUS / JACOBI / BELLINI / VENETI.

Formerly the panel appeared to be a precocious early work, but the evidence of refined technical command, including the engraved cherubim on gold ground, the foreshortened parapet, and the repoussoir cushion and book suggest the fruit of the artist's mature years in the 1450s.

Not only do the heads of the cherubim show up in Jacopo's drawing book owned by the Louvre (leaves 48 and 49), they also appear in the background of the Butler *Madonna and Child* attributed to Andrea Mantegna (Metropolitan Museum of Art, New York), who would undoubtedly have been inspired by the work seen here.

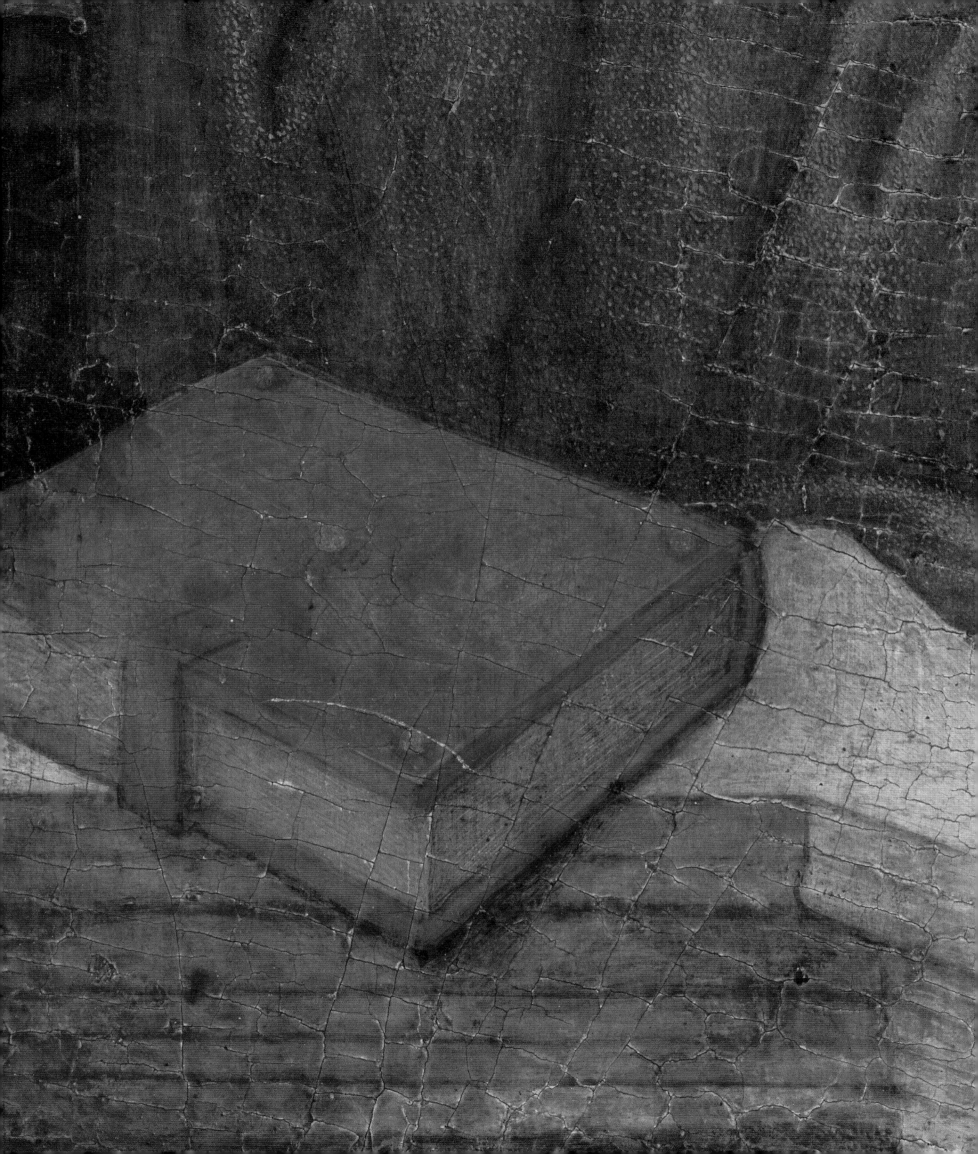

ANTONIO VIVARINI 15

Murano, 1415/20—Venice, 1476/84
Madonna and Child Blessing
Panel, 22 x 16" (cat. no. 1236)
Last restored 1958-59

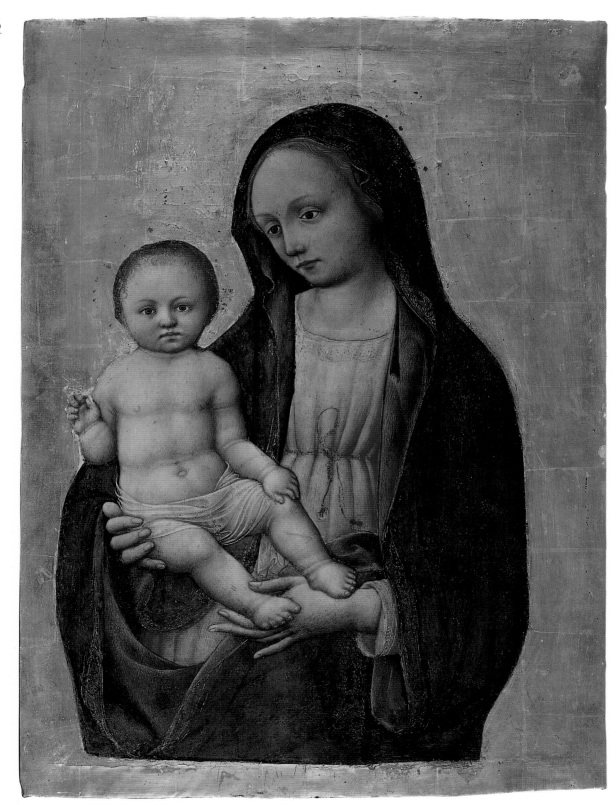

This panel came to the Gallerie in 1959 following its removal from the Church of San Giorgio delle Pertiche, to which it had been consigned in 1846. Since the little devotional panel was state property, it must have been commissioned for a public building, albeit which one is not known. Such assumption gains support from a reference, dated 1711, on the back to a court order issued at the time of the work's restoration.

   This is an extremely unified work, notable, despite the old-fashioned gold ground, for the artist's mastery of the new illusionism and for his soft, luminous palette, suggesting influence from Tuscany as well as from Jacopo Bellini. It can be dated around 1440.

Murano, 1415/20—Venice, 1476/84
The Marriage of Saint Monica
Panel, 12 x 18" (cat. no. 50)
Last restored 1951

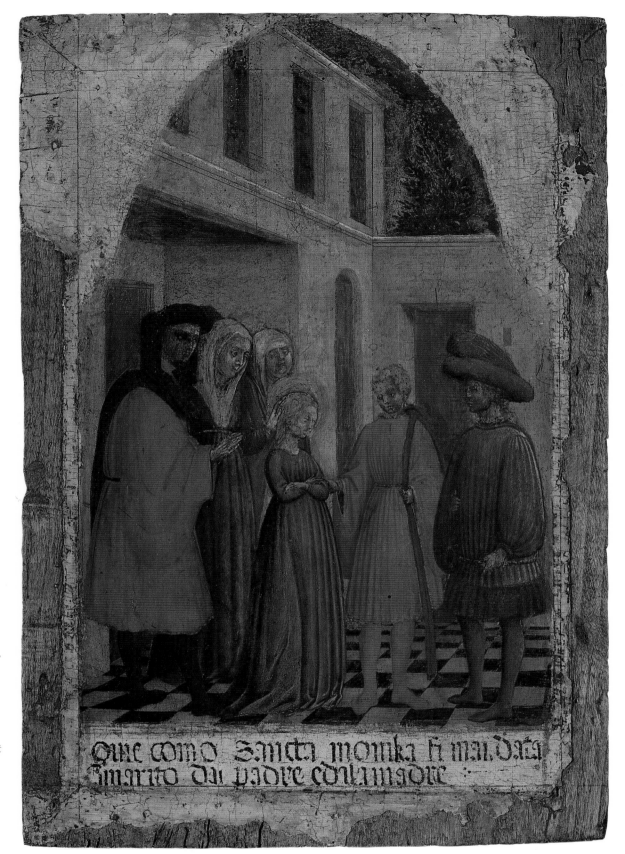

Although the Gallerie acquired this panel as early as 1816, through bequest from Girolamo Molin, it remained in the reserve until 1852. In 1932, the Gallerie lent the work to Murano's Museo Vetrario for a period that ended only in 1951. The Gothic inscription at the bottom reads: QUI È COMO SANCTA MONIKA FU MANDATA A MARITO DAL PADRE E DA LA MADRE ("Here is Saint Monica being given in marriage to her husband by her father and mother").

The painting originally served as an altarpiece in the Church of San Stefano, where, according to Ridolfi (1648), a wooden statue portraying the Saint stood surrounded by "little stories from her life." These small panels were dispersed in 1733 when the altar was rededicated to Saint Stephen. From this narrative group there survive the *Birth of Saint Augustine* at the Courtauld Institute of Art in London; the *Baptism of Saint Augustine* at the Carrara Academy in Bergamo; the *Conversion and Death of Saint Monica's Husband* at the Detroit Institute of Arts; and *Saint Monica at Prayer* in a private Milanese collection.

With its Masolinesque tonalities, the autographic work seen here would appear to reflect a desire on the part of the artist for a more spacious, perspectival, or illusionistic ambience, while the contemporary dress worn by the figures recalls the images of Paolo Uccello. By 1581, however, this would strike Sansovino as "antique clothes of the Venetians."

The entire series should probably be dated to the early 1440s.

Murano, 1415/20—Venice, 1476/84
Mentioned, 1441-1450(d.)
*Madonna and Child Enthroned between Saints
Gregory, Jerome, Ambrose, and Augustine*
Triptych: central canvas, 138 x 81"; two wings, 138 x
55" each; all with gilt-plaster decorations
(cat. no. 625)
Last restored 1950

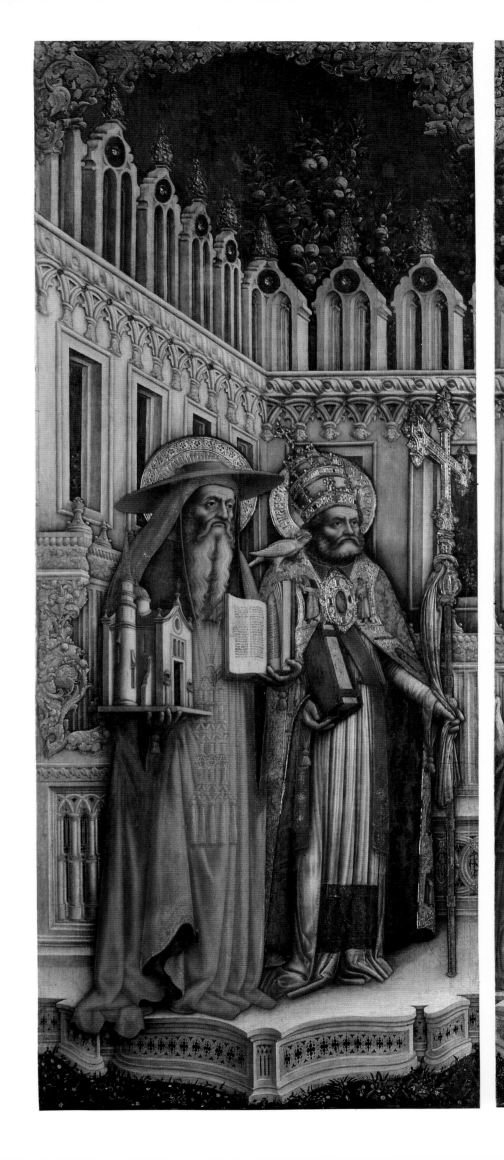

Signed and dated on the step leading to the
throne: M / 4 / 46 / IOHANES / ALAMANUS /
ANTONIUS/ D / MURIANO. The Gallerie acquired
this triptych in 1807 following the Napoleonic
secularization. It too originated in the *sala
dell'albergo* at the Scuola della Carità, where it
hung opposite Titian's *Presentation of the
Virgin in the Temple*. The altarpiece had been
framed in carved wood, which was destroyed
at the same time as the altar, in 1811, when
Selva opened a connecting passage through the
various buildings in the complex and installed
a brief flight of stairs.

   Among the oldest surviving Venetian
paintings on canvas, the triptytch is certainly
as well the most unified and significant of the
problematic collaborations carried out by
Antonio and Giovanni. But here, at least, one
may securely attribute to the former both the
Virgin and the angels, images closely related to
the figures of Masolino. In this "sacred
conversation," the iconography is unusual for
being set within a *hortus conclusus*. However
innovative, the rationalized perspective is all
but overpowered by the opulent décor, which
must have been even richer when still
supplemented by the original frame and the
now-lost stucco ornament on the copes of
Saints Augustine and Gregory. Inasmuch as
Antonio and Giovanni painted their triptych at
the same time that Donatello was beginning his
work at the Santo, their treatment of space
may reflect knowledge of the Paduan's
preparatory drawings for the sculptural
project.

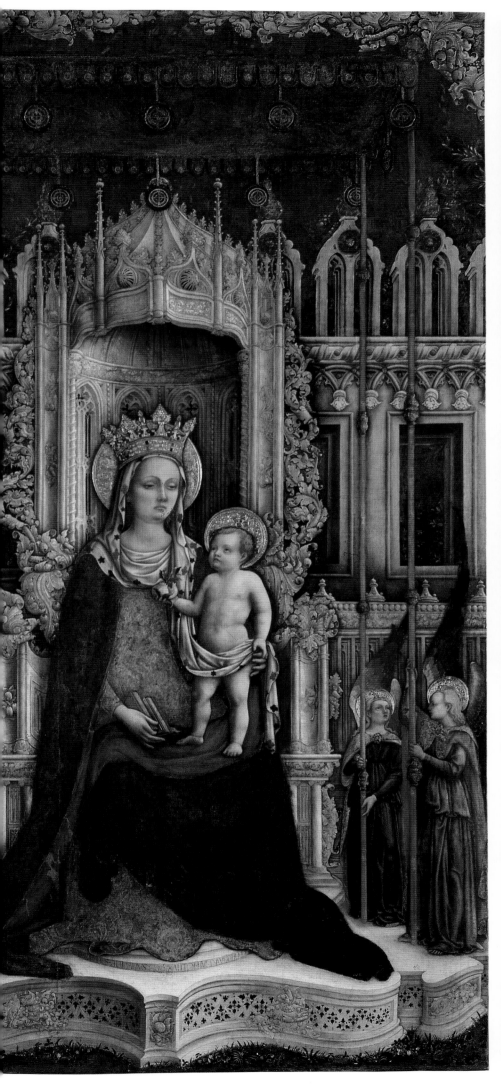
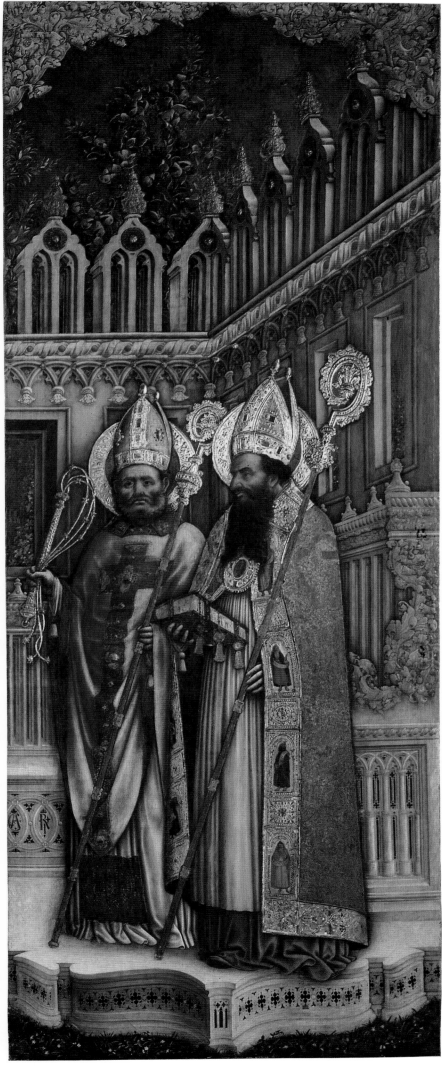

PIERO DELLA FRANCESCA 18

Sansepolcro, 1416/17—October 12, 1492
Saint Jerome with a Donor
Panel, 20 x 17" (cat. no. 47)
Last restored 1948

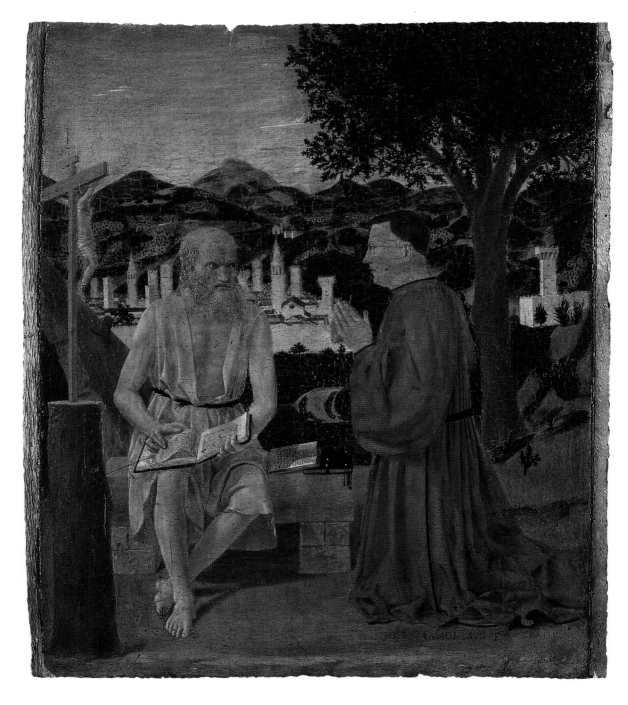

On the trunk of a tree at left appears a clearly authentic signature: PETRI DE BŪ /GO SCI SEP / ULCRI OPUS. Below the donor to the right we find: HIER - AMADI - AUG - F -. This refers to Girolamo Amadi, son of Augusto, whose wealthy family had come from their native Lucca to settle in Venice, where they financed the building of the Church of Santa Maria dei Miracoli. The difference in the lettering of the two inscriptions has caused some to doubt that the signature could be of the same date as the other name, which was believed to cite some later owner rather than the donor. However, the painting, which in 1833 entered the collection of Felicità Renier, who left it to the Gallerie in 1850, may have been commissioned "by someone in a Romagnola or Marche court for which Piero painted many pictures of beautiful little figures," as Vasari put it in

1568. From there the panel seems to have made its way to Girolamo Amadi. The artist very likely executed *Saint Jerome with a Donor* around 1450, following his stay in Ferrara. This would make it contemporaneous with the small panel entitled *The Penitent Saint Jerome* (Staatlichemuseen, Berlin), which is not only signed and dated 1450 but is also like the work seen here in its size, in the character of its landscape, and in the harmonious integration of the Saint with his natural environment. This picture, like that in Berlin, evokes Piero's native Tuscany. Thus, the figures stand silhouetted against the Alpe di Luna, while the tower or goblet-like chimneys and slender bell-towers withdraw into depth just as they do in the artist's *Baptism* (National Gallery, London). In other ways, however, such as the relationship between the Saint and

the donor, the panel reflects influence from Flemish painting, particularly that of Rogier van der Weyden, which Piero could have seen at the Ferrarese court. The colors of our little panel have deteriorated rather considerably. The green (a resinate of copper) used for the tree foliage and for the background landscape has now turned to burnt chestnut. Even so, within this crystalline microcosm—nature stilled and rigorously defined by two cylindrical volumes, one a tree stump bearing the Crucifix and the other a full-grown tree— forms reveal themselves in all their incorruptible purity and abstract perfection. This "synthesized illusionism of form, color, and light" would prove fundamental to Giovanni Bellini and the whole of Venetian painting, already on its way towards a vision of pictorial art steeped in the most exquisite color.

Isola di Cartura, 1431—Mantua, 1506
Saint George
Panel, 26 x 13" (cat. no. 588)
Last restored 1933; conservation 1979

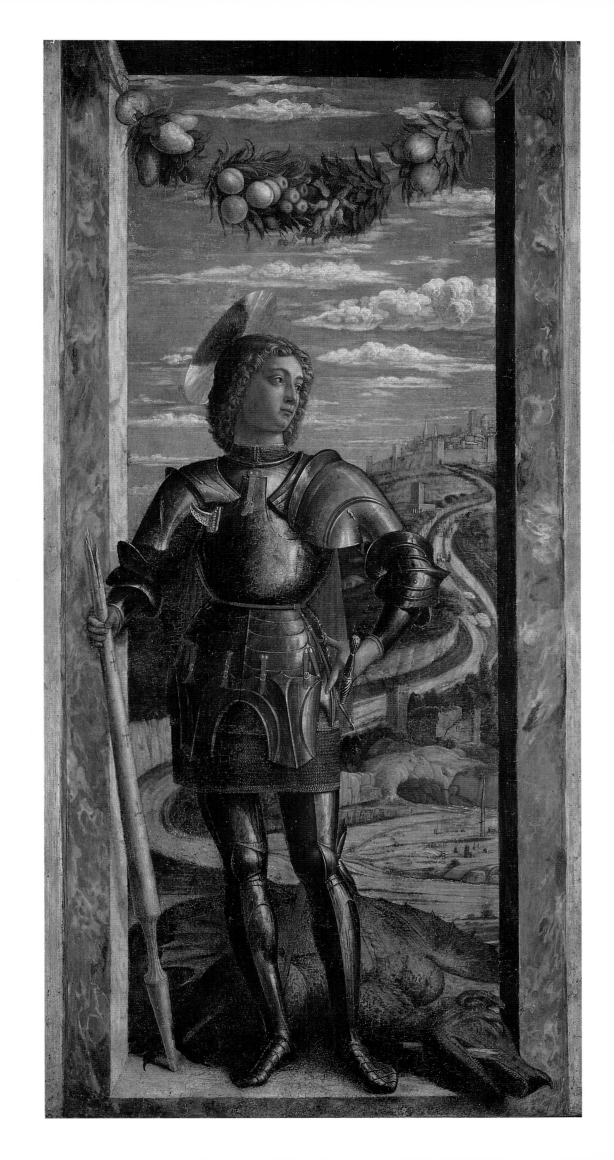

Acquired from the Manfrin collection in 1856, the painting is in a good state of preservation, despite a bit of retouching on the Saint's armor and on the dragon's snout. The provenance is unknown, but it must have involved a larger whole of which the work seen here constituted a part.

Art historians have dated the painting variously, as contemporary with the Eremitani frescoes and the *San Zeno Altarpiece*, from the artist's first Mantuan period, or, in view of certain Donatellesque and Castagnesque qualities, directly to his Florentine sojourn of 1466-67. However, affinities with the *Sant' Eufemia* in Naples' Galleria di Capodimonte, a work signed and dated 1454, suggest that the *Saint George* would fall more comfortably between *Sant' Eufemia* and the *San Zeno Altarpiece* in Verona. In the imperturbable young Saint, more a mythological hero than a model of Christian piety, the lingering symptoms of the artist's early training under Squarcione combine with the glyptic, Donatellesque consistency of the forms to generate, through rigorously exact perspective, an idealized, humanistic vision of serene beauty, without need of influence from Tuscan artists, present though these now were in Padua.

The fortified town represented in the background is Selene, under whose walls Saint George, according to the *Legenda Aurea*, slew the dragon.

Ferrara, 1430-95
Madonna and Sleeping Child, called The
Madonna of the Zodiac
Panel, 24 x 16"; with original frame, 48 x 27";
including lunette, 8 x 22" (cat. no. 628)
Last restored 1982

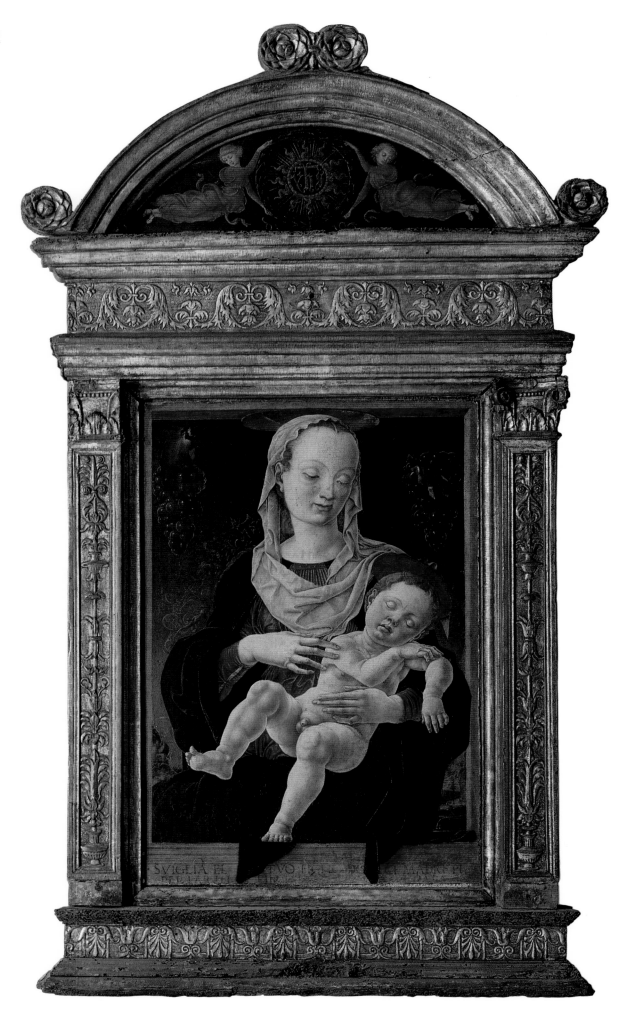

Inscribed on the parapet: SVIGLIA EL TUO
FIGLIO DOLCE MADRE PIA / PER FAR INFIN FELICE
L'ALMA MIA ("Sweet pious Mother, watch over
your child to bring infinite joy to my soul").

Purchased in 1896 from the Coen Rocca-
Luzzato family of Venice, Tura's panel once
hung in the Bertoldi farmhouse in Merlara nea
Padua, and it may very well have been a kind
of altarpiece intended for private use. The
contemporary frame in the style of Donatello
includes a tympanum embellished with the
device of San Bernardino supported by two
angels.

On the ground to the left of the Madonna,
the four zodiacal signs of Aquarius, Pisces,
Sagittarius, and Virgo have been traced in
gold, a series that must have continued
towards the right, where some fragments of it
can still be detected.

Although recently likened to the paintings
that Tura completed in 1469 for the organ
shutters in the Ferrara cathedral, the work
seen here was probably executed just after the
artist's *Primavera*, or, more correctly, *Erato*
(National Gallery, London), which would make
it datable between 1459 and 1463. Composed
with perfect clarity, the figures have been
painted in layers of transculent pigment that
on their own virtually assume a volumetric
quality. Moreover, the images display none of
the unsettling formal distortions or haunted
expressionism characteristic of the organ
shutters in Ferrara, or of the artist's later work
in general.

Tura would repeat the Sleeping Christ Child
theme almost entirely in the Roverella
polyptych, a work of his maturity.

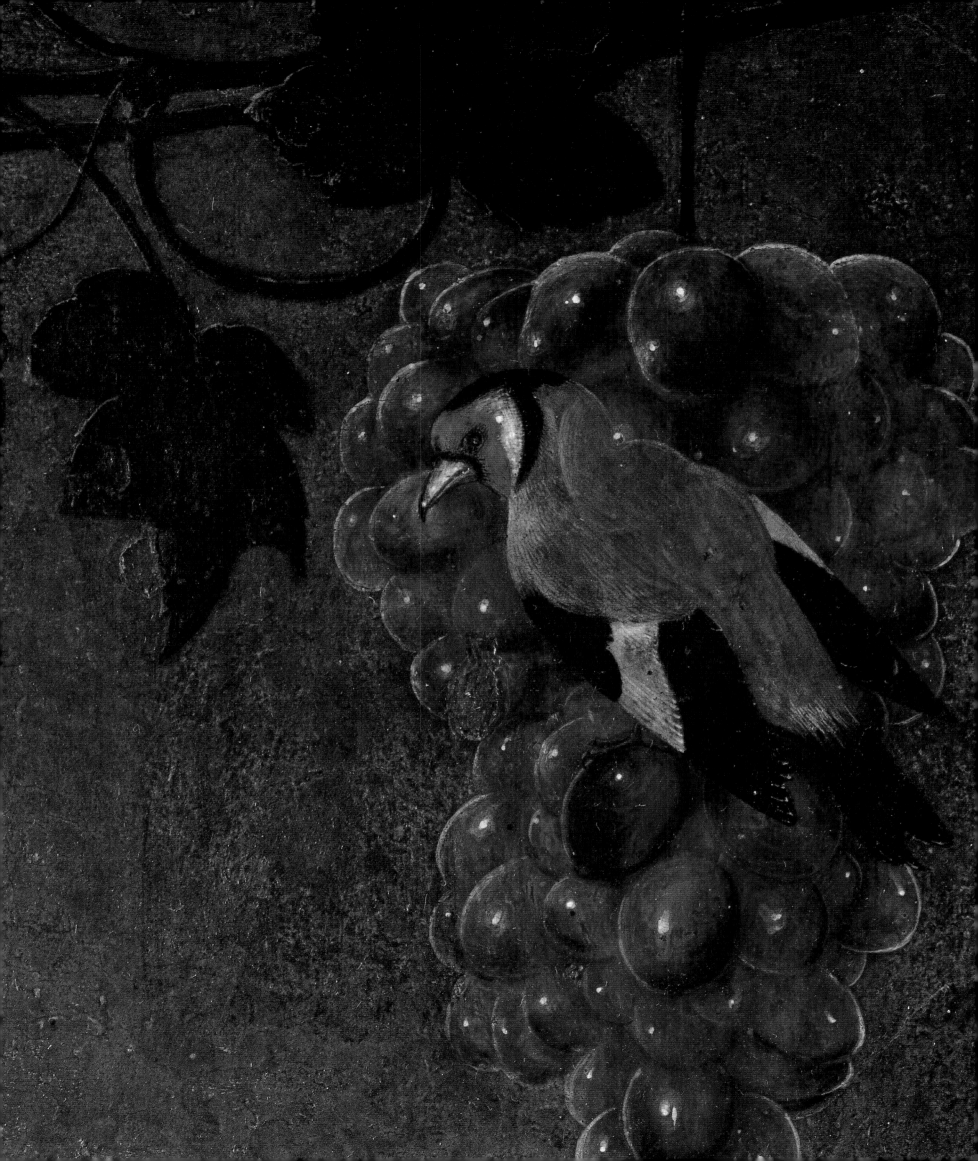

Murano, c.1430—after 1491
*Enthroned Madonna with Sleeping Child
between Saints Andrew, John the Baptist,
Dominic, and Peter*
Five-panel polyptych: central section, 52 x 6"; side
panels, 43 x 13" (cat. no. 615)
Currently in restoration

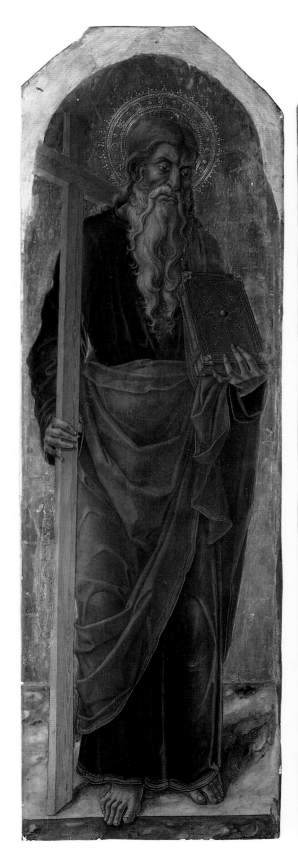
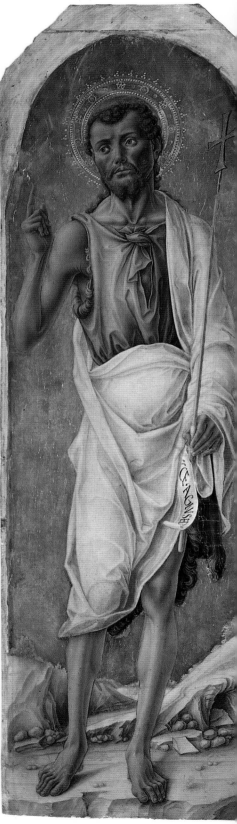

The inscription at the bottom of the central panel, which signs and dates the painting 1464, reads: OPUS / BATOLOMEI VA RINI / DE MURANO / MCCCCLXIIII.

This polyptych counted among the first acquisitions made for the Gallerie in 1812, following secularization. It came from the Venetian Church of Sant'Andrea alla Certosa, where it served as the altarpiece in the Ca' Morosini Chapel, known as the *Capitole*, or "Chapter." An engraving by G. Sasso informs us that the original frame, now lost, had been carved with a Crucifixion flanked by half-length prophet figures along the top.

Here, Mategna's new conception of the human figure has been modified by a bright, polychrome background, as well as by the Gothic linearism that continues to enclose shapes with hard-edged contours. The result is a most expressive work from the hand of an artist who otherwise could not resist an overriding need to make allusive use of his material. But even Giovanni Bellini had to acknowledge Bartolomeo's *Enthroned Madonna and Sleeping Child.*

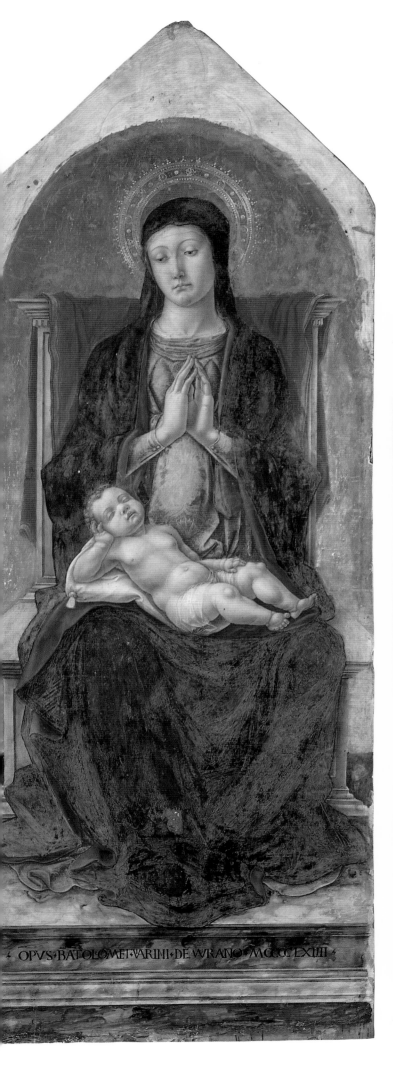

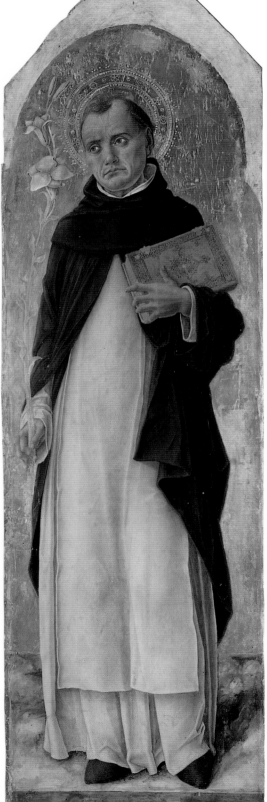

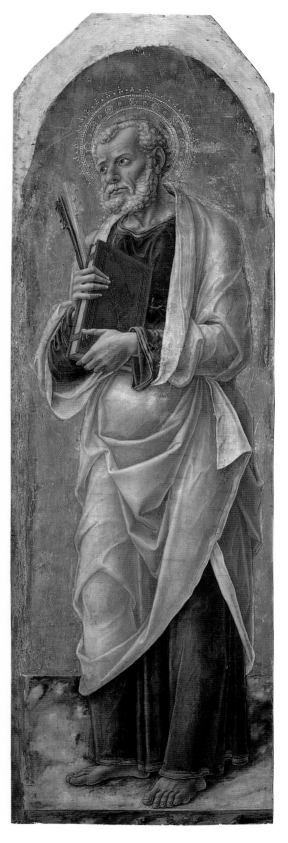

OPVS·BATOLOMEI·VARINI·DE·VRANO·MCCCCLXIIII·

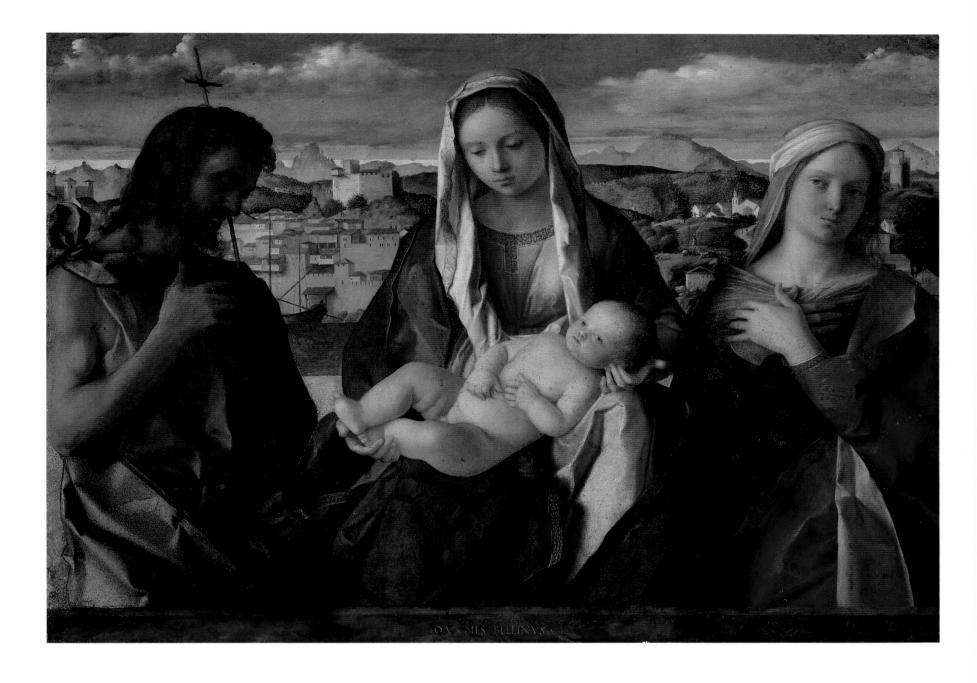

GIOVANNI BELLINI   34

Venice, 1430-1516
Madonna and Child between Saint John the Baptist and a Female Saint
Oil on panel, 22 x 30" (cat. no. 881)
Last restored before 1926

Signed on the parapet at center: JOANNES BELLINUS. This painting—acquired by the Gallerie in 1926 from the Giovanelli collection in Venice, by special arrangement with the State—is of the highest caliber, despite the effects of overcleaning at some time in the past. It also gives witness to a phase of the artist's development at the outset of the 16th century, a phase characterized by extreme freedom of invention and an effort to place his figures in an ampler, more luminously atmospheric space. This period, which culminated in 1505 in the *San Zaccaria Altarpiece*, brought such works as the *Madonna del Prato* (National Gallery, London)

and the *Pietà* from the Donà dalle Rose collection (ill. no. 35), all paintings whose innovative horizontality long delayed their attribution to Giovanni Bellini. Notwithstanding the splendid vignette of the riverside city and the distant, pale-colored Alpine foothills, this canvas, like the others, had yet to achieve perfect harmony between figures and background setting, which would come only around 1510, after Bellini had undergone the influence of Giorgione. Andrea Previtali's *Marriage of Saint Catherine* (1504) in the National Gallery, London, provides a *terminus ad quem*, thanks to its exact copy of Giovanni's John the Baptist.

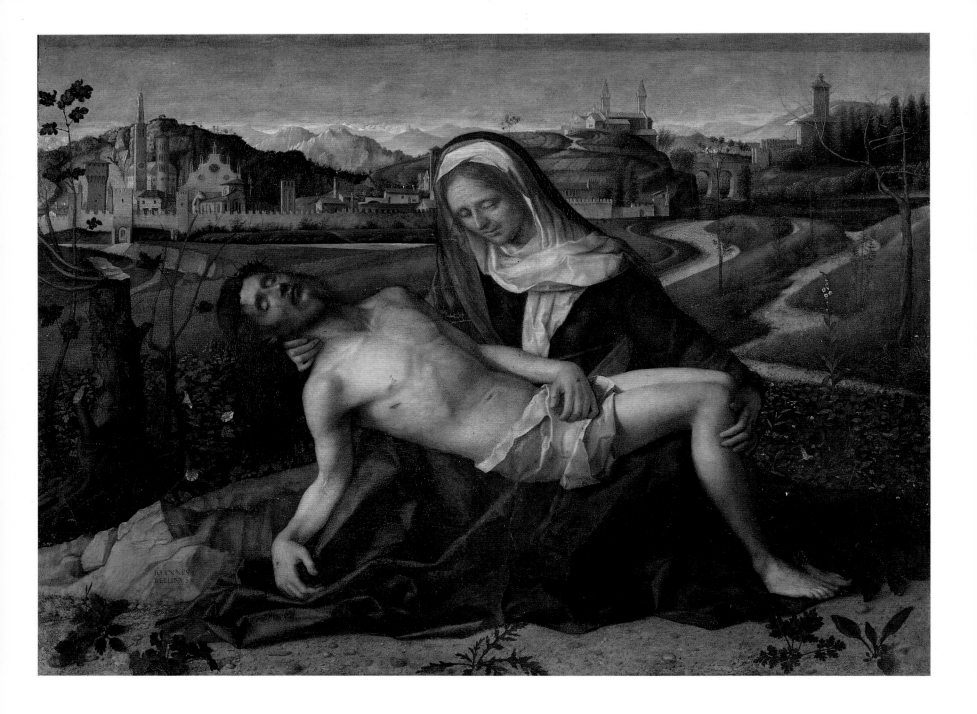

GIOVANNI BELLINI 35

Venice, 1430-1516
Pietà
Oil on panel, 26 x 35" (cat. no. 883)
Last restored 1935

Inscribed on the rocks at lower left: JOANNES / BELLINUS. Although acquired in 1935, by agreement, from the Donà dalle Rose collection, the painting had belonged to the Martinengo family in 1866, when it underwent restoration with lamentable results. A thick tinted varnish now coats the painted surface, giving it a golden tonality far removed from the brilliant luminosity originally achieved by the artist, the quality of which we know from small areas cleaned in 1978.

The work can be dated around 1505, a time when Giovanni demonstrated Northern or "Düreresque" tendencies not only in his closely observed meadow and translucent palette, but also in his effort to place figures in an ampler landscape.

However, the naturalism of the setting remains far from objective, in that it combines buildings from many places: the pre-Palladian Basilica, the cathedral and campanile at Vicenza, a view of Cividale's Natisone, and the Sant'Apollinare Nuovo campanile in Ravenna.

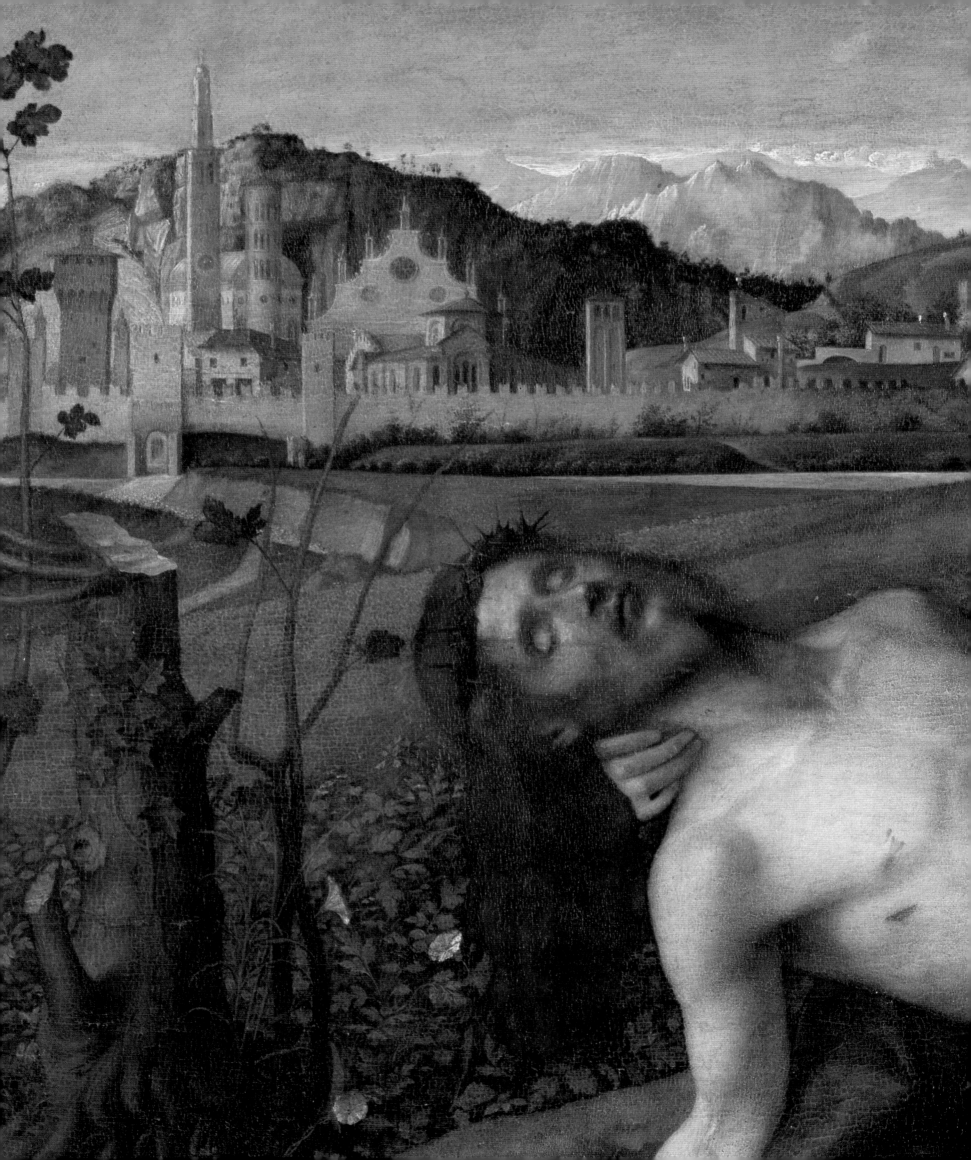

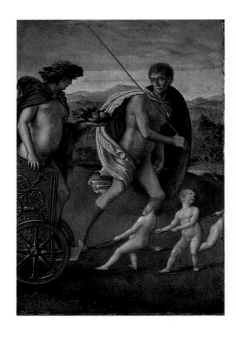 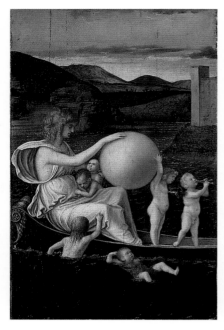 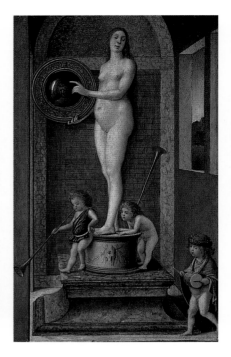 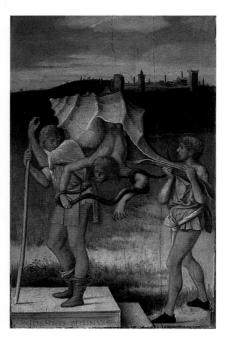

GIOVANNI BELLINI 36

Venice, 1430-1516
Allegories
Four walnut-veneered fir panels, 13 x 9" (a) and 14 x
9" (b,c,d) (cat. no. 595)
Last restored 1979

The *Allegories*, given to the Gallerie in 1838
by Girolamo Contarini, must originally have
formed part of a small piece of mirrored
furniture meant to serve as a dressing table,
which may be the very "furniture in walnut
adorned with certain little paintings by Messer
Zuan Belino" mentioned in Vincenzo Catena's
will of 1530 (leaving the piece to Antonio
Marsili). While still in the Contarini collection,
the suite possessed a fifth panel, which may
not have come from the same furniture but
merely resembled the panel it replaced. The
presence of a *Fortune* among the first four
panels would seem to obviate the need for a

second provided by the fifth panel. Already in
1489, the Venetian market had become so
flooded with small furniture of this sort that
the Senate passed a law (ineffectively) against
such work being either ordered or executed.
Given the complex moral symbolism of the
decorative panels, these may have been added
in an effort to redeem the furniture's frivolity
of purpose.

From left to right

(a) Tradition held that Bacchus in his chariot
offering a bowl of fruit to a warrior (an image
freely adapted from drawings by Jacopo
Bellini) represented Sloth and Perseverance, or,
better yet, Lasciviousness tempting the heroic
warrior—that is, the Man of Virtue. What we
have, then, is the allegory of "Heroic Virtue."

(b) The woman on the small boat with a great
sphere, surrounded by *putti*, signifies the
"Allegory of Fickle Fortune" or "Melancholy."

(c) The nude woman standing on a pedestal
and holding a mirror may be understood as the
"Allegory of Prudence" or, even more perhaps,
as "Vanity." Northern European in origin, the

iconography corresponds precisely to that in an
engraving by Jacopo de' Barbari of 1504, as
well as in a painting by Hans Baldung Grien of
the same year, a work now in Vienna. The
person reflected in the convex mirror is
probably the client.

(d) The symbolism of a man caught in the coils
of a serpent slithering from a great shell held
by another figure is more difficult to
understand. In the past, it was often
interpreted negatively, as "Infamy Unmasked,"
"Calumny," or "Falsehood." Recently, it has
assumed a more positive meaning, as the
"Allegory of Courage and Wisdom," with the
shell signifying life and procreation.

Thanks to its painterly refinement, as well as
to its light-suffused spaciousness, where the
figures come together with such limpid
elegance, this little suite constitutes a nonpareil
among the artist's works. Dating has varied
between the early 1480s and the early 16th
century, although the latter seems more
probable, given the echoes of certain Northern
European works produced in 1504.

Venice, 1430-1516
*Mourning the Dead Christ, with Joseph of
Arimathea, One of the Marys, the Magdalene,
and Filippo Benizi of the Servite Order
(Benedictine)*
Oil on canvas, 178 x 125" (cat. no. 166)
Last restored 1964

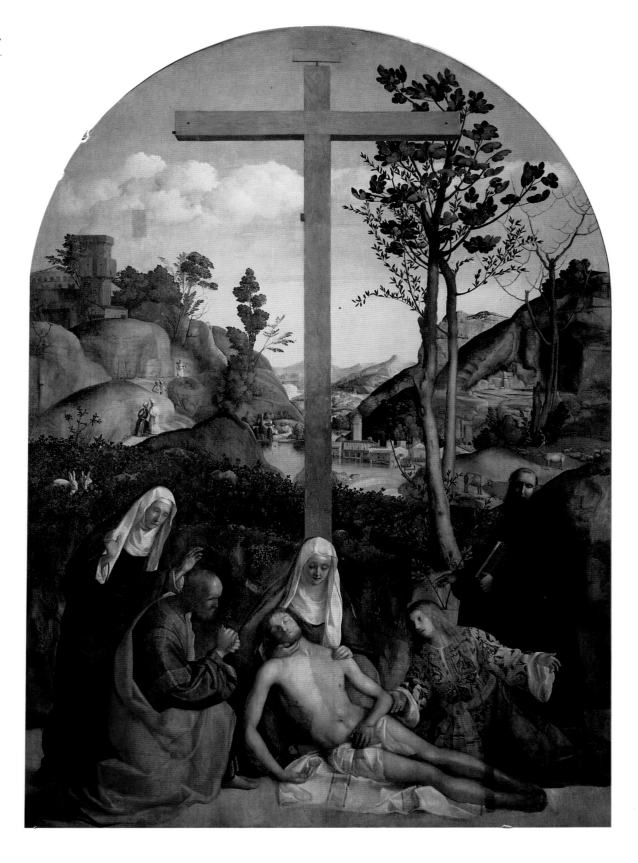

In the wake of secularization, when it became State property in 1814, this painting was rolled up and eventually sent to the Commenda for storage before being assigned to the Gallerie in 1829. Originally in Venice's Church of Santa Maria dei Servi, the work long survived as the masterpiece of Rocco Marconi, to whom Boschini had attributed it in 1664, until the catalogue of 1903 reclaimed it for Giovanni Bellini. By now this attribution is almost universally accepted, provided it allows for other hands on parts of the landscape as well on the figures of Saint Monica and Filippo Benizi. The work seen here may have been the artist's last attempt at a large altarpiece, the marvelous chromatic transparency of which recalls the canvases executed for San Zaccaria and San Giovanni Crisostomo, while also anticipating the *Drunkenness of Noah* in Besançon and the *Feast of the Gods* in Washington.

Venice, 1430-1516
*The Archangel Gabriel and The Virgin
Annunciate*
Canvas, each 90 x 43" (cat. no. 734)
Last restored 1908 (*The Virgin Annunciate*)

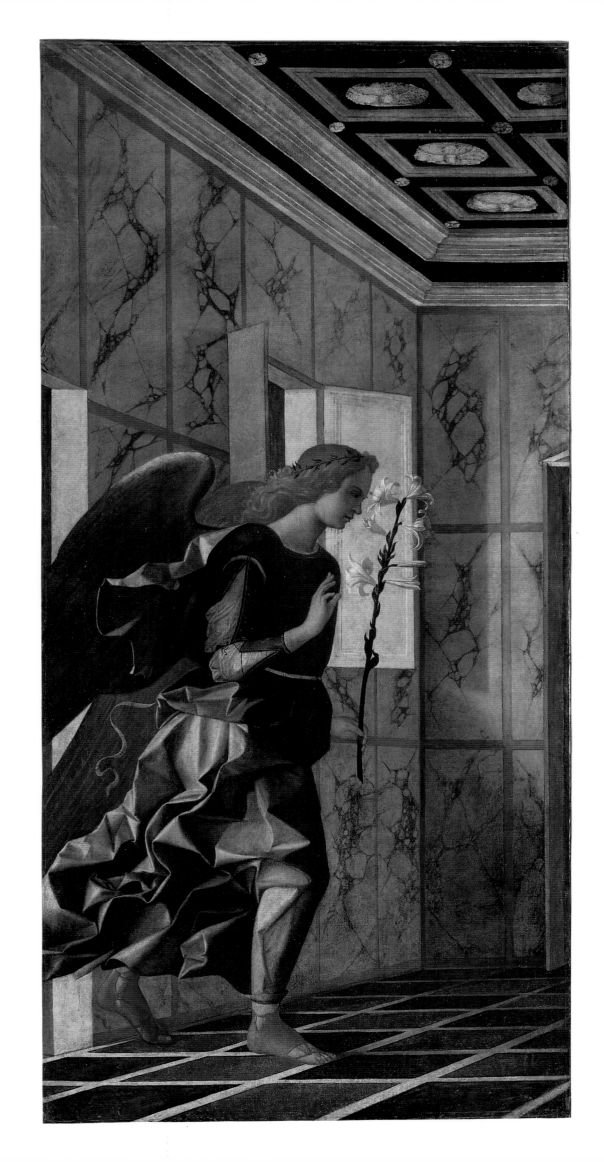

These two canvases once adorned the outer
doors of the organ case in the Venetian Church
of Santa Maria dei Miracoli. The inner panels
bore a *Saint Peter* (now in the Gallerie reserve)
and a *Saint Paul*. The latter was lost along
with some *chiaroscure* that were once on the
organ loft.

At the time of the church's secularization in
the early 19th century, the *Virgin* canvas was
stored at San Francesco della Vigna and the
Saint Paul at the Frari. After purchasing the
Archangel Gabriel in London in 1907, the
Gallerie exhibited it side by side with the
Virgin canvas in the same year.

Boschini, writing in 1664, attributed the two
paintings to Pier Maria Pennacchi, an artist
from Treviso whose role as a go-between
among Venetian painters at the turn of the
15th and 16th centuries remains controversial.
Later attributions moved steadily closer
towards Giovanni Bellini, whose touch is
clearly discernible, until the recent claim made
for Carpaccio, to whose *Dream of Saint Ursula*
(ill. no. 68) the diptych visibly refers,
particularly in the treatment of the angel. In
conclusion, however, we take the work to
derive from the master's own drawing, but
then to have been completed with certain
contributions by others.

As for dating, it cannot be earlier than 1489,
the year of the church's completion, with a
marble-clad interior recorded in paintings
datable in the opening years of the 16th
century.

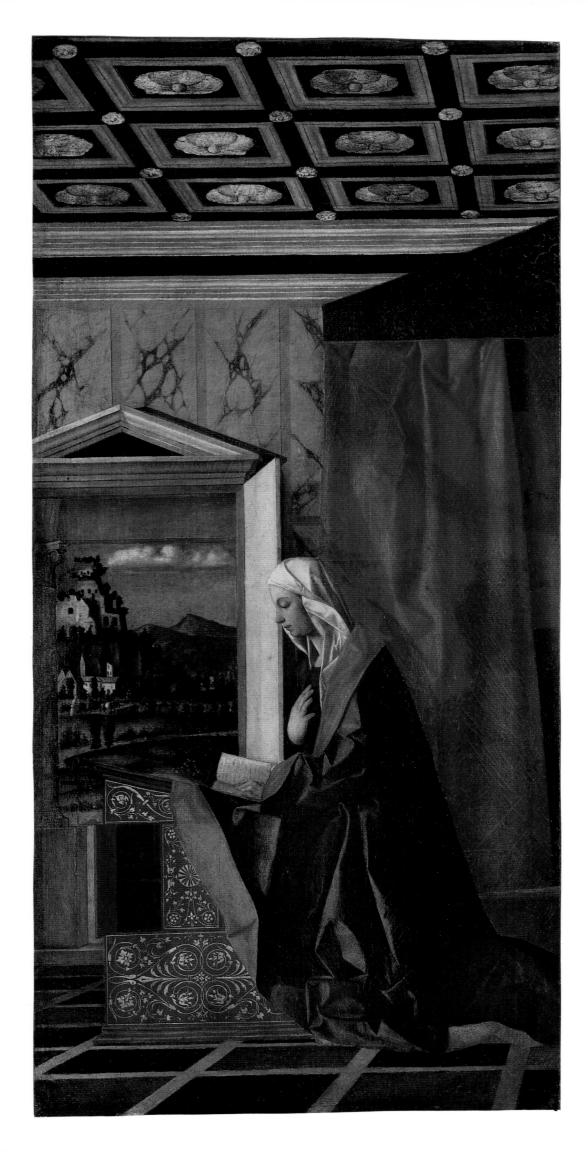

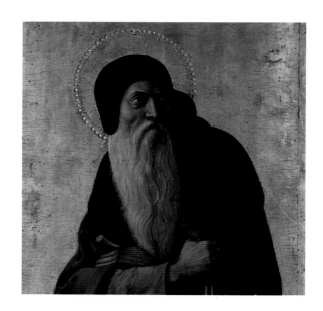

GIOVANNI BELLINI
AND WORKSHOP   39

Triptych of Saint Sebastian
Central panel 68 x 18", side panels 68 x 18" and 51 x
19", lunette 24 x 68" (cat. no. 621/a)
Last restored 1948-49

Here we find Saint Sebastian flanked by Saints Anthony Abbot and John the Baptist, while in the lunette above hover God the Father and the Annunication. This triptych, along with three others (a *Nativity*, a *Saint Lawrence*, and a *Madonna*) originally hung in Venice's Santa Maria della Carità, whose interior underwent reconstruction at the end of the 15th century. All four triptychs constituted altarpieces for family chapels built in 1460-64 against the *barco*, a structure setting off the church's elevated choir. It appears that by the time of the chapels' consecration in 1471, the paintings had already been installed. Dismembered as a result of secularization, when the church, along with the entire Carità complex, became a home for the Accademia, the triptychs remained scattered until their reassembly got under way in the late 19th century, a process completed only in the mid-1950s. Those responsible for the task relied on a record made at the time of the panels' dismantling and removal from the church. Numbers marked on the individual pieces correspond with this record, as well as with descriptions of the four triptychs given by Boschini in 1664.

Still, the arrangements pose problems even today, mainly because of no evident or direct correlation between the Saints depicted in a triptych and those over whose altar the painting hung. Traditionally attributed to the Vivarini, the paintings were later thought to have come from the Bellini family—first the workshop of Jacopo, whose drawings the panels sometimes recall, then the workshop of Giovanni—and to have been executed in the late 1450s. The surviving presence of certain archaisms, such as the gold ground, could be explained by the involvement of assistants from Murano or by the wishes of the clients themselves.

This particular triptych was the altarpiece in the Saint Sebastian Chapel belonging to the Zaccaria Vitturi family. The Saint Sebastian and Saint Anthony Abbot panels entered the Gallerie in 1812, while the Baptist panel arrived in 1834, from storage at the Church of San Giovanni Evangelista. The lunette, sent to Vienna in the early 19th century, returned to Venice in 1919, after World War I.

The reconstruction of the present triptych's main or, lower, parts is unquestionably correct, since the landscape continues across all three panels. Considered the most important of the triptychs, it is almost unanimously attributed to Giovanni Bellini, at least as far as the Saints are concerned, especially the figure of Saint Anthony Abbot. The latter's piercing gaze, further pressured by the cramped space of the panel, echoes a drawing by the artist in the Royal Library, Windsor, although the main inspiration seems to have come from Donatello's *Saint Prosdocimus Altarpiece* in Padua. The drawing may have served as a means of translating Donatello's sculpture into Bellini's painting. Despite its gold field, the *Triptych of Saint Sebastian* displays complete mastery of Florentine and Paduan innovations, particularly the articulation of figures in relation to the spaces they occupy, the sense they give of a new-found spirituality, and the purity of the background colors.

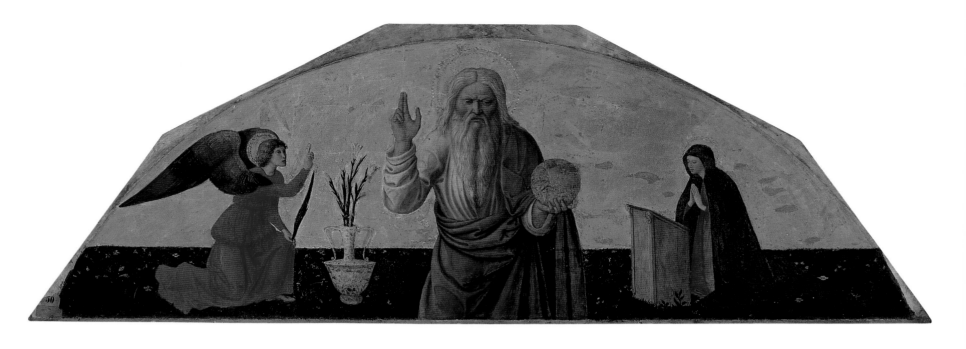

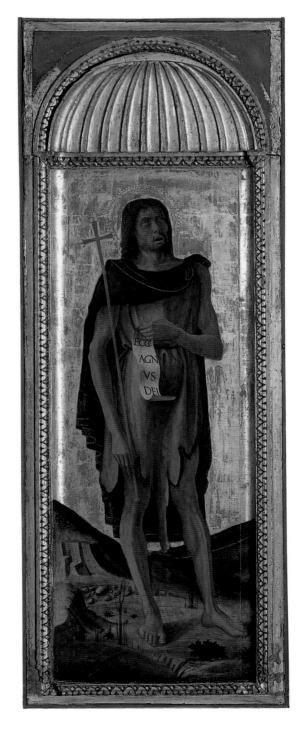
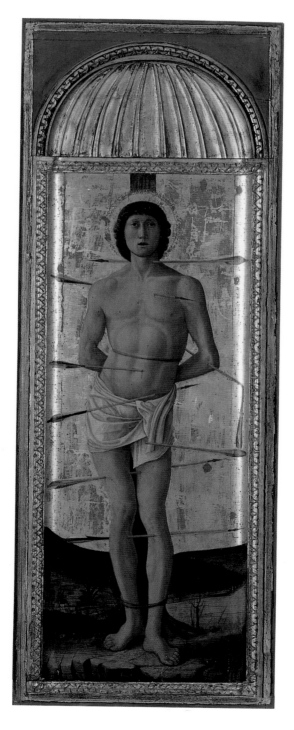
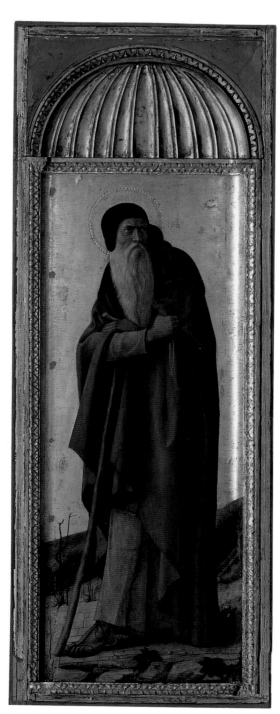

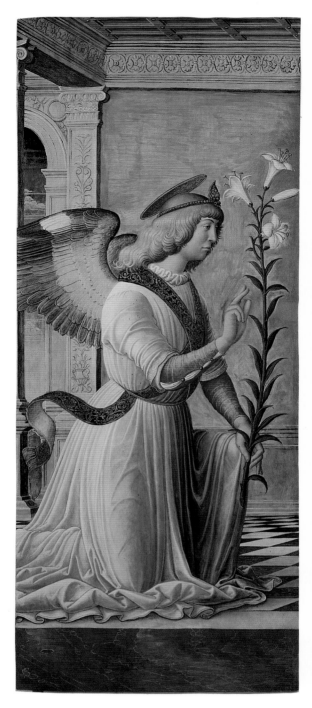 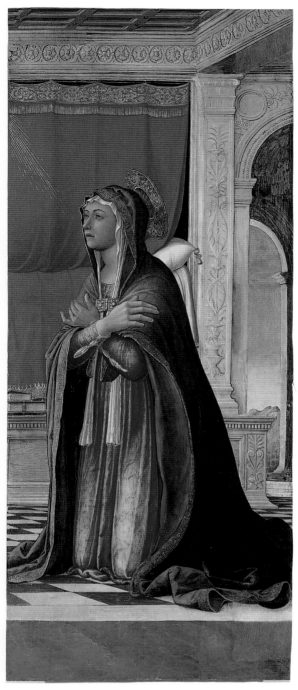

JACOPO PARISATI CALLED DA MONTAGNANA   40

Mentioned 1458-99 (d. Padua)
The Archangel Gabriel and The Virgin Annunciate
Two partial panels, 75 x 30" and 74 x 74" (cat. nos. 606, 608)
Last restored 1984-91

Originally in the Paduan Church of Monteortone, these two paintings must have formed part of a larger whole. Thanks to the composition's linear perspective, we can infer an absent central part measuring about 44 inches wide, an inference confirmed by the amputated state of the red-curtained bed in the background of the *Virgin Annunciate*. In addition to the implications of the recessional axes, we may also assume further excisions to the right of the Virgin and to the left of the Archangel, of about 10 inches each. In 1550, Vasari wrote that "Montagnana, who painted in Venice, did a picture for the Church of Santa Maria di Monteortone in Padua."

While translating Mantegna's great legacy into decorative linearism, Montagnana also proved himself no stranger to the aesthetic innovations of Giovanni Bellini. Further, his uncommon mastery of perspective and spatial depth may reflect some acquaintance with the marquetry of Pietro Antonio degli Abati. The *Virgin Annunciate* is probably contemporary with the frescoes executed by the artist at Monteortone between 1494 and 1497. The lambent color—particularly evident in the backgrounds and revealed only after a later grayish wash had been removed during the latest restoration—may owe something to the Northern European painters and sculptors who were active in Padua at this time.

Reflectography discloses a delicate preliminary line drawing, done in silverpoint on the primed surface.

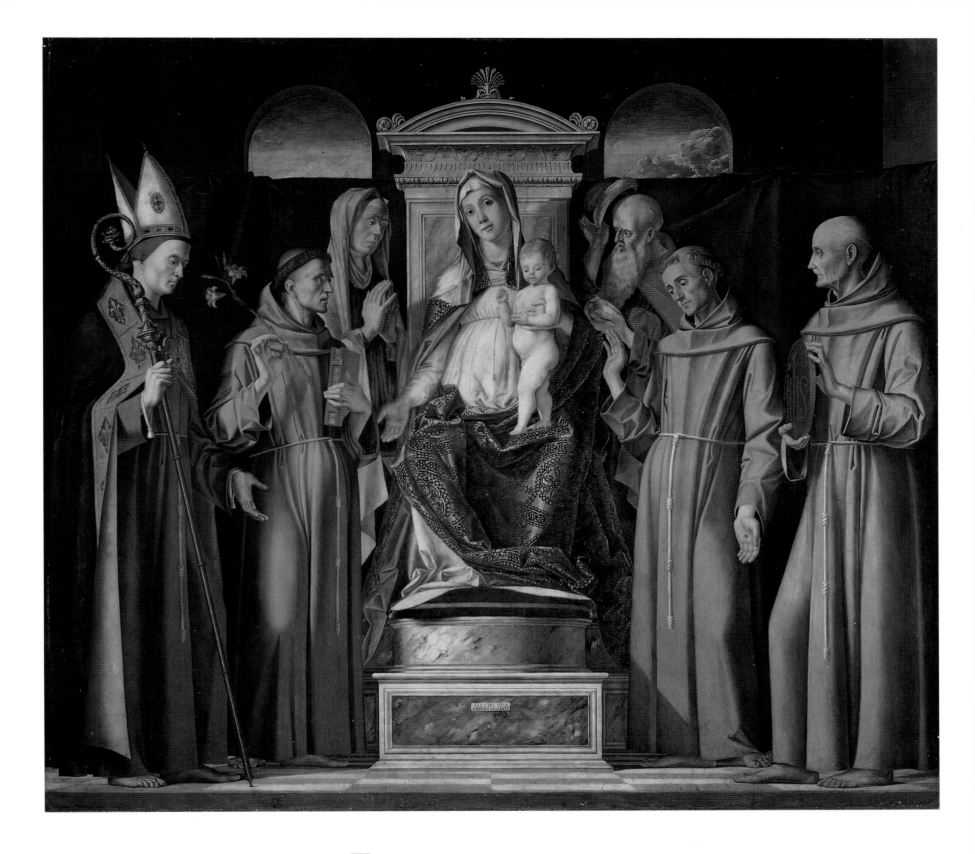

ALVISE VIVARINI   41

Murano, 1442/53—d. between 1504 and November 4, 1505
Madonna and Child Enthroned between Saints Louis of Toulouse (or Bonaventure), Anthony of Padua, Anna, Joachim, Francis, and Bernardino of Siena
Panel, 70 x 78" (cat. no. 607)
Last restored 1979

The panel has been signed and dated 1480 on the base of the throne: ALVIXE VIVA / RIN / P / MCCCCLXXX.

It was among the core group of works acquired by the Gallerie in 1812, following secularization.

The green canopy, although old, is a later addition, whose dense pigment cannot be penetrated by radiography.

In the initial composition, the two windows must have been wide open to a landscape beyond, as in the *Madonna Adoring the Sleeping Child* in the Venetion Church of San Giovanni in Bragora. The work seen here—a *Sacred Conversation*—constitutes the crowning event in the career of Alvise, who became not only a sensitive interpreter of the lessons taught by Antonella da Messina, but also an harmonious synthesizer of all the cultural streams flowing through his art.

The Fondation de Costade in Paris owns a study for the Saints' heads, while the bust of Saint Anthony reappears in a small picture now in the Museo Correr in Venice.

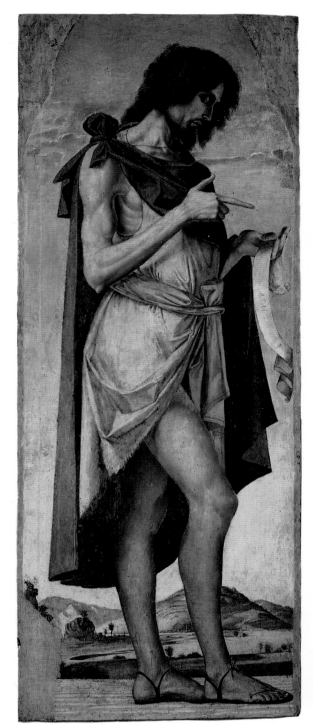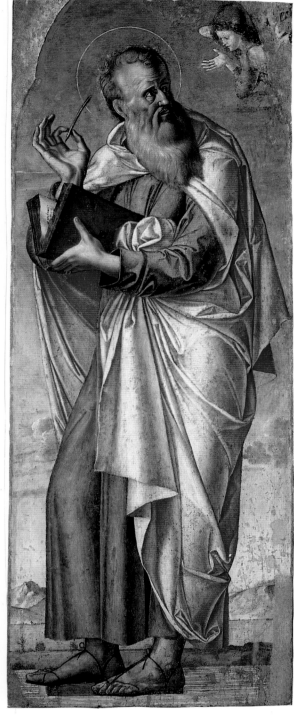

ALVISE VIVARINI   42

Murano, 1442/53—d. between 1504 and November 4, 1505
Saint John the Baptist and Saint Matthew
Panels, 54 x 21" and 53 x 20" (cat. nos. 618, 619)
Last restored 1949

The two panels came to the Gallerie in 1812, among the first to arrive there following the Napoleonic secularization. Originally they hung in the Church of San Pietro Martire on Murano.

By the time they reached the Gallerie, the pictures had been damaged along the top. The latest restoration removed some old overpainting, and thus made it possible to confirm the attribution to Alvise, as well as date the panels just after the *Sacred Conversation* of 1480 (see ill. no. 41).

The cool, crystalline palette, the subtly agitated brushwork, and the depth of the bare, timeless landscapes at the feet of the Saints (particularly in the Baptist panel) make these paintings two of the artist's most evocative works.

Probably b. Vicenza; mentioned 1459-1523
Saint Peter Blessing, with Donor
Panel, 24 x 16" (cat. no. 1343)
Last restored 1978

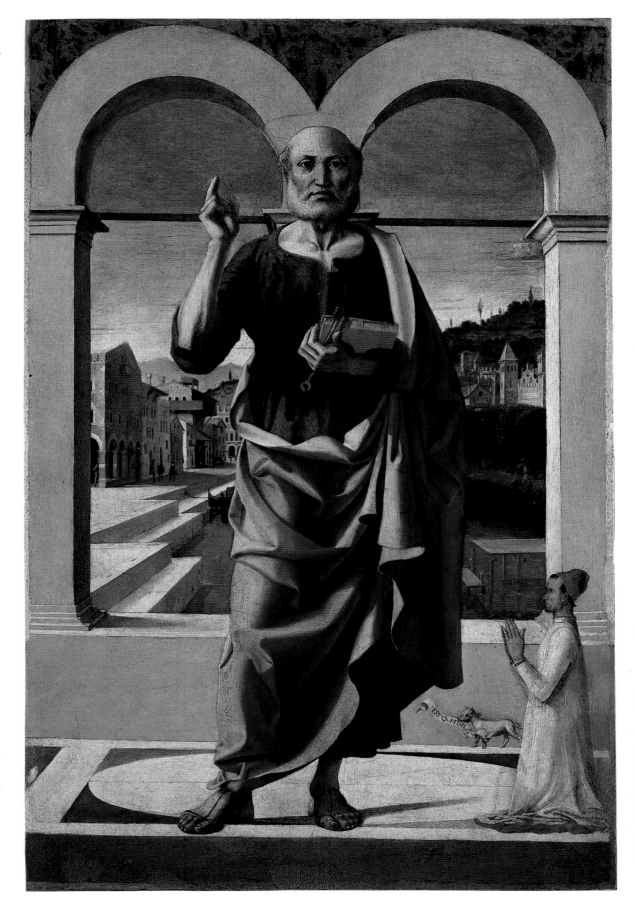

The inscription on the scroll carried by the little dog in his mouth reads: ESTO FIDELIS ("Be faithful"). At the end of 1871, Crowe and Cavalcaselle cite the painting in the Papafava collection in Padua. In 1971, the State exercised its right of preemption in favor of the Gallerie when Count Novello Papafava dei Carrersi proposed to sell the painting to Robert George Powler of Florence.

Most informed opinion attributes the work to Montagna because of its close stylistic and iconographic links to the artist's other works, most of all the frescoes in the Church of Santi Nazaro e Celso in Verona. Like these murals, *Saint Peter Blessing* dates from around 1505, and exhibits an extraordinary capacity to synthesize the human figure with the natural and human-made environment. The artist's *antonellismo*—his debt to Antonello da Messina—is enriched by elements drawn from Giovanni Bellini, most evident in the delightful fragment of Veneto landscape, where among various borrowed buildings one finds the façade of the Duomo in Vicenza and the Arena in Pola.

Conegliano, c.1459-1517
Pietà, with the Virgin, Nicodemus, Saint John, and the Marys
Panel, 29 x 46" (cat. no. 604)
Last restored 1990

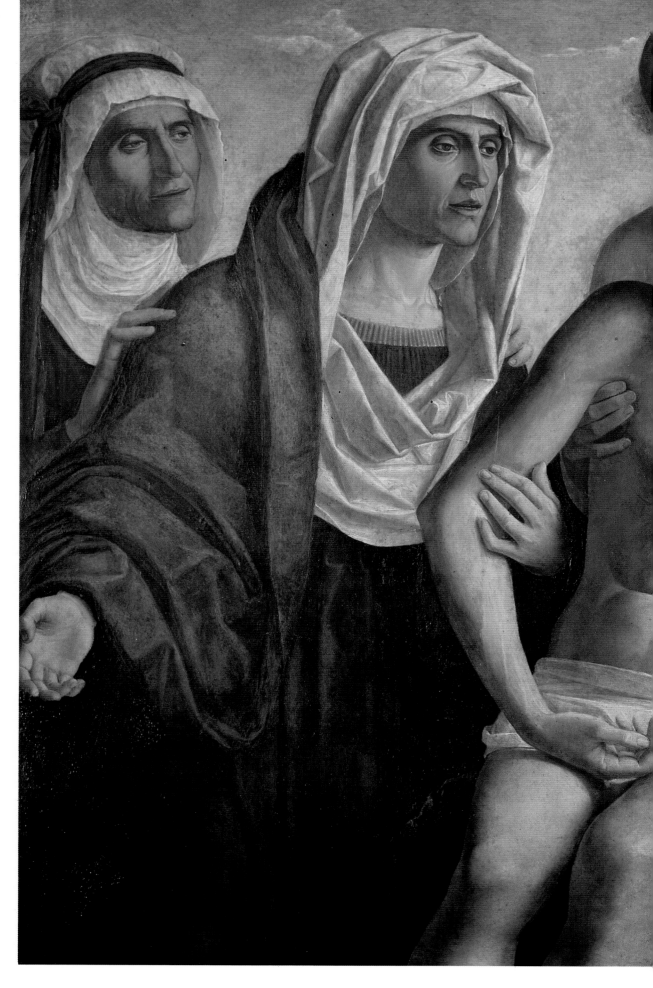

An inscription along the lower right edge reads: IOANNIS BAPTISTE CONEGIANENSIS OPUS. The Gallerie received the painting in 1850 through a bequest from Felicita Renier. Although its original provenance is not known, the work is generally assumed, without much confirming evidence, to have come from the Capitolo del Carmine on Murano. With the help of certain landscape features, most commentators have also considered the painting a youthful effort, by an artist who would become one of Venice's leading painters of religious subjects.

Having borrowed from Alvise Vivarini, Antonello da Messina, and Giovanni Bellini, particularly the latter's *Dead Christ with Angels* in the Museo Civico, Rimini, Cima made them his own in a synthesis of genuine equilibrium and dignity.

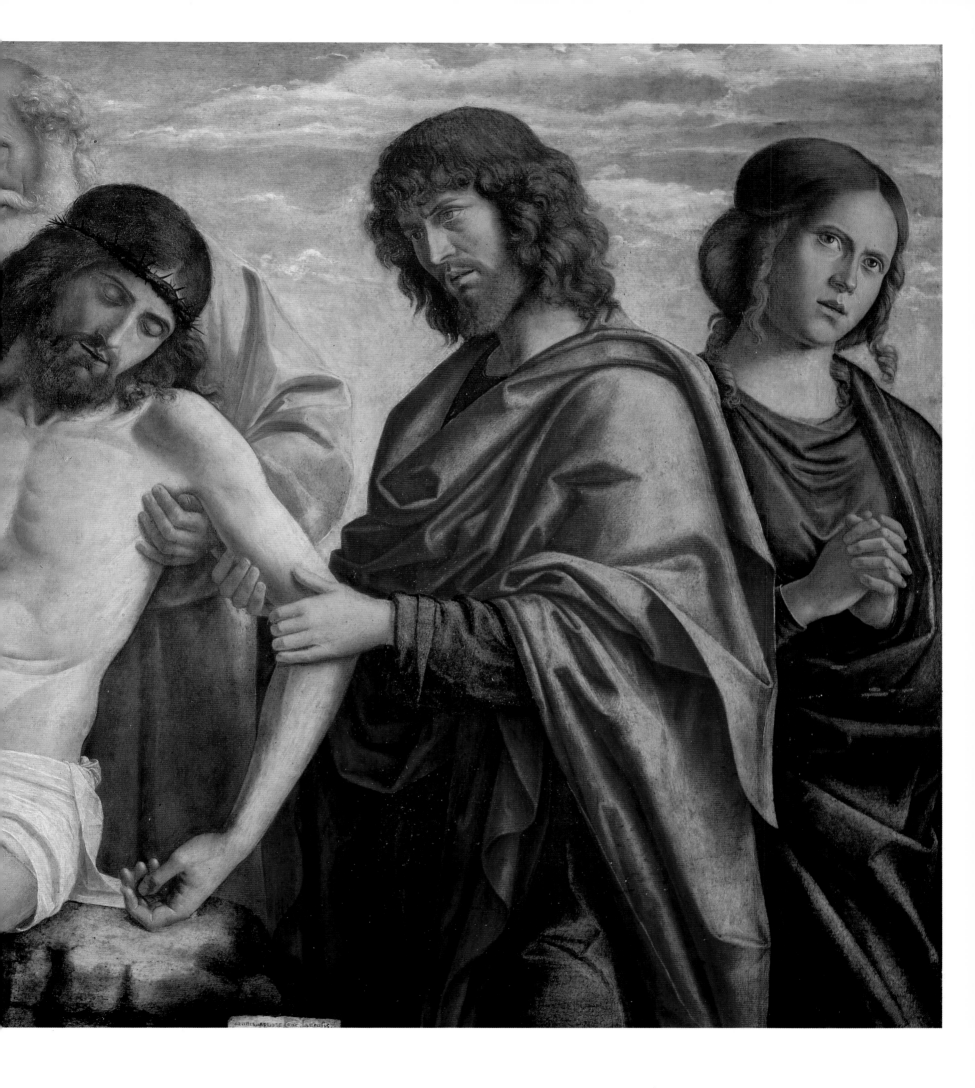

Conegliano, 1459/60-1517/18
*Madonna of the Orange Tree, with Saints Jerome
and Louis of France*
Panel, 85 x 56" (cat. no. 815)
Last restored 1979

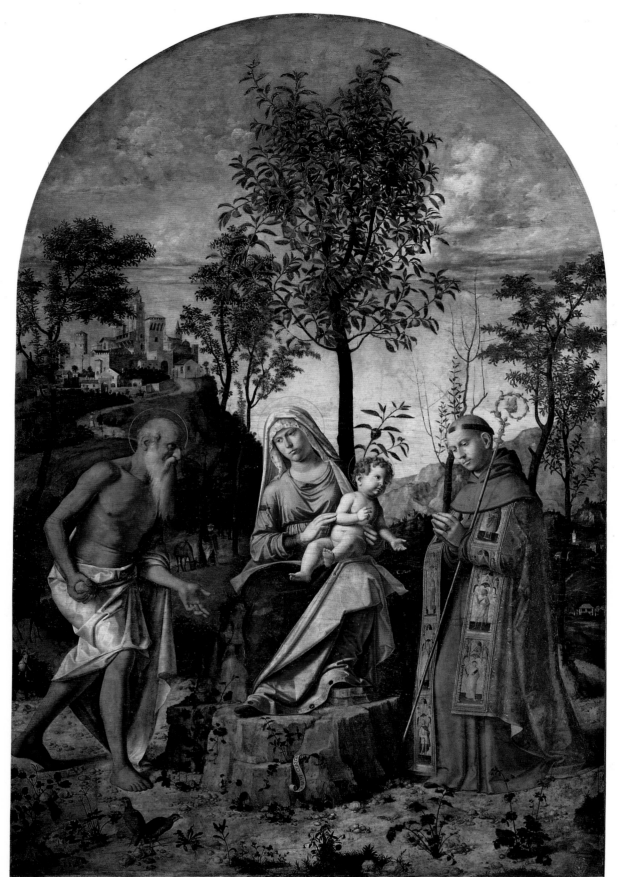

The artist's signature is inscribed on a scroll at the Virgin's feet: JOA-BPT-CONGL-. Made State property by the Napoleonic secularization, Cima's *Madonna of the Orange Tree* was appropriated for Vienna in 1816, restored to Venice after World War I, and finally assigned to the Gallerie in 1919. It originally hung in the Church of Santa Clara on Murano, where it would have been understood as a variation on the Flight into Egypt theme, a narrative completed by the little figure of Saint Joseph with his donkey in the background. This unfolds just left of the eponymous orange tree, which is probably an emblematic reference to the Virgin herself.

Without question, Cima harvested some of his ideas for this painting from the votive picture that Giovanni Bellini had painted for Doge Agostino Barbarigo in 1488, a work now in the Church of San Pietro Martire on Murano.

Given the similarity of the central group to that in the artist's *Sacred Conversation* in Lisbon, the *Madonna of the Orange Tree* can be dated between 1495 and 1497. The terse clarity of the drawing, the crystalline purity of the color, and the delightful landscape, the latter dominated by a castle reminiscent of San Salvatore di Collato, combine to make this one of Cima's most felicitous achievements.

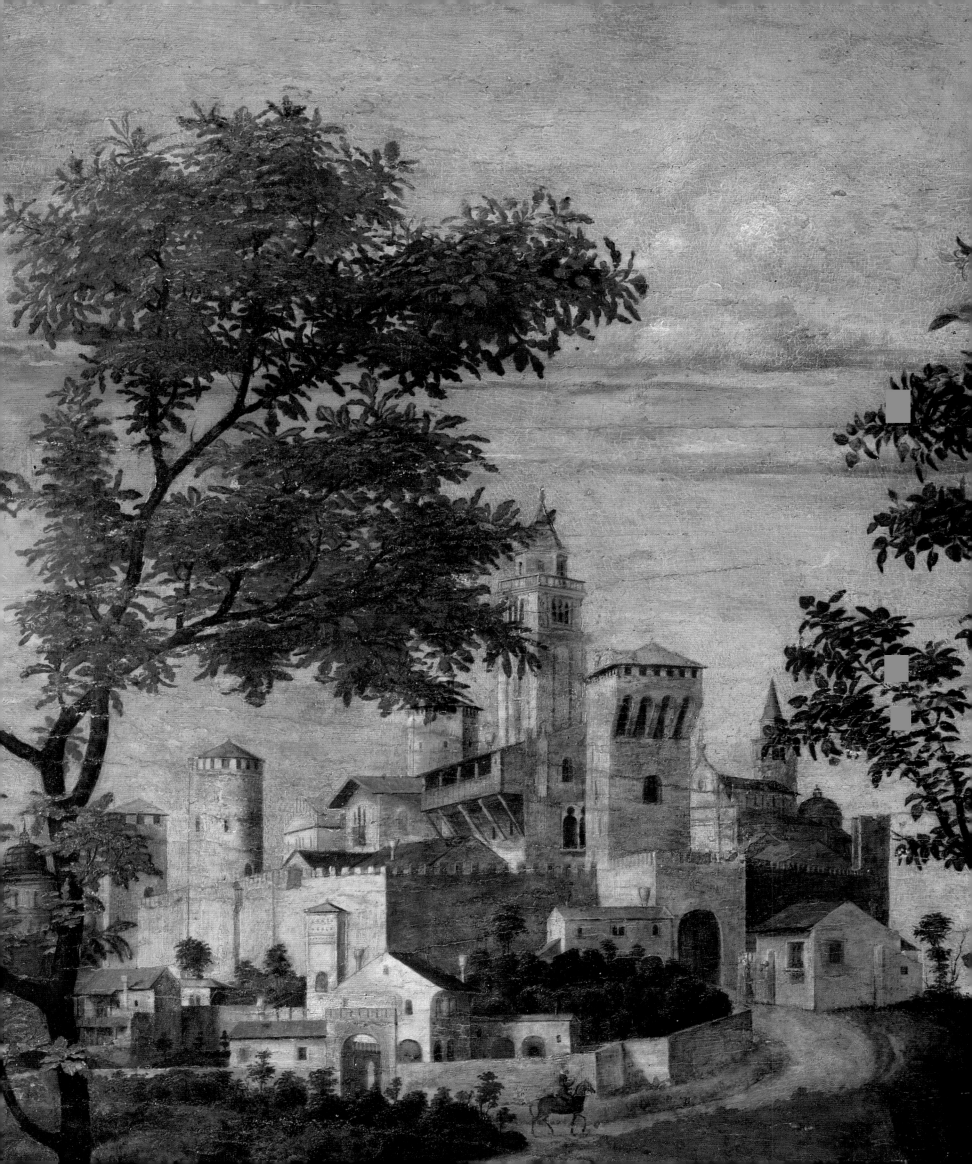

Conegliano, 1459—c.1517
*Madonna and Child Enthroned, with Musical
Angels and Saints Catherine, George, Nicholas,
Anthony Abbot, Sebastian, and Lucy*
Panel, 165 x 84" (cat. no. 36)
Last restored 1982

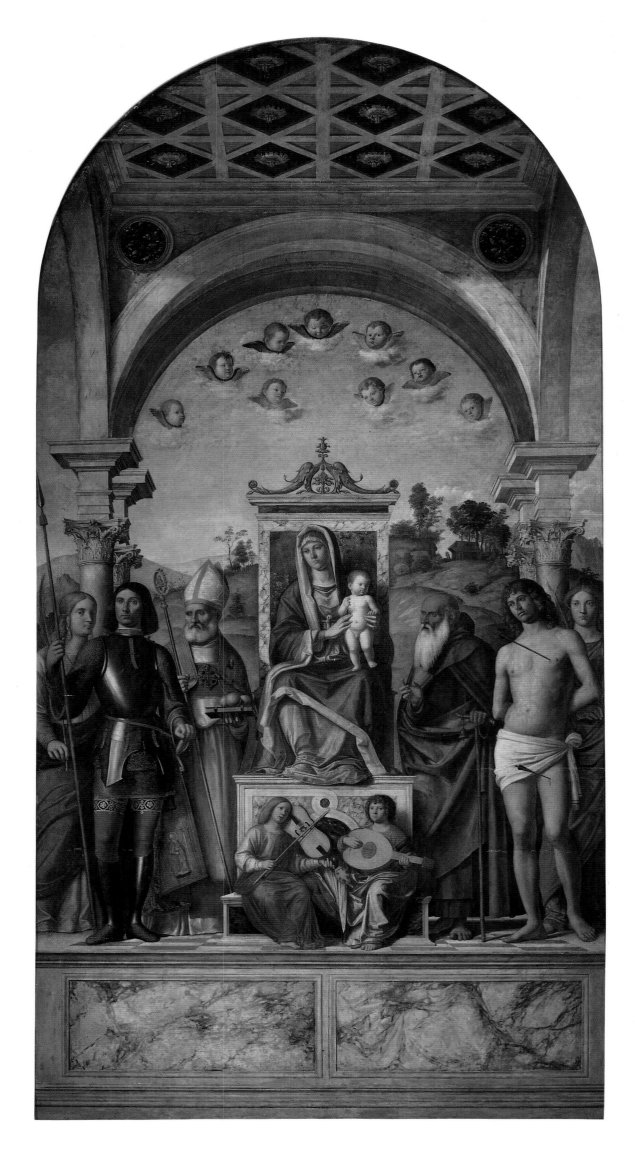

Part of the core collection transferred to the
Gallerie in 1812, following secularization, this
altarpiece had originated in the Carità Church,
where it rested above a marble altar made by
Giorgio Dragan under commission from a
Milanese, Crisoforo Solari. The altar itself was
installed in 1495, the year during which Solari
entered service at the court of Ludovico il
Moro. Given its stylistic closeness to the
mature *Miglionico Polyptych*, which Cima
executed in 1499, the *Madonna and Child
Enthroned* must date from between 1496 and
1499, the latter being the year the donor died.
Very likely, as in other Venetian works of this
period, Cima made his trompe-l'oeil
architectural space consistent with the real
environment, so that the painted columns
would have appeared to continue the marble
ones. The effect so impressed Francesco
Sansovino that, in 1581, he described the
complex as follows: "the marble altarpiece of
Saint George, joined to a most beautiful altar
with rich and noble columns, was designed by
the Milanese architect Cristoforo Gobbo. . . ."

Yellowed varnish and much repainting now
hamper our ability to examine the picture,
making it difficult to assess the quality of the
original colors.

In any case, Cima had been inspired by
Giovanni Bellini's *San Giobbe Altar*, as well as
by the same artist's *Sacred Conversation* for
the Santi Giovanni e Paolo Church (now
known only through a 19th-century copy),
where the space behind the throne became
something other than an apse. Cima, however,
enriched the arrangement by filling the sky
with a floating ribbon of his customary sweet,
angel-faced clouds. The drawing is especially
precise, as revealed by radiographic analysis,
which also disclosed a *pentimento* under the
face of Saint Catherine, originally conceived in
profile.

Conegliano, 1459—c.1517
The Incredulity of Saint Thomas with Saint Magnus Bishop
Panel, 86 x 60" (cat. no. 611)
Last restored 1979

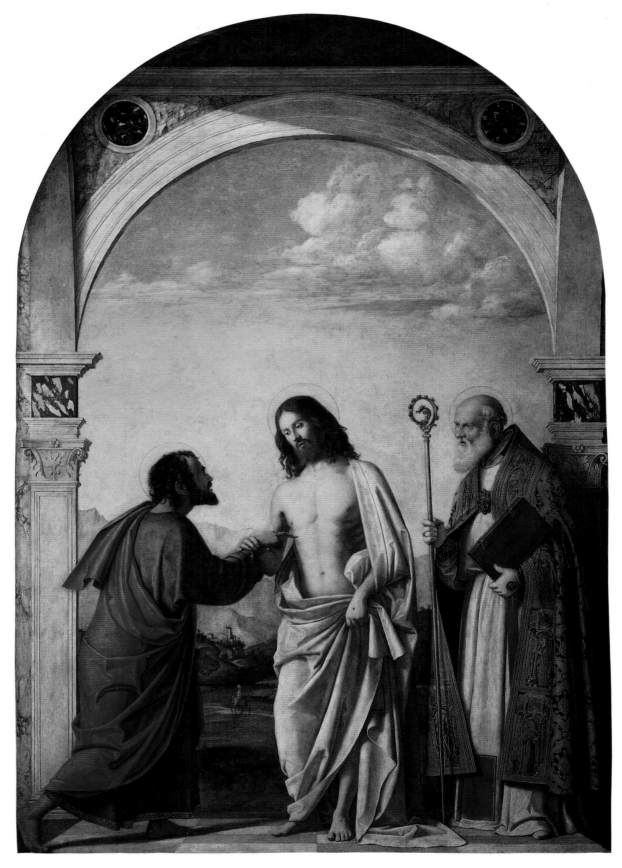

Once made state property by the Napoleonic secularization, this painting went into the Commenda reserve, where it remained until consigned to the Gallerie in 1829.

Cima had realized it for the Scuola dei Mureri altar in the San Samuele Church, whose patrons happened to be Saints Thomas and Magnus.

Ranked among the most important of the works that Cima painted in Venice during the first decade of the 16th century, *The Incredulity of Saint Thomas* came into being just after the artist had done the same subject for a Thomite confraternity of flagellants at Portogruaro, a picture dated 1504 and now in London's National Gallery.

In the present instance, Cima created a splendid study in light and shade, where figures stand cleanly silhouetted against a luminous sky and the distant village below. With its compositional balance and truly classical dignity, Cima's altarpiece seems completely innocent of the tonal innovations that Giorgione was making at this very time.

GIOVANNI AGOSTINO DA LODI
(PSEUDO BOCCACCINO)   48

Active late 15th—early 16th century
Christ Washing the Feet of the Apostles
Panel, 52 x 44" (cat. no. 599)
Last restored 1979

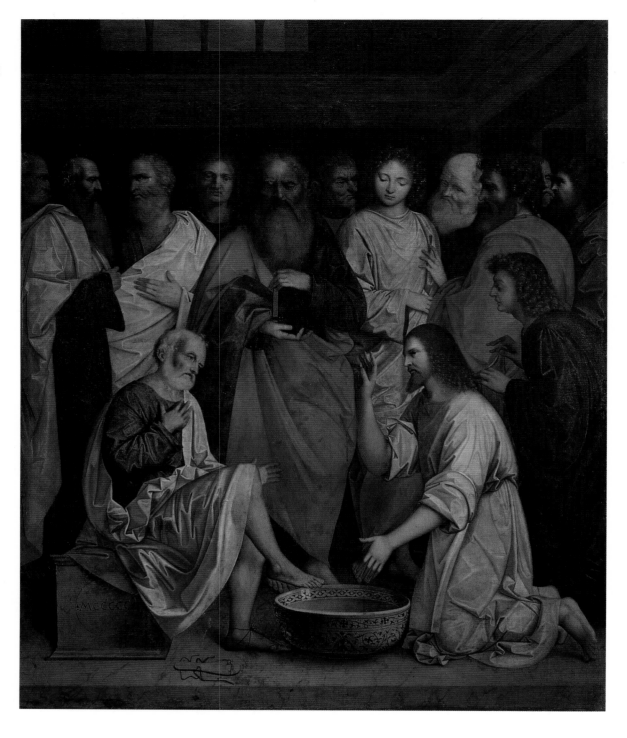

The date has been inscribed on the seat at the left: MCCCCC. The Gallerie acquired this painting in 1856 from the Manfrin collection, along with an attribution to Perugino. Then, it appeared to be from the hand of Boccaccino and thus from the so-called "Pseudo Boccaccino," by now identified as Giovanni Agostino da Lodi, whose presence in Venice is documented on March 25, 1491. What took

him there was a commission for the altarpiece of the ferry boatmen of Murano, to be installed over their altar in the destroyed Church of San Cristoforo della Pace, today San Pietro Martire. Giovanni Agostino is one of the figures in Venice who, at the turn of the 16th century, stood in marked contrast to the surrounding culture, the consequence of his introduction of Bramantesque and Leonardesque forms.

These, meanwhile, are fully evident here— especially in the heads of the Apostles, which recall Leonardo's *Last Supper* at Santa Maria delle Grazie in Milan—but reinterpreted in a highly personal manner as well as in a Venetian key. The only dated work by this artist, *Christ Washing the Feet of the Apostles* would be not only noted but also imitated in Venice.

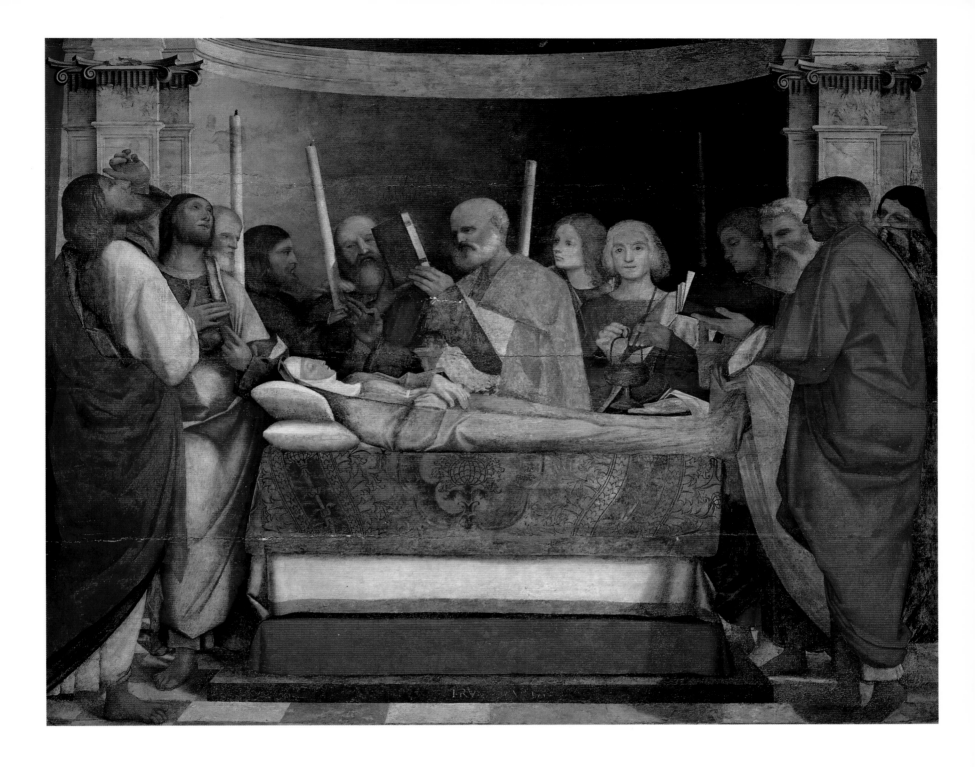

PIER MARIA PENNACCHI 49

Treviso, 1464-1514/15
Dormition of the Virgin
Oil on panel, 54 x 68" (cat. no. 657)
Currently in restoration

Fragmentary signature on the lowest step: (PE)TRUS (M)ARIA. The Gallerie acquired this painting in 1912 from the seminary at Udine, which had received it from the Cernazai collection. Generally considered a work of the Trevisan painter's late maturity, *Dormition of the Virgin* seems close in time to his *Salvator Mundi* in the Santissimo Chapel at Treviso Cathedral, a fresco commissioned in 1511.

The amplitude of the present composition, the obvious allusions to Lotto, to Giovanni Agostino da Lodi's *Christ Washing the Feet of the Apostles* (ill. no. 48), and perhaps to Cesare da Sesto reflect the eclectic tradition upon which Pennacchi drew. Meanwhile, the artist's original chromatic effects have become almost atonal, thanks to irreversible abrasions suffered by the painted surface.

ANTONELLO DA SALIBA 50

Messina c.1467—c.1535
The Virgin Annunciate
Oil on panel, 19 x 14" (cat. no. 590)
Last restored 1979

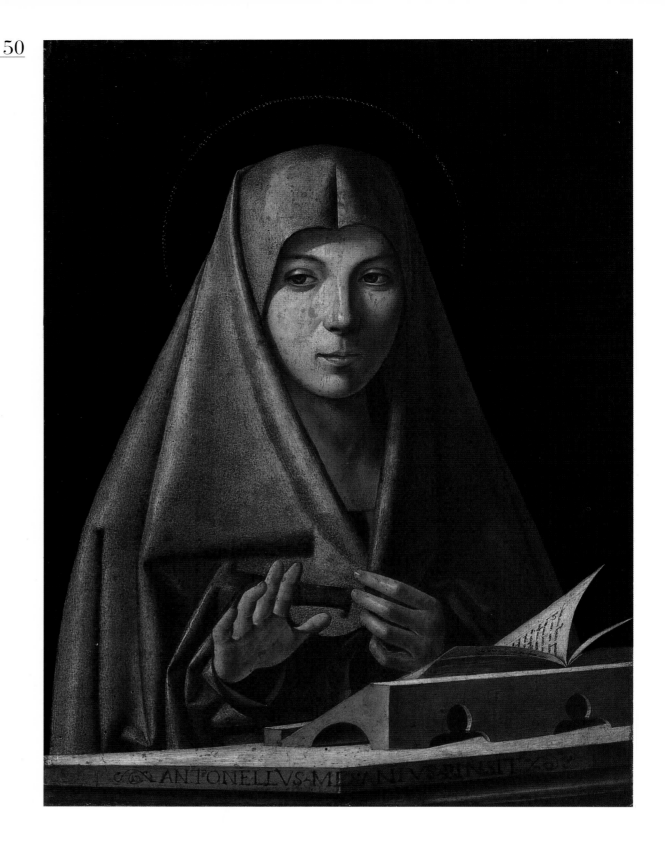

Inscribed at bottom on the parapet:
ANTONELLUS / MESANIUS / PINSIT.
The painting entered the Gallerie in 1812, among the first acquisitions made in the wake of the Napoleonic decrees. It originally hung in the hall of the Anticollegio at the Palazzo Ducale, having arrived there with a group of paintings given to the Republic by Bertuccio Contarini. Probably the "image of Our Lady" recorded by Ridolfi in 1648 as present in the Contarini mansion, the picture is a copy of

Antonello da Messina's *Annunciata* now in the National Gallery, Palermo. It was long held to be by the Early Renaissance master himself, and even the prototype of the Palermo painting. Only towards the end of the 19th century could the correct authorship be established, and the work excluded from the oeuvre of Antonello da Messina. The presence of motifs reminiscent of Bellini, Montagna, and Cima da Conegliano, as well as a certain stiffness in the mantle's fall and in the facial

features, has confirmed the attribution to Antonello de Saliba (the son of Antonello da Messina's brother-in-law Giovanni de Saliba or Resaliba), who was probably in Venice from 1480 to 1497, the years for which there is no mention of him in Messina. However abstract or geometric the overall conception, the expressive face, framed in the folds of the mantle, has been scrupulously observed, with light giving firm definition to the beautiful hands in the foreground.

Venice, 1429-1507
Blessed Lorenzo Giustiniani
Tempera on canvas, 88 x 62" (cat. no. 570)
Last restored 1965

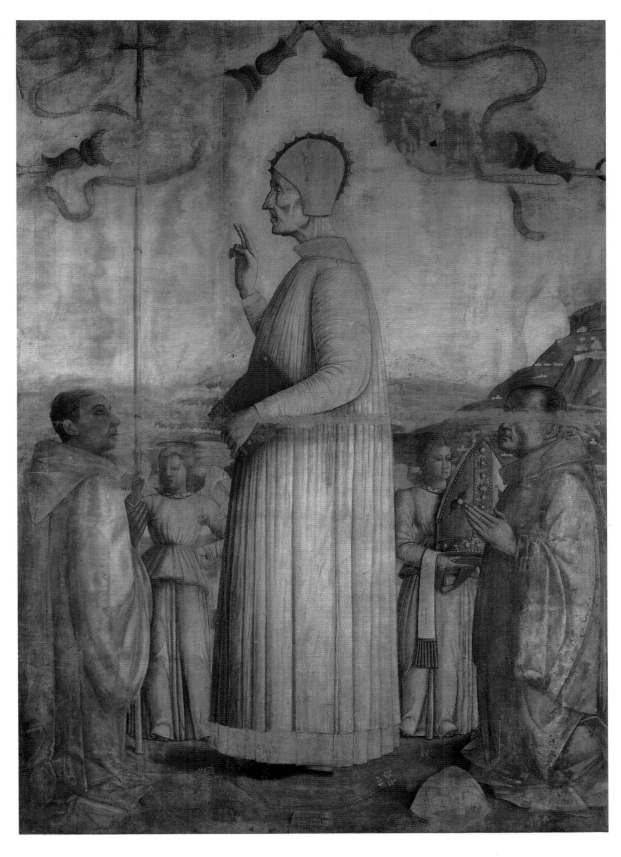

An inscribed label at lower center reads: MCCCCXLV / OPUS / GENTILIS / BELLINI / VENETI. The painting originally hung in the Church of the Madonna dell'Orto, where Ridolfi (1648) and Martinoni (1663) recorded having seen it. At the time of the church's restoration in 1850, *Blessed Lorenzo Giustiniani* was taken to the Gallerie, where it has remained in continuous exhibition since 1887. Painted, perhaps, as a processional standard, the work survives as one of the oldest Venetian paintings on canvas. Its entire surface, particularly the background, has been badly damaged.

Blessed Lorenzo Giustiniani is Gentile's earliest dated work, executed nine years after the death of the first Patriarch of Venice. The iconographical source must have been the "figure" of Lorenzo Giustiniani realized by Jacopo Bellini in 1456 for the subject's tomb, a figure now identified with the sculpture in the Lando chapel at San Pietro di Castello. The unsparingly veristic rendering of the ascetic, in sharply outlined, monolithic profile, declares the artist's respect for Mantegna, at the same time that it also announces a gift for objective observation, which would eventually make Gentile the Signoria's official painter.

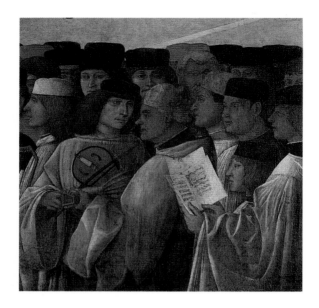

GENTILE BELLINI   52

Venezia 1429-1507
Procession in Piazza San Marco
Oil on canvas, 147 x 298", with two insertions
below, 29 x 58" and 28 x 67" (cat. no. 567)
Last restored 1989-90

This painting forms part of the *Miracles of the Cross Cycle* that once hung in the *sala dell'albergo*, or *della croce*, in the Scuola di San Giovanni Evangelista, which still owns a relic of the True Cross, presented to the confraternity in 1369 by Philippe de Mézières, Grand Chancellor of the Kingdom of Cyprus. The new paintings were to replace decorations from the early 15th century, by then hopelessly old-fashioned, and to record the new miracles attributable to the relic.

Originally the cycle comprised ten paintings: Carpaccio's *Miracle of the Relic of the Cross at the Rialto Bridge*, Bastiani's *Donation of the Relic of the Cross to the Scuola di San Giovanni Evangelista*, Mansueti's *Miracle of the Relic of the Cross in Campo San Lio*, and Pietro Perugino's *Miracle of the Vendramin Ships* (all completed by 1494); Gentile Bellini's *Procession in Piazza San Marco, Miracle of the Cross on the Bridge of San Lorenzo*, and *Miraculous Healing of Pietro de' Ludovici* (1496, 1500, and 1501); Mansueti's *Miraculous Healing of the Daughter of Benvegnudo da San Polo* (after 1502); and Diana's *Miracle of the Relic of the Cross* (after 1502). Only eight of them reached the Gallerie (see also ill. nos. 53-59). The painting executed by Perugino, while in Venice for work in the Palazzo Ducale, was destroyed and replaced in 1588 with a canvas by Andrea Vicentino, now also lost. A picture by Mariscalco had already disappeared by the time Boschini made his inventory in 1664. The most detailed, though not always exact, source available to us is a little book printed in 1590 describing the miracles wrought by the relic, and citing not only the name of the painter who illustrated each of them but also the date of his work.

By the Napoleonic decree of 1806, the Scuola di San Giovanni Evangelista and its assets became State property, but the *Miracle* pictures remained *in situ* for several years, before being transferred to the Gallerie in 1820. Although exhibited on various occasions, they did not appear together as an ensemble until 1947.

The painting seen here is inscribed on a cartouche at lower center: MCCCCLXXXXVI / GENTILIS BELLINI VENETI EQUITIS - CRUCIS / AMORE INCENSUS OPUS ("1496/the work of Gentile Bellini of Venice, knight, afire with love of the Cross"). Although reworked, this has certainly not been changed in substance.

Two large passages added at the lower left and right of the *Procession in Piazza San Marco* probably correspond to the two doors in the wall opposite the altar where both Ridolfi (1648) and Boschini (1664) remembered having seen the picture. The work would then have been patched up at the time of its placement opposite the window following Massari's reconstruction of the space.

We see here the solemn Saint Mark's Day procession, in which each Scuola took part carrying their holy relics. Specifically the painting represents the rite of April 25, 1444, when Jacopo de' Salis, a Brescia merchant, sought and received help for his gravely injured son. The date and signature, however reworked, match the information given in the *Opuscolo dei Miracoli* (1590) and other early sources. The painting is not only the first of those done by Gentile for the Scuola; it is certainly the best known as well, if only because of the unrivaled documentation it provides of the Piazza's appearance before the changes made in the 16th century. The Basilica still glittered with its original mosaics, only one of which survives, just as the great arches and the Porta della Carta still blazed with gilt and polychromy, whose onetime existence restoration has now confirmed. On the left, we see the houses of the Procurators as they had been since Doge Sebastiano Ziani (1172-78) built them, long before reconstruction began around 1514.

There is no sign of the Clock Tower, undertaken only in the year of the painting itself and not completed until after the turn of the century. In 1505, Leopardi would recast the flagstaffs in front of the Basilica in bronze. On the right, near the campanile, is the Antico Ospizio Orseolo, pulled down about fifty years later in the course of Sansovino's remodeling of the Piazza and the construction of the new Procuratie. As the procession moves from right to left across the rose-colored brick pavement, which Tirali would replace in 1723 with today's gray-and-white, the Doge and his retinue wind their way from the Porta della Carta.

The miracle, with its protagonist kneeling behind the baldachin, all but disappears right before our eyes, thanks to the overwhelming importance assumed by the procession, the Basilica of San Marco, and the Piazza, the very symbol of Venice.

As we know from the latest restoration, Gentile's picture has been extensively repainted, albeit in a manner largely faithful to the original scheme. Among a number of drawings cited in connection with the work, the British Musèum's *Procession in Piazza San Marco* seems more likely to have derived from Carpaccio's treatment of the subject.

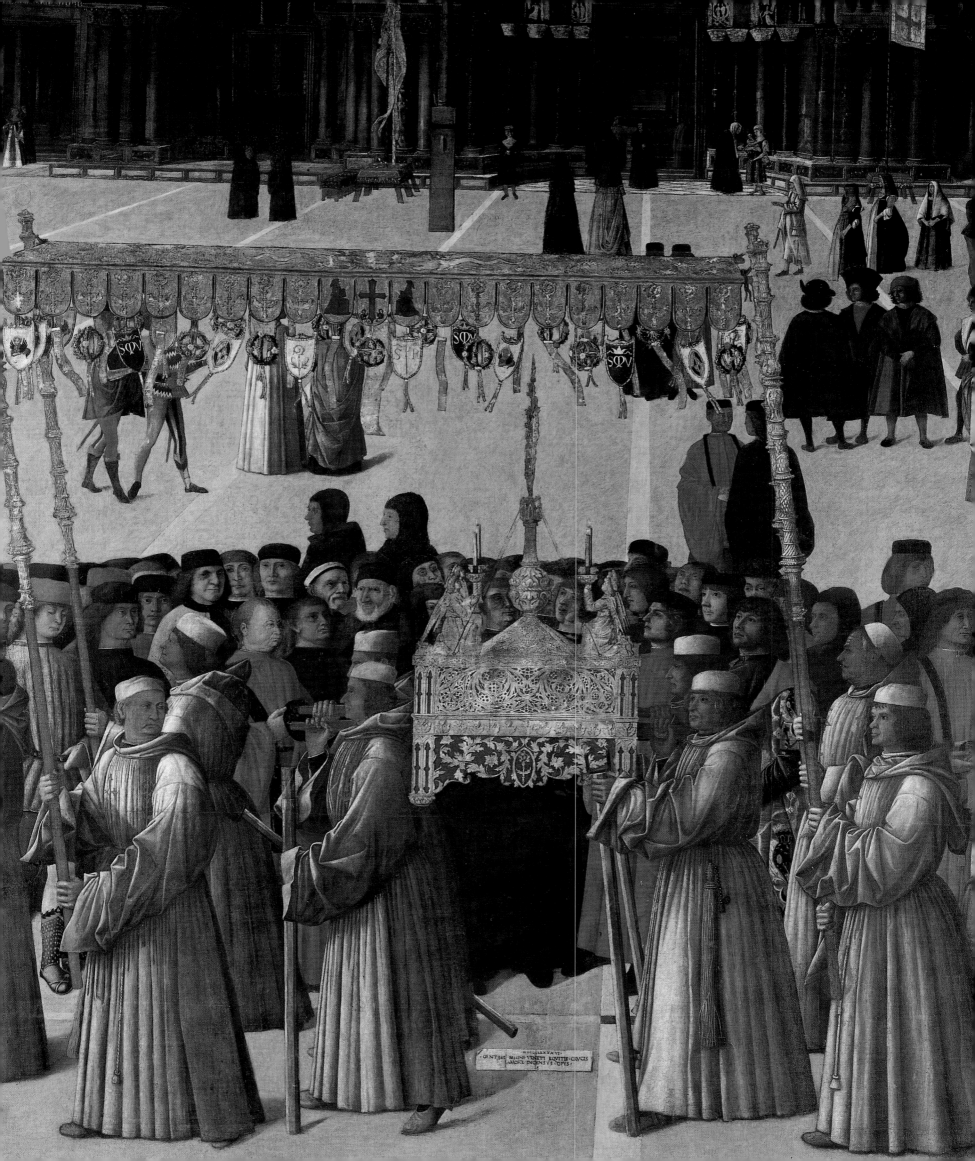

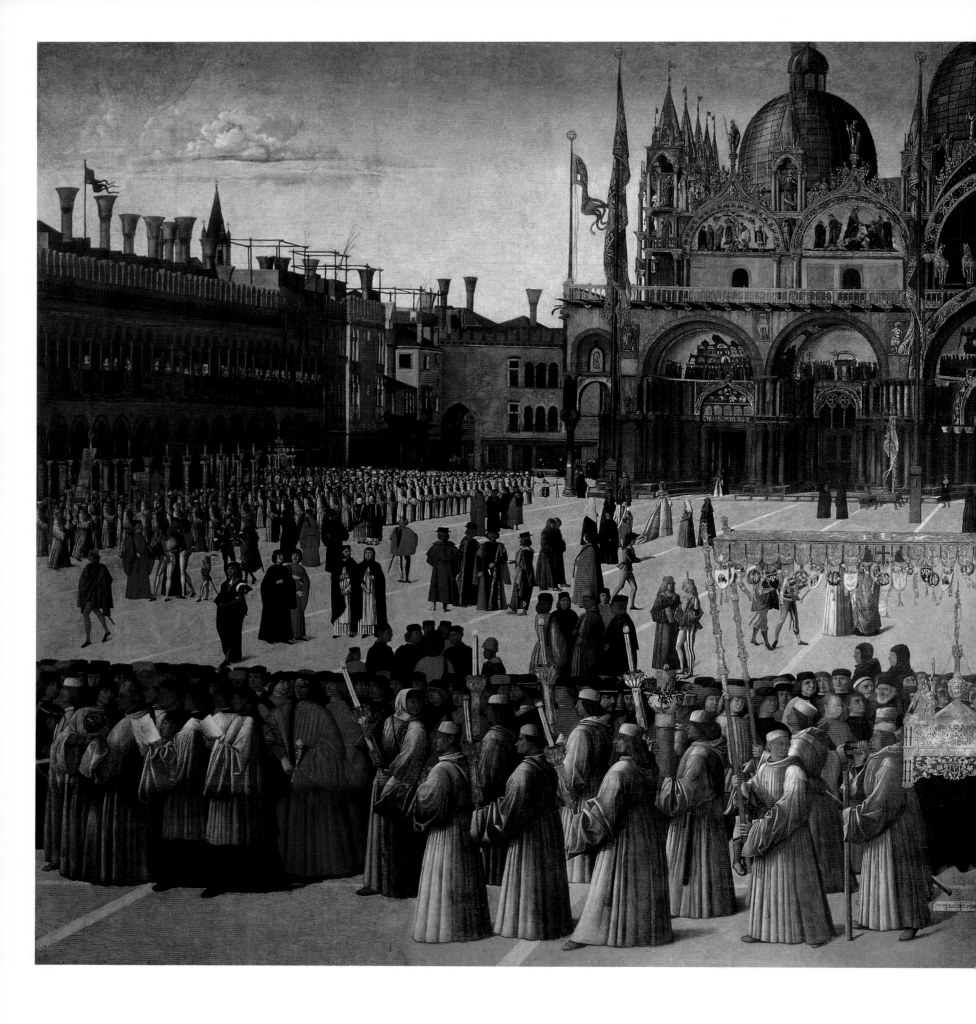

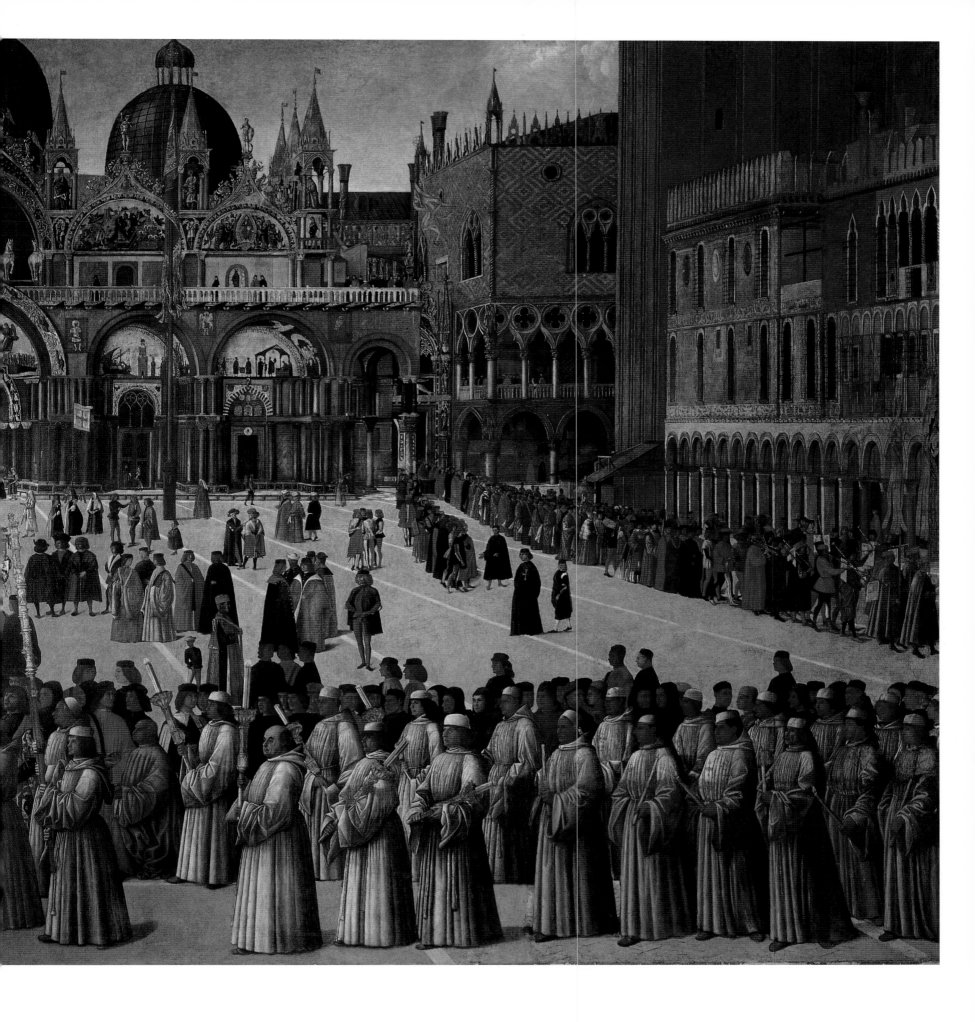

Venice, 1429-1507
*Miracle of the Cross on the Bridge of San
Lorenzo*
Oil on canvas, 130 x 172" (cat. no. 568)
Last restored 1989-90

Inscribed at center below: GENTILI BELLINI
VENETI F / MCCCCC. This has been much
reworked but not substantially altered.

Before its acquisition in 1820, following
secularization, the painting hung in the *sala
dell'albergo*, or *della croce*, at the Scuola of
San Giovanni Evangelista (see ill. nos. 52, 54-
59), where it held the central position on the
wall opposite the window. According to legend,
the relic accidentally fell into the canal during
a procession at the Church of San Lorenzo
some time between 1370 and 1382. There it
floated, resisting the attempts of all would-be
rescuers but those of the *Guardian Grande*,
Antonio Vendramin.

The date and the artist's name, although
certainly retouched on the label, are the same
as given in the *Opuscolo dei Miracoli* (1590),
by Ridolfi (1648), and by Zanetti (1771). In
this painting too, the urbanscape proves most
interesting. The buildings still sprout their
goblet-shaped, characteristically Venetian
chimneypots as well as their murals and
painted plasterwork. The water is like a green
mirror, whose reflections fill the scene with an
air of magical enchantment. In the colorful
throng on the left, we can detect Caterina
Cornaro and her ladies, and, in the right
foreground, five kneeling figures who, it has
been suggested, may represent members of the
painter's own family. Portraits these
undoubtedly are, but more probably of officers
of the Scuola confraternity, conceivably from
the Cornaro family.

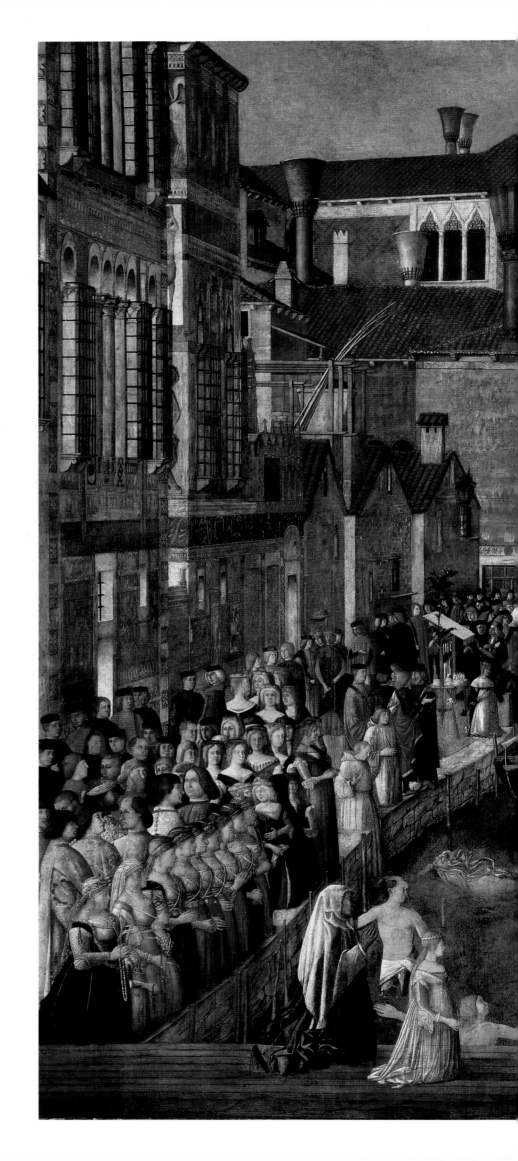

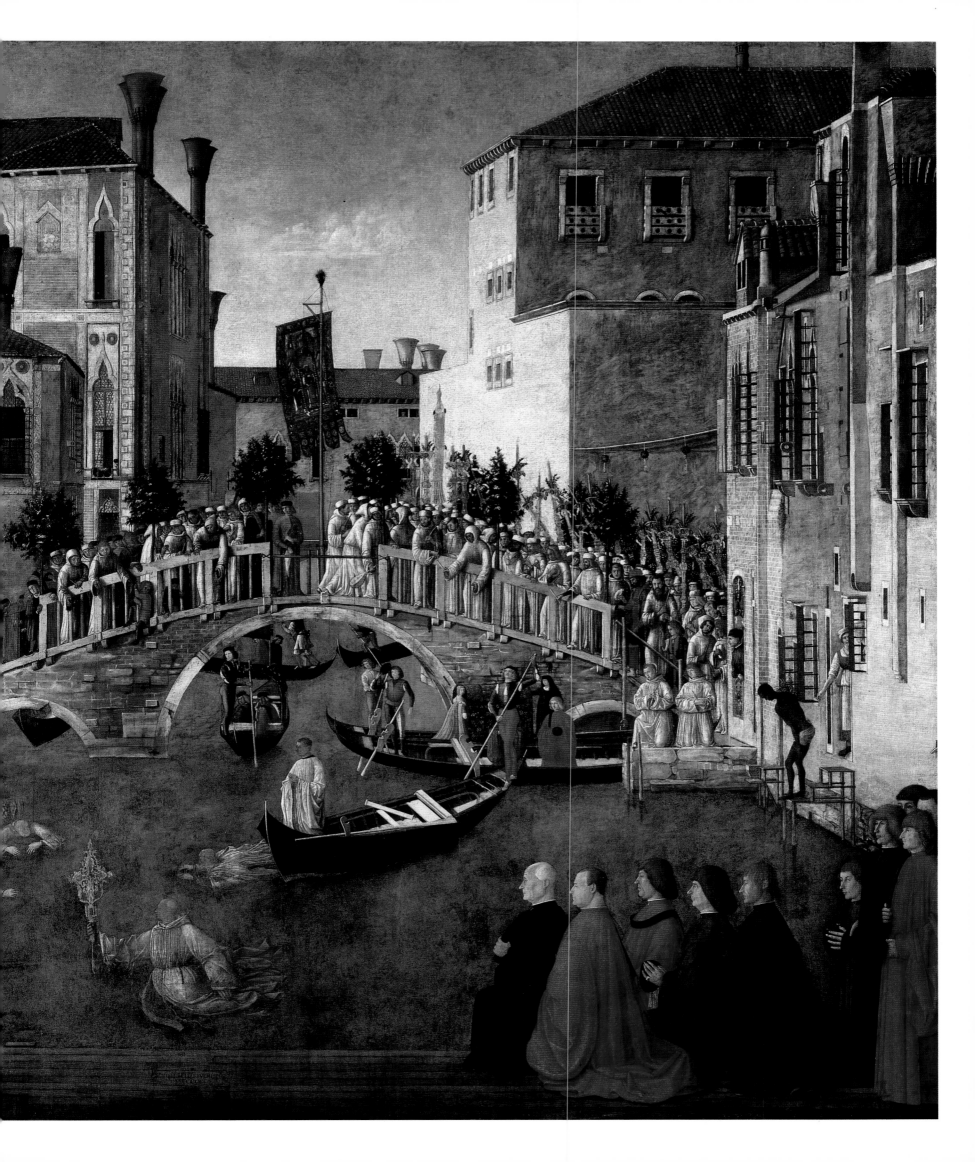

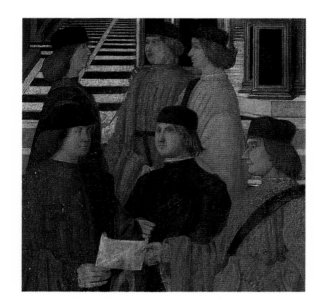

GENTILE BELLINI 54

Venice, 1429-1507
Miraculous Healing of Pietro de' Ludovici
Oil on canvas, 148 x 104", with an insert below 3 x
60" (cat. no. 563)
Currently in restoration

Although not original, the inscription on the steps—GENTILIS BELLINI / VENETI F.—follows an old tradition. Whatever the reason, such as cutting a doorway, for the passage added at the bottom, it resulted in considerable abrasion and repainting. Like the rest of the *Miracles of the Cross Cycle*, this work entered the Gallerie in 1829, after securalization (see ill. nos. 52, 53, 55-59).

The narrative concerns Pietro de' Ludovici, a devotee of the relic, who was cured of a quartan fever merely by touching a candle that stood near the reliquary. According to the *Opuscolo dei Miracoli* of 1590, Gentile painted the picture in 1501, which made it, probably, the first of the cycle to be completed following the Scuola's request to the Senate for permission to recruit an additional fifty members and thus raise money for "continuing the paintings that have been begun on canvas for the adornment of the business quarters."

As for the episode, Gentile appropriated an idea of his father's found in a book of drawings now in the British Museum (f.68r). Sketches in Munich's Graphische Sammlung (nos. 12552, 12554, 14644, 14647, 14648), as well as architectural studies of the church interior, a tabernacle, and a ciborium, all attributable to Gentile, demonstrate the extensive preparation involved in getting the perspective exactly right for the representation of a church's interior elevation. The setting may well be San Giovanni Evangelista as it appeared in Gentile's time, and the triptych above the altar a work by Bastiani known as the *Donation of a Relic* (see ill. no. 55).

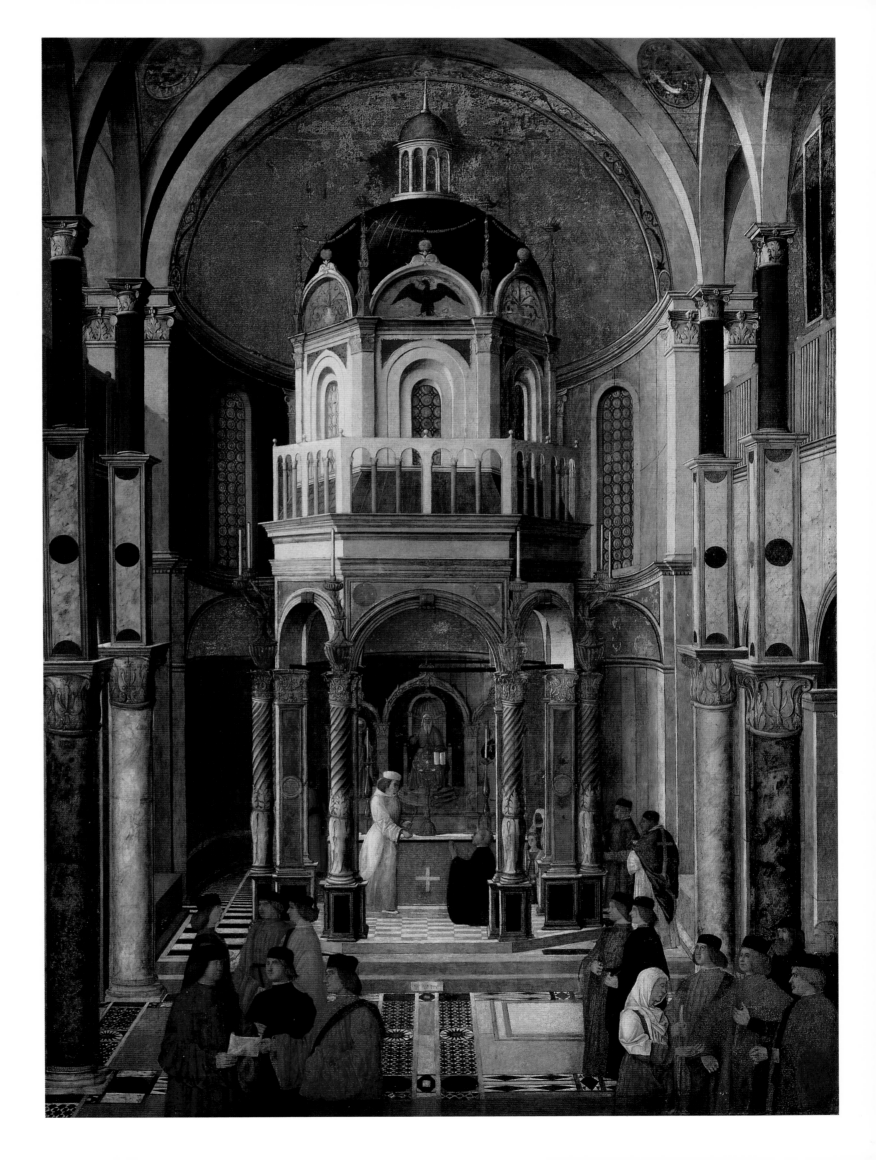

1449 (mentioned)—1512 (d.)
*Donation of a Relic of the Cross to the Scuola di
San Giovanni Evangelista*
Oil on canvas, 133 x 180" (cat. no. 561)
Currently in restoration

The work seen here depicts Philippe de
Mézières' presentation of the relic (see also ill.
nos. 52-54, 56-59) as if the event had
occurred in the Church of San Giovanni
Evangelista, albeit viewed from without so that
the painting becomes a valuable record of
public buildings long since altered or
destroyed. The artist gives us the church's
original brick façade, behind its portico
crowned with a statue-studded terrace leading
to the graveyard. One of the sculptures derives
from a cartoon for the signed mosaic of Saint
Sergius in San Marco. Through the door we see
the polygonal apse and the altar surmounted
by a polyptych, perhaps the one by Gentile
Bellini (ill. no. 54). At left, along the side of
the Scuola, are the round windows whose
existence was confirmed during the most
recent restoration, as well as the first 6 feet of
the Sala Grande, erected in 1495. Such details
represent a *terminus a quo*, despite the
Opuscolo, which assigns the picture to the year
1494.

 The Bastiani picture interests us mainly as a
record, since its punctilious description is a far
cry from the imaginative visions of Bellini and
Carpaccio.

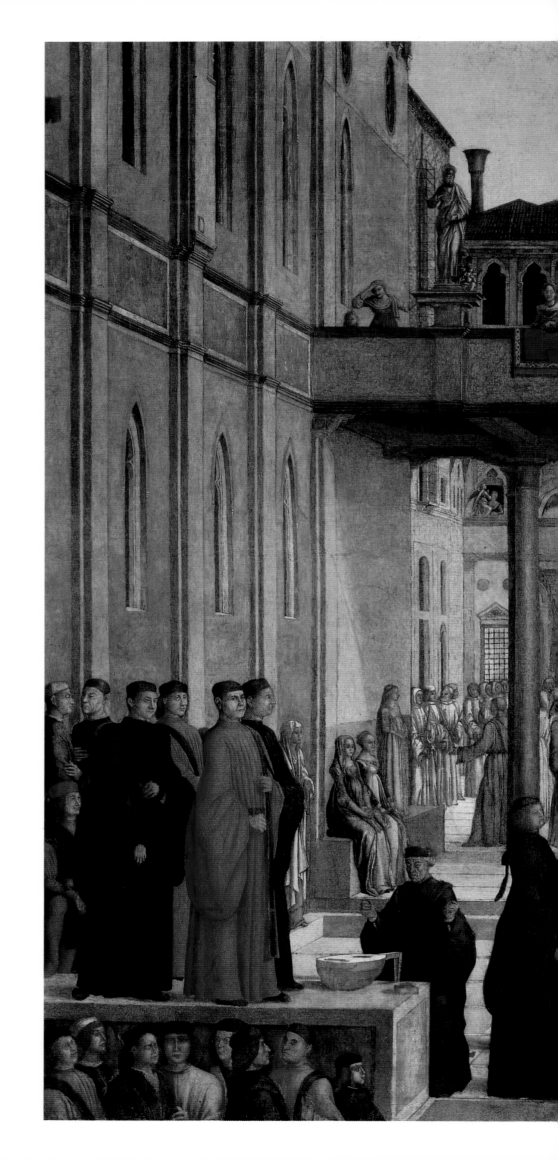

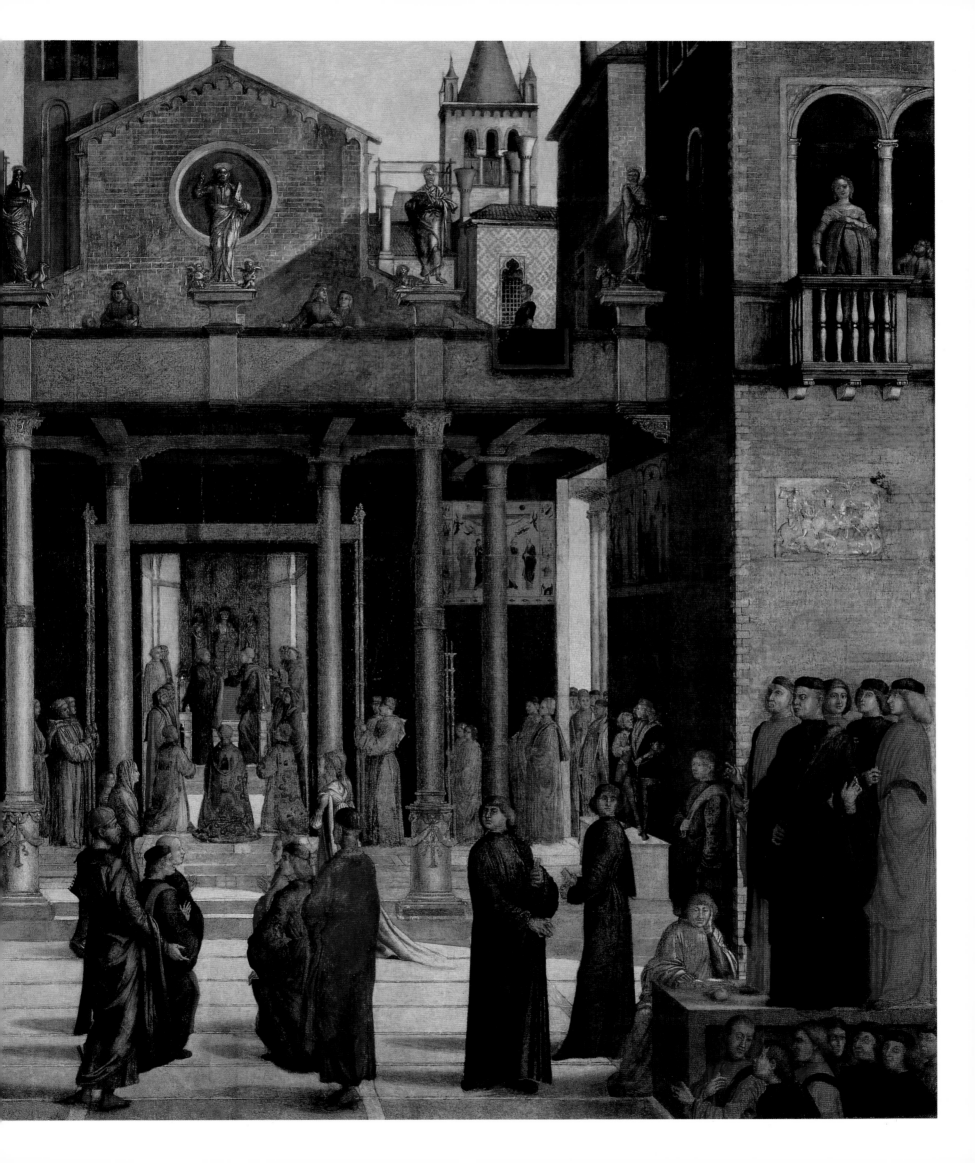

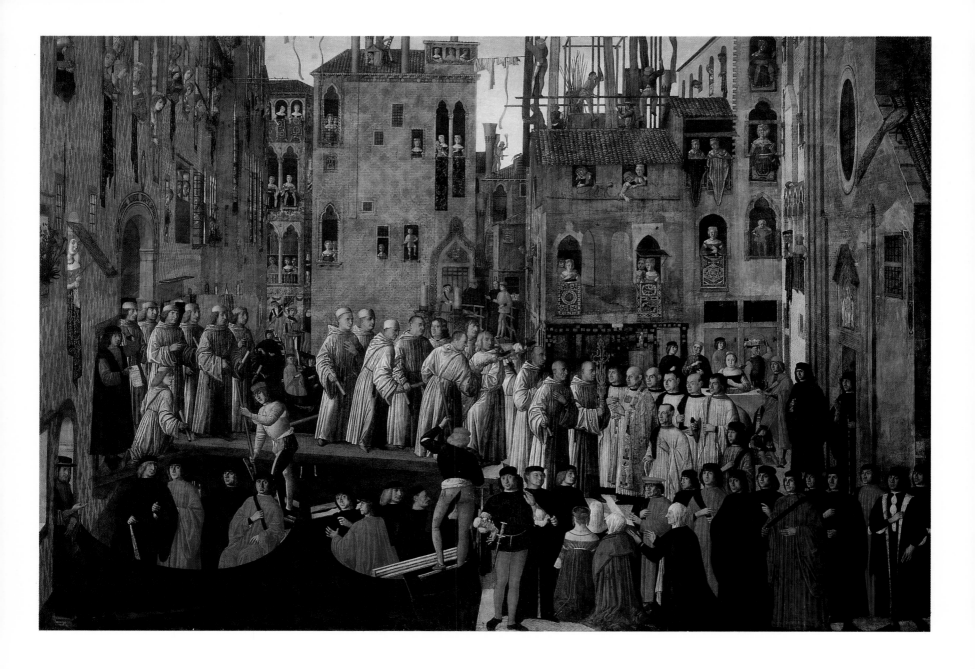

GIOVANNI MANSUETI   56

Mentioned, 1485-1527
Miracle of the Relic of the Cross in Campo San Lio
Oil on canvas, 127 x 183" (cat. no. 564)
Currently in restoration

The figure at left raising a hand to his cap (probably a self-portrait) holds a label inscribed: OPUS / JOANNIS D / MANSUETI / S VENETI / RECTE SE / NTIENTIUM BELLI / NI DISCIPULI ("By Giovanni Mansueti of Venice, believed by right-thinking persons to be the disciple of Bellini").

Acquired at the same time as well as from the same source as the preceding works, and part of the same *Miracles of the Cross Cycle* (see ill. nos. 52-55, 57-59), the painting recounts an extraordinary event that occurred in 1474 during the funeral for a member of the brotherhood who had been less than fervent in his devotion to the relic. Suddenly, the holy object became so heavy that, for a while, it had to be entrusted to the parish priest of San Lio.

The *Opuscolo dei Miracoli* of 1590 tells us that the canvas was painted in 1494 "by the hand of Master Zuane di Mansueti Zotto." The artist may have drawn, in part, on a preparatory study by Gentile Bellini now in the Uffizi (no. 1293).

For his somewhat naïve urbanscape, Mansueti may have borrowed not only from Gentile but also, to a lesser extent, from Carpaccio.

An unusual feature is the sign at extreme left at the side of the church: CASA DA FITAR DUCATI 5 ("House to let, 5 ducats").

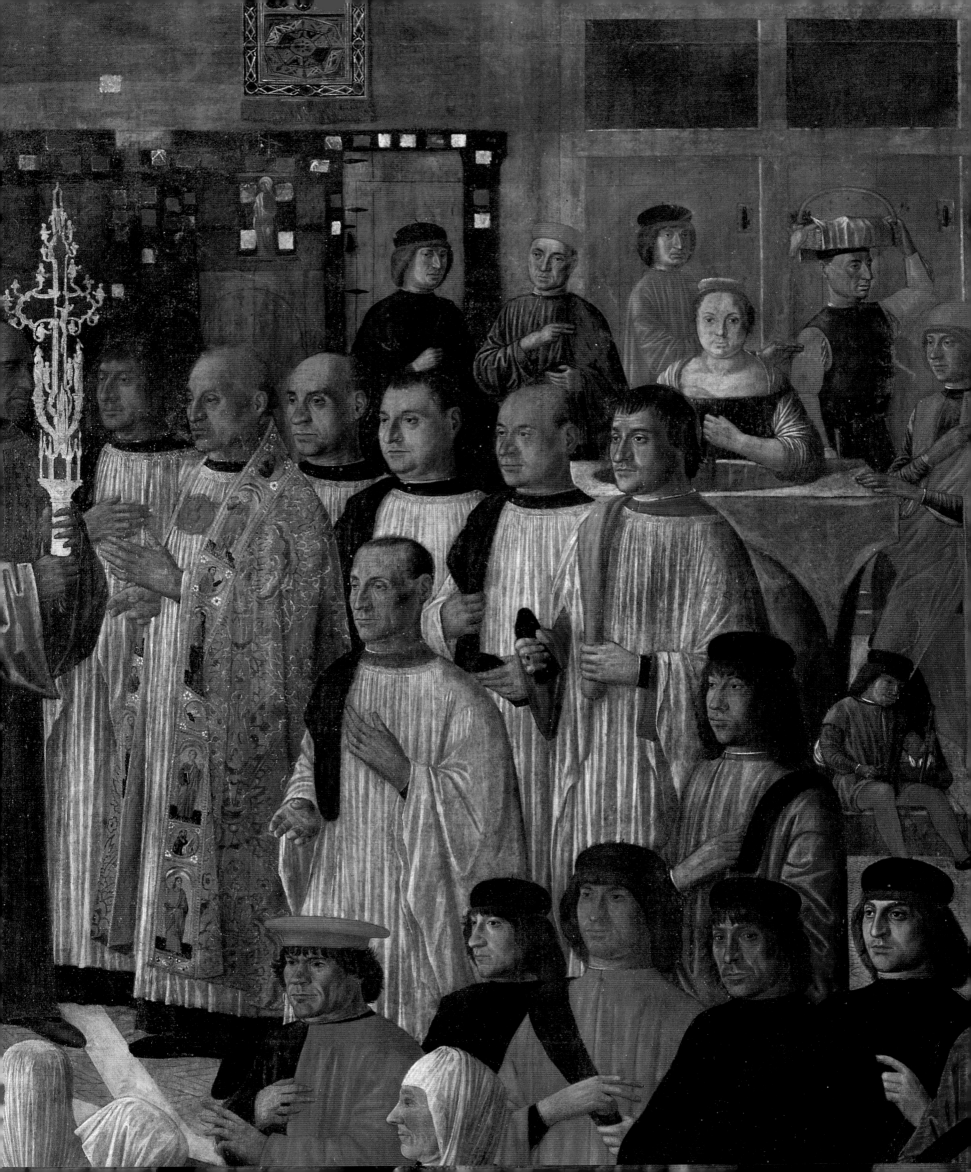

Mentioned, 1485-1527
Miraculous Healing of the Daughter of
Benvegnudo da San Polo
Oil on canvas, 144x 118" (cat. no. 562)
Currently in restoration

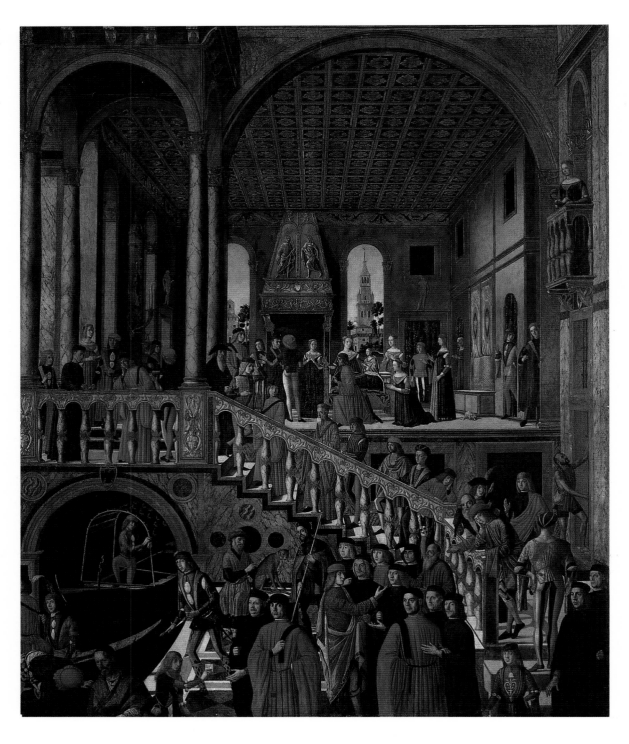

W ith the same provenance as the preceding work (ill. no. 56), this painting narrates a miraculous cure that took place in 1414. It involved the daughter of one Benvegnudo, paralyzed from birth but then instantly healed when touched by three candles that her father had placed near the relic of the Cross.

The Renaissance setting constitutes an interior elevation of great historical interest, echoing some of the solutions devised by Carpaccio in the *Saint Ursula Cycle*, which

may provide a *terminus a quo* for dating Mansueti's picture.

In the letter delivered by the boy in the left foreground, we can now decipher only *Spettabili domino Franc. . . fidelis* ("To the esteemed Sir Franc . . . faithful"), but in 1833-34, Zanotto claimed that he could also make out the name "Duodo." This would throw further light on the dating, since Francesco Duodo served as *Guardian Grande* of the Scuola around 1506. Too, the work must

postdate the 1502 permission granted by the Senate to recruit fifty more members and thus raise funds for finishing the decoration of the *sala* (see ill. no. 54).

None other than Paolo Veronese, while working on the *Feast in the House of Levi* (ill. no. 104), saw fit to adopt several of the solutions devised by Mansueti for the work seen here, such as allowing the action to unfold between an arcade and a flight of stairs.

BENEDETTO RUSCONI
CALLED DIANA 58

Venice, 1482 (mentioned)—February 9, 1525
Miracle of the Relic of the Holy Cross
Oil on canvas, 144 x 58" (cat. no. 562)
Currently in restoration

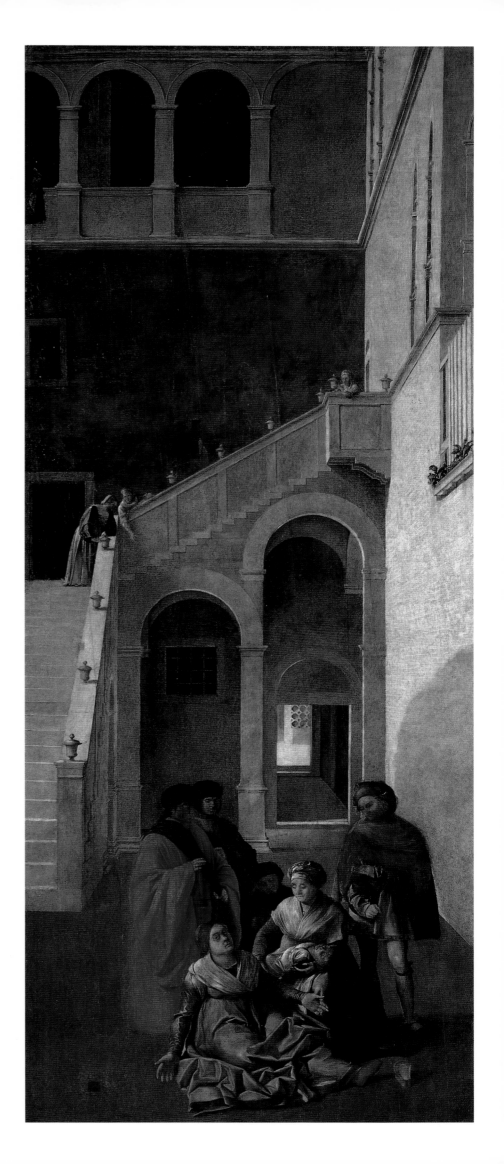

With the same provenance and acquisition date as its companion works (ill. nos. 52-57, 59), this painting has hung in the Gallerie since 1828, despite a huge blank space on the right side of the pictorial field. The subject, variously interpreted in the 17th and 18th centuries, has to do with an episode that, according to the *Opuscolo dei Miracoli* (1590), transpired on March 10, 1480. The four-year-old son of "Ser Alvisi Finetti, accountant to the *Camera degli Imprestidi* ['Loan Office']," found himself instantly cured after having been severely injured by falling from an attic. The 1787 inventory of the Scuola's paintings describes a work corresponding exactly to the one seen here, a work that already embodied developments symptomatic of the new century, especially the innovations of Giorgione and Lotto. Thus, treatment of the interior courtyard, with its subtle play of light and shade, invites visual exploration deep into illusionistic depth. The picture should be dated in the first decade of the 16th century, but certainly after the Senate's decree of 1502 permitting the confraternity fifty additional members as a means of finishing the painting cycle for the *sala dell'albergo*.

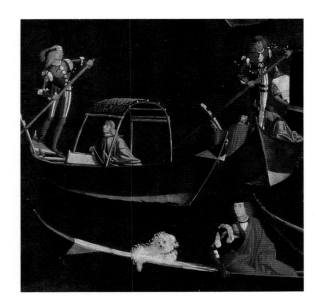

VITTORE CARPACCIO   59

Venice, 1465—c.1526
Miracle of the Relic of the Cross at the Rialto Bridge
Canvas, 143 x 160" (cat. no. 566)
Last restored 1990-91

The painting comes from the Scuola of San Giovanni Evangelista, where it formed part of the *Miracles of the Cross Cycle* (ill. nos. 52-58). Following secularization, it entered the Gallerie in 1820 and has remained on display since 1830. The painting recounts the miraculous cure of insanity brought about by Francesco Querini, patriarch of Grado, through a relic of the True Cross.

In 1544, after consulting the "judicious painter Master Titian," those in charge removed a portion of the painting's lower left corner for the sake of a doorway opened into the new *albergo* built about this time. Later, the empty corner was rather clumsily painted in or reconstructed, as we know from a preparatory drawing, in Vienna's Albertina, for the figure with his back turned and the small boy at his left.

The miracle, witnessed by a foreground audience of Venetian patricians, members of the contrafraternity, and the *Compagnia della Calza*, or "Hosiers' Guild," becomes almost lost in the kaleidoscopic portrait of the city itself, viewed from one of its nodal points at a

moment virtually contemporary with the bird's-eye plan drawn by Jacopo de' Barbari. The wooden bridge of 1458 still spanned the Rialto, with its movable central section open to allow the passage of larger craft. The structure collapsed in 1524 and was replaced by the stone bridge that exists even today. At left, a sign announces the *Albergo dello Storione* ("Sturgeon's Inn"), next to the loggia and its crowded market. At right are the *Fondaco dei Tedeschi* ("German Warehouse"), destroyed by fire in 1505, the Ca' da Mosto, whose ground-floor entrance yet survives, and the campanile of San Giovanni Crisostomo as well as that of Santi Apostoli, the latter rebuilt in 1672. Even compared with the meticulously descriptive realism of the artist's other paintings, this one excels in its coloristic brilliance and narrative spontaneity.

The most plausible date continues to be 1494, as given in the *Opuscolo dei Miracoli*.

Recent X-ray evaluation has disclosed a beautiful preparatory drawing beneath the paint, done with silverpoint on a priming coat of adhesive gesso.

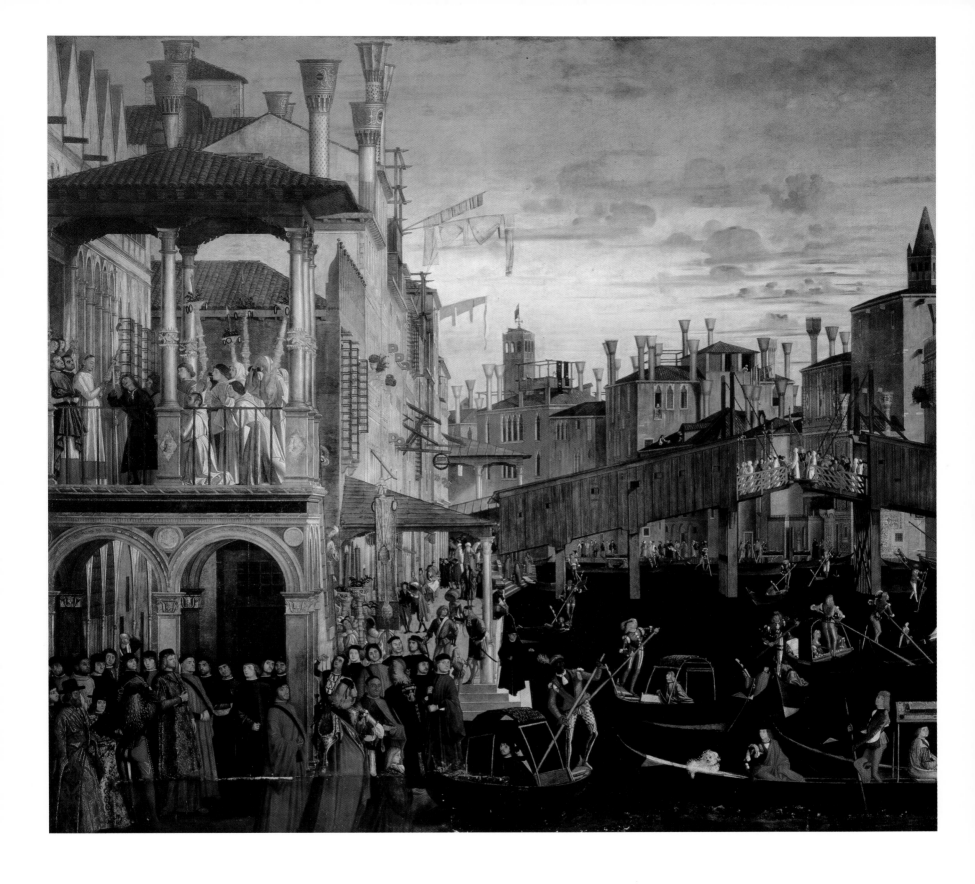

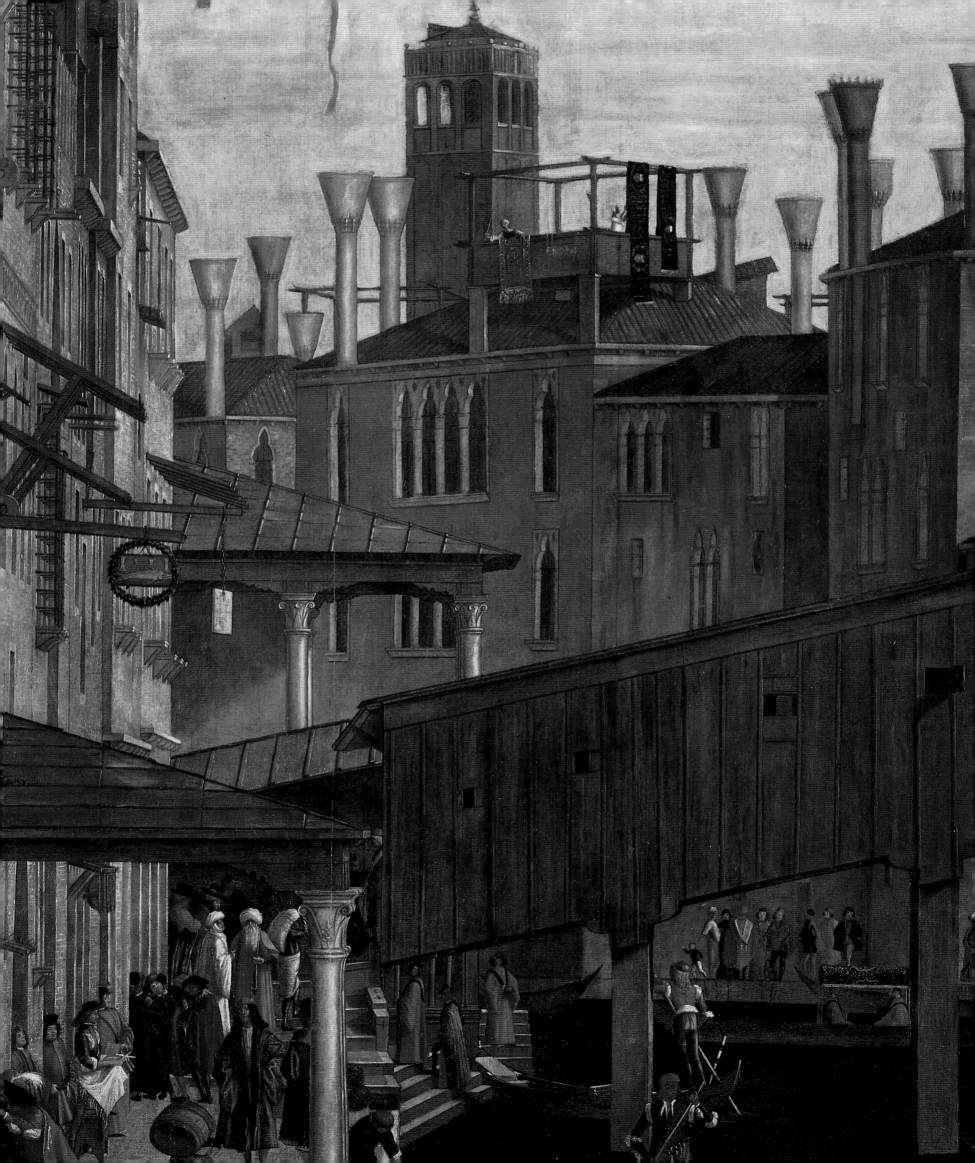

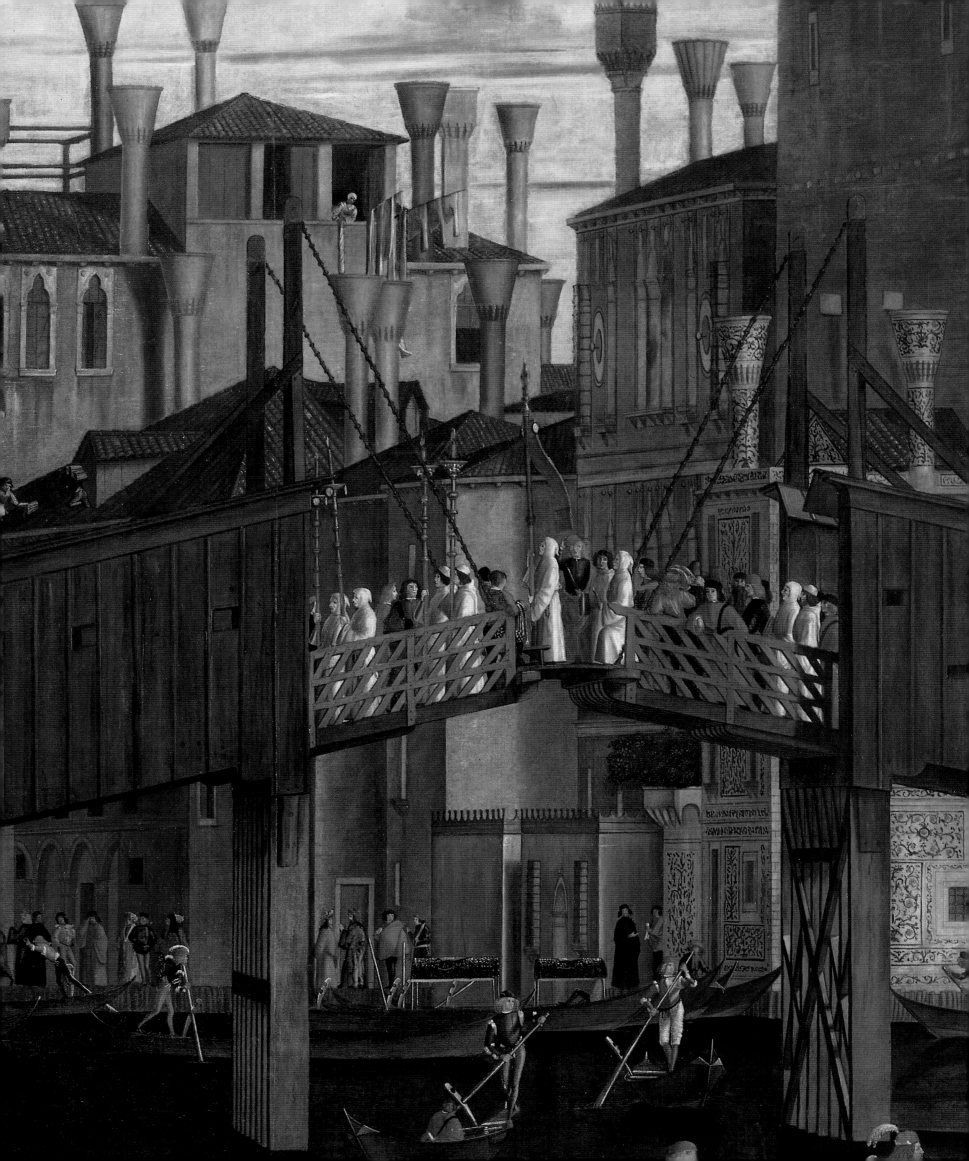

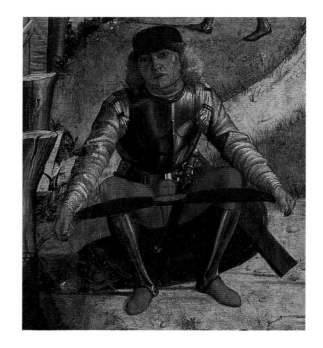

VITTORE CARPACCIO   60

Venice, c.1465—1526
Arrival at Cologne
Oil on canvas, 112 x 102" (cat. no. 579)
Last restored 1984

At the lower left, an inscribed label or scroll reads: OP. VICTORIS / CARPATIO / VENETI - MCCCCXXXX.M / SEPTEMBRIS. This painting, like the eight others that follow here, came to the Gallerie in 1812 with the first group of works affected by the Napoleonic secularization. All originated in the Scuola di Sant'Orsola (now the rectory for the monastery of Santi Giovanni e Paolo) whose noble brethren decided in 1488 to decorate their residence with "the story of the lady Saint Ursula," knowing that they could count on not only contributions from their own membership but also the largesse of such patrician families as the Loredans. Altogether, Carpaccio executed eight canvases and an altarpiece (see ill. nos. 61-68), all dated between 1490 and 1495. Meanwhile, informed opinion has tended to hold that the project took longer, moreover that the *Embassy* paintings (ill. nos. 64-66), at least, were done only at the very close of the century. In the light of the latest restorations, however, Carpaccio's *Saint Ursula Cycle* would indeed appear to have been realized at dates very close to those inscribed on the individual canvases, leaving stylistic differences to be explained by the involvement of other hands in completing the series. What seems to have escaped notice is a 1493 note in Marin Sanudo's *De origine, situ . . . urbis Venetae* ("Concerning the Origin, Site . . . of the City of Venice") recalling that among the "notable sights of the city is the chapel of Saint Ursula at San Zuanne Pollo with its very beautiful historical figures and scenes."

With some freedom, Carpaccio narrates the Ursula epic as recounted in the Venetian edition of Jacobus de Voragine's *Golden Legend*, published in 1475. Ursula, a Christian Princess of Brittany, agrees to marry Ereus, Prince of England, on condition that he be baptized and that the couple, accompanied by a long train of young women, undertake a pilgrimage to Rome. There the Pope joins them for the journey to Cologne, where they are all massacred by the Huns, a disaster already revealed to Ursula in a dream.

The canvases have been much tampered with and restored, as we know from engravings by G. del Pian, in order to make them accommodate successive modifications of the host building. As exhibited, the narrative began at the *Cornu Epistolae* (to the right of the altar) and ended across from it, an arrangement confirmed by the discovery of a door, on the right side of the chapel, corresponding exactly to a gap in the *Arrival of the Ambassadors* (ill. no. 65). Carpaccio did not execute the paintings in the order of the narrative sequence itself; rather, he began with the last stage of the journey before the martyrdom, perhaps because the Loredan altar and tombs had not yet been removed from the other wall.

Thus, the *Arrival at Cologne* lacks the complex spatial articulation characteristic of the other canvases, which makes for an uncomfortable, crowded scene in whose restricted space the artist attempted to give simultaneous representation to several different episodes.

Cleaning has uncovered a material quality previously only guessed at, a quality that merely accentuates the atmosphere of bemused expectancy that gives the story its true fascination.

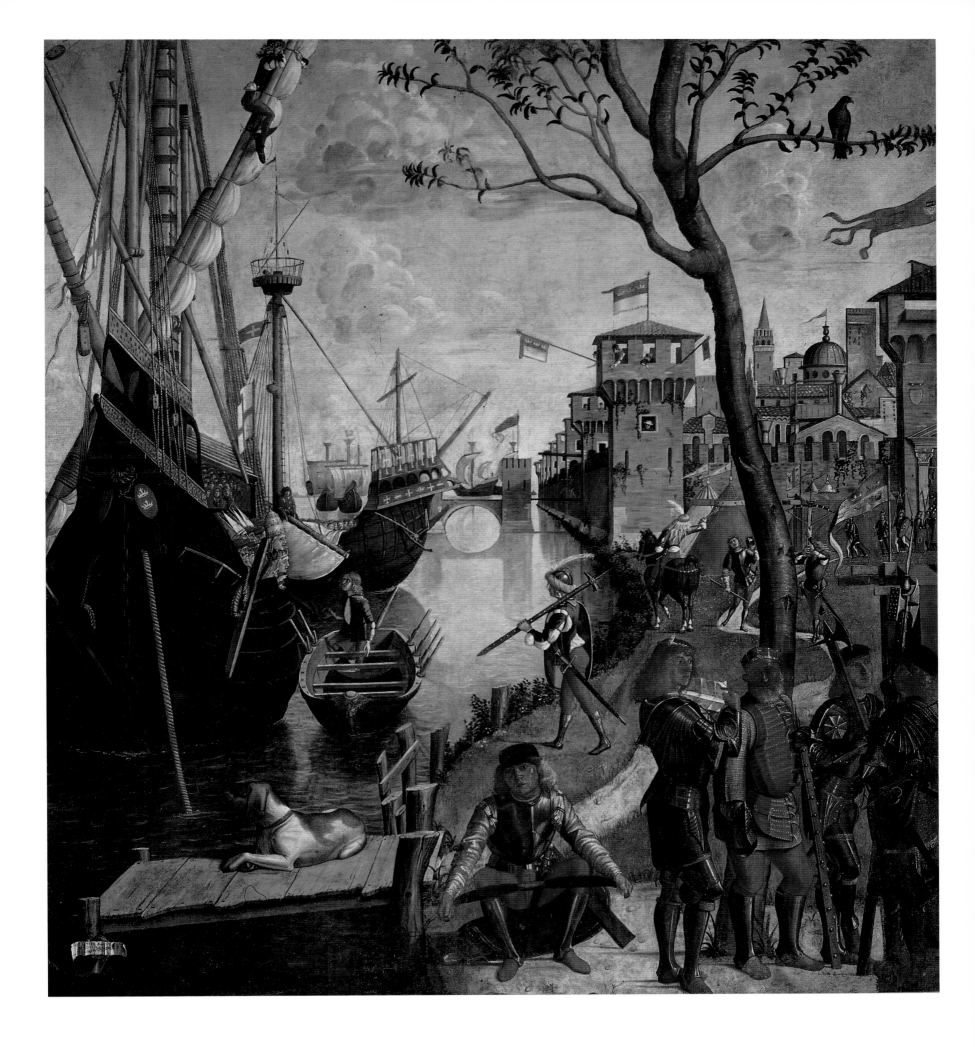

Venice, c.1465-1526
Apotheosis of Saint Ursula and Her Companions
Oil on canvas, 192 x 134" (cat. no. 576)
Last restored 1982-83

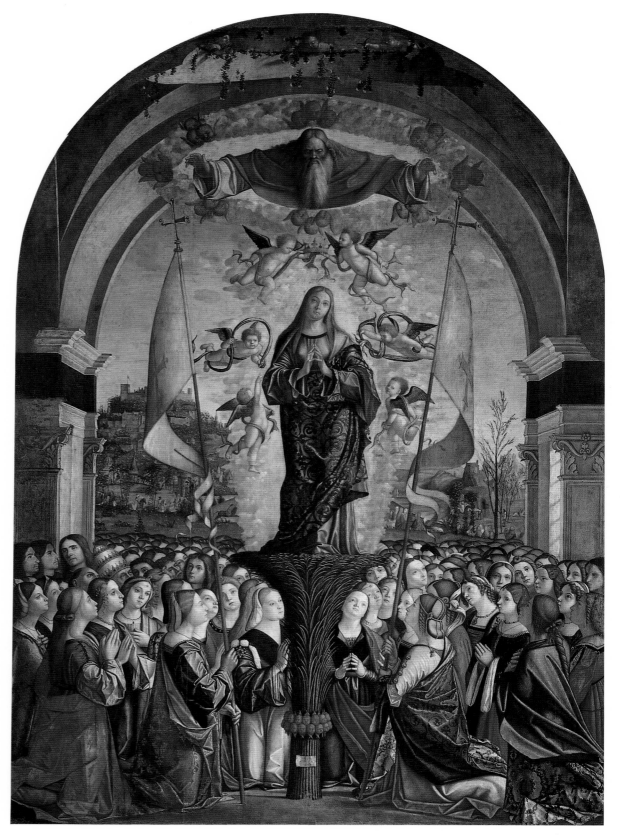

At bottom, on a sheaf of palm leaves, is a label reading: OP. VICTORIS / CARPATIO / MCCCCLXXXXI. Much controversy surrounds the dating of this altarpiece, which represents the apotheosis of Ursula, received in Heaven by God the Father, who encircles her with a celestial crown, as her companions attend and participate in the event. The date 1491 inscribed on the scroll, which is not original but certainly in keeping with an old tradition, has been much debated, mainly because the naïve and somewhat tired imagination at work in the *Apotheosis* seems more suited to a later date. Thus, the inscribed year may simply record the date of the commission, leaving the *Apotheosis* to become contemporary with the artist's *Presentation of Jesus in the Temple* for San Giobbe (ill. no. 69). Both works involved two drawings once in the Gathorne-Hardy collection at England's Donington Priory and now in the Ashmolean Museum, Oxford. Or perhaps the painting seen here was begun in 1491 and resumed later in connection with the rebuilding of the presbytery in 1504, at which time the three male faces—undoubtedly portraits of leading figures in the confraternity—would have been added. Too, since the canvas has not yet undergone methodical stratigraphic examination, the possibility of a later insert cannot be excluded. Be that as it may, the splendid wealth of color revealed by the latest cleaning would seem to support the inscribed date, while the underdrawing pounced onto the canvas, discovered reflectographically, suggests that the artist may have prepared both the drawings and the cartoons personally but then assigned much of the remaining work to his assistants.

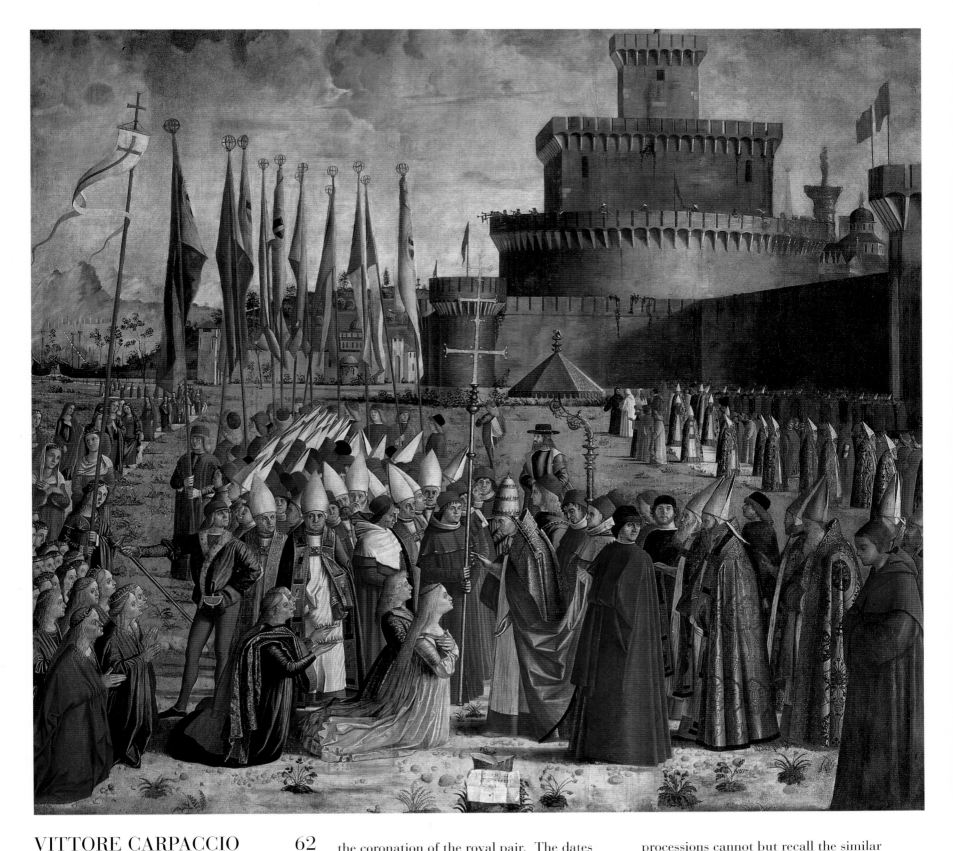

VITTORE CARPACCIO   62

Venice, c.1465-1526
The Pilgrims Meet with Pope Cyriacus before the Walls of Rome
Oil on canvas, 112 x 123" (cat. no. 577)
Last restored 1984

The inscription on the scroll at bottom center reads: VICTORIS / CAR / PATIO - VENETI / OPUS. Here, in Rome before the Castel Sant'Angelo, Ursula and her pilgrims meet the Pope, who decides to join them after Ereus' baptism and the coronation of the royal pair. The dates proposed for this painting vary widely. However, a *post quem* element could be the presence, on the pontiff's right, of a personage in a red toga. This is the Venetian humanist Ermolao Barbaro who died in official disgrace in 1493, after which it would have been risky for the artist to include his portrait. The procession is punctuated by brilliant banners, white miters, and red skullcaps, while the virgins wind their way in from an horizon blocked by blue mountains.

Further, the parallel course of the two processions cannot but recall the similar solution adopted by Jacopo Bellini for his *Procession in Piazza San Marco* of 1496 (ill. no. 52), which may therefore provide a *terminus ad quem* for dating Carpaccio's picture. Equally recalled, meanwhile, is the *Adoration of the Mystic Lamb* panel in Jan van Eyck's *Ghent Altarpiece*, as well as Perugino, who, in 1494, was at work in both the Palazzo Ducale and the Scuola di San Giovanni Evangelista. The British Museum in London owns a preparatory study for the Pope and the two bishops.

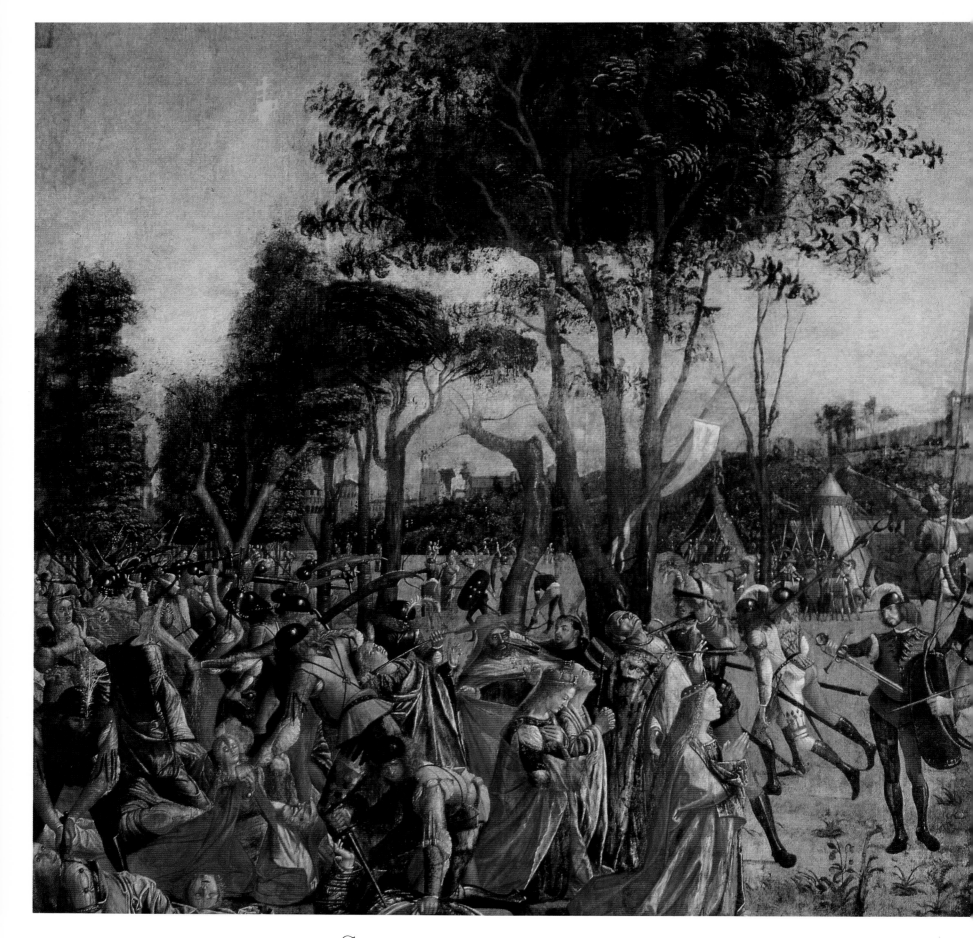

VITTORE CARPACCIO   63

Venice, c.1465-1526
The Martyrdom of the Pilgrims and the Funeral of Ursula
Oil on canvas, 108 x 234" (cat. no. 580)
Last restored 1984

Signature and date have been inscribed on the column base: VICTORIS CARPATIO / VENETI - OPUS / MCCCCLXXX/XIII. The column crossed with the arms of Loredan and Caotorta divides the two episodes: at left, the slaughter of the pilgrims culminating in the martyrdom of Ursula; at right, the Princess' funeral. A splendid warrior—perhaps Julian, son of the Hunnish King—gives the picture its focal point. Accompanying the cortege are bishops, Dominican friars, nobles, and members of the Scuola, some of their images certainly

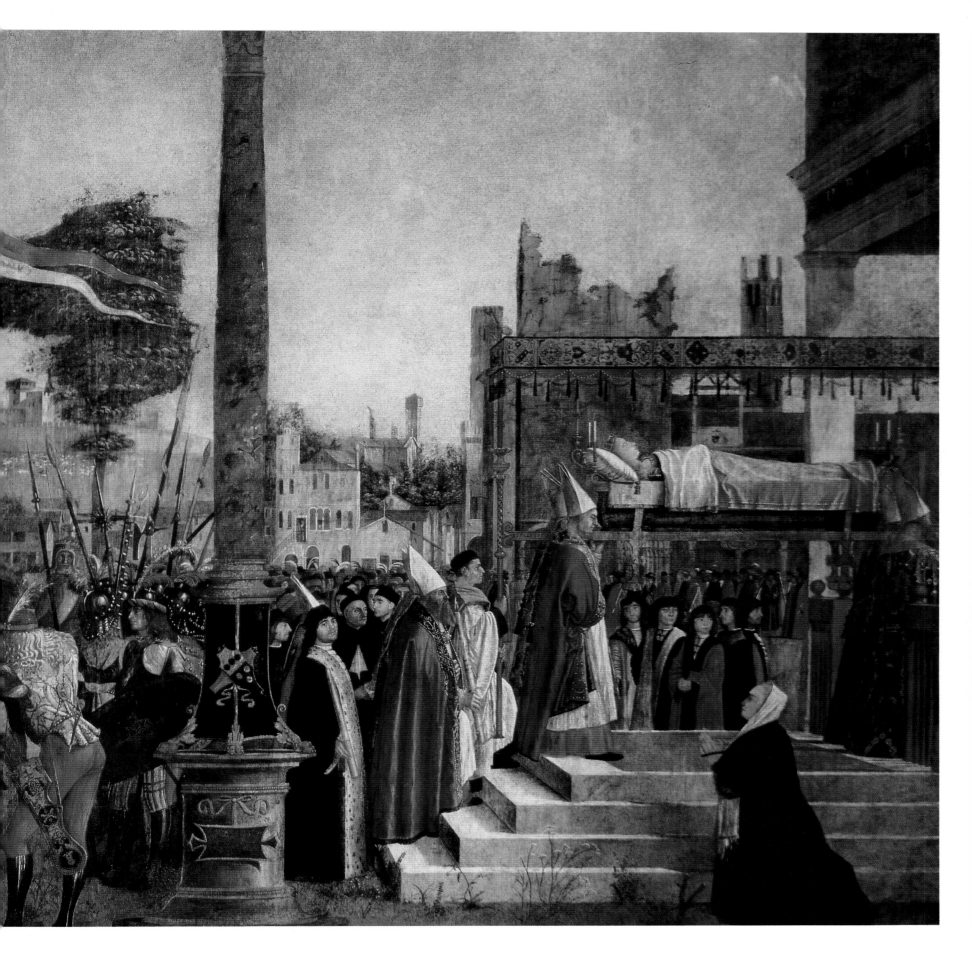

portraits, though it would be rash to attempt precise identification.

As such efforts go, however, the most persuasive may be the designation of the veiled woman kneeling at the side of the catafalque as Eugenia Caotorta, wife of Nocolò Loredan, who had already died when the painting was done. Wearing the zealot's garments in which she chose to be buried, Lady Loredan appears to be something of an outsider at the holy event.

In this composition, Carpaccio demonstrated extraordinary skill, orchestrating the complex space with utmost clarity, while so fusing microscopic descriptions, worthy of the Flemings, with images of Umbrian and Ferrarese derivation that they coexist in perfect harmony.

Venice, c.1465-1526
Return of the Ambassadors
Oil on canvas, 118 x 211" (cat. no. 574)
Last restored 1983

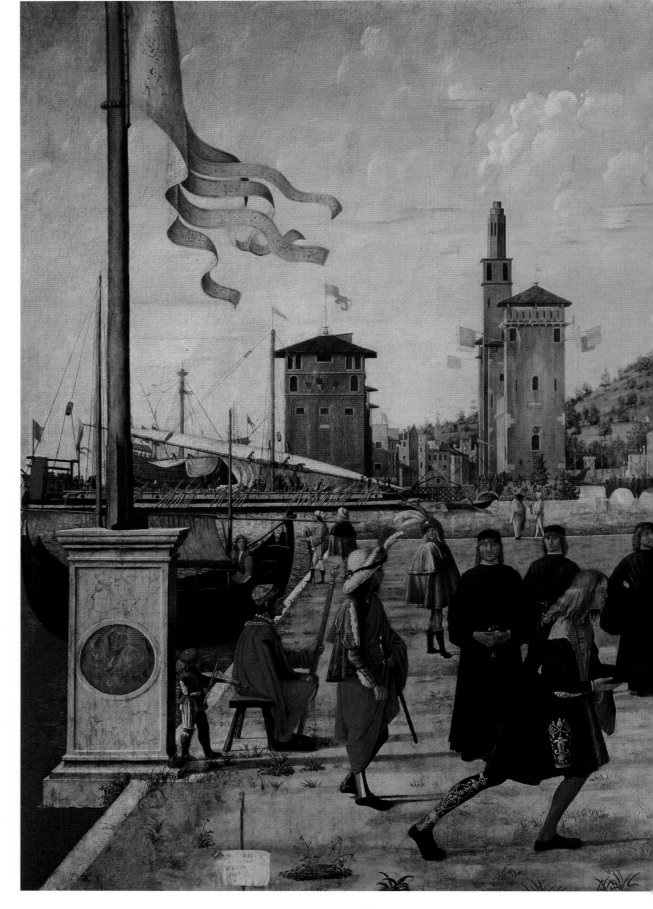

The inscription on the scroll in the lower left reads: VICTORIS / CA ... TIO / VENETI / OPUS. Also noted, this time on the base of the mast at left, is the restoration carried out in 1623.

The picture seen here may be the best preserved of the *Ursula* canvases. It narrates the return of the English ambassadors to their King with Ursula's reply. The person seated on the riverbank next to a pageboy trumpeter is *Lo Scalco*, or "Steward," whose function was to introduce the ambassadors into the Doge's banquet hall by accompanying them with music. A little beyond him a youth advances with the insignia of the *Compagnia della Calza* ("Hosiers' Guild") embroidered in pearls, while the shoulder of the next young man seems to serve as the focal point of the composition, around which fragments of Venetian buildings cluster as if viewed through a scenic kaleidoscope. Within this setting, the towers of the Arsenal can be recognized on the left, while one of the reliefs on the façade of the large building at center comes from a metal plaque attributged to Bertoldo. In his *Return of the Ambassadors*, Carpaccio achieved color of a particularly vibrant and luminous order.

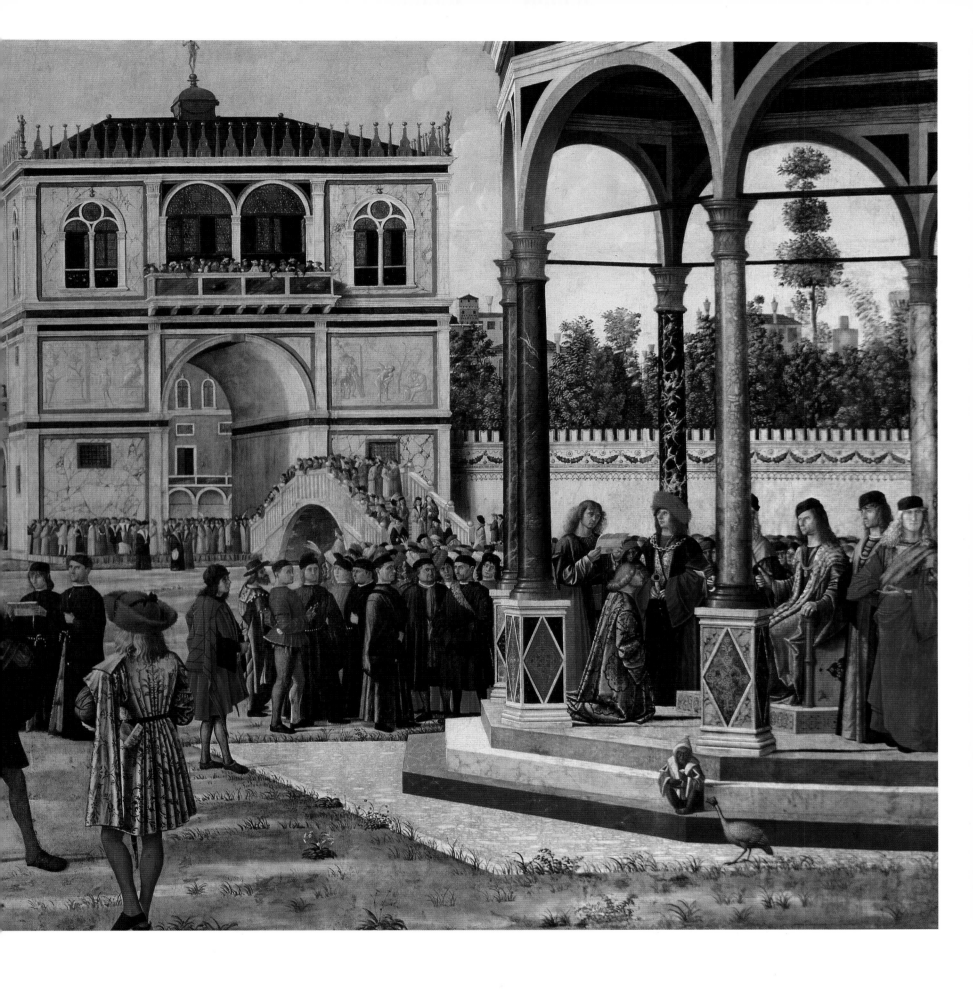

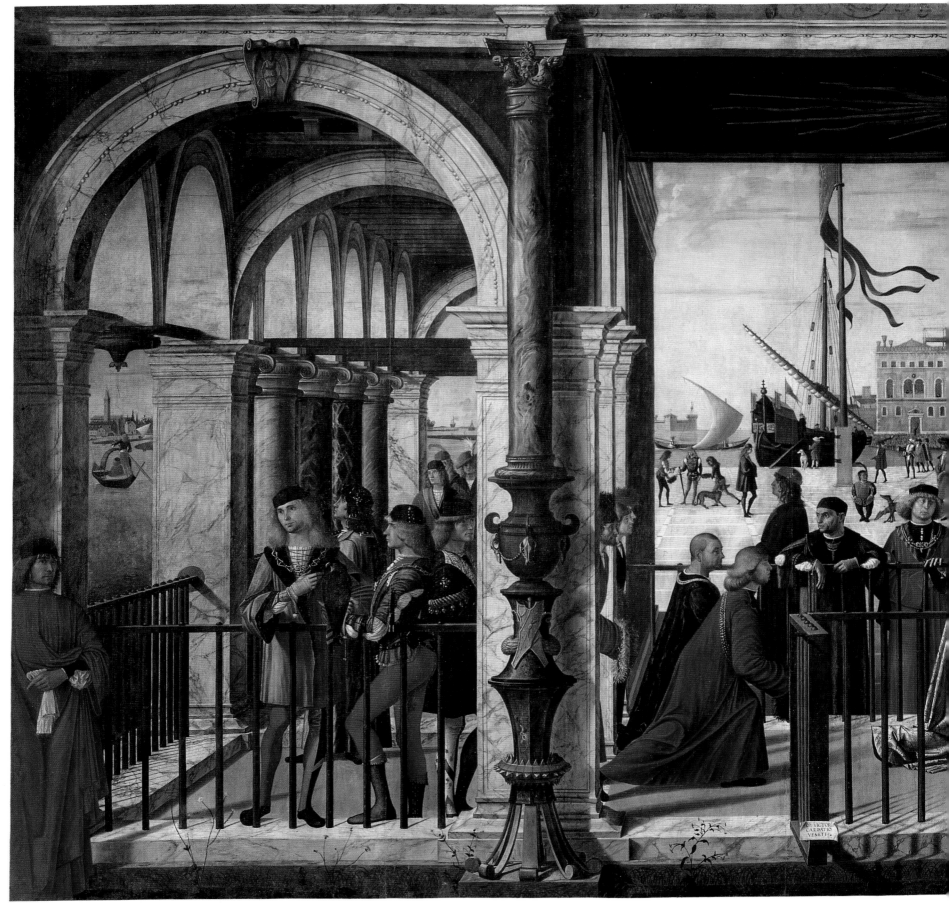

VITTORE CARPACCIO 65

Venice, c.1465-1526
Arrival of the Ambassadors
Oil on canvas, 110 x 236" (cat. no. 572)
Last restored 1983

The inscription at lower center reads: OP.

VICTORIS / CARPATIO / VENETI. This painting is the first in the narrative sequence of the *Saint Ursula Cycle*, its three "chapters" each distinguished by a different kind of architecture. After arriving at the Breton court in the left scene, the English ambassadors present Prince Ereus' marriage proposal at stage center. In the next act, on the right, Ursula meets her father in her room to discuss conditions, while her nurse waits at the foot of the stairs. The gap in the lower central zone corresponds to a door opened in the early 16th century, obscuring the wonderful head of a pageboy and damaging the figure that recent

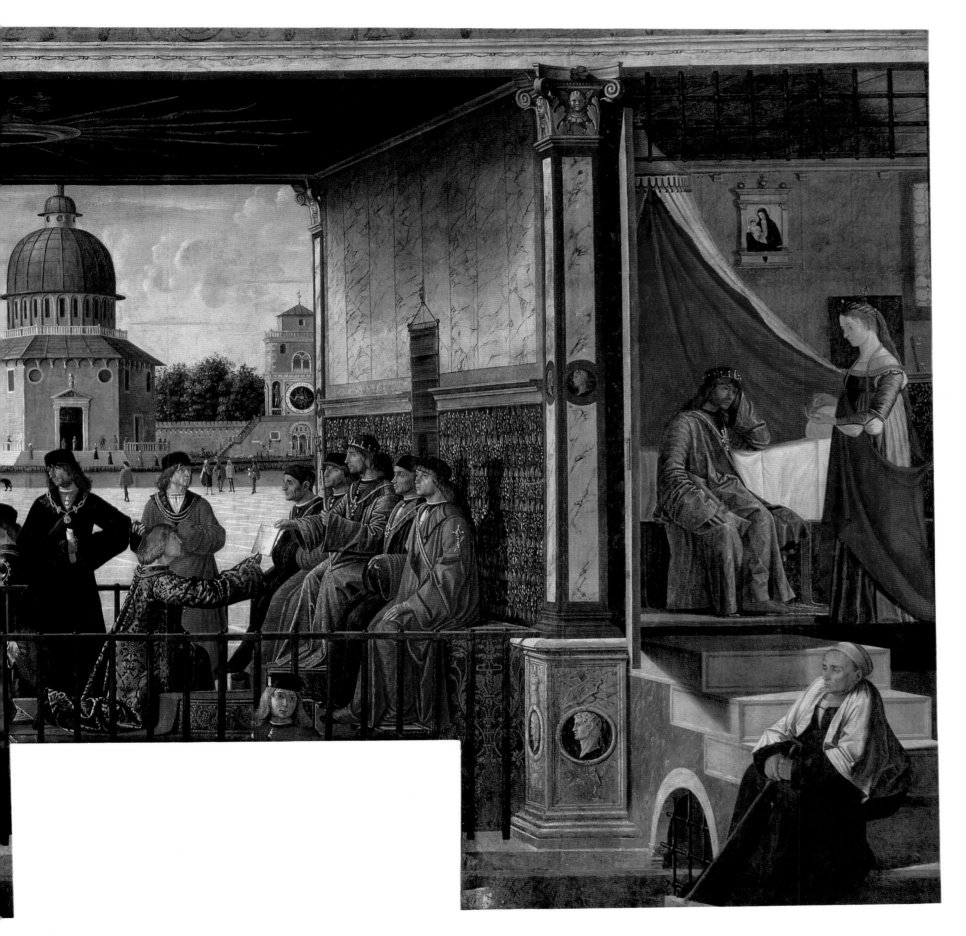

restoration has somewhat recovered. Also reconstituted is a fragment of the candelabra marking off the first scene, a fragment known from Del Pian's engraving. Conceived and executed almost as a theater spectacle, the *Arrival of the English Ambassadors* is perhaps the most complex painting in the cycle. Its

many portraits have inspired a multitude of identifications, all of them, however, difficult to confirm, even though the images clearly represent members or patrons of the Scuola. The abundance of perspective devices and the freedom of invention show that Carpaccio had absorbed the latest Renaissance discoveries in

rationalized illusionism. Thus, the influence of Perugino can be seen in the building at center rearground and in the withdrawing series of arches on the left. There are preliminary drawings in the Christ Church Library, Oxford, in the Museo Nazionale of La Valletta, Malta, and in the British Museum, London.

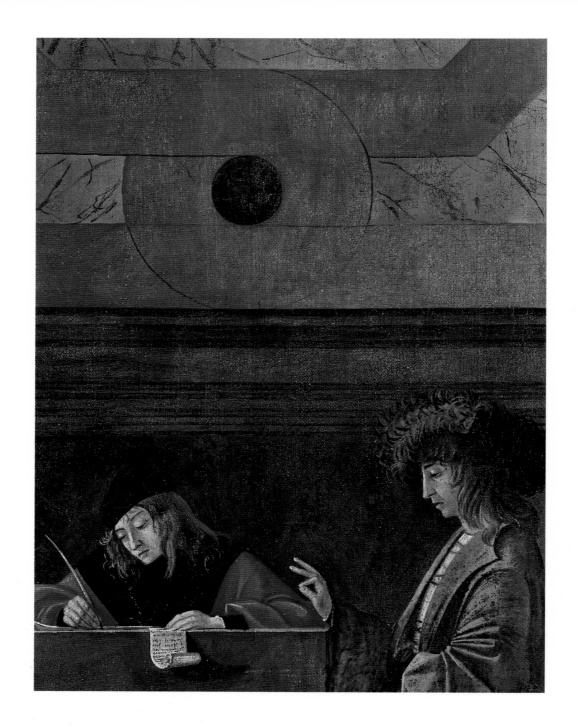

VITTORE CARPACCIO   66

Venice, c.1465-1526
Departure of the Ambassadors
Oil on canvas, 112 x 101" (cat. no. 573)
Last restored 1984

The inscription on the bottom step at left reads: VICTORIS CAR / VENETI / OPUS. Here we find the English ambassadors taking their leave of Breton King Mauro, who hands them his reply to the King of England, while the scribe, to whom the monarch has dictated his message, stands in the left foreground. The episode unfolds in a Lombard-style hall resplendent in marble of many colors.

Exquisite artifice, a subtle luminary play, and, above all, the wealth of decorative architectural features endow the scene with endless fascination.

Although worn in some places, to the point of becoming almost tonal, the color remains astonishing yet consistent with the overall design, which finally is the structural foundation of this brilliant painting.

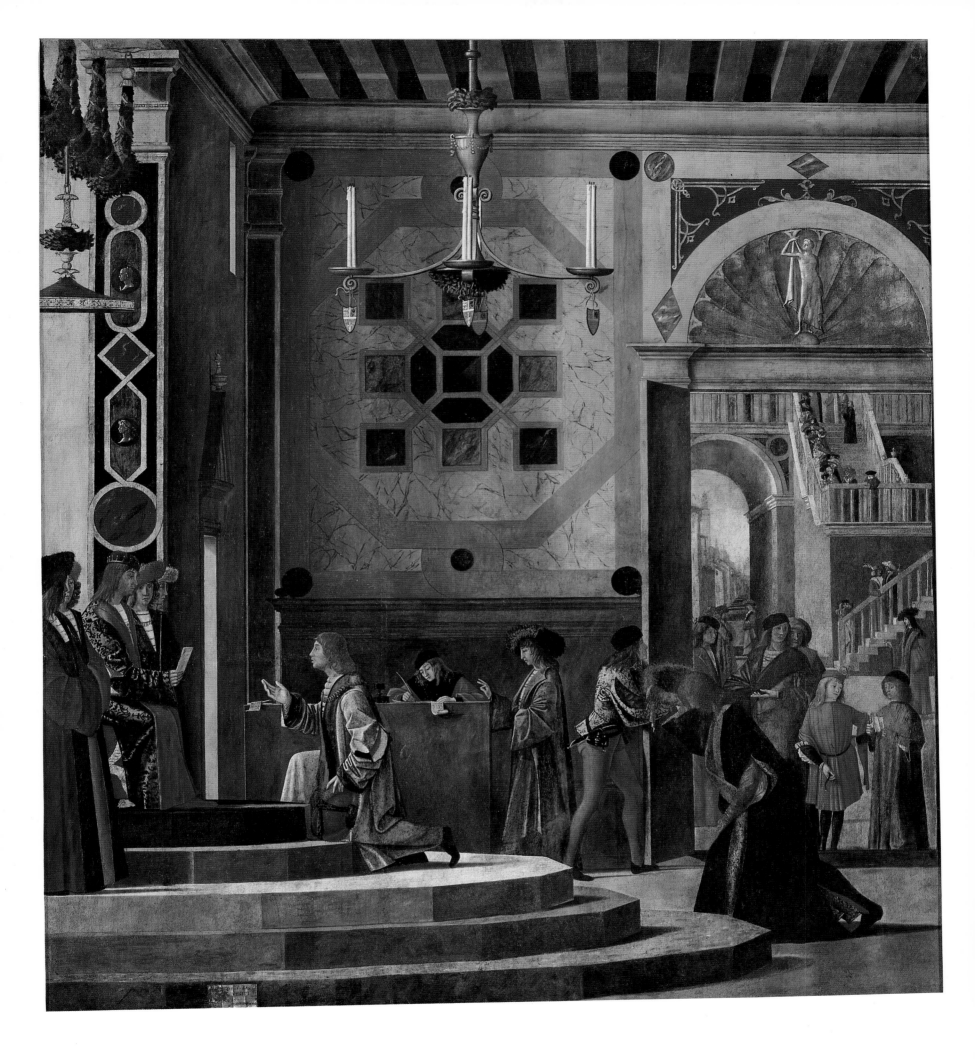

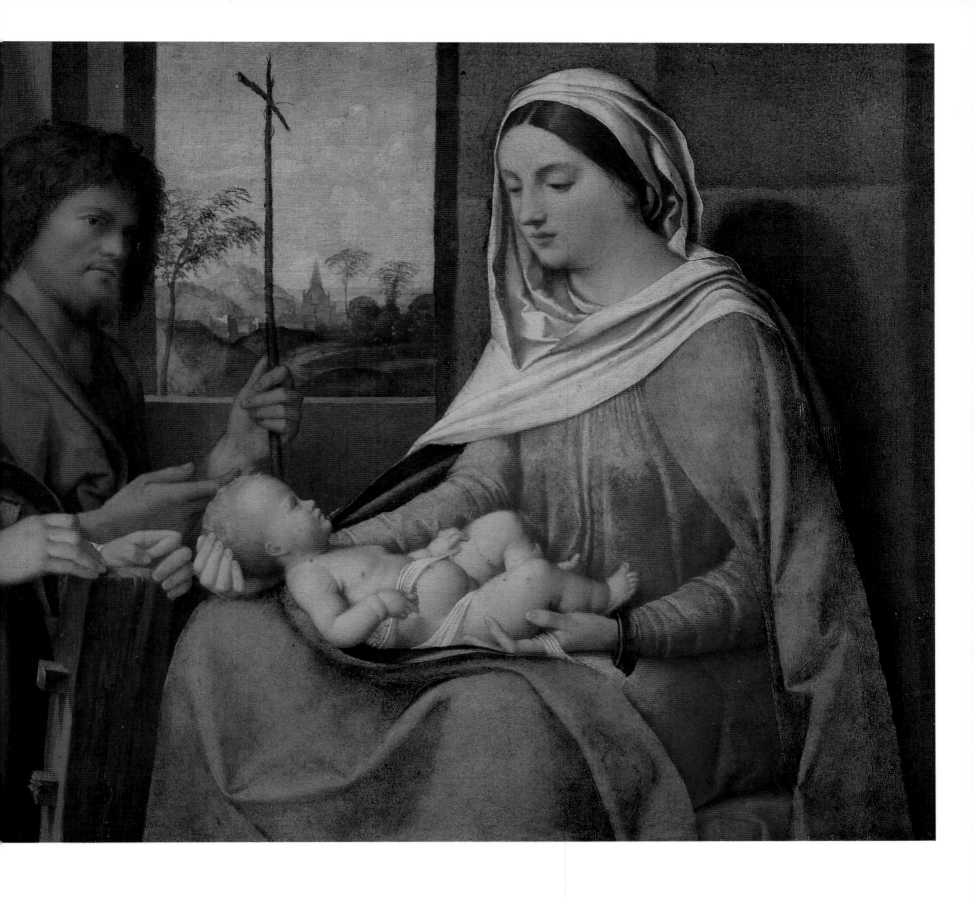

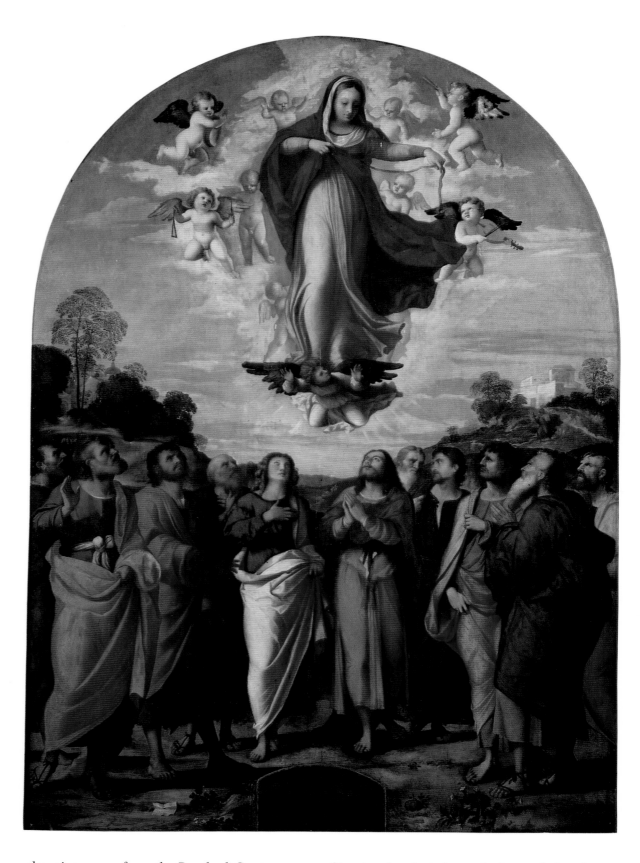

JACOPO NEGRETTI CALLED PALMA IL VECCHIO 74

Serina, near Bergamo, c.1480—Venice, 1528
Assumption of the Virgin
Oil on panel, 76 x 55" (cat. no. 315)
Last restored 1963

Among the first works acquired by the Gallerie in 1812, following secularization, this

altarpiece came from the Scuola di Santa Maria Maggiore, which still exists, on foundations in front of the homonymous church. An insert at the center of the lower zone no doubt corresponds to what must have been a tabernacle. Although now invisible, a label or scroll in the lower left probably displayed a signature. On February 5, 1513, Palma received a payment of 50 ducats for the little altarpiece, suggesting that by then he had finished and delivered the work. A youthful effort, it represents an artist struck by

Giorgione's coloristic revolution and already under the spell of Titian's powerful personality. The composition combines two episodes: the Assumption of the Virgin and the legend of the girdle, the garment said to have been given by Our Lady to "doubting" Thomas as proof of her ascent to Heaven. Mary, curiously borne aloft on the shoulders of a tiny angel, appears less intent on Heaven above than humanly inclined towards the minuscule Apostle scurrying along the hillside to participate in the holy event.

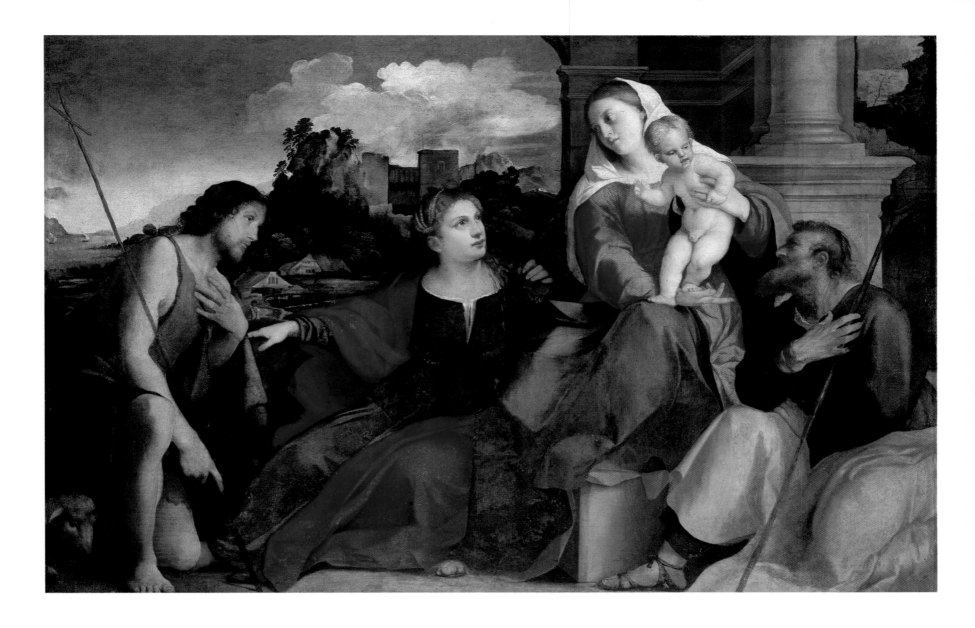

JACOPO NEGRETTI CALLED
PALMA IL VECCHIO   75

Serina, near Bergano, c.1480—Venice, 1528
Holy Family with Saints Catherine and John the Baptist
Oil on canvas, 51 x 78" (cat. no. 147)
Last restored 1947

Purchased in 1900 from Alessandro Bedendo, who had it in turn from the Pizzamano family, this is almost certainly the picture described by Ridolfi (1648) and Martinioni (1663) as being in the *casa* Widmann in Venice. There are several gaps in the painted image, affecting Saint Catherine's face and neckline as well as the sky along a horizontal swath. The painting remained incomplete at the artist's death, as the unfinished hands of the Saint and the Baptist show, and it may have been none other than Titian who gave Catherine her face and brought the landscape with its castle to conclusion.

Radiographic and reflectographic analysis seems to confirm this separation of hands, while also revealing a variety of preliminary work, towards an arcaded portico, in the background behind Saint Catherine, as well as towards a different, early conception of that figure's face. In this, one of Palma's last works, the sheer breadth of the colorism, the pyramidal composition, cleverly borrowed from Titian's *Pesaro Madonna* in the Frari, and the quality of the light, a light not unlike Lotto's, combine in a coherent and harmonious whole, despite the damage and division of hands. A variation on the theme, attributed to Titian, hangs in the Musée des Beaux-Arts in Dijon.

GIOVANNI ANTONIO DE' SACCHIS
CALLED PORDENONE

Pordenone, 1483/84—Ferrara, 1539
Blessed Lorenzo Giustiniani and Saints
Oil on canvas, 168 x 88" (cat. no. 316)
Last restored 1965

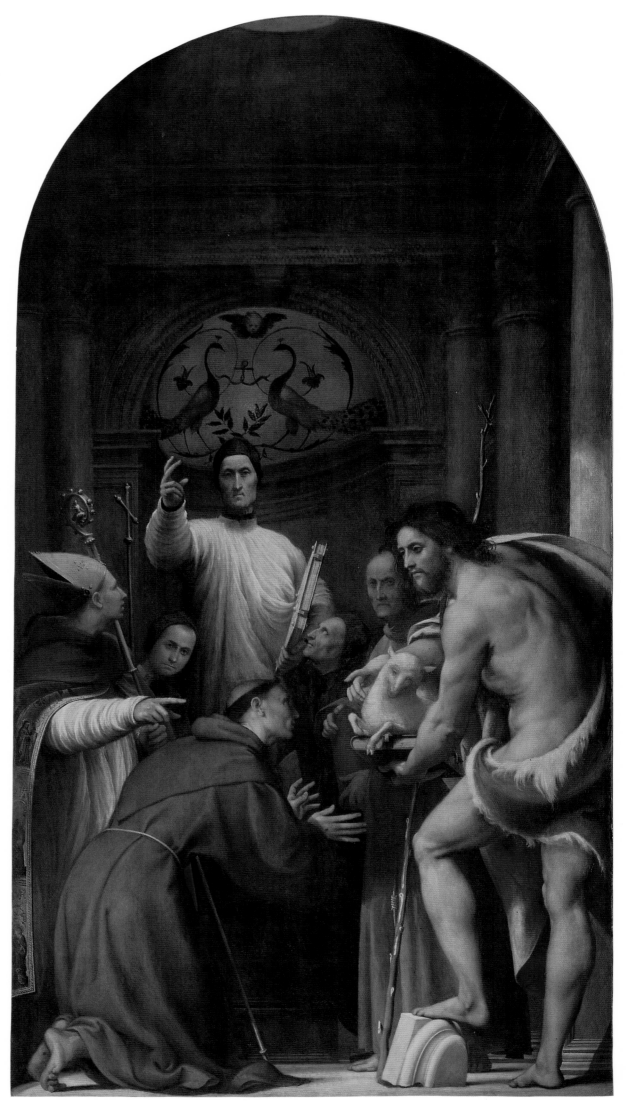

The signature has been inscribed on the step at the base: JOANNIS / ANTONII / PORTUNA / ENSIS. Originally, the painting served as an altarpiece in the Renier chapel, to the left of the presbytery, in the Venetian Church of the Madonna dell'Orto. Transported to Paris in 1797, it returned to Venice in 1815 and entered the Gallerie. Meanwhile, a copy by the painter Dalla Valentina replaced it at the Madonna dell'Orto.

At the center Pordenone represented Blessed Lorenzo Giustiniani, canonized in 1690 and here flanked by two *fratelli turchini*—brothers dressed in Turkish blue—as well as accompanied by Saints Augustine and Francis on the left and by Saints Bernardino and John the Baptist on the right.

In 1532, Pordenone undertook the great altarpiece for the canons of San Giorgio in Alga, known as the *fratelli turchini*, who at the beginning of the 16th century officiated at the Church of the Madonna dell'Orto. The painting replaced another devoted to the same Beatus and executed by Girolamo Santacroce in 1525, then moved to the Church of San Giorgio in Alga. While greatly admired in the 17th and 18th centuries, Pordenone's altarpiece did not attract scholarly attention until the end of the 19th. Now the innovative composition, the grandly modeled volumes, the dramatic power, and the organ-like play of color and light won appropriate recognition. In paintings such this one, the artist achieved a kind of proto-Mannerism that could not have failed to impress the young Tintoretto.

Arezzo, 1511—Florence, 1574
Justice
Oil on panel, 31 x 74" (cat. no. 1370)
Patience
Oil on panel, 31 x 73" (cat. no. 1371)
Last restored 1989/90

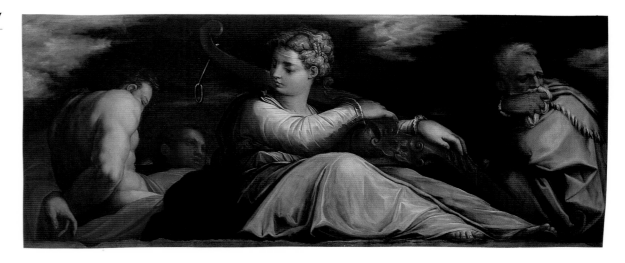

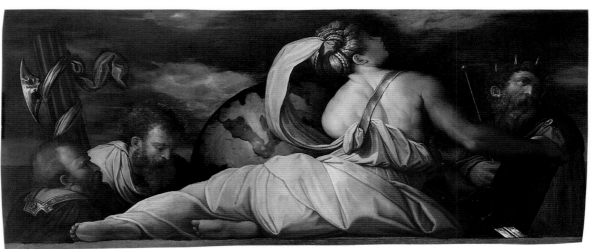

Acquired in 1987 from Signora Giovanna di Capua Sestieri, these two *Virtue* paintings had, in 1908, been in the Giovanelli collection in Venice. Originally they hung in what is now the Palazzo Corner Spinelli, purchased by Giovanni Corner in January 1542. The building, thought to have been designed by Marco Coducci, was restored by Michele Sanmicheli, who introduced a new ceiling "of carved wood, richly gilt," for which Vasari, according to his own account given on April 8, 1542, executed "nine large paintings . . . in oils": *Charity* (now lost), *Hope* (Lord Weidenfeld collection, London), *Faith* (H. Trainé collection, Zurich), *Patience*, and *Justice*. At the four corners there were also

four "*putti* bearing scrolls," derived (at least in the case of the two acquired by the Gallerie at the same time as the two *Virtues*) from high reliefs now in the Archaeological Museum, but, as noted by Samuolo (1532), briefly installed in a building on Piazza San Marco. A third *putto* belongs to a private collector in Venice, while the fourth has disappeared.

The work must have been completed during August 1542, when Vasari left Venice after designing the sets and costumes for *La Talanta*, a comedy by Aretino. For this project he received 120 ducats, the wooden panels themselves, and four "ounces of ultramarine blue."

Foreshortened to be viewed from below, all the allegorical figures appear to lean over an invisible parapet, their consummately elgant figures silhouetted against a blue sky. In them, Vasari undoubtedly brought to perfection a Pordenone scheme for a lost ceiling painting once installed at the Scuola di San Francesco ai Frari.

Venetian painters must have studied the work with great interest, not least the young Paolo Veronese for his small ceiling in the San Sebastiano sacristy. And Vasari himself had difficulty matching the felicitous and refined formal elaborations of his Venetian project. He would reutilize the drawings for some of the Virtues in his frescoes for the Sala dei Cento Giorni in Rome's Cancelleria.

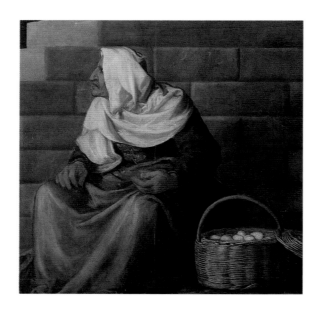

TITIAN
(TIZIANO VECELLIO)   78

Pieve di Cadore, 1488/90—Venice, August 27, 1576
Presentation of the Virgin in the Temple
Oil on canvas, 133 x 310" (cat. no. 626)
Last restored 1981

The canvas was painted by Titian for the *albergo* at the Scuola Grande della Carità, now part of the Gallerie dell'Accademia, where it is still exhibited. The artist probably began the picture some time after August 29, 1534, and evidently finished it before March 6, 1538. The *sala dell'albergo* also held, on the adjacent wall, Giampietro Silvio's *Marriage of the Virgin*, and Girolamo Dente's *Annunciation*, both of which are in the parish church of Mason Vicentino. The canvas has been cut along its lower edge to fit the two doorways. The portal on the viewer's right already existed when Titian set to work, as we know from the painting itself, where a frame of rusticated stone voussoirs acknowledges the old Gothic entrance to the Scuola's ground floor, now walled up. The door on the left was cut on March 10, 1572, evidently requiring that part of the canvas be sacrificed.

From the very start, the *Presentation of the Virgin* has been much praised. In 1568, Vasari wrote that it depicted "all kinds of heads, taken from life." Ridolfi (1648) and Boschini (1664) went so far as to name some of the figures, claiming to recognize Andrea de' Franceschi and Lazzaro Crasso, officers of the Scuola. However, their identity cannot be confirmed in the light of current knowledge. Still, the figures on the left, included by the artist as courtesy, are indeed senior members of the Scuola's governing body, among them the *Guardian Grande*, the Vicar, and the *Guardian del Matin*, who can be identified by their garments. Yet, since these functionaries held office for one calendar year only, whereas Titian worked on the canvas from 1534 until early 1538, they cannot be identified by name. The suggestion that Pietro Bembo and Pietro Aretino are among them must be rejected out of hand, in the light of their well-known features. More recently, the couple facing the window have been recognized as Titian himself and his wife Cecilia (d. 1530), while the little girl in the dress of the period, leaning against the window, may be their daughter Lavinia.

The painting's most recent restoration was undertaken only after complete X-ray, stratigraphic, and reflectographic studies established that, generally speaking, the paint is in good condition. However, the right side has sustained severe damage, across a 62cm (25") band running the entire height of the canvas. Moreover, the truncated sculpture of a male torso, in the lower right corner, has been completely overpainted in an attitude different from the one originally adopted. There can be little doubt that the figure is from Titian's own brush, or that it plays an important role in the painting's iconographical scheme. The torso and the old woman selling eggs are thought to personify pagan antiquity and Judaism. Consequently, it has also been suggested that the picture signifies the three eras—*Before the Law, Under the Law*, and *Under Grace*. And just as the subject is the Presentation of the Virgin, the painting itself becomes a kind of sacred representation. The fires on the mountainside—the *Marmarole* of the artist's native Cadore—also symbolize Mary's virginity, believed to be as eternal as the burning bush seen by Moses.

A complete X-radiograph permits us to clarify the genesis of the work itself, showing how Titian initially projected the architectural setting about 20cm, or 8 inches, lower. *Pentimenti* under the window on the left reveal that the artist had begun with two fully clothed female figures placed a little higher on the canvas than the two spectators, a man and a woman, now in the painting. In lieu of the present, truncated sculpture, Titian originally intended a bas-relief or a mural with centaurs. While the picture's horizontal dimensions (as well, no doubt, as the client's preference) may account for the traditional Venetian narrative scheme, the artist handled it in a remarkably "modern" spirit. The composition, deriving most immediately from Carpaccio, shows a profound understanding of the new architecture designed by such contemporaries as Sansovino and Serlio. The perfect balance between landscape and architecture, as well as between these and the isocephalic procession led by portraits of the confraternity brethren (all portraits), joins with the exceptional resonance of the artist's palette to unify the work as an innovative variation on 15th-century models, a fresh departure that would hold great significance for the future development of figure painting.

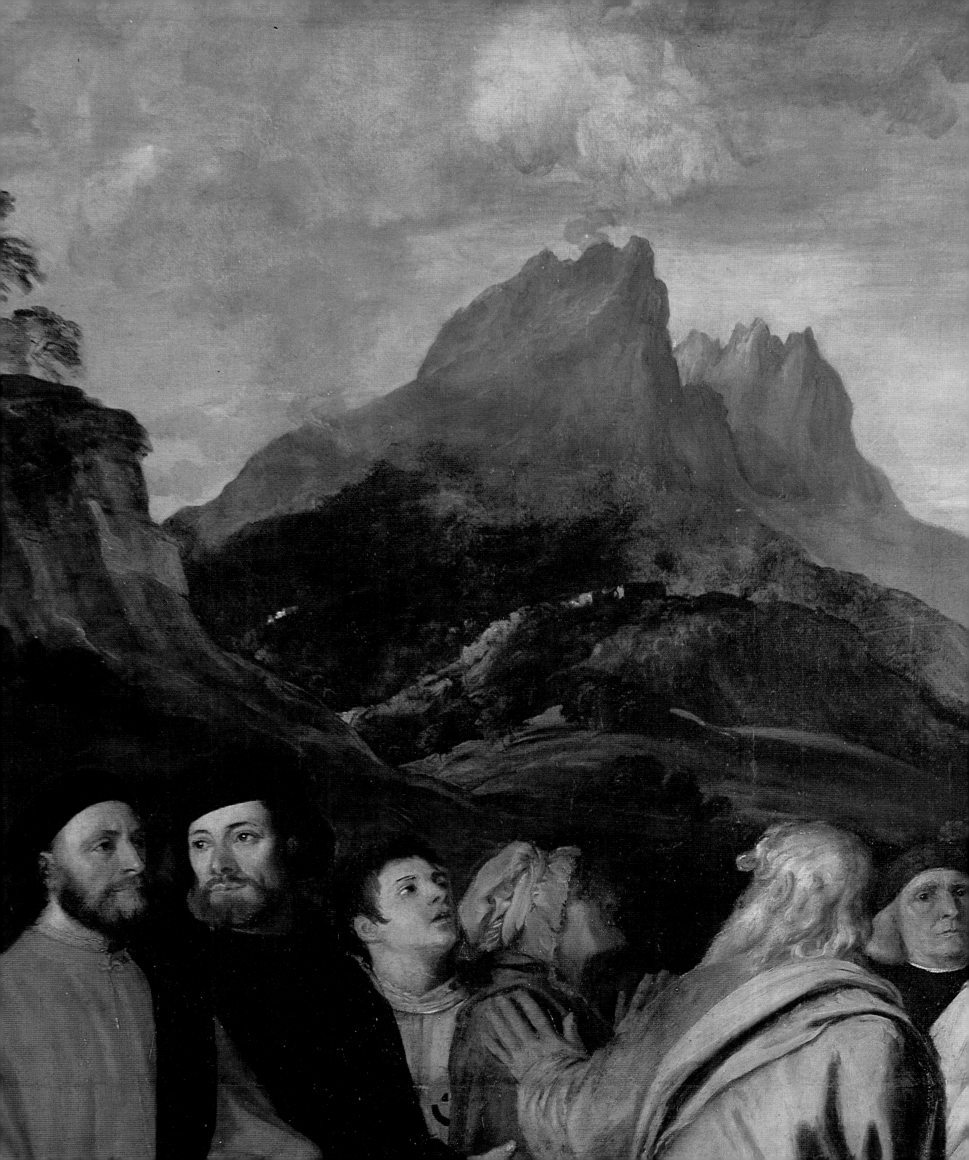

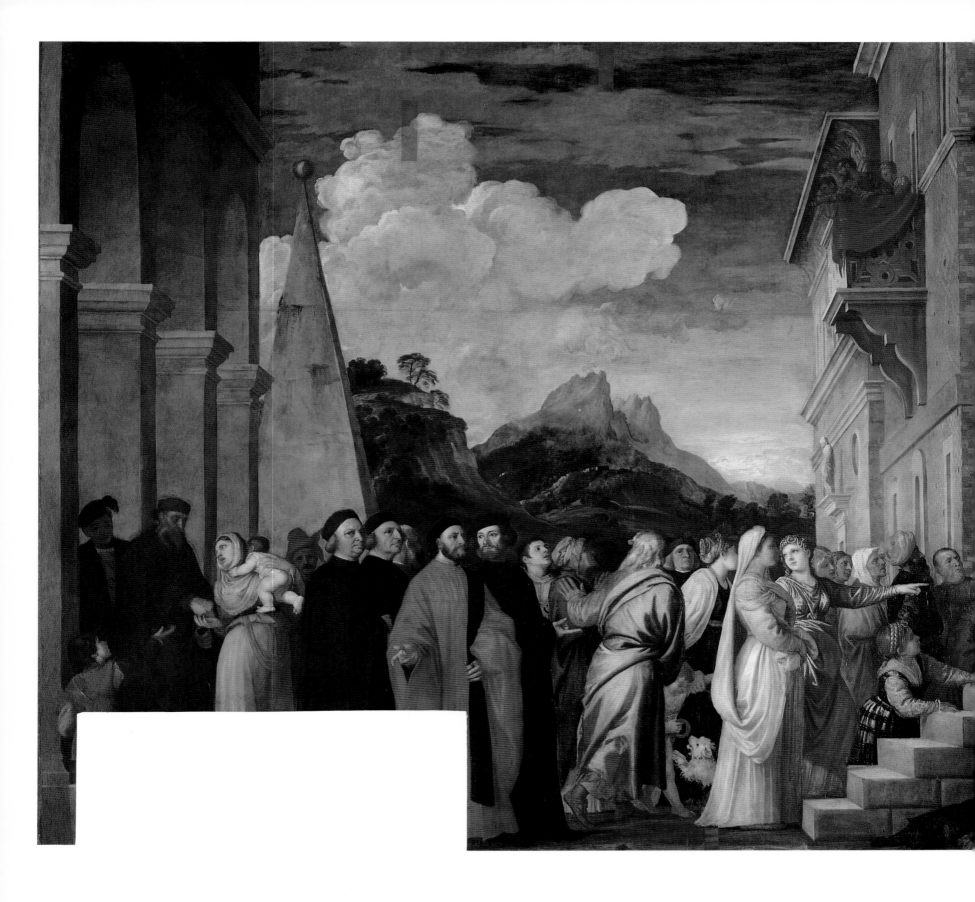

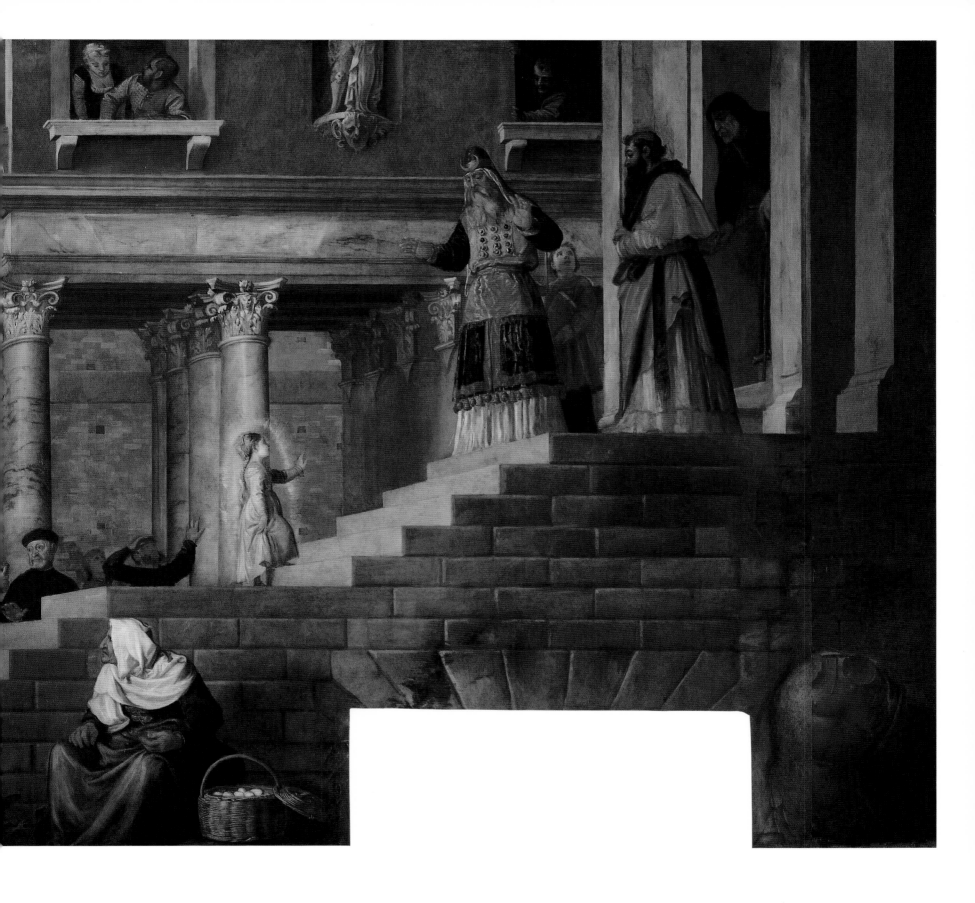

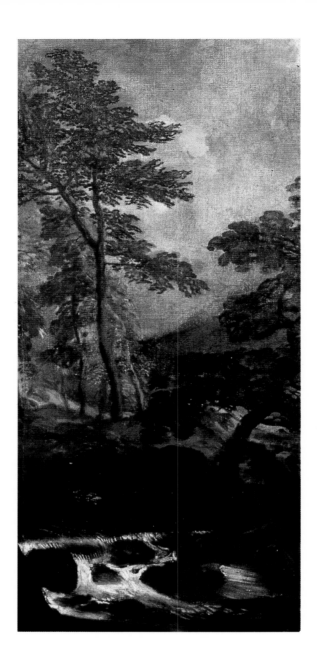

TITIAN
(TIZIANO VECELLIO)   79

Pieve di Cadore, 1488/90—Venice, August 27, 1576
Saint John the Baptist
Oil on canvas, 81 x 54" (cat. no. 314)
Last restored 1981

From its place in the richly adorned Church of Santa Maria Maggiore (in the chapel to the right of the presbytery), this altarpiece was removed in 1807 to the Gallerie in their first consignment of paintings, works saved from exile at Milan's Brera by the concerted protest of the Venetian people.

Signed TICIANUS, on the rock where John the Baptist plants his left foot, the picture has been acclaimed by authorities from the very beginning. In 1557, Lodovico Dolce, writing in his *Dialogue on Painting*, declared that he had never seen "anything more beautiful, or with better drawing and coloring." And here, in the interest of a carefully conceived metaphor, Titian does indeed weave together drawing, color, and imagination, finally endowing his subject with a slightly bucolic quality. It is as if he had explicitly set out to refute Florentine allegations that Venetian painters scarcely knew how to draw.

Now revealed by reflectography, the very powerful preliminary drawing of the Saint begs comparison with both Michelangelo and Classical art. The strong, alert, masculine body, its musculature evincing a sure grasp of anatomy, departs dramatically from the conventional image of an ascetic wasted by fasting.

Exemplary in its academic correctness, the work would delight any 17th- or even 19th-century critic; yet, for the very same reason, it constitutes something of a puzzle for us today. In any case, the potent draftsmanship and rich coloring still apparent beneath the traces of successive restorations, together with the freshness of the landscape, suggest that the work belongs with the Gallerie's own *Presentation of the Virgin* (ill. no. 78) and the Louvre's *Christ Crowned with Thorns*, which recent research has been able to date to 1540. Thus, the present picture was probably painted in the 1540s.

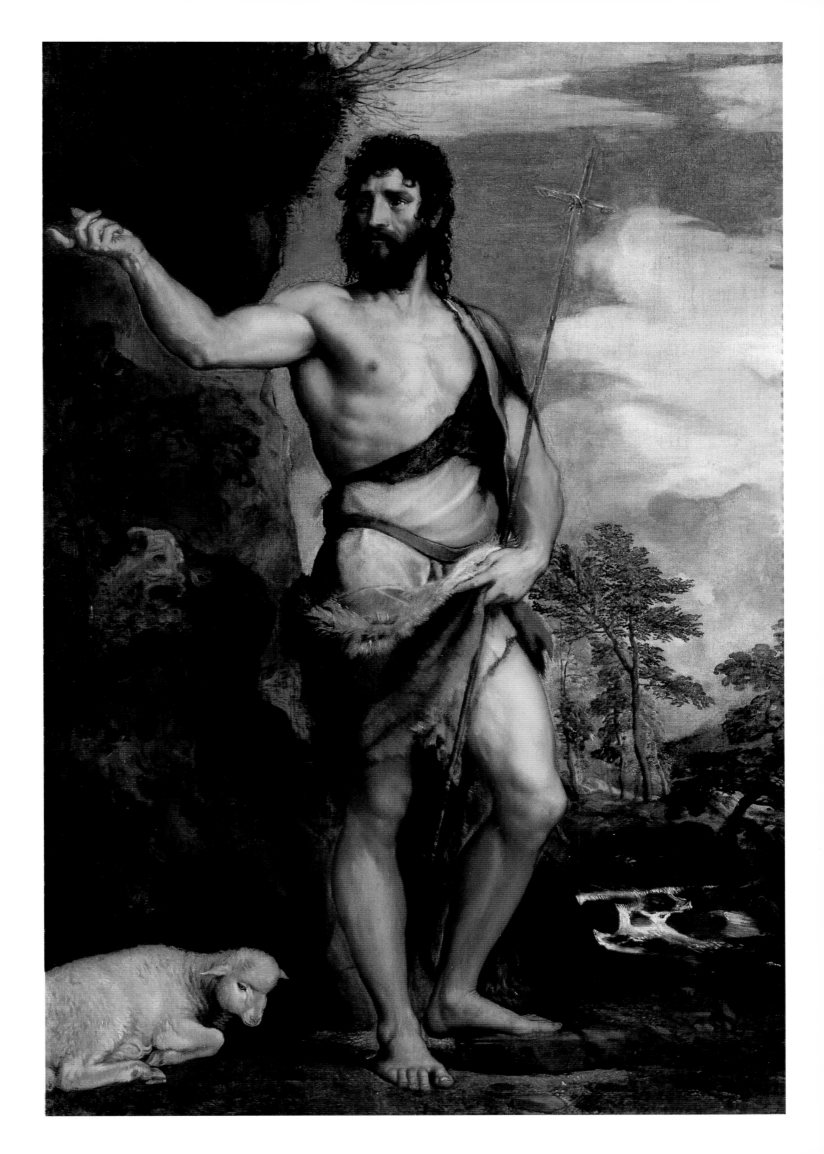

Pieve di Cadore, 1488/90—Venice, August 27, 1576
Madonna and Child
Oil on canvas, 50 x 39" (cat. no. 1359)

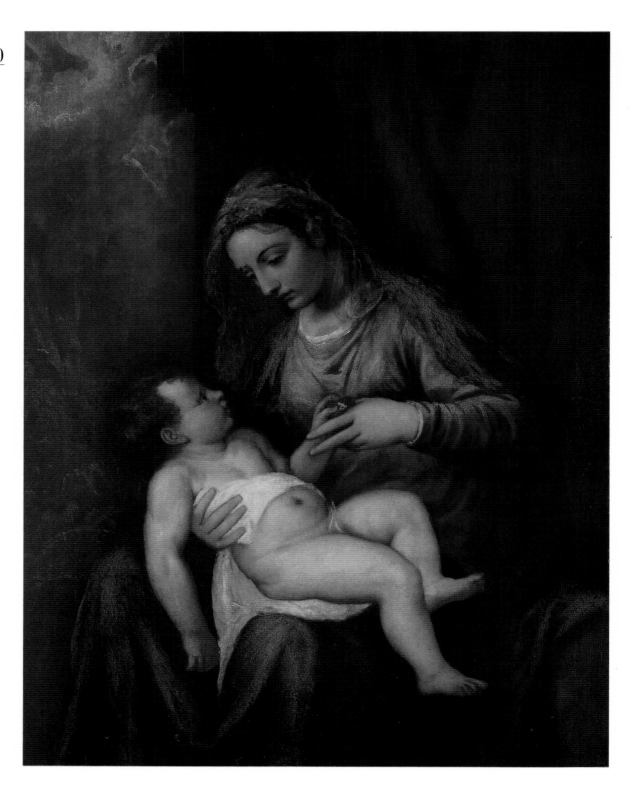

The work appears under the name of Titian in a catalogue compiled in 1616 for the Milanese collection of Marchesi Mazenta (Milan, Castello Sforzesco). A 1628 appraisal, made by the painter Giambattista Cerano of certain paintings from the same collection, includes Titian's *Madonna and Child*, described as "two cubits across," or about the size of the picture seen here. The work appears yet again in an inventory taken on December 30, 1678, at the instance of the brothers Ludovico and Alessandro Mazenta. It stayed with this family until 1879, then passed to their descendants, the Pinetti of Martinengo (Bergamo). In 1916, the canvas was acquired by Luigi Albertini, whose son Leonardo bequeathed it to the Gallerie in 1981.

Still generally attributed to Titian, the painting was exhibited as such in London in 1930, but some critics have reservations, seeing it rather as a copy of one of the master's lost works.

Numerous reproductions attest to the great popularity of this devotional image. An engraving was published by Pietro Daret in the 17th century (Modigliani, 1942), and there is an almost identical painting in the sacristy of the Duomo in Padua, attributed to Padovanino.

The work reproduced here is certainly by Titian, a fact established by reflectographic and X-ray analysis, which discloses a composition realized with quick, layered brushstrokes typical of the artist's work, especially in the 1560s. It is akin to the *Madonna and Child* authenticated by the Alte Pinakothek in Munich, as well as to the San Salvador *Annunciation*, but the worn-down texture of the colors and the reworked passages make the picture hard to decipher, all of which may account for the doubts of some art historians. Notwithstanding the problematic surface, the figures are clearly depicted in vibrantly luminous impasto, further brightened by the unexpected glow of the burning bush (Exodus 3:2). Seen at the left of the picture, this symbol of Mary's perpetual virginity also figures in the almost-contemporary painting at San Salvador. X-ray analysis reveals that the canvas had already been used for another subject, probably a praying Saint or perhaps a Magdalene.

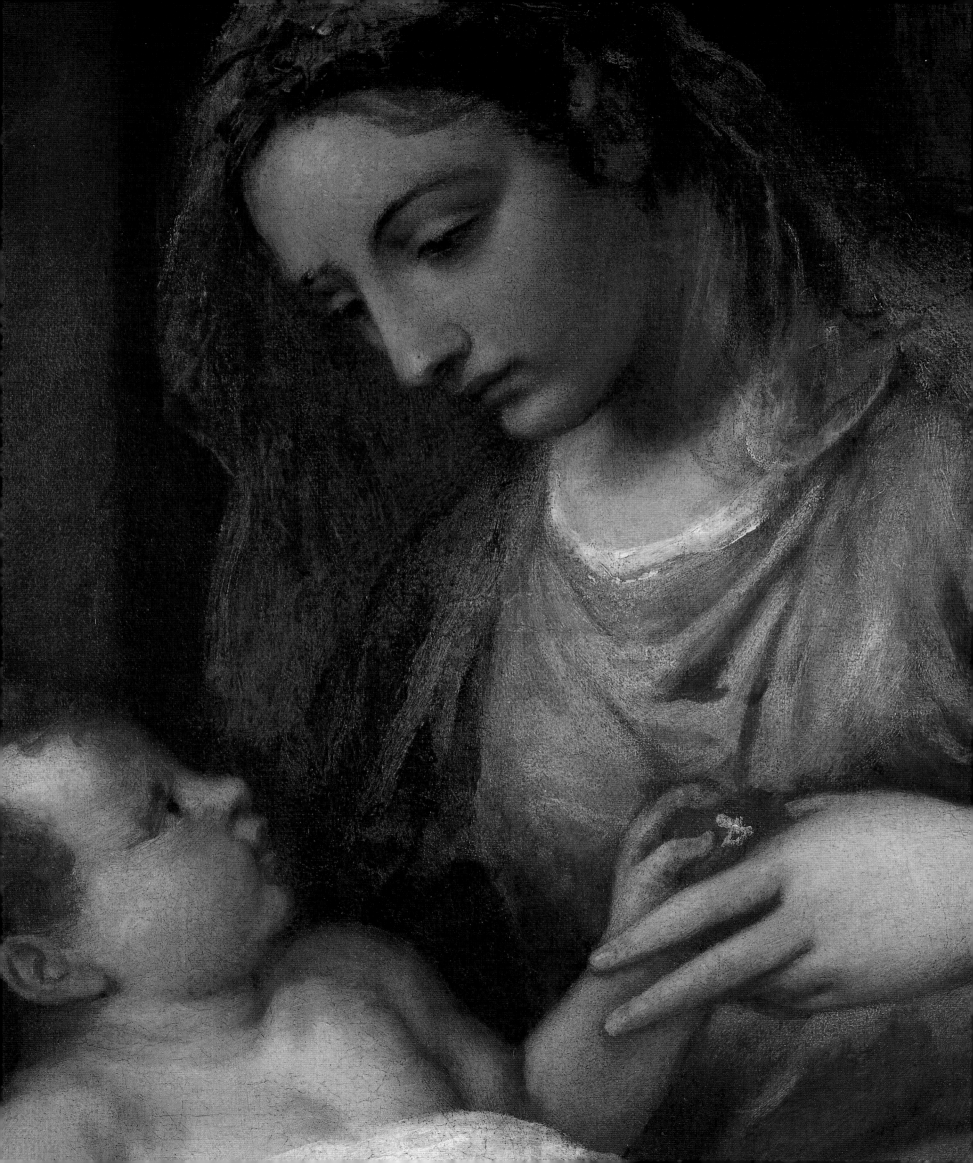

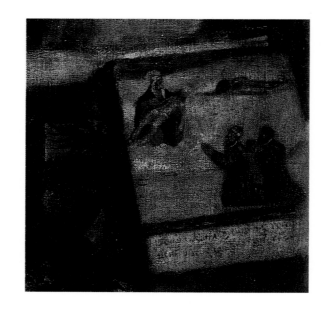

TITIAN (TIZIANO VECELLIO)   81

Pieve di Cadore, 1488/90—Venice, August 27, 1576
Pietà
Oil on canvas, 151 x 150" (cat. no. 400)
Last restored 1984-85

In 1648, Ridolfi wrote that Titian intended this work for the Chapel of Christ at the Frari, as a consideration for his being buried there. The negotiations, however, went on at great length, possibly because the friars had reservations of their own, with the result that the artist never completed the picture. "After his death," it "fell into the hands of Palma [Giovane], who finished it, adding a few small angels and this modest inscription: QUOD TITIANUS INCHOATUM RELIQUIT/PALMA REVERENTUR ABSOLVIT/DEOQ. DICAVIT OPUS ("What Titian left wanting Palma reverently completed, and dedicated the work to God"). In 1664, Boschini described it for the first time, as standing in the Church of Sant'Angelo "on the left hand," and asserted that it had been initiated by Titian and then completed by Palma: "The chiaroscuro is wholly Titian's, but the other figures are in many places retouched or repainted by Palma."

Titian died on August 27, 1576, at the height of the plague in Venice, and was buried the next day in the Frari "at the foot of the altar of the Crucifix." Although much inhibited by circumstance, the ceremony nonetheless constituted a State funeral since the Canons of San Marco officiated.

At the death of Titian and his son Orazio, the mob sacked his richly furnished mansion at the

Biri, which another son, Pomponio, sold on October 27, 1581, to Cristoforo Barbarigo. Presumably the house contained certain of the artist's works, since Barbarigo, in a will dated March 13, 1600, bequeathed to his younger brother Domenico four paintings by Titian: "Christ carrying the Cross, the Magdalene, the Madonna framed in ebony, and Venus." The next mention of the *Pietà* does not occur until 1675, when Joachim Sandrart erroneously described it as originally intended for the Church of San Pantalon, going on to say that it was finished by Palma but signed in the name of Titian by order of the Senate. Since Palma finished the picture "with his own hand," it presumably stayed with him until his death in 1628. By 1631 it had arrived at the Church of Sant'Angelo, where the end of the great plague of 1630 was celebrated with unusual pomp and devotion inasmuch as it occurred on the feast of the Archangel Michael, the church's patron. Here Titian's "especially personal painting"—almost an *ex voto*, given the circumstances of its completion—could find a logical and worthy placement.

Between 1581 and 1622, records of pastoral visitations to Sant'Angelo make no reference to the painting, which was presumably still in Palma's studio. But following a long period during which such records were not kept, the transcript of a visitation by Baoder in 1690 cites "a large painting of the Madonna of the Pietà, by Titian, in the Chapel of the Most Holy" (Archivo Patriarchale, Venice, *Visite pastorali*).

An unconvincing theory holds that the *Pietà* was at least begun under commission from the Marques de Ayamonte, who, while Resident in Milan, had been made responsible, by Philip II,

for paying a pension to Titian. On January 27, 1575, Ayamonte expressed to Guzmán de Silva a desire for a painting by the artist with "a dead Christ in a winding sheet, his Mother standing" (Ferrarino, 1975, n. 164). Nor can it be established that Titian originally conceived the painting as smaller, with only the Christ and the Virgin, but then gradually enlarged it to include the architecture, the Magdalene, and the other figures. After a recent cleaning, in the course of which seven inserts were counted on the back, it became clear that the central zone was not large enough to contain even the Madonna group.

However, Ayamonte's letter of April 27, 1575, to Guzmán de Silva is of the greatest interest, since the writer mentions a large painting with Mother, Son, and Magdalene, which, by accurately describing the *Pietà*, would appear to be the earliest recorded reference to it. Perhaps after negotiations broke down with the Frari, for which Titian had casually composed his votive picture bit by bit, the artist toyed with the notion, in 1575, of letting the Marques de Ayamonte have it. The following year, as pestilence raged, he reconsidered and made the painting into an *ex voto* against the epidemic, or at least into an important piece of autobiography. The Church of Sant'Angelo, suppressed in 1810, was destroyed in 1837, well after the *Pietà* had been assigned to the Gallerie in 1814.

During the picture's most recent restoration, it became evident that Titian, besides using several different types or weaves of canvas and thus creating a surface of varying thicknesses, appropriated for the central zone (where perhaps he anticipated the need for a more densely chromatic surface) a piece of canvas

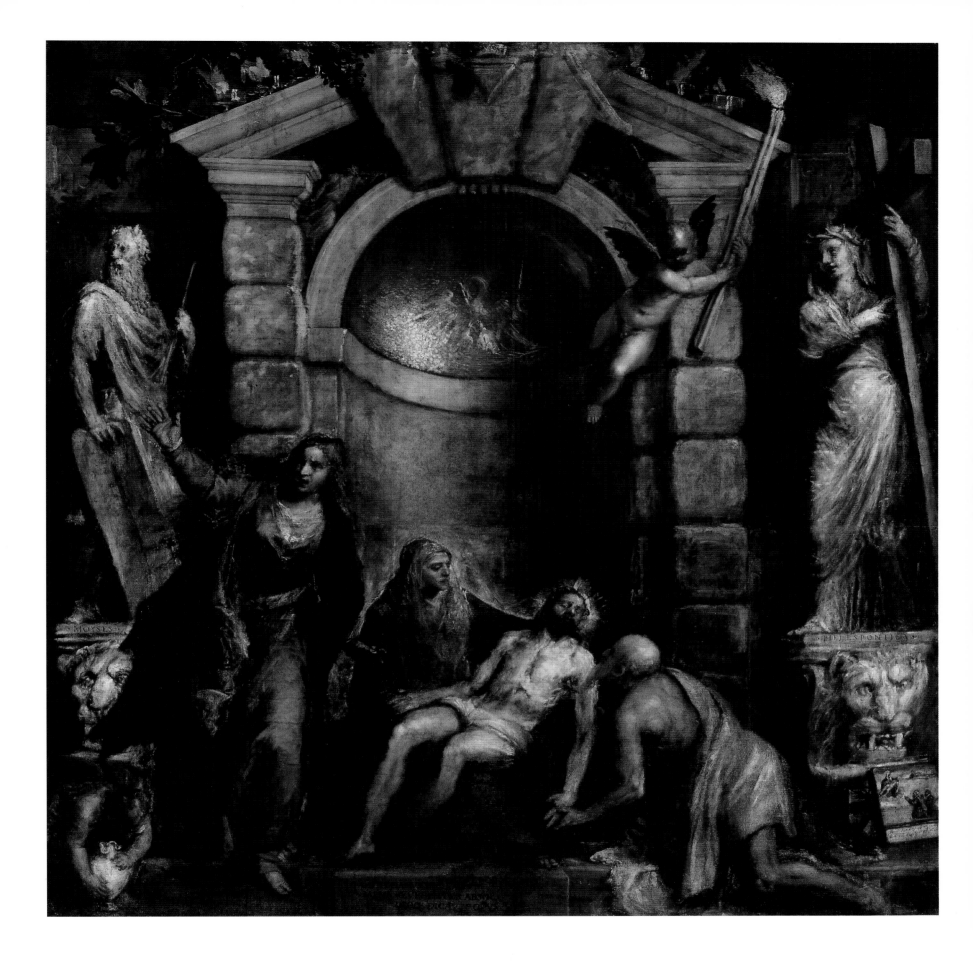

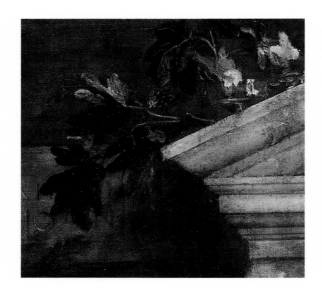

already painted to represent the face of a man. With the tinted varnishes stripped away, it becomes clear that Palma's contribution was very small, limited to a few glazes, added for the sake of disguising the seams of the several inserts, to the face of the angel (applied over Titian's own far less conventional but unfinished *putto* whose back-bent leg can be seen by X-ray), to the inscription, and possibly to a retouching of the pediment. The last is evidenced by a high finish quite different from that of the rustication below or from the nine lamps above, which are rendered in thickly impastoed, overlapping colors. Still, it is not impossible that even such a detail as the pediment came from Titian himself at some earlier moment in his artistic development, comparable, for instance, to the *Presentation of the Virgin in the Temple*, also in the Gallerie (ill. no. 28).

Further, once we consider the particular influences at work in the *Pietà*, there can be no question that Titian was its author. For instance, the niche enframing the central group reflects the architectural blend of rustic and sacred elements typical of Giulio Romano at his most accomplished, as in the Palazzo del Te in Mantua. This same interplay captivated even Andrea Palladio, but found its strongest exponent in Sebastiano Serlio. In addition, the mosaic half-dome with its image of a pelican (symbol of the Sacrifice on the Cross) amounts to a homage, as does the entire central part of the composition, to Giovanni Bellini.

The *Pietà* includes three types of inscription, the most elegant of which can be found in the Latin inscriptions on the statue bases: Moses

(MOYSES) and the Sibyl (ELLESPONTICAS). The Greek inscriptions above the statuary are virtually illegible. Several times reworked and altered in the course of restoration, they can be partially deciphered only by means of infrared reflectography:
ΔI... ΘEO(Σ)
HO...N over the Moses, and ANO corresponding to the Sibyl. Finally, the phrase in dialect on the panel at the bottom right—appropriately enough, written in a contemporary hand—can also be made out with the aid of reflectography. "Dona Katta venir nostra pecata bene pixt. Sig[navit?][natur?]..."

Much has been written about the iconography of the *Pietà*, which is concerned, above all, with death, the Eucharistic sacrifice, and the Resurrection. The painting is rich in symbols, all of them variously interpreted, from the lions' heads, which may signify Titian's family or Saint Mark, or possibly the Resurrection, or yet divine wisdom, to the spectral statuary, entirely autograph, of Moses the Jewish legislator, representative of the Old Testament and Precursor of Christ the Redeemer, and of the Hellespontine Sibyl who prophesies, both the Crucifixion and the Resurrection.

Like Michelangelo, Titian portrayed himself in a *Pietà*, destined for his own tomb. The half-naked old man—variously called Joseph of Arimathea, Saint Jerome, Nicodemus, or, more accurately, Job—prostrate before the Virgin holding Christ, is in fact a self-portrait. The picture thus becomes, in the fullest sense of the word, a "devotional" painting, intended

as it initially was for the artist's tomb and then recast as an enormous *ex voto* (earlier even than the *Grace Received*) wherein not once but twice Titian genuflects to Mother and Son, asking intercession by the Father in this life as well as in the next.

If we consider that in Venetian political thinking Venice was identified with the Virgin, it is clear how the *Pietà* came, by the official will of the Republic, to be a monument to Titian himself.

As justly noted, the painting, with its inherent drama, emerges as a true testament, illuminated by the artist's "magical expressionism," by the extraordinary "chromatic alchemy" that dissolves even as it resolves the imagery, at times verging on the very threshold of the inchoate. In no way a later addition, the little votive panel in the lower right corner—a painting within a painting—depicts Titian, together with his son Orazio, begging the Virgin for immunity from the plague and, by this means, draws us more powerfully into the larger narrative. Also raised against evil is the tragic gesture of the arm thrust up from the feet of the Sibyl, its hand clasped about a globe surmounted by a cross. Around this time, and perhaps for the same reason, the master resumed work on his *Saint Sebastian* (formerly in the Barbarigo collection and now in Leningrad) because of the subject's potent, miracle-working efficacy.

Such agonized attempts to appease Heaven proved unavailing. The plague, growing worse even as Titian made his last brushstrokes, struck down both the artist and his favorite son, Orazio.

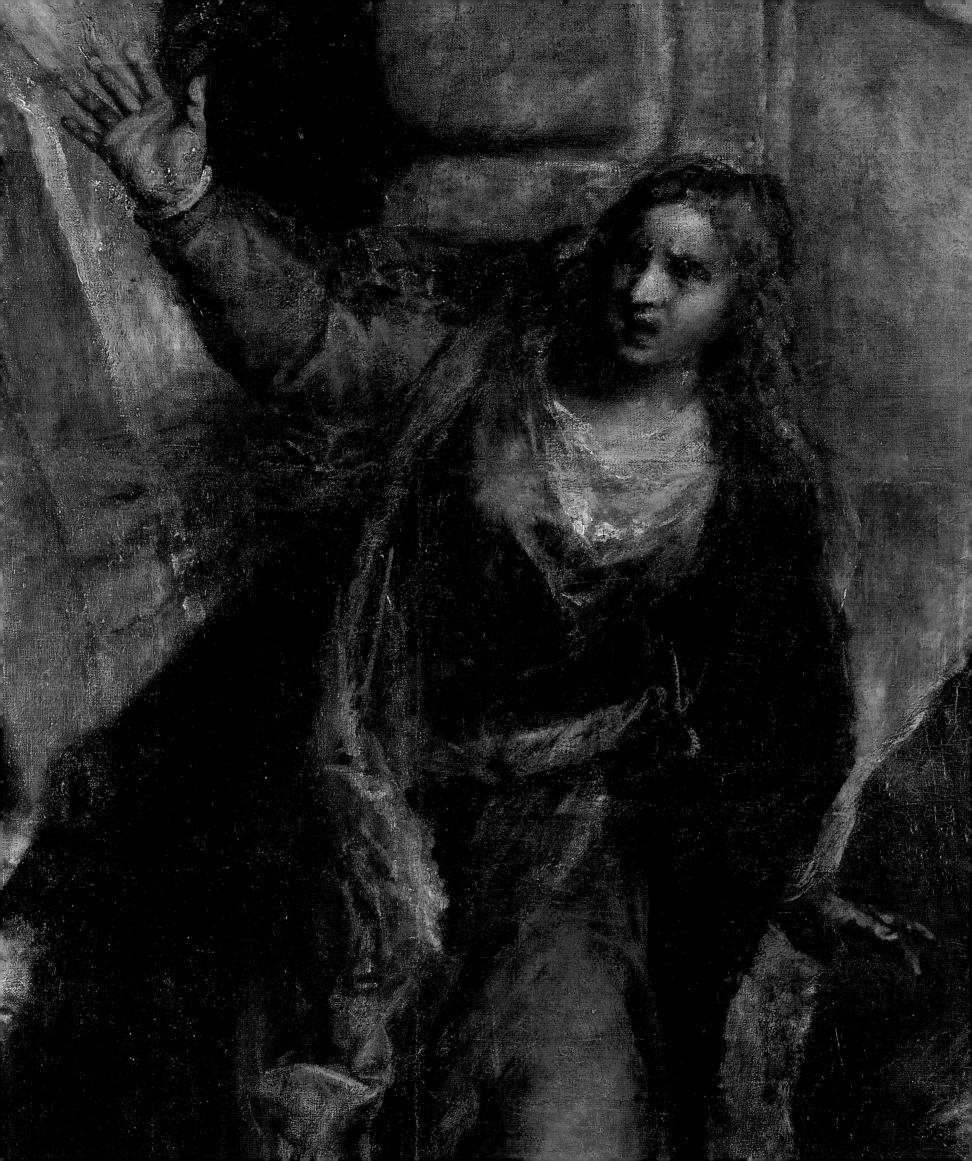

Venice, c.1480—Loreto, 1556
Portrait of a Young Man in His Study
Oil on canvas, 39 x 45" (cat. no. 912)
Last restored 1982

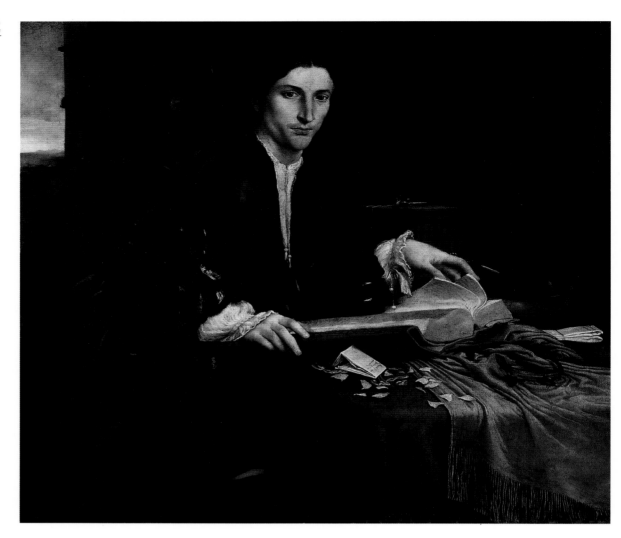

Acquired in 1930 from Count Eduardo di Rovero of Treviso, this painting evinces a psychological insight and a subtle melancholy that may well qualify it as Lotto's finest essay in portraiture. The latest restoration revealed, beneath layers of old varnish, a characteristically cool palette, as well as the objects over the sitter's shoulder (a purse and perhaps a horn) that had been almost impossible to make out. It also disclosed the lower part of the body, which had been readily visible under X-rays. The sitter is caught at a moment when his attention has wandered away from his reading to pursue some passing and elusive thought.

Illumination pouring in from the left highlights the beautiful still-life on the writing table, comprising objects charged with symbolic meaning: ink pot, green lizard, letter with broken seal, defoliated rose. Taken together, the allegory may well refer to a lost love, especially the ring lying on the table, a touch that also reflects the refined sensibility of the underrated Lotto.

It has been suggested that the subject of the portrait is Alessandro Cittolini, who, together with the painter, witnessed the will of Sebastiano Serlio on April 1, 1528, at the Dominican monastery of Santi Giovanni e Paolo in Venice, where Lotto was staying at the time.

Compare this with the artist's portrait of Andrea Odoni at Hampton Court, dated 1527.

GIROLAMO ROMANI
CALLED ROMANINO   83

Brescia 1484/87—c.1566
Deposition
Panel, 73 X 74" (cat. no. 737)
Last restored 1965

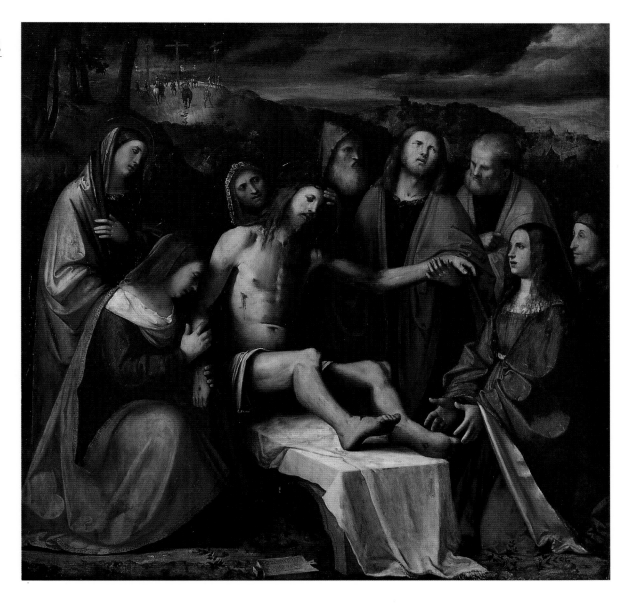

The signature and date are inscribed on a scroll at bottom center: HIERONYMI RU / MANI BRIXIANI / OPU. M.D.X. MENSE DECEMBRI ("Girolamo Romani, December 1510"). This originated as the altarpiece for the Passion Chapel in the old Church of San Lorenzo in Brescia, and it remained there in 1791 after the church had been completely renovated during the 18th century.

By 1852, the painting was in the Manfrin collection in Venice, whence it passed to Canford Manor, home of Sir Ivor Guest, later Viscount Wimborne. Through private sale, the work returned to Italy, where the Gallerie acquired it in 1909 from Marquis Strozzi Ridolfi of Florence. It is the earliest known and dated work by Romanino.

Under a livid, stormy sky, the deposed body of Christ is attended by the two Marys at left and, on the right, by Joseph of Arimathea, Saint John, Nicodemus, the Magdalene, and a donor. Calvary looms in the left background.

Fundamental to our understanding of the artist's youthful activity, the *Deposition* shows him in full command of his expressive means and perfectly at one with the Venetian pictorial tradition. Still, if the chromatic sonorities, the composition itself, and certain physiognomic types betray a debt to Giovanni Bellini, Giorgione, and the young Titian, Romanino owed just as much to his own Lombard background.

Some of the round faces, the ghostly light, the flickering shapes of the executioners on Golgotha, and the very objectivity with which the donor has been described recall Bramantino, Altobello Melone, and Paduan art in general.

All these components blend in a mature, coherent work, certainly one of finest by Romanino, who was between twenty-three and twenty-six years old when he painted it.

Orzinuovi(?), c.1480—c.1550
Saints Anthony Abbot and Paul the Hermit
Oil on panel, 66 x 55" (cat. no. 328)
Last restored 1977

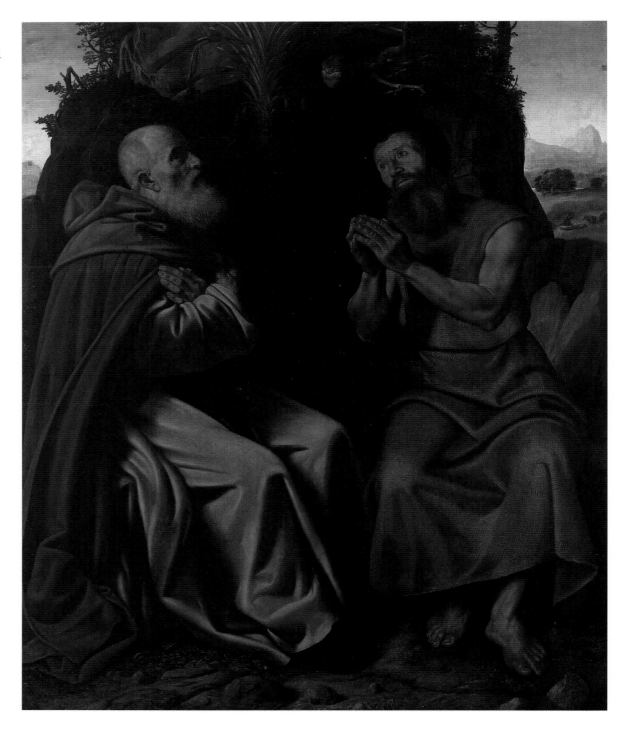

A fragmentary signature and date can be found inscribed on a stone in the lower foreground: OPUS JOVAN.JERONI. / BRIXIA DE … ALDIS 1520 (?).

Acquired in 1856 from the Manfrin collection, the painting yielded its original, albeit now fragmentary, signature and date in the course of the last restoration. A work of such stylistic and chromatic maturity would seem to be more at home somewhat later than 1510, the year provided by the pre-restoration reading. Furthermore, the new dating helps account for the evident reference to the figure of Saint Paul in Titian's *Assumption*. And even when brought forward by ten years, the picture remains the earliest dated work that we have for this artist. However informed Savoldo may have been about the innovations of the Tuscans, of Dürer, Giorgione, and Leonardo, he also drew significantly from Lombard precedents, such as those set by Foppa and Bergognone.

Bathed and clearly defined in a limpid light, the powerful figures stand forth with a proto-Caravagesque plasticity and naturalism. Thus, it is not by chance that the painting seen here has been described, paradoxically, as "the first Caravaggesque picture in Italian art." The Prado owns a picture in which Velázquez took up the same subject and also composed the Saints very much as Savoldo did.
Independently of one another, the two artists may have looked at a Dürer woodcut of 1504.

Treviso, 1500-71
Presenting the Ring to the Doge
Oil on packing canvas, 148 x 120" (cat. no. 320)
Last restored 1988

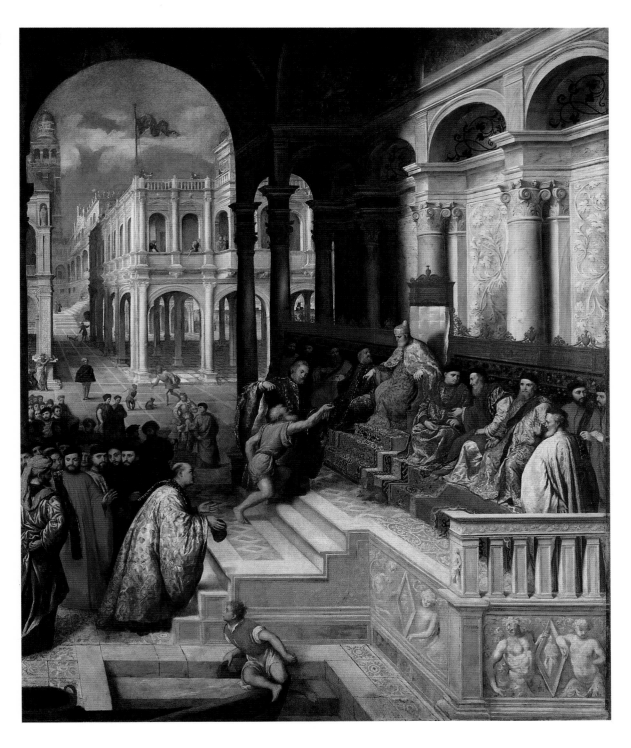

The painting once hung in the *sala dell'albergo* at the Scuola Grande di San Marco, centered on the wall just left of the entrance, along with Gentile Bellini's *Saint Mark Preaching in Alexandria*, now in the Brera (Milan), the *Martyrdom of Saint Mark* by Giovanni Bellini and Vittore Belliniano, Mansueti's *Baptism of Arian* and *Mark Heals Arian Again*, and Palma Vecchio's *Tempest*, still *in situ*. The cycle recapitulated the theme of a now-vanished decorative arrangement in the Palazzo Ducale, whose courtyard appears, somewhat modified, in the painting seen here.

Presenting the Ring to the Doge figured among the objects shipped to Paris in 1797 and returned to Venice in 1815. Inasmuch as the confraternity had in the meantime been suppressed, the painting was consigned to the Gallerie. It concerns the fisherman who, according to legend, offered the Doge the ring of Saint Mark (still preserved, tradition says, in the Basilican treasury), after having received it from the Apostle's own hand, as proof of certain miraculous happenings he had witnessed the night before. Around the Doge stand the Senators, facing the Scuola's *Guardian Grande* and members of the confraternity. The artist signed his painting on the little corner pilaster of the platform base: O / PARI DIS / BORDONO. While the complex architectural setting derived from Sebastiano Serlio, the campanile is real—that of the Church of Madonna dell'Orto, erected in 1503.

Since the time of Vasari (1568), *Presenting the Ring to the Doge* has been hailed as Bordon's masterpiece, and rightly so. A recent restoration—the latest of many, which culminated when the painting was relined, perhaps during the picture's sojourn in France—recovered something of the cool refinement with which the artist handled color. Bordon was once thought to have painted this work in 1534-35, following a decision by the Scuola in 1534 to complete the decoration of the *sala dell'albergo*. Now the picture appears more likely to have come later than Titian's *Presentation of the Virgin* (1534-39; ill. no. 78). The staircase has its direct source in Sebastiano Serlio's Book Two, published in Paris in 1545. Now it seems clear that the paintings in which Bordon emphasized the architectural setting generally date from 1545-50, when the artist decisively joined the Mannerist camp.

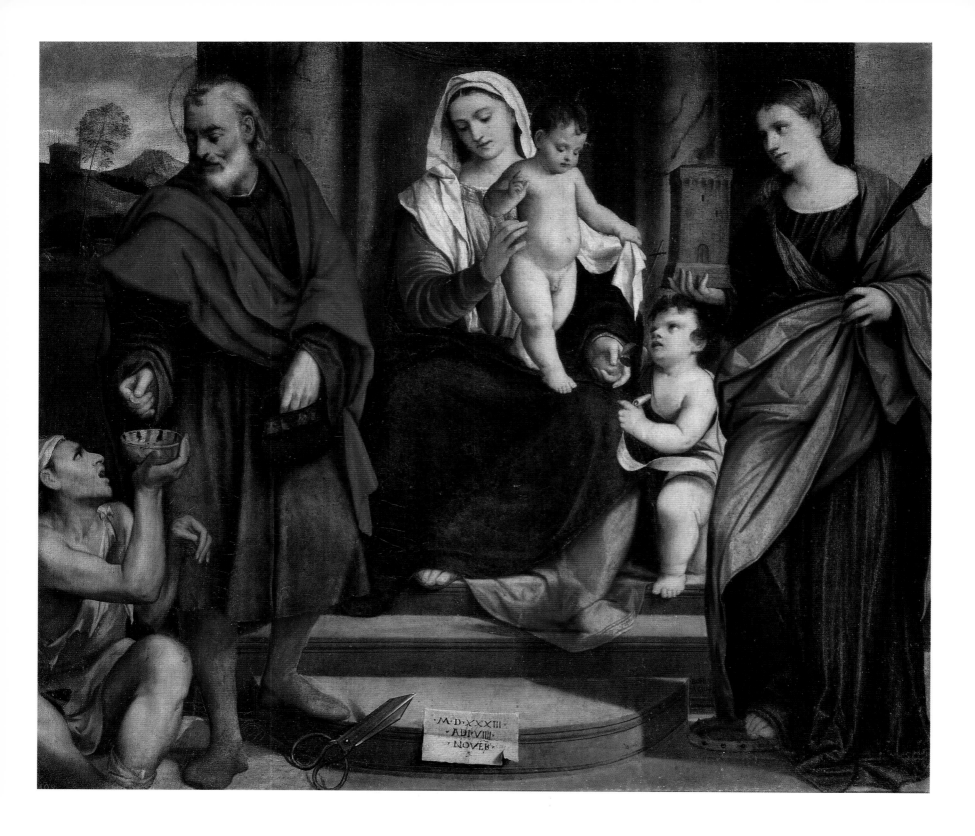

BONIFACIO DE' PITATI
(BONIFACIO VERONESE) 86

Verona, 1487—Venice, 1553
The Madonna of the Tailors
Oil on canvas, 52 x 60" (cat. no. 1305)

Painted for the altar on the ground floor of the Tailors' School near the Jesuit Church in Venice, the canvas depicts Saint Omobono, patron of tailors, whose great shears (on the pavement at the Saint's feet) help to confirm the work's original location. After secularization, the painting reverted to the State, which sent it to the Palazzo Reale, whence it came to the Gallerie only in 1945.

Flanking the Madonna and Child with Saint John the Baptist at the center are Saint Barbara on the right and, on the left, Saint Omobono, the latter giving alms to a poor cripple. The date is inscribed in a cartouche just above the picture's lower edge: M.D.XXXIII / ADI. VIIII / NOVEB. A signature appears on the second step: BONIF. / CIO, F.

With a date of 1533, this is the earliest confirmed work by Bonifacio, and thus fundamental to any consideration of his importance. Over and above the influence of Palma Vecchio and of Titian's palette, it shows the artist to have been inspired by Mannerist doctrines, which are particularly evident in the treatment of the Saint and of the beggar holding his bowl.

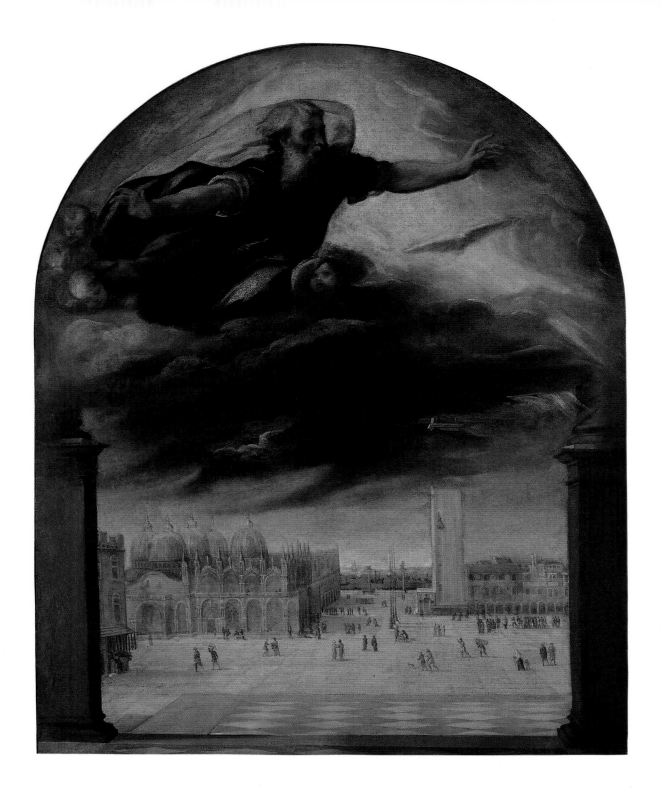

BONIFACIO DE' PITATI
(BONIFACIO VERONESE)   87

Verona, 1487—Venice, 1553
God the Father over the Piazza San Marco
Canvas, 75 x 53" (cat. no. 28)
Last restored 1991

This is the central part of a triptych, with flanking panels devoted to the *Archangel Gabriel* and the *Virgin Annunciate*, the whole of which once hung in the Camera degli Imprestidi ("Loan Office") in the Palazzo dei Camerlinghi. Its mutilation and separation into three parts (the other two also at the Gallerie) took place at an uncertain date, but not before 1808, the year of an inventory identifying the work as still united.

The bird's-eye view of the Piazza San Marco—showing the Basilica, the Palazzo Ducale, the Piazzetta with its twin columns, the roadstead with the Island of San Giorgio and part of the Giudecca, the Campanile with the adjoining old buildings—also includes the Loggetta, which means that the painting could not have been executed before 1540, the year the Logetta was finished.

Recent cleaning has revealed delightful scenes which can now be seen; a long line of postulants waiting before the Porta della Carta, a group of saltimbanks near the campanile, luggage carriers, a fur shop on the first floor to the left. Certainly the Vedutisti in future centuries must have been aware of this "modern" and forward looking tranche of Venetian life.

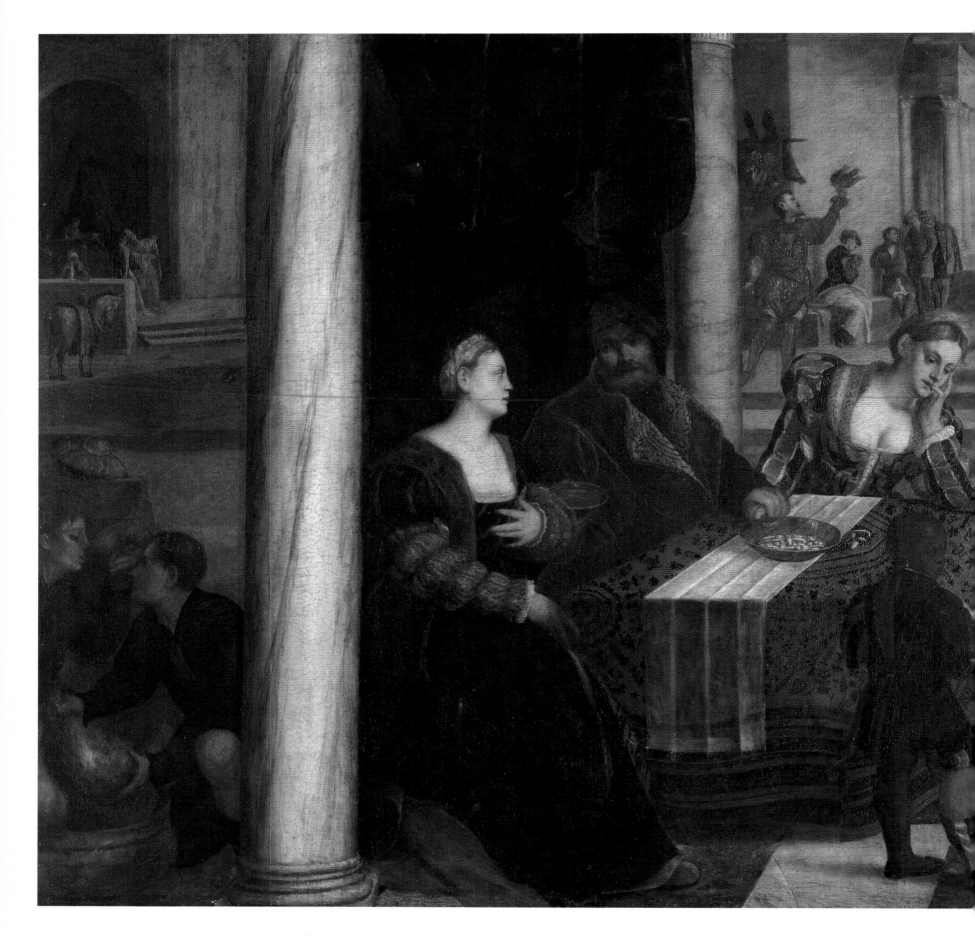

BONIFACIO DE' PITATI
(BONIFACIO VERONESE)   88

Verona, 1487—Venice, 1553
Parable of the Rich Man and the Beggar
Oil on canvas, 82 x 175" (cat. no. 291)
Currently in restoration

Through the good offices of Viceroy Eugène de Beauharnais, the Gallerie acquired the painting from the Grimani family on October 31, 1812. Boschini mentioned it in 1660 as belonging to the Giustiniani family, in whose palace it remained in 1763, according to

Monaco's catalogue of 112 engravings.
   The rich epicure (Dives) sits on the portico of his sumptuous villa surrounded by cheerful company and a group of musicians, including a lute player and a violist da gamba. Meanwhile, at right, a ragged Lazarus vainly

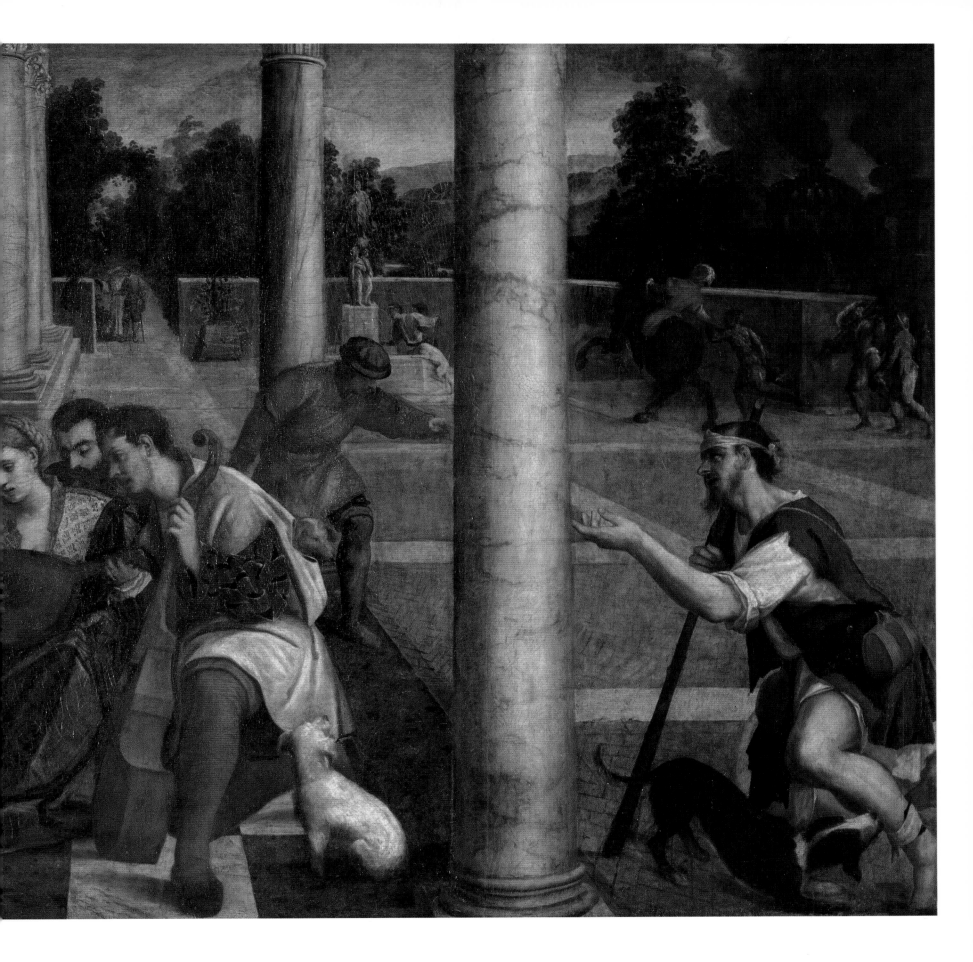

solicits alms while a dog licks his sores (Luke 16:19-31).

The fire-swept farm buildings in the background may allude to the hell fire that awaits the wealthy Dives. At left a hunter carries his hawk on his wrist, while a pair of lovers move towards a garden in the distance.

Generally ranked as the artist's masterpiece, by reason of the narrative genius it displays and the delicate blend of its colors, despite the baleful effects of old varnish, the painting is also one of the most evocative of 16th-century Venetian paintings, especially for its exact and delightful description of villa life. By 1543-45, about which time he painted the *Parable*, Bonifacio had managed to synthesize the lessons of both Titian and Tintoretto in a mature interpretation all his own.

Venice, 1514-94
Saint Mark Freeing the Slave
Oil on canvas, 166 x 216" (cat. no. 42)
Last restored 1965

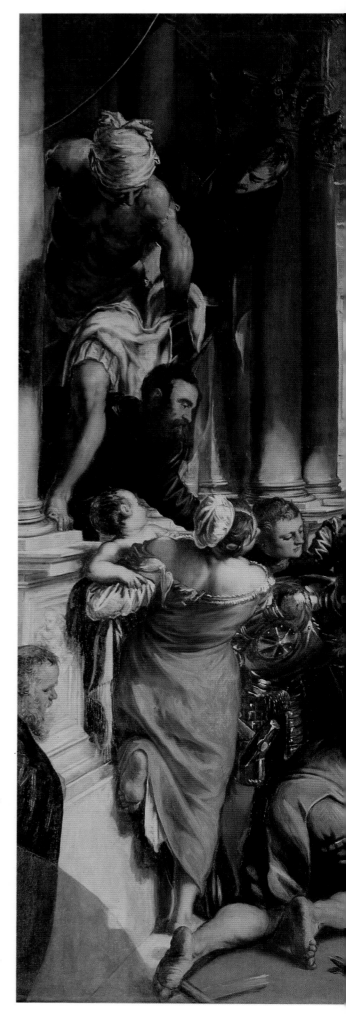

Signed at lower right: JACOMO TENTOR F. This is the artist's first painting for the Chapter Hall at the Scuola Grande di San Marco. Taken to Paris in 1797, *Saint Mark Freeing the Slave* was returned to Venice in 1815, when, owing to the supression of the sodality, it was assigned to the Gallerie.

On November 30, 1542, the Scuola di San Marco decided to decorate its *sala capitolare* with a series of paintings depicting the legends of its patron Saint. Tintoretto probably received the commission for the work seen here in 1547, when the *Guardian Grande* was Marco Episcopi, father of the artist's future wife, Faustina. Tintoretto had finished by April 1548, the time of Aretino's letter to him praising the work.

Tintoretto found his miraculous theme in Jacobus de Voragine's *Legenda Aurea*, which tells of how the Saint's intercession won freedom for a slave. The slave-owner, a Provençal gentleman, had ordered that his servant be blinded and his legs broken, because he had defied his master and venerated the relics of the Saint.

The bold foreshortening of the Saint Mark's figure, the unprecedented intensity of the colorism, the novel composition, and the dramatic urgency of the whole won immediate admiration for the work—as well as dissenting opinions. According to Ridolfi, writing in 1648, an argument raged within the confraternity as to whether they should keep the painting, until, finally, the affronted artist carried it off to his house. Later, after tempers had cooled all around, he returned it.

In *Saint Mark Freeing the Slave*, Tintoretto virtually summarized his experience as a figure painter, especially the Michelangelism, cultivated through the most rigorous draftsmanship, with an originality of mind and an intensity of vision that could not but generate both admiration and dismay. The complexity of the composition—leading the eye inward, from the massive foreground figures to the sketchy urbanscape in the background—is matched by powerful contrasts of color and chiaroscuro, as well as by two competing sources of light, one external, flowing from the right, the other internal and originating in the depth of the pictorial space itself. With this, the observer "is suddenly engaged, and made to participate, in the scene."

The Pinacoteca in Lucca owns a workshop copy; the Uffizi has a partial copy attributed to Antonio Zannoni; and another, much smaller one hangs in the sacristy of Venice's Tolentini Church.

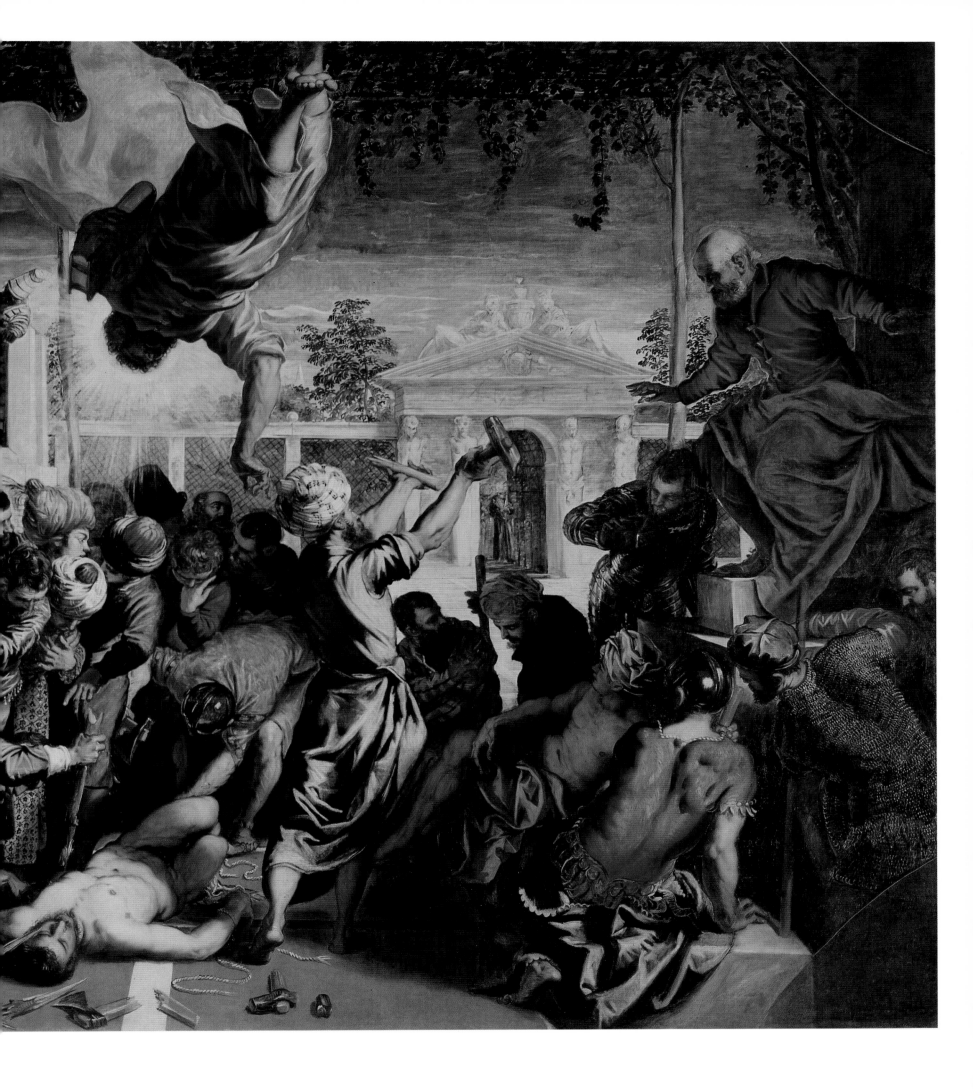

JACOPO ROBUSTI
CALLED TINTORETTO

Venice, 1514-94
The Procurator Jacopo Soranzo
Oil on canvas, 42 x 36" (cat. no. 245)
Last restored 1957

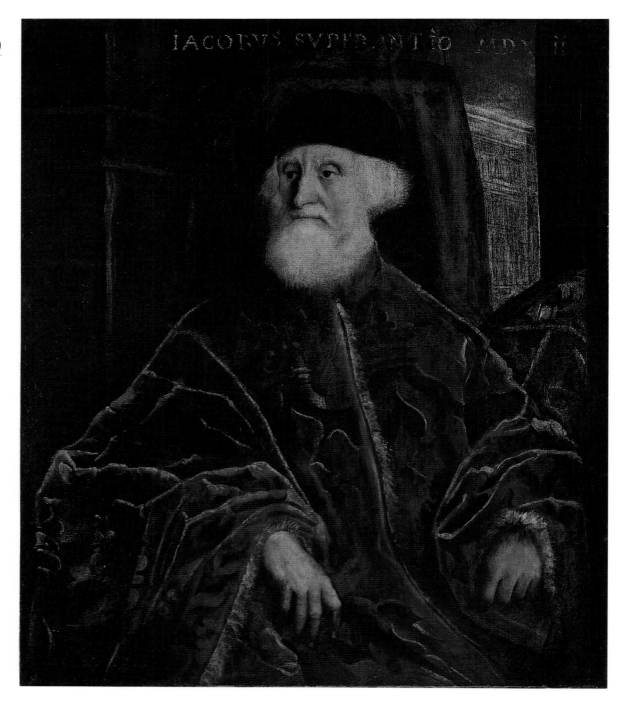

An inscription above the sitter's head reads: JACOBUS SUPERANTIO MDX[X]II. The painting originally hung in the Procuratorie de Supra, where Boschini (1674) cites the work and Tintoretto as its author. Among the first paintings assigned to the Gallerie in 1812, it is probably the "Portrait of a Senator, half-length" attributed to Titian in Edwards' inventory.

The inscribed date, as revealed by restoration, is 1522, the year in which Soranzo was elected Procurator; however, the painting must have been executed closer to 1550, shortly before the subject's death in 1551, like the other portrait of Soranzo in Milan's Castello Sforzesco. The latest restoration, in addition to confirming the attribution to Tintoretto, has shown the picture to be a fragment of a compositon once large enough on the right to include another figure, a part of whose sleeve is still visible. The mutilation probably occurred at the end of the 16th century, when Tintoretto himself or his son Domenico trimmed the paintings in the Procuratorie to fit the agency's reconstructed quarters in the Palazzo Ducale. This canvas is typical of Tintoretto's portraiture, which, with the same expressive power known from more celebrated works, presents the sitter in all his special identity and character.

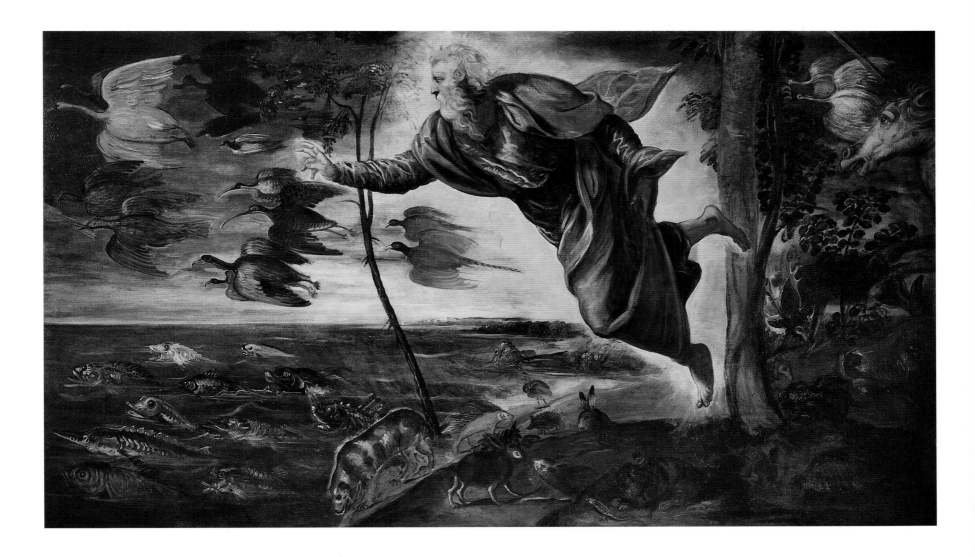

JACOPO ROBUSTI
CALLED TINTORETTO   91

Venice, 1514-94
Creation of the Animals
Oil on canvas, 60 x 103", slightly trimmed on both
height and width (cat. no. 900)
Last restored 1967

This painting, like the next two, came from the Scuola della Trinità, whose building was pulled down during the 17th century to make way for the Basilica della Salute. Once the Scuola's new premises had been made ready, the paintings were transferred into them.

Following secularization, Pietro Edwards claimed the *Temptation of Adam and Eve* and *Cain and Abel* for the Gallerie in 1812, but the State placed the *Creation* in reserve from whence it did not rejoin the other two pictures until 1928.

Originally, a total of five paintings narrated the Book of Genesis, all part of the decorations ordered for the Scuola's *sala dell'albergo*, a program that had got under way in 1547 with four paintings by Francesco Torbido. A document of March 23, 1550, mentions additional works, and on November 25, 1553, another reference indicates that the project lacked only two paintings, both for the sides of

the altar. Thus, 1553 represents a *terminus ad quem*, and most critics date Tintoretto's Trinità pictures around 1550.

Only four of Tintoretto's five Trinità canvases survive—the three seen here and a fragmentary *Adam and Eve before God the Father* in the Uffizi reserve. For the lost *Creation of Eve*, a record exists in a drawing by Paolo Farinati, now in the Janos Scholz collection in New York. Included on the sheet is quite an exact copy of the *Temptation of Adam and Eve*.

By contrast with the articulated plasticism of the Gallerie's other two Trinità paintings, the *Creation of the Animals* seems woven "like a tapestry," as if a single breath animated the whole rapid movement of Creator and creatures alike: the birds ploughing the sky in parallel lines, the fish in phosphorescent water, and the land animals rushing headlong to some unseen goal.

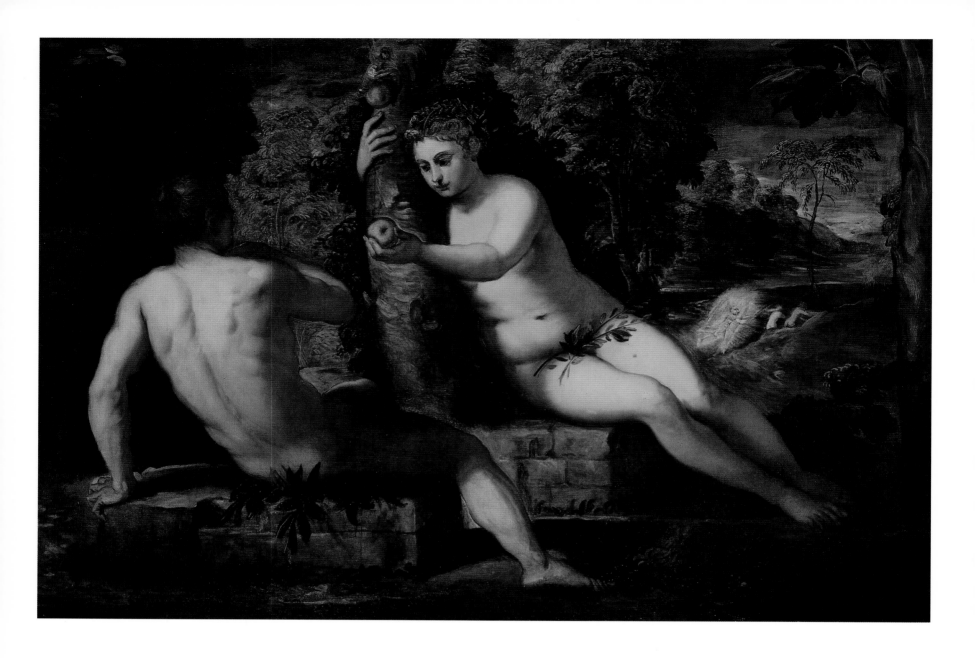

JACOPO ROBUSTI
CALLED TINTORETTO   92

Venice, 1514-94
The Temptation of Adam and Eve
Oil on canvas, 60 x 88", slightly trimmed on both
height and width (cat. no. 48)
Last restored 1967

Silhouetted against a thickly foliated
background, two nude bodies confront one
another along a beautifully nuanced Mannerist
diagonal. They appear radiant with light at
the final moment before their lapse into fatal
sin. The consequences unfold at right, where
the first two mortals flee Eden, pursued by an
avenging angel haloed in light. The work
provides a key document in the artist's growing
involvement with landscape, which from now
on would become a constant factor in his
pictorial language (see also ill. no. 91).

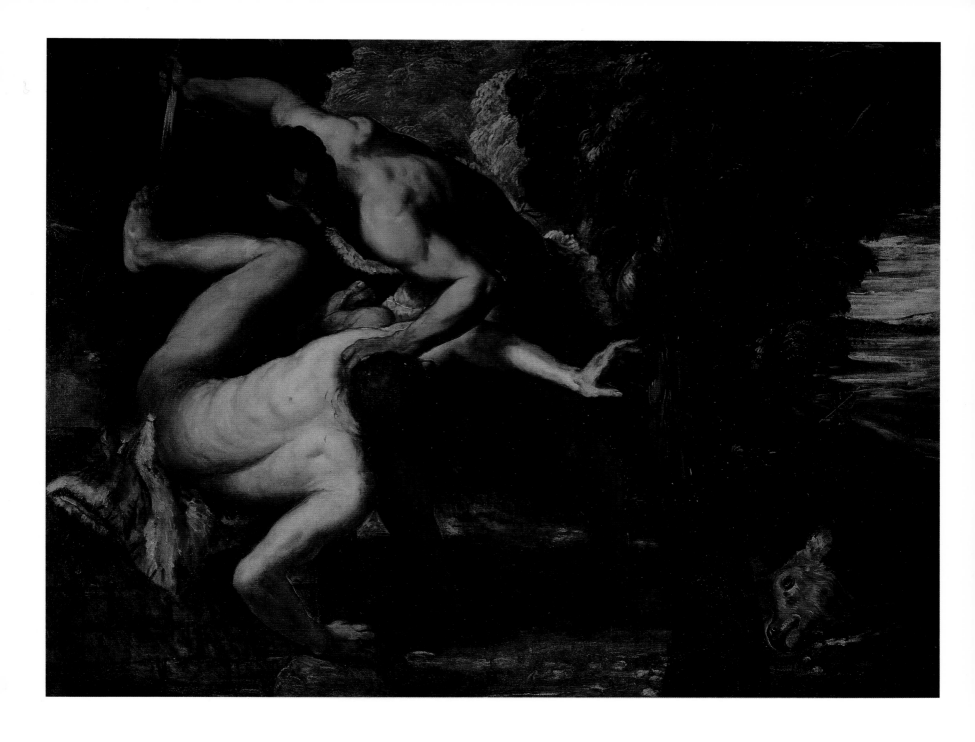

JACOPO ROBUSTI
CALLED TINTORETTO 93

Venice, 1514-94
Cain and Abel
Oil on canvas, 78 x 60", slightly trimmed at right (cat.
no. 41)
Last restored 1967

Once again (see also ill. no. 92, as well as 91) Tintoretto has set two naked bodies against dense vegetation, which opens at the right upon a bit of deep landscape. The artist had very likely taken account of Titian's version of the subject, painted about ten years earlier for the ceiling of Santo Spirito in Isola. This can be sensed above all in the dramatic counterpoise of the two figures. However,

Tintoretto placed his own Mannerist mark on the arrangement through the softer painterliness of his touch combined with more dramatic light/dark contrast. The figure of Cain appears to have influenced Paolo Veronese when, in 1552, he painted the demon in the *Temptation of Saint Anthony* for the cathedral of Padua, a painting now in the Caen Museum.

Venice, 1514-94
Assumption of the Virgin
Oil on canvas, 96 x 54" (cat. no. 219)
Last restored 1988

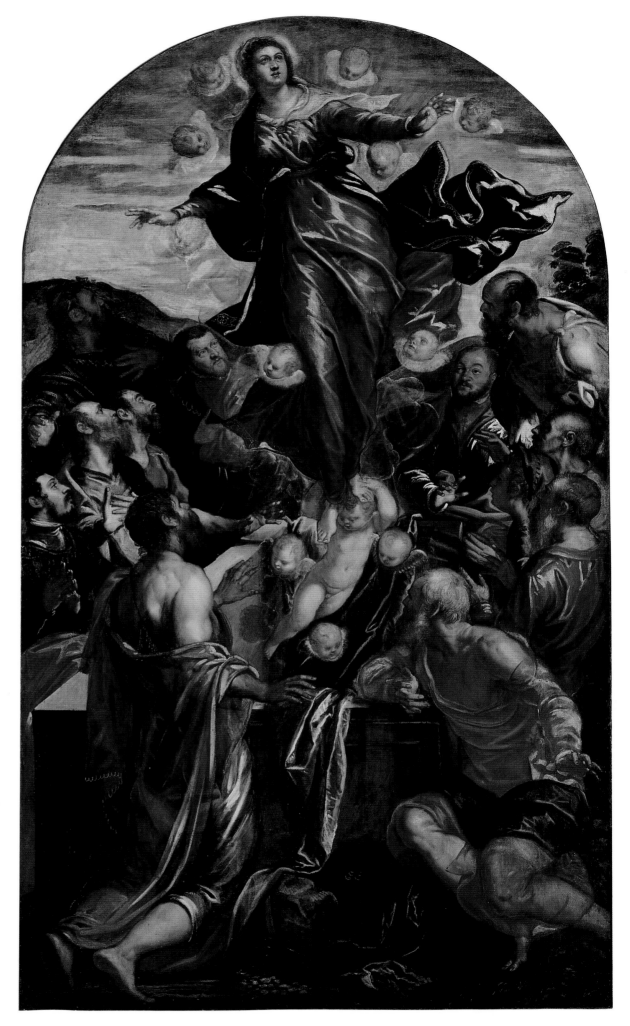

The painting once hung in the Venetian Church of San Stin, or Saint Stephen Priest, a structure that was torn down shortly after its secularization in 1810. The picture entered the Gallerie in 1814, only to be lent to the Cathedral in Torcello from 1928 to 1955. Once returned to the Gallerie, it underwent restoration, thereupon recovering its original round-headed format. The work is generally dated around 1550, by reason of its stylistic consistency with a group of paintings that includes the *Saint Martial Altarpiece* in Venice, *Saint Augustine Curing the Lame Men* in Vicenza's Museo Civico, and the *Madonna in Glory with Child and Saints* in the Galleria Estense, all from about the same time.

Within the brilliantly calculated composition—a vortex of rotary movement— we can distinguish among the Apostles at least three portraits, no doubt representing the picture's commissioners.

The drawings on the back, revealed by the most recent cleaning, depict an altar and a bit of cornice or baluster, which probably relate to plans for hanging the canvas in its original location.

Venice, 1514-94
Saint Louis, Saint George, and the Princess
Oil on canvas, 90 x 58" (cat. no. 899)
Last restored 1986

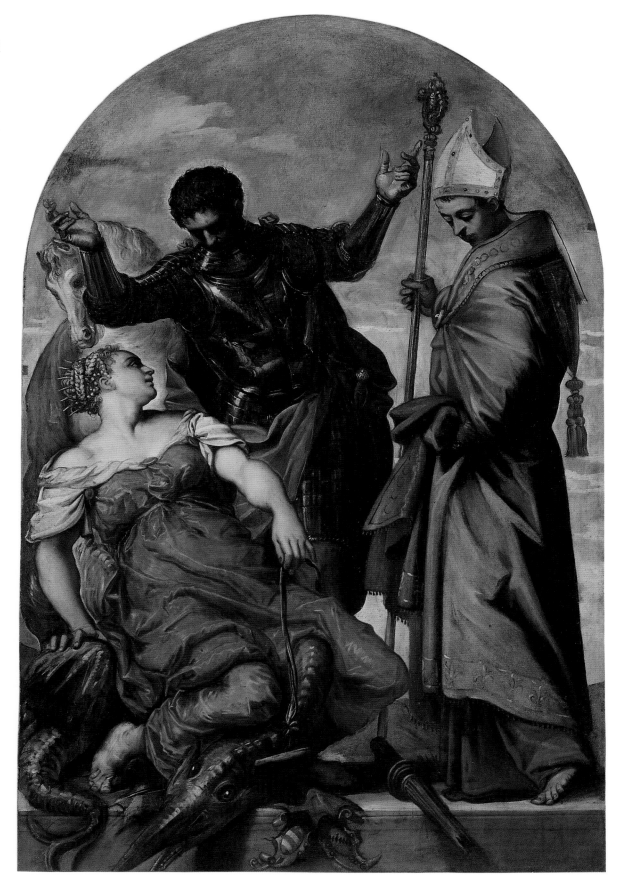

Like the *Saints Jerome and Andrew* about to be seen (ill. no. 96) and the *Madonna and Child with Four Senators* now on loan to the Istituto Veneto (cat. no. 243), this painting was executed for the main room at the Magistrato al Sale ("Salt Magistracy") in the Palazzo dei Camerlenghi on the Rialto, where Boschini mentions having seen it in 1664. In 1777, all three canvases were modified into rectangles and installed in a chapel at the Palazzo Ducale. For the great Tintoretto exhibition in 1937, they regained their original round-headed formats and, following the show, made their way to the Gallerie.

Following local custom, two "salt" magistrates, Giorgio Vener and Alvise Foscarini, commissioned the pictures to mark their respective departures from office, on September 13, 1551, and May 1, 1552. A few years later (1557), Dolce, mistaking the Princess for Saint Margaret, took issue with Tintoretto for his "want of good taste, when he set Saint Margaret astride a serpent." The remark suggests the notoriety and controversy, that the painting, with its unconventional iconography, quickly stirred up in Venetian artistic circles. The lady rides her dragon with consummate horsemanship, posed with such virtuosity that she can twist back towards her rescuer while simultaneously, even arrogantly, admiring her reflection in his polished armor. Saint Louis of Toulouse standing apart, in a pensive attitude, constitutes a scenographic aside of considerable contrast and dramatic effect. And there may well be connections with the contemporary theater here, not excluding the possibility that the artist took cues from the sets that Vasari had designed in 1542 for Aretino's play *La Talanta*. The palette, with its play of light/dark relations, exemplies the Mannerist/Roman character of the artist's style at this time.

JACOPO ROBUSTI
CALLED **TINTORETTO** 96

Venice, 1514-94
Saints Jerome and Andrew
Oil on canvas, 90 x 58" (cat. no. 898)
Last restored 1986

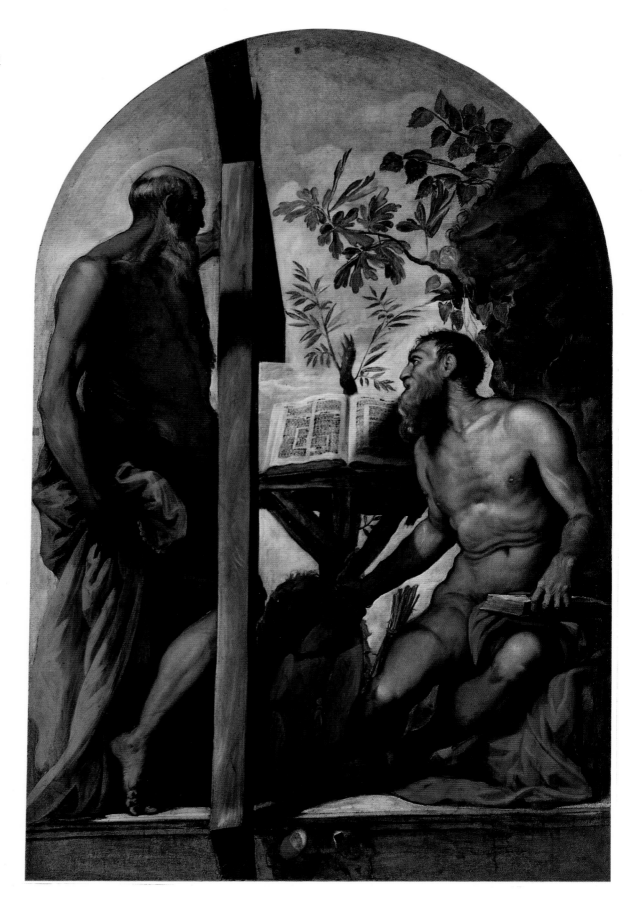

This painting was commissioned by "salt" magistrates Andrea Dandolo and Girolamo Bernardo to note the expiration of their respective terms of office on September 6, 1552, and October 9, 1552.

The latter date provides a *terminus a quo* for the work, which came only a bit later than *Saint Louis, Saint George, and the Princess.* Here the two Saints, stripped naked, flank a tall cross, viewed athwart in order to create an optical illusion of great depth.

The latest restoration has clarified the picture's colors, which nevertheless remain sharply contrasted in their ligh/dark values (see also ill. no. 95).

Venice, 1514-94
The Stealing of the Body of Saint Mark
Oil on canvas, 159 x 126" trimmed both left and right
(cat. no. 831)
Last restored 1959

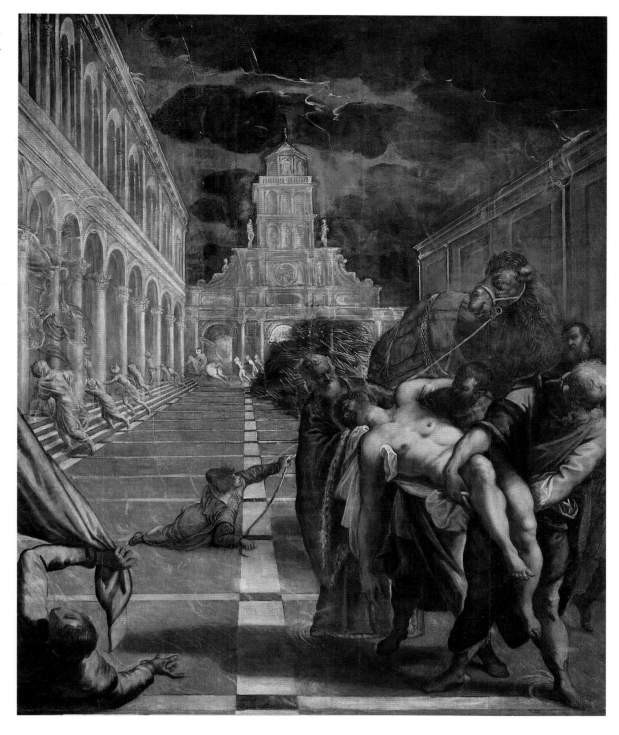

Together with the Gallerie's *Saint Mark Saves a Saracen* (cat. no. 831) and the *Rediscovery of Saint Mark's Body* now in Milan's Brera, this painting formed part of the *History of Saint Mark Cycle* executed for the chapter hall at the Scuola Grande di San Marco. All three pictures were commissioned and paid for by a famous physician, Tommaso Rangone, then the Guardian Grande of the Scuola, whose members gave their authorization on June 21, 1562. The paintings had already been hung by 1566, when Vasari saw them during his sojourn in Venice. Following some unrecounted dispute, they were removed a few years later and, on August 10, 1573, sent to the house of Rangone himself. On September 8 the donor returned them to Tintoretto, who

now undertook to "finish them perfectly." Once restored to the Scuola, they remained in place until 1807, when, as a consequence of secularization, Edwards took charge of them. In 1882, the Brera received the *Rediscovery*, while in 1815 the other two went into the Salone Sansoviniano. Taken thence to Vienna in 1866, these pictures were soon returned to the Salone, finally coming to the Gallerie on March 6, 1920.

The canvas seen here narrates an episode in which, according to legend, the Christians of Alexandria, unexpectedly set free by a hurricane, stole the body of Saint Mark from the pyre where it had been laid for burning. The restoration of 1959 disclosed on the back of the canvas traces of drawing that in several

ways diverge from the finished picture, especially as regards the paving and the position of the Saint's body.

Thrust into the foreground and drenched in light, the moribund figure appears in stark relief, while the spooky architecture (a transfiguration, as has been noted, of Sansovino's plans for systematizing the Piazza San Marco) and the images of fleeing figures become ever more fluid and spectral as they race into depth, the better to heighten the illusionistic distance between them and the principal group on the frontal plane. Meanwhile, the entire drama unfolds in a knowing, calculated play of light.

A drawing of the Saint Mark figure was sold at Sotheby's in London in June 28, 1979.

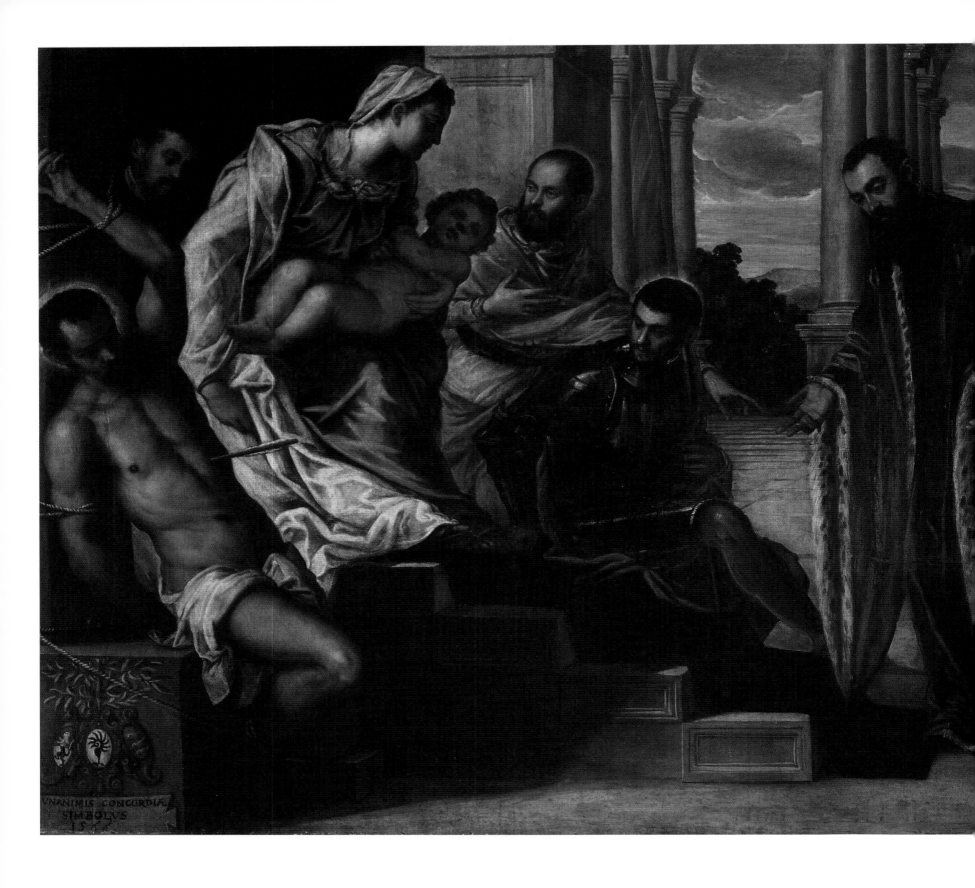

JACOPO ROBUSTI
CALLED TINTORETTO   98

Venice, 1514-94
Madonna and Child with Saints Sebastian,
Mark, and Theodore, Venerated by Three
Camerlenghi, called *Madonna of the Treasurers*
Oil on canvas, 88 x 208" (cat. no. 210)
Currently in restoration

An inscription in the lower left with a date reads: UNANIMIS CONCORDIAE / SIMBOLUS / 1566 ("Symbol of Universal Concord, 1566"). Commissioned for the Magistrato dei Camerlenghi di Comune in the Palazzo dei Camerlenghi on the Rialto, where Ridolfi took note of it in 1648. Tintoretto's *Madonna and Child* went into the Commenda reserve following the Napoleonic suppression, but then found its way to the Church of Santi Giovanni e Paolo. From there the Gallerie claimed it in 1883. On the plinth in the lower left corner appear the arms of Pisani, Malipiero, and Dolfin; thus, the inscribed date must refer to the magistracy of Michele Pisani, Lorenzo Dolfin, and Marino Malipiero. Tintoretto probably painted the work a bit later, around 1567, when Marino Malipiero's term expired.

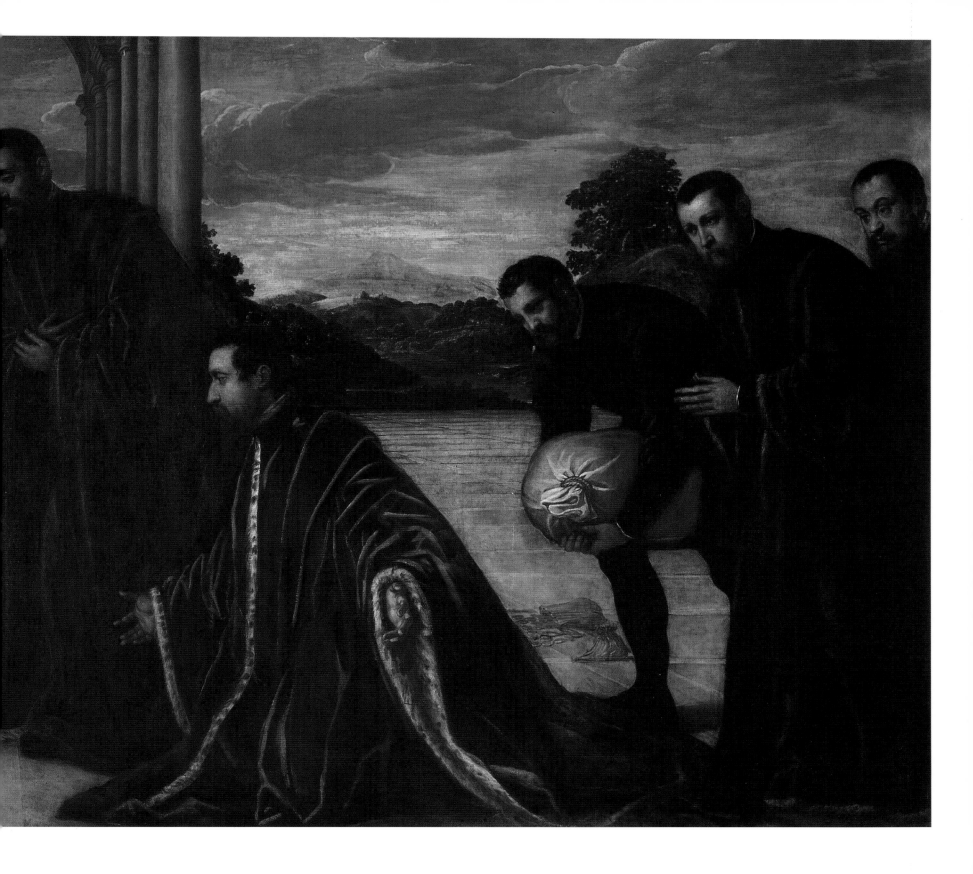

The three magistrates who commissioned the votive canvas take their place in the foreground in full veneration before Mary, while, behind each, a secretary follows bearing bags of coin. The long, horizontal format evolved in response to the great tradition of Venetian narrative painting, whose composition, in this instance, unfolds to the beat of a peaceful, solemn rhythm that seems all the more resonant because of the wonderful landscape opening up beyond the colonnade. The aperture, together with the "perspectival scansion of the floor," illusionistically dilates the space in depth.

The encounter between the Virgin and her devotees sponsored by Saints, while a familiar theme in Venetian painting, received an entirely novel treatment in the hands of Tintoretto, a treatment marked by the refreshing presence of nature, the dignified attentiveness of the donors, and the articulate group within the "Sacred Conversation" (the Madonna and Child accompanied by Saints). The painting, which, until the recent restoration, had not been touched since 1780-81, during the curatorship of Edwards, is in an exceptional state of preservation.

JACOPO ROBUSTI
CALLED TINTORETTO 99

Venice, 1514-94
Doge Alvise Mocenigo
Oil on canvas, 46 x 39" (cat. no. 233)
Last restored 1959

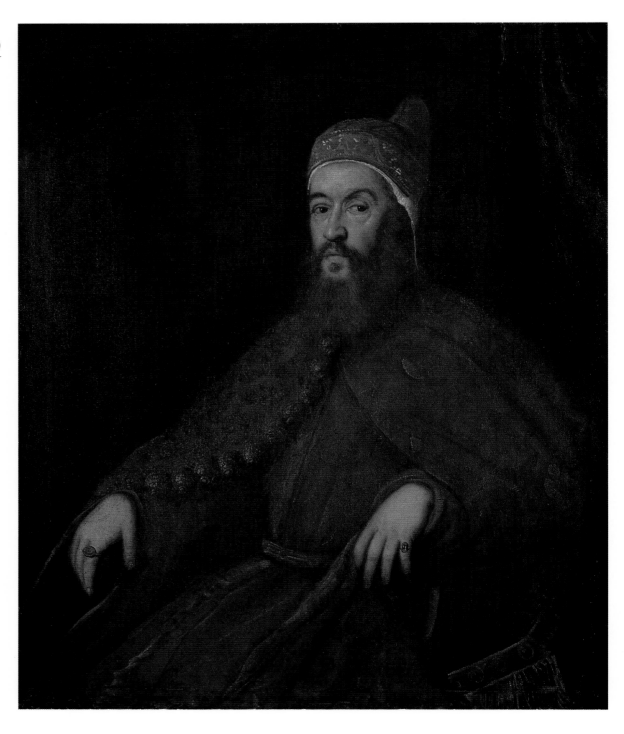

Boschini, writing in 1664, mentions this portrait as by Tintoretto, hanging in the last room of the Procuratoria de Ultra.

Following the Napoleonic suppression, it entered the public domain and finally, by 1817, the Gallerie.

Alvise Mocenigo, born in 1507, served as Doge from 1570 to 1577. The portrait may very well have been painted around 1570, near the time of the subject's election.

Tintoretto portrayed this Doge on another occasion, in a painting now at the National Gallery in Washington. Still later, he executed a votive portrait, with the help of his studio, for the *sala del collegio* in the Palazzo Ducale.

The Metropolitan Museum of Art in New York owns a preparatory study from the artist's own hand. A rather weak replica of the present painting is in Berlin's Staatliche Museen.

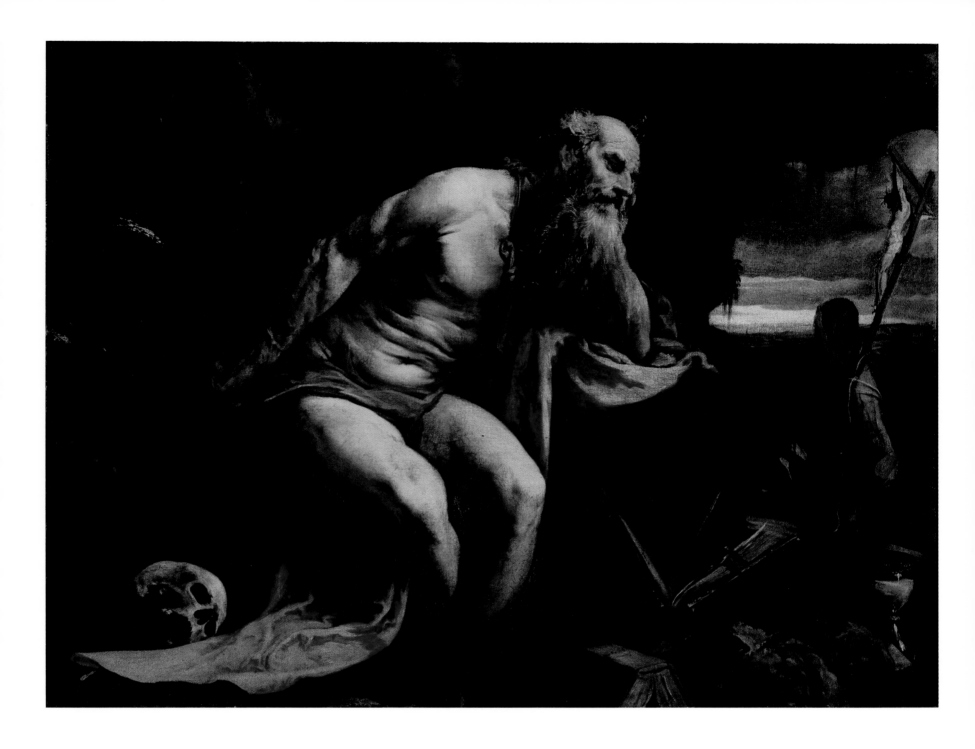

JACOPO DA PONTE
CALLED BASSANO   100

Bassano, 1517-92
Saint Jerome in Meditation
Oil on canvas, 48 x 50" (cat. no. 652)

Acquired in 1900 from Alessandro Bedendo of Mestre, along with Palma Vecchio's *Sacred Conversation* (see ill. no. 75), this is almost certainly the *Saint Jerome* mentioned by Ridolfi (1648) and Verci (1775) as present in the Palazzo Widmann in Venice (where the Palma Vecchio definitely was).

Saint Jerome in Meditation is one of the artist's capital works, dating from the late 1560s when his Mannerism was slowly giving way to careful analysis of the natural world. While the Saint deliberates in his grotto, a setting sun glows unforgettably on the right. The aged Jerome, his every wrinkle picked out by the chill light and his wasted loins barely covered by a rose and violet cloth, is surrounded by the symbols of his condition: the crucifix on a stump, bound volumes, an hour glass, a skull in shadow. The cleverly chosen canvas, with its coarse texture, accentuates the play of light and color.

A copy of the painting, which once passed for a work by the young El Greco, belongs to Verona's Museo di Castelvecchio.

Bassano, 1517-92
Adoration of the Shepherds
Oil on canvas, 38 x 56" (cat. no. 1360)

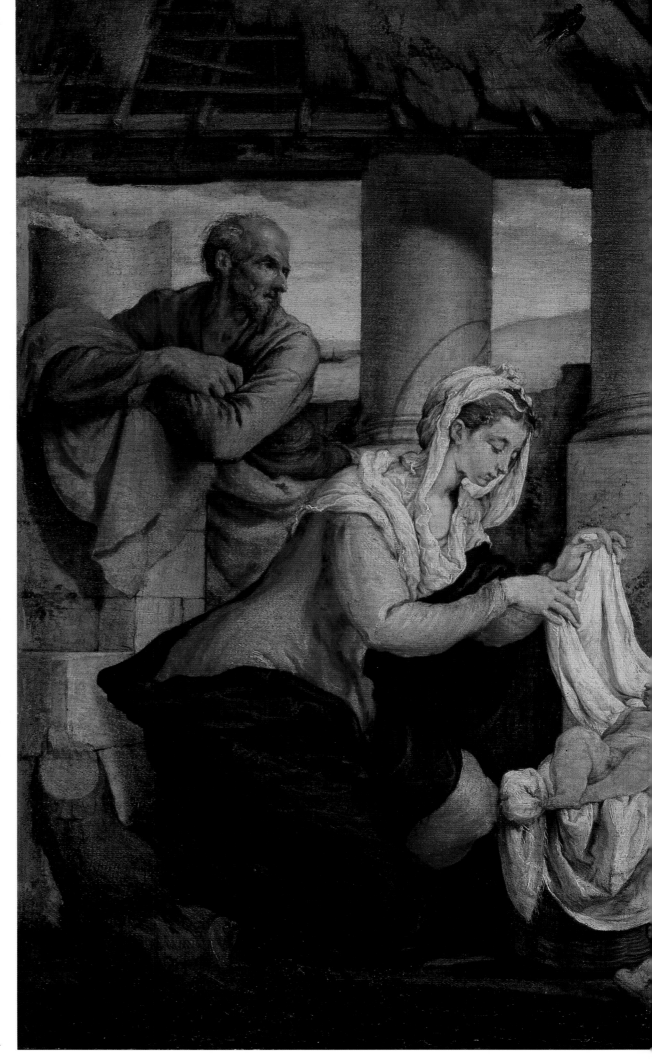

This may be the painting on the same subject mentioned by Pona in his little poem *Il Sileno* (1620) as present in the Giusti del Giardino collection. And it was from Count Justo Giusti del Giardino that the Gallerie acquired the work in 1983. The *Adoration of the Shepherds* dates from the late 1540s, which makes it contemporary with the artist's *Flight into Egypt* at the Norton Simon Museum in Pasadena and a bit later than his *Adoration of the Shepherds* at Hampton Court. However, the Gallerie picture departs from those works in its closer alliance with the style of Parmigianino, as well as in its more balanced composition and warmer atmosphere. Here *maniera* and realism encounter one another in singularly harmonious rapport. The refined, attenuated forms of the figures may derive from Mannerism, and the palette and the taste for ruins from Northern Europe, probably through Pieter Aetsen, but what makes the picture datable around 1550 is the loving, closely observed naturalism with which the animals have been depicted, a characteristic common to an entire group of Bassano's paintings.

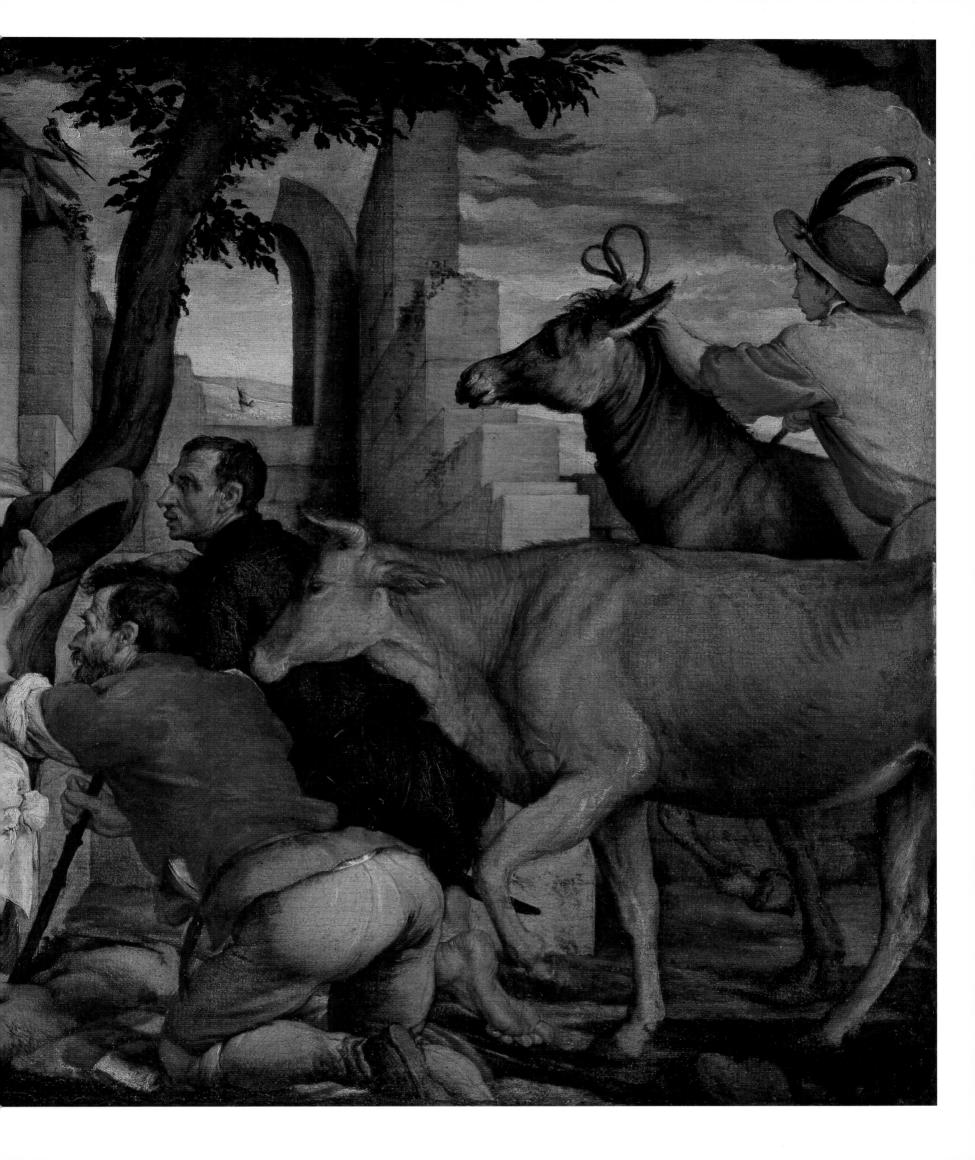

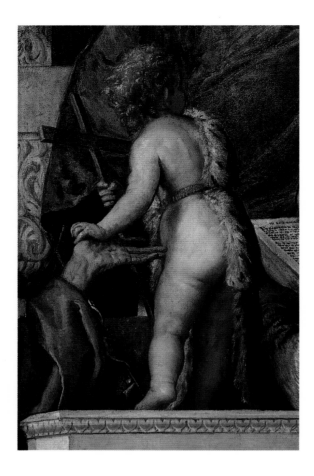

PAOLO CALIARI
CALLED VERONESE   102

Verona, c.1528—Venice, 1588
Madonna and Child Enthroned, with Saint Joseph, the Infant Saint John the Baptist, and Saints Justina, Francis, and Jerome
Oil on canvas, 134 x 76" (cat. no. 37)
Last restored 1969-70

From its original place over the altar in the sacristy of the Church of San Zaccaria, this "Sacred Conversation" was requisitioned for Paris in 1797 and then consigned to the Gallerie in 1815, along with three other paintings from the same church.

In 1562, Francesco Bonaldo, procurator for the monasteries, undertook to spend 200 ducats to rehabilitate the San Zaccaria sacristy, while also creating a sepulcher for his brother Girolamo and his son Giovanni. The execution of the altarpiece seen here has generally been understood as involved with the rebuilding and thus dated around 1562. However, a sketch for the picture's essential concept, now at the Boymans van Beuningen Museum in Rotterdam, also includes studies for the *Marriage of Saint George* in Verona's Church of San Giorgio in Braida, with a notation of expenses on the back dated June 1564. This consequently becomes a *terminus post quem* for the painting, which must have been done around that time. In the altarpiece, now decontextualized, Veronese appears to have been especially concerned for the relation of his imagery and composition to the real, ambient space, which today we can appreciate only by means of photomontages.

In the chapel, natural light fell in a manner consistent with what Veronese conceived as a passage of sky, which once opened above the curtain before being painted over, possibly because it had been damaged. This remarkable luminary effect can still be found in engravings, particularly in the one by Wagner.

Much praised by historiographers, beginning with Sansovino (1581), this *Sacred Conversation* signaled the climactic moment of Veronese's youthful production. Here, Mannerism seems foreshadowed not only in the asymmetrical composition, which recalls that of Titian's *Pesaro Altarpiece* at the Frari, but also in the dramatic gestures of Saint Francis, the Saint John viewed from the back, the improbable plinth, and the tonality of the colors. Still, the whole has been composed with harmonious, quasi-classical equilibrium, thanks to the artist's assimilation of the grand Venetian tradition of 15th- and 16th-century devotional art, from Giovanni Bellini, also represented at San Zaccaria, to Titian.

Infrared reflectography has disclosed several *pentimenti*: the base of the column now covered by Saint Justina's palm, a longer mantle for Saint Jerome, the lion's muzzle placed lower, in contrast to the current position that allows a quasi-dialogue with Saint Jerome. The analysis also revealed a preliminary drawing in charcoal for the architecture.

The critical fortune of the work may be judged by the number of copies made from it. Gradenigo (1756, 1942 ed.) mentions one commissioned by the English Consul in Venice and another by the Elector of Saxony, who wanted to purchase the original, which the Venetian public authorities prevented by stamping the picture with the seal of Saint Mark. Then too, Gian Antonio Guardi copied the altarpiece for Marshall Schulenburg, while Napoleone Nani made yet another copy. Waagen (1852) cites a replica in England in the collection of the Earl of Cowper. Further, a contemporary copy hangs in Rome's Capitoline Museum, a small-format version in a private collection in New York, and a late 17th-century one at Christ Church, Oxford.

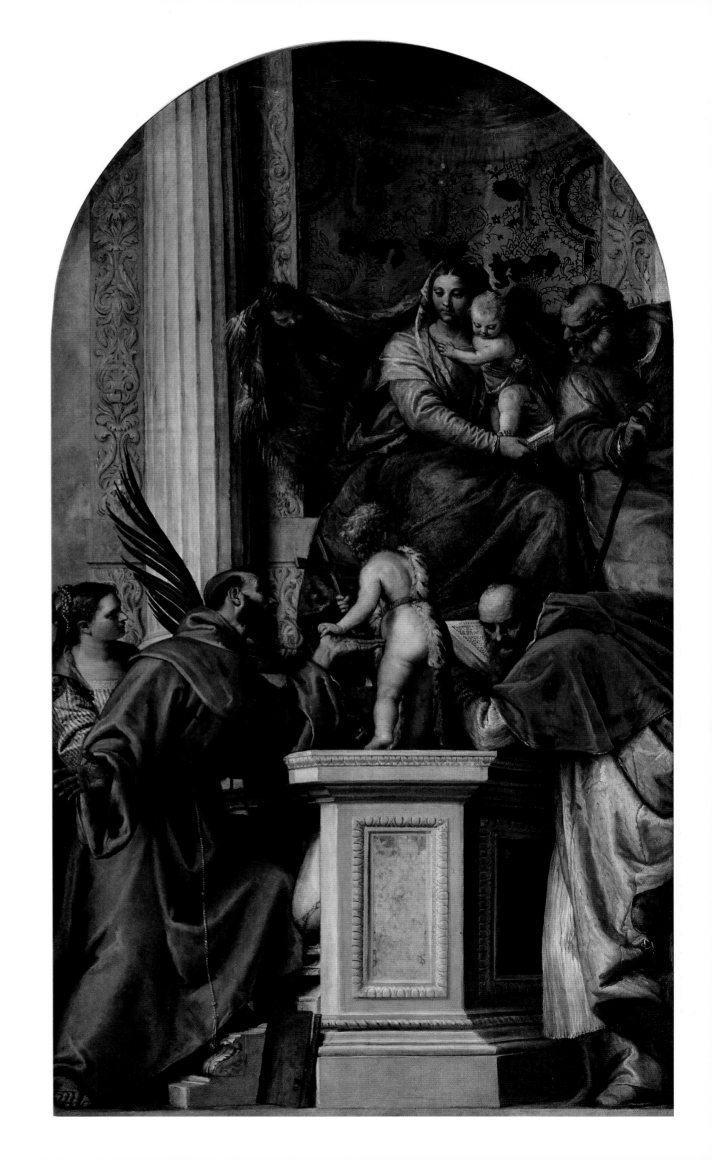

Verona, c.1528—Venice, 1588
Allegory of the Battle of Lepanto
Oil on canvas, 67 x 54" (cat. no. 212)
Last restored 1983

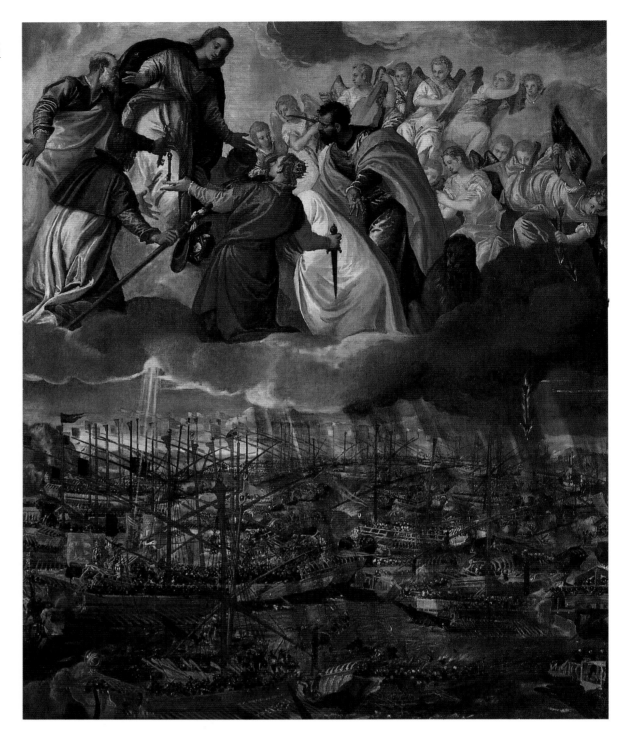

Veronese's *Battle of Lepanto*, thrust into the public domain by the Napoleonic decrees, arrived at the Gallerie in 1812, with the first group of art works assigned there. Its original home had been the Church of San Pietro Martire on Murano, where Boschini (1664) records its presence above the Rosary altar, which still exists. On the right, according to Ridolfi (1648), hung the *Madonna del Rosario* painted by Veronese and his workshop, which also ended up in the Gallerie following the Napoleonic secularization, but today is on loan to the Museo Vetrario on Murano (cat. no. 207).

In the lower zone, Veronese narrates the Battle of Lepanto, a naval confrontation of 1571 between the Holy Alliance, in which the Venetian Republic played a major role, and the Turkish fleet. The artist drew on the cartographic and illustrational sources with which the tactical plan of the sea skirmish was disseminated to the world at the end of 1571. The same sources would be used as well by contemporary followers of Tintoretto. In the upper zone, above a cushion of thick clouds, a peronsified Venice, flanked by Saints Mark and Justina (whose feast day, the 17th of October, would commemorate the battle), addresses the Virgin, while on the left Saints Peter and Roch, the latter a compatriot of the city, intercede for her. Accompanying them on the right is a choir of angels who hurl flaming arrows at their nemesis. A ray of light penetrates the cloud bank to illuminate the standard of Saint Mark on a Venetian galley.

It has been assumed that the painting was commissioned as an ex-voto by a certain Pietro Giustinian of Murano, who had been in the famous battle and whose patron Saint plays an important role in the narrative. Or it could have been commissioned by another member of the same family, Onfrè Giustinian, who had been the official in charge of bearing the news of victory back to Venice.

In the small but well-balanced, entirely autographic composition, the artist clearly aimed for stylistic difference between the two parts, more or less using the point of his brush for the heroic scene, where he had been conditioned by the imagery in prints, and then a melting, luminous, fresh, painterly colorism for the sacred allegory.

It seems likely that the canvas dates from about the time of the battle—that is, close to 1571. A few years later, in 1578, Veronese executed the large votive canvas in memory of the Lepanto victory, a work commissioned by Doge Sebastiano Venier for the *sala del collegio* in the Palazzo Ducale.

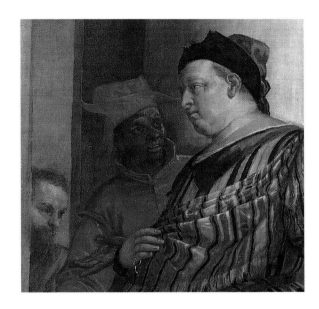

PAOLO CALIARI
CALLED VERONESE   104

Verona, c.1528—Venice, 1588
Feast in the House of Levi
Oil on canvas, 222 x 524" (cat. no. 203)
Last restored 1980-82

Veronese executed this enormous painting for the refectory of the Santi Giovanni e Paolo monastery to replace a *Last Supper* by Titian that, like the refectory itself, had been destroyed by fire in 1571. The commission was underwritten by one of the friars, a certain Andrea De' Buoni or Buono, who had also helped to defray the cost of replacing the lost buildings. According to the inscription on the base of the pillar in the lower left of the canvas, Veronese completed his work on April 20, 1573. Three months later, the artist found himself charged with heresy before the Holy Office (Inquisition), for having treated the Last Supper with such extreme liberty and such disregard for canonical tradition. The artist was interrogated, in particular, about certain of the figures in his composition: "the man with the nosebleed"; "the buffoon with the parrot on his fist"; "the man who picks his teeth"; "the armed men dressed like Germans." In reply, Veronese claimed artistic freedom: "We artists . . . give ourselves the same license as poets and lunatics." Moreover, "I fill my canvas as I must, according to my instructions and my imagination." But, he asserted, everything scurrilous takes place "outside the house of the banquet"; moreover, he could not but follow the example set by his betters, among them Michelangelo. Clearly, Veronese had yet to learn the rules for sacred art that,

only a decade earlier, had been promulgated by the Council of Trent.

Despite his vigorous defense, Veronese was enjoined to correct and amend the painting, within three months and at his own cost, "so that the Last Supper of Our Lord may be as is seemly." In actuality, however, he appears to have made only one correction, probably after consultation with the learned Dominicans who had commissioned the work. At the top of the pilaster with the date below he inscribed: "fecit D. Covi Magnum Levi—Luca Cap. V." And indeed we find in Luke 5:29: "Levi made Him a great feast in his own house."

Subsurface examination with X-ray, infrared, and especially reflectography has discovered neither significant corrections nor major *pentimenti*. Those that do appear derive from the normal creative process, amounting to alterations or erasures of architectural details, or slight changes of attitude in the diners. A young page who was holding a puppy in his right arm while resting his left hand on the table has been overpainted, as already noted by Zanetti in 1771, so that the white tablecloth could remain free. Scientific analysis also eliminated the possibility that the two figures on the near side of the table—Levi himself, according to Ridolfi (1648), and the man in red—could have been painted in at a later stage. In fact, both appear to have been conceived right along with the other figures, who were painted just after the tablecloth. There is even a *pentimento* under the figure of Levi. Further *pentimenti* survive beneath the columns, which were very likely given their final form *in situ*; below the tympanum of the building seen through the first arch on the left; and, most of all, beneath the structure visible beyond the first arch on the right.

Reflectography has also shown, with extreme clarity, the underlying design of the architecture. As for the tribunal's order, Veronese acknowledged it merely with an inscription alluding to Levi's feast, which justified all the "scurrility" in the picture, so pervasive that it includes the very bread on the table, but, most of all, the mocking face of Levi, whose eyes, ears, and gaping mouth are witnesses to human stupidity.

In 1697, the San Giovanni e Paolo refectory burned down again, at which time the huge painting could be saved only by cutting it in three parts and carrying them out rolled up. Thus, before the latest restoration the picture was in three pieces, with tatters and fragments of the original canvas folded under the surface.

When the Venetian Republic fell, the Napoleonic victors passed up Tintoretto's *Paradiso*, even though it had just been restored, in favor of Veronese's *Feast in the House of Levi*. Once returned from Paris to Venice in 1815, the painting was assigned to the Gallerie.

During its most recent restoration, the great picture regained its true scale as measured from one seam to another among the subdivided canvas' three parts. This was achieved by calculating or projecting modular spatial relationships from architectural elements. The original proportions of the work could also be deduced from an engraving by Stenredam made before the fire and damage of 1607, as well as from a late-16th-century copy now in a Turin collection. This would seem to confirm that the floor and double balustrade once continued beyond the present bottom edge. It also indicates the loss of a band along the upper edge, a reality corroborated not only by the engraving but, in addition, by an 18th-

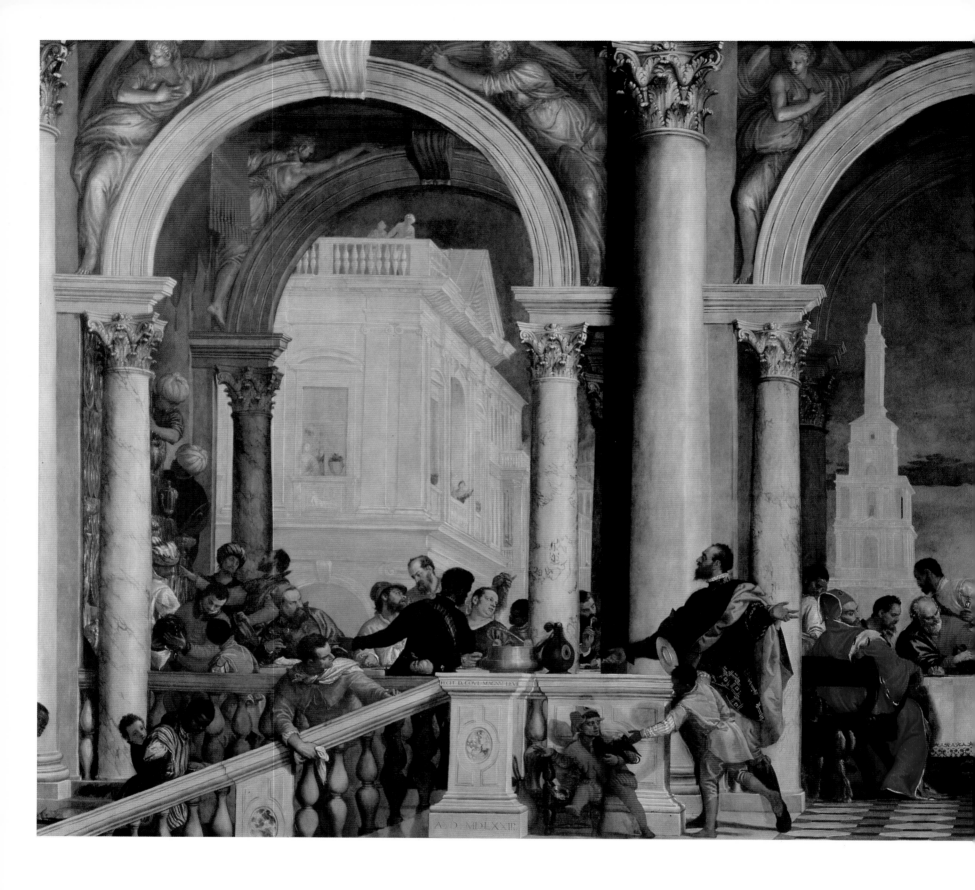

century copy (perhaps from the hand of Sebastiano Ricci) in the Ashmolean Museum at Oxford.

For the triple arcaded setting of his Biblical episode, the artist appears to have taken inspiration from contemporary Palladian ideas in general, especially as evinced in Falconetto's Loggia Cornaro, and even more from Sansovino's Libreria, to whose interior decoration Veronese himself had contributed.

Other influences could be cited in the Venetian figurative tradition, in the drawings of Jacopo Bellini, and in narrative painting, with the latter exemplified by Giovanni Mansueti's *Miraculous Healing of the Daughter of Benvegnudo da San Polo* (ill. no. 57).

For such a vast undertaking, the painter must have made preparatory studies, traces of which were indeed found on the back of the original canvas when the old lining was removed. They constituted squaring used for scaling up a

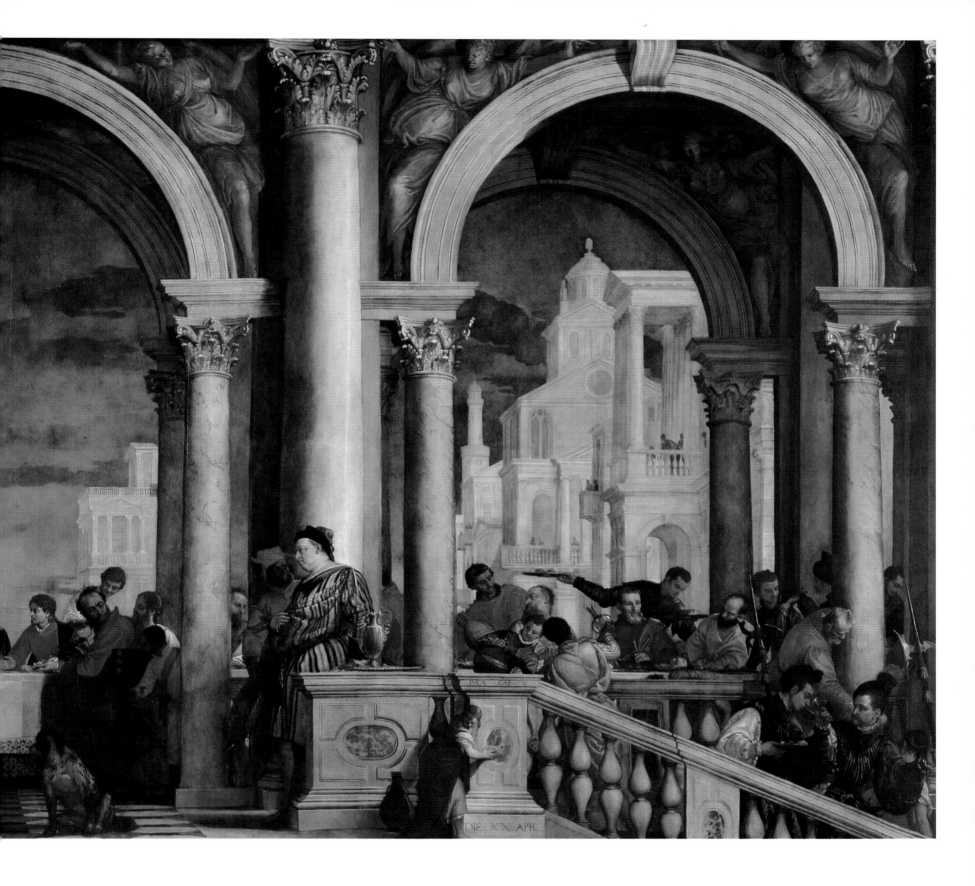

small sketch to the dimensions of a large painting. Then, there are the Louvre's *Five Figures Turned to the Left* drawings and Kassel's early drafts for the servants, which must date from the very beginning of the project.

Despite the amplitude of the composition, which might suggest the need for assistants, the sheer quality of style and color, the technical virtuosity displayed in the figures, and the masterful handling of the architectural masses make it almost impossible to detect the presence of hands others than Veronese's.

The *Feast in the House of Levi* marks the close of the artist's explorations of the banquet theme, a series distinguished by perfect equilibrium between architectural ambience and its human inhabitants. Quite plausibly, the masterpiece seen here has been termed "the finest, most mature essay in this pictorial form."

Verona, c.1528—Venice, 1588
Mystic Marriage of Saint Catherine
Oil on canvas, 135 x 97" (cat. no. 1324)
Last restored 1986

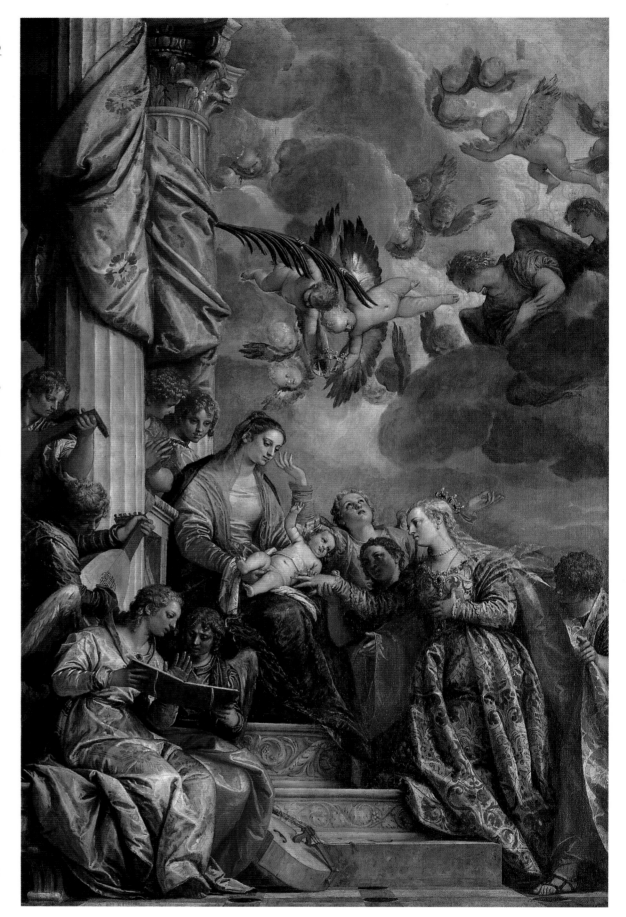

Painted for the high altar of the Venetian Church of Santa Caterina (called *dei Sacchini*, or "of the sackcloth wearers"), part of the homonymous convent that originally belonged to the Sacchini Order before passing in 1274 to the Augustinian Nuns, this work not only enjoyed great favor but also great renown, thanks to Agostino Carracci's 1582 engraving.

The picture is proto-Baroque in its exuberant rejoicing, in the dazzling quality of its colorism, and in the serene beauty of its figures. The special appeal it held for the 17th century is perfectly caught in a verse by Boschini (1660):

A painting could work so strongly on you
Only if its pigment were of pearl and rubies,
Of emeralds and sapphires finer than any,
And of pure and perfect diamonds.

With the suppression of the Augustinian Order in 1807, the church and its contents became State property, but remained in place. In 1915, when the complex served for a military hospital, the convent-school faculty believed that the best protection for the painting would be to leave it on the altar. However, the authorities disagreed and took the picture to a wartime shelter. In 1925, it was sent to the Gallerie, remaining there until replaced by a copy in 1960. It was the copy, not the original, that was destroyed by fire in 1977.

In 1895, Lattanzio Querena (according to the archives of the Accademia di Belle Arti in Venice) completed a restoration that for decades left the painting obscured under a thin gold varnish. The latest restoration, however, has recaptured its pristine integrity, including the splendid chromatics so eulogized by early authorities. Re-established as one of the artist's best-preserved works, at least in Venice, the *Mystic Marriage of Saint Catherine* has now been dated around 1575, more or less contemporary with (or a little later than) the Collegio ceiling in the Palazzo Ducale, whose first payment was made in December 1575.

Reflectography has disclosed the head of a *putto* on the left of the Virgin's face, completely finished and then painted out in the final version. This *pentimento* is particularly interesting in that it can be compared with a 16th-century drawing in Boston's Isabella Stewart Gardner Museum, a sheet once assumed to be a preparatory sketch for the *Mystic Marriage of Saint Catherine* but now thought more likely to be a copy of one of Veronese's preliminary studies for it.

The three unfinished coats-of-arms on the lowest step offer no evidence for dating the picture more precisely.

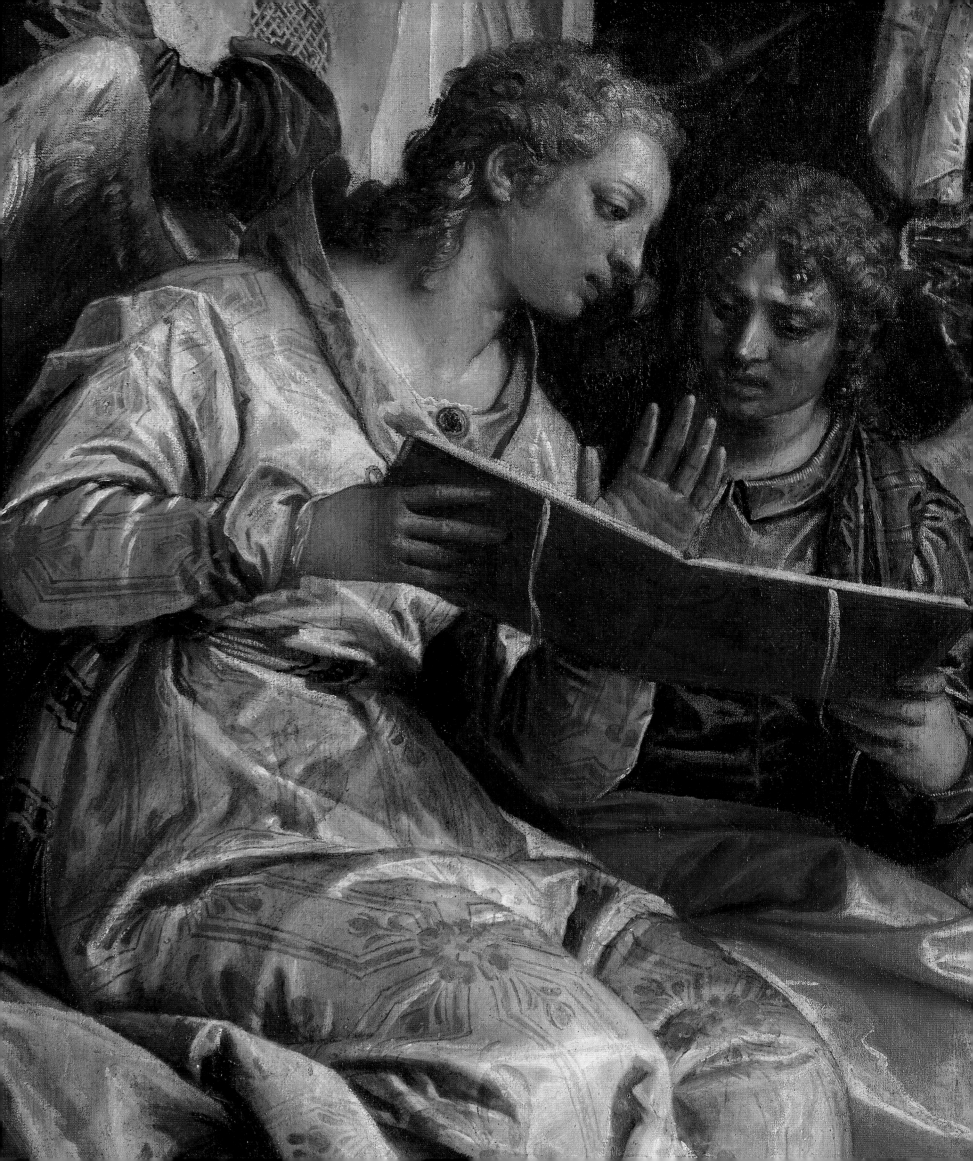

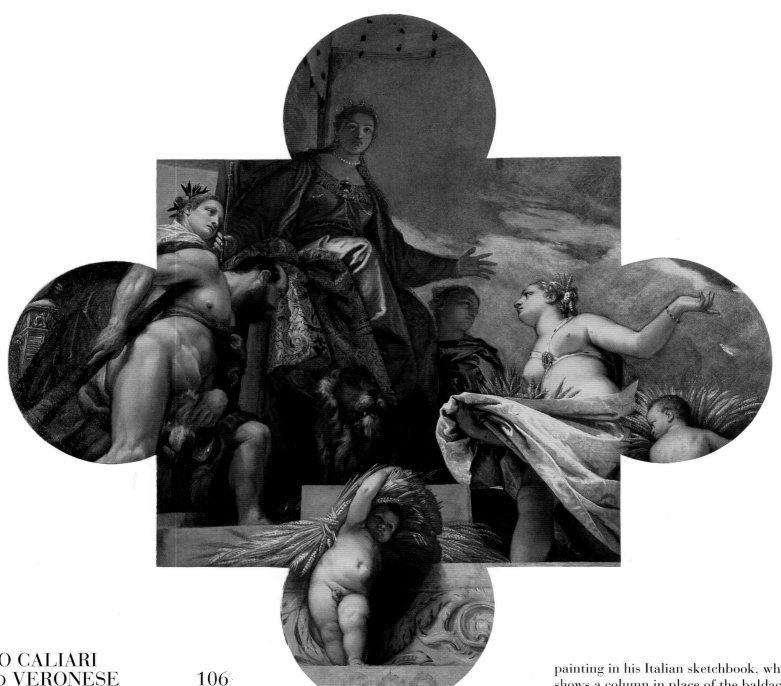

PAOLO CALIARI
CALLED VERONESE   106

Verona, c.1528—Venice, 1588
*Venice Receiving the Homage of Hercules and
Ceres*
Oil on canvas, 124 x 131" (cat. no. 45)
Last restored 1986

As Ridolfi recorded in 1648, Veronese painted this canvas for the ceiling of the *Magistrato alle Biade* in the Palazzo Ducale. Concerned with the import, storage, and sale of grain, the "Cereals Office" was located at the far end of the loggia floor overlooking the San Marco dock. The exact quarters occupied by the Office were probably those still adorned with a 15th-century bas-relief known as *Our Lady of the Harvest*.

On January 23, 1570, the premises were reconstructed at a cost, "for wood, metal and labor," of 323 lire 5 soldi. Since this information yields no hint of the amount disbursed for the painting itself (Lorenzi, 1868), we must assume that it was executed several years later. The work remained in place until 1792, when it was restored by Pietro Edwards and hung in a room adjoining the main hall of Sansovino's Library. A later transfer left it in the anteroom of the great building designed by Sebastiano Santi on the site of the Church of San Geminiano. In an attempt to prevent its removal to Vienna, the Venetian authorities finally assigned the painting to the Gallerie around 1895.

The odd, quatrefoil format may not be that of the original painting, or may have been reworked, since it obscures many iconographical details.

Anthony van Dyck, during his Venetian sojourn in 1622-23, made a copy of the painting in his Italian sketchbook, which shows a column in place of the baldachin behind the figure of Venice. This has been confirmed by stratigraphic, as well as reflectographic, analysis revealing the baldachin to have been a later addition. Originally, the personification of Venice stood under the open sky, barely set off by the pilaster base and the column, while Ceres and Hercules offered her a wheatsheaf symbolizing the prosperity and good governance of the Republic.

Despite considerable damage, particularly to the sky, the quality of the figures, the subtly luminous colors, the expert illusionism, and the beauty of the nude figures (especially Ceres, an image that would later influence Tiepolo) combine to transform the allegory into one of Veronese's greatest works.

The painting can be dated to around the time of the artist's canvases in the Palazzo Ducale Collegio, especially *Venice Flanked by Justice and Peace* (1575-77).

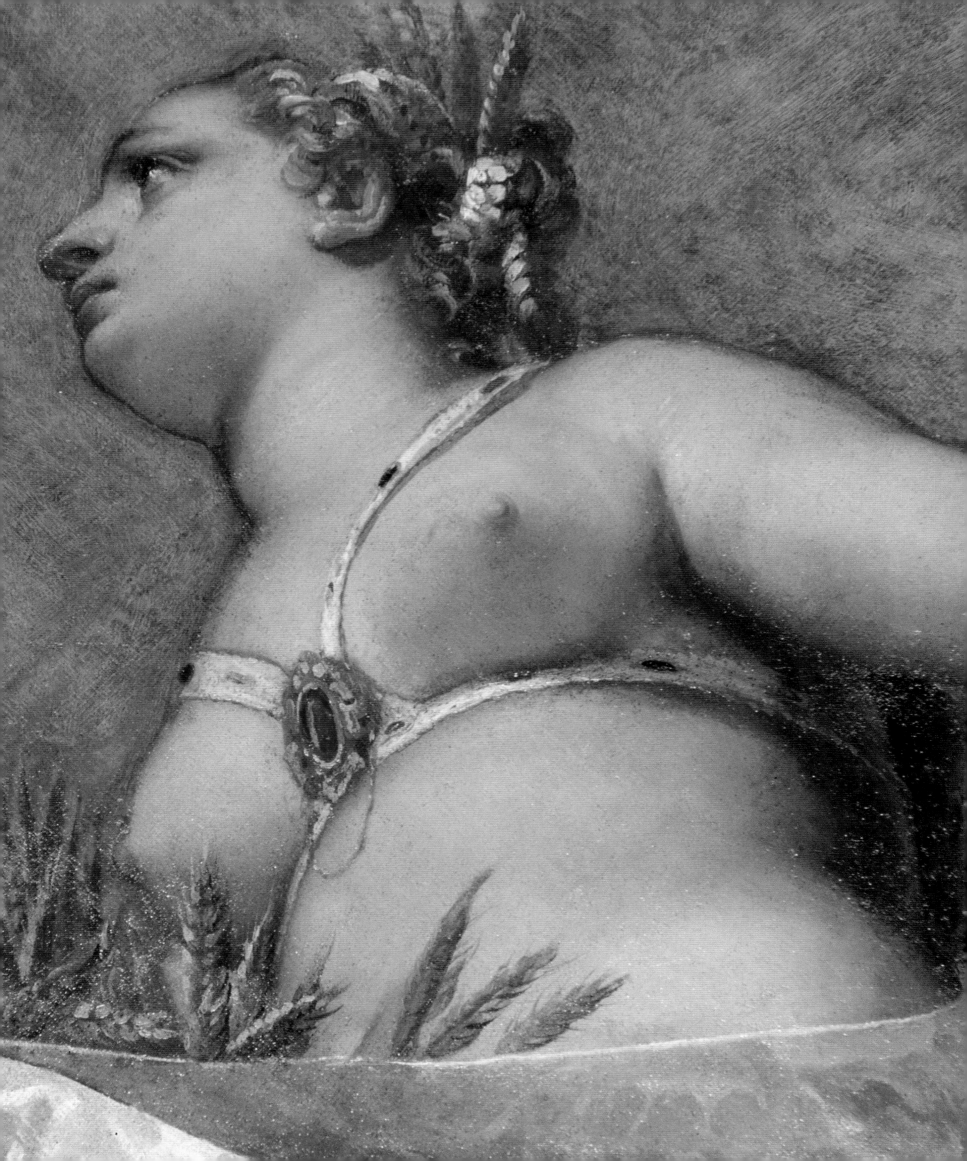

Verona, c.1528—Venice, 1588
The Annunciation
Oil on canvas, 110 x 217" (cat. no. 260)
Last restored 1970

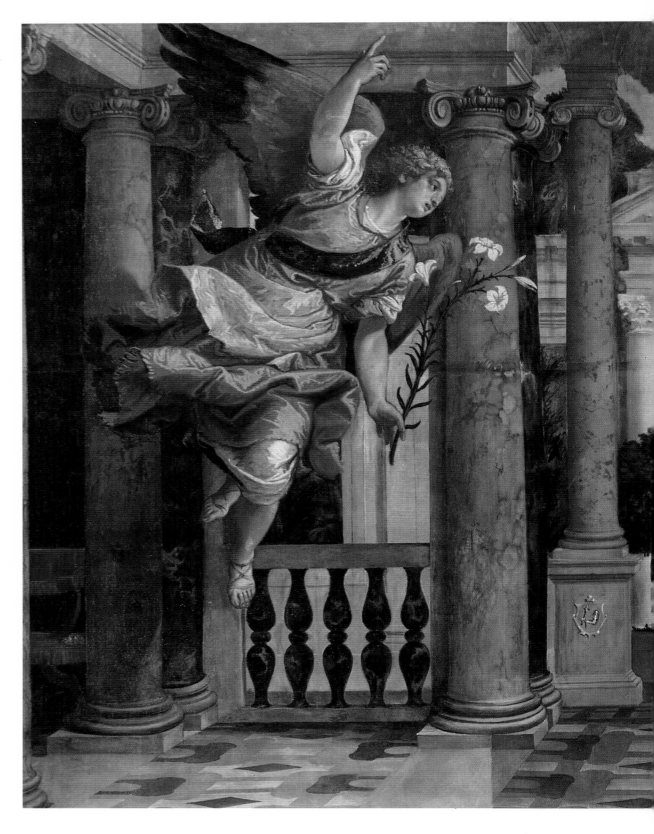

This picture came to the Gallerie in 1811 from the Scuola dei Mercanti, where it had hung above the door in the *sala dell'albergo*, flanked by grisaille personifications called *Charity* and *Faith*, now exhibited in the Sansovino room at the Biblioteca Marciana.

The Scuola's emblem—a hand blessing the Cross—rests just below the apex of the midground tympanum, while in the foreground, on either side, the arms of the donors, the Cadabrazzo and Cottoni families, adorn the bases of two columns.

A once-powerful institution, the Scuola dei Mercanti still stands as an edifice, just to the left of the Church of Madonna dell'Orto. The *sala dell'albergo* was rebuilt between 1575 and 1580, during which period its program of pictorial decorations was carried out.

The *Annunciation* was painted in 1578, as we know from reflectographic examination below a thick layer of repainting. Contemporaries, who lavished praise on the picture, ascribed it to Veronese almost without exception. More recent critics are not so sure,

and have postulated a collaboration with the artist's younger brother Benedetto.

In reality, however, present readings of the work are conditioned by a canvas that has suffered much tampering and repainting, even though some of this was removed during the last restoration in 1970. An addition to the central portion of the lower zone camouflages the irregularity of the original format, evidence of which can be found in the statue crowning the tympanum, now truncated as a result of the canvas' having been cut down. Thanks to

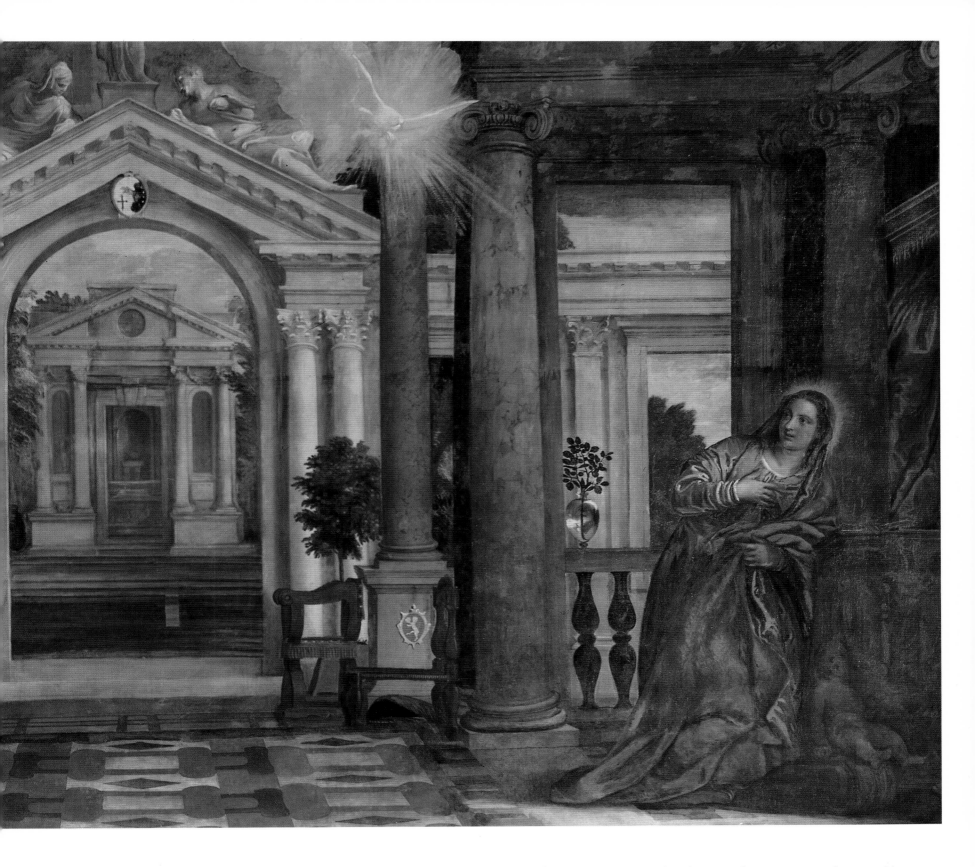

a fragment of the Cross revealed by reflectographic analysis, we know that the sculpture symbolized Faith, flanked by the surviving personifications of Old and New Testaments recumbent on either side of the tympanum. Moreover, the cloud radiant with the dove of the Holy Ghost conceals—as, again, we know from reflectography—a column capital on the midground right—corresponding to the still-visible capital on the left—as well as an impost block, both of which supported the springing of an arch that must

have once been complete. Thus, the picture—the brilliance of whose original colorism can be seen even now in the extraordinary vase resting on the balustrade—becomes an ensemble of five successive scenes that recede towards and close upon a small temple very likely inspired by the Church of San Francisco della Vigna. Clearly, the architectonics of the composition had their source not only in Palladio but also in contemporary carnival and theatrical design. The two allegorical figures on the tympanum have been identified with some

sketches in a drawing presently owned by Christ Church, Oxford (no. 341). However, since this sheet includes preparatory studies for works datable to 1586—among them the *Coronation of the Virgin* for the Ognissanti Church (now part of the Gallerie's collection but on loan to the Museo Provinciale in Torcello)—its connection with the picture seen here must be regarded as problematic at best. On the other hand, the Old Testament figure is referred to quite explicitly in a drawing privately owned in France.

Verona, c. 1528—Venice, 1588
Crucifixion
Oil on canvas, 115 x 179" (cat. no. 252)
Last restored 1969

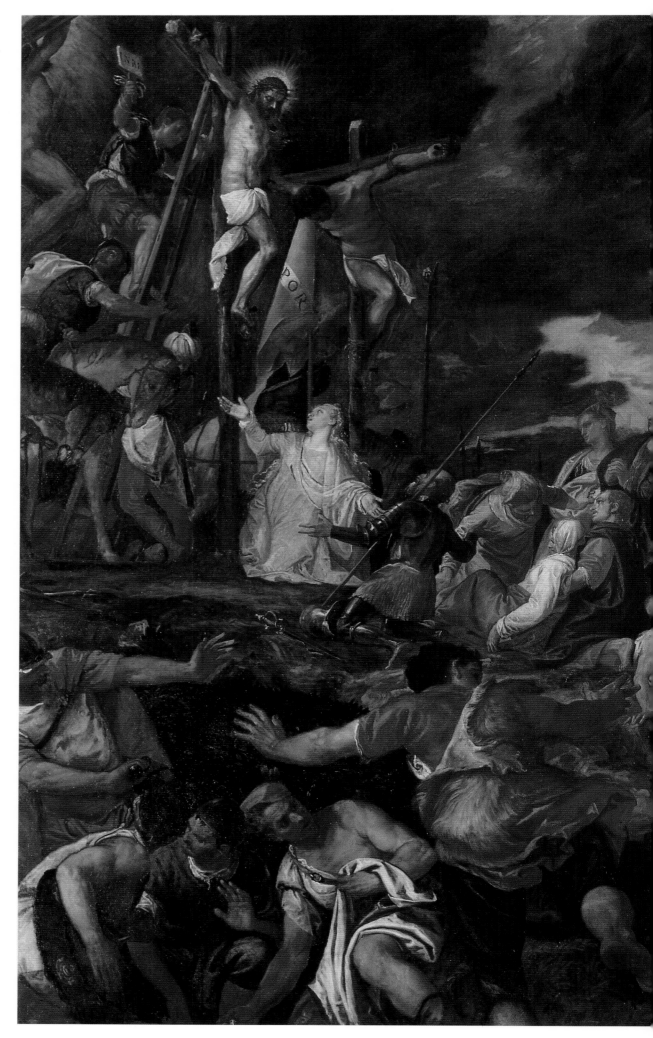

Veronese's *Crucifixion* hung in the Church of San Nicolò della Lattuga, "above the altar of Saint John the Baptist," according to Zanetti, writing in 1733 and again in 1771. After secularization in 1806, the painting was expropriated by the State. However, only in 1834 did it reach the Gallerie, where it long remained rolled up in the reserve, until restored in 1852-53 and then exhibited. The latest restoration, which stripped the heavy 19th-century varnish from the surface, has eliminated all doubt about the attribution.

This *Crucifixion*, in contrast to its important counterpart in the Louvre (painted between 1570 and 1580), leads us through a long, episodic narrative held together by the view of Jerusalem in the background. It anticipates the landscape conventions so characteristic of the succeeding century, especially in the huge repoussoir cavalry, as well as in the doleful, disorderly procession moving towards the starkly lit figure of Christ crucified. In certain particulars—the seated women in the background or the dead rising from their open graves—the image becomes a literal transcription of the scene described in Saint Matthew's Gospel.

Now the inventive iconography of the *Feast in the House of Levi* has been replaced by strict adherence to Scripture, reflecting a powerful change in the political and religious climate of Venice.

The melancholy mood (which Tintoretto also evinced) and the emphatic drama of the composition, so unlike the utter serenity of the artist's earlier works, are all characteristic of his last phase, from which this painting comes (c. 1582).

Reflectography has disclosed several *pentimenti*, the most significant of which is a tilted ladder at the center, above the female devotees.

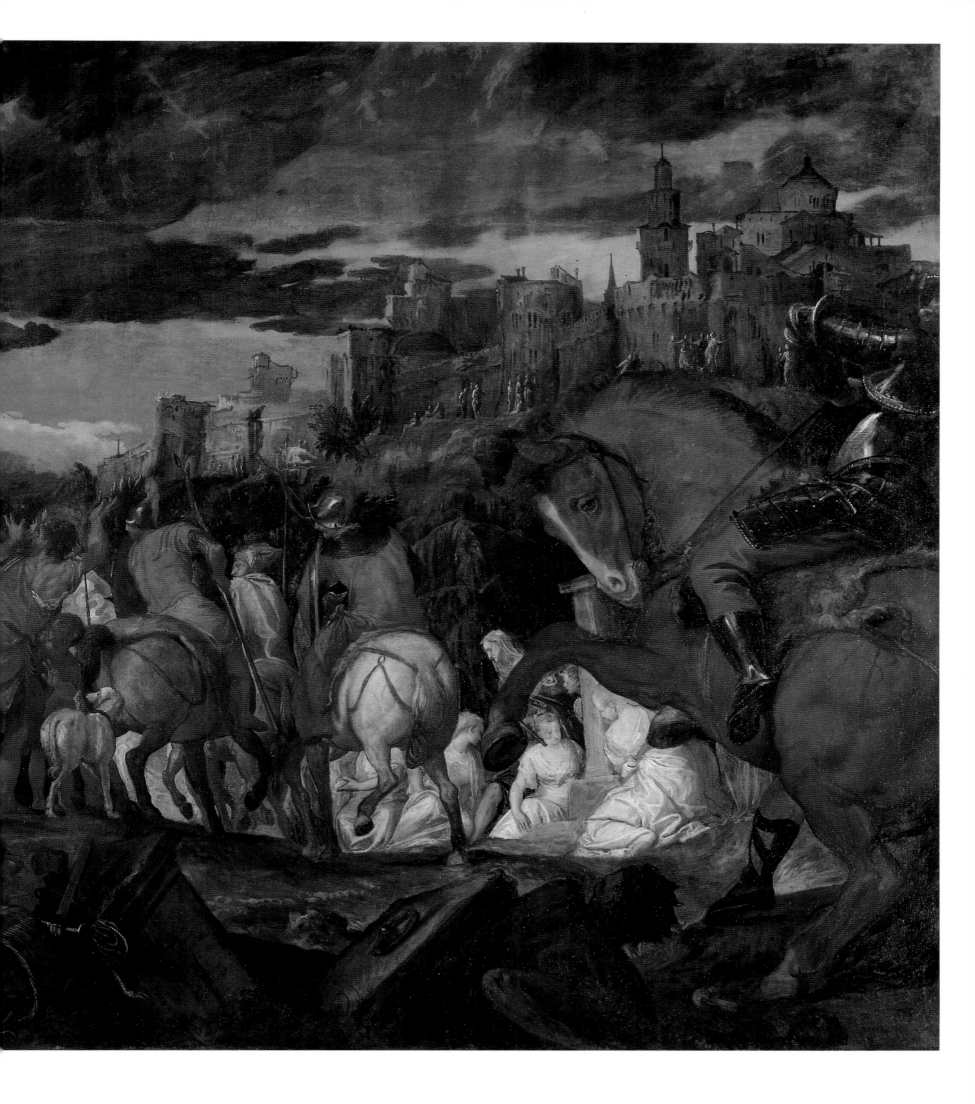

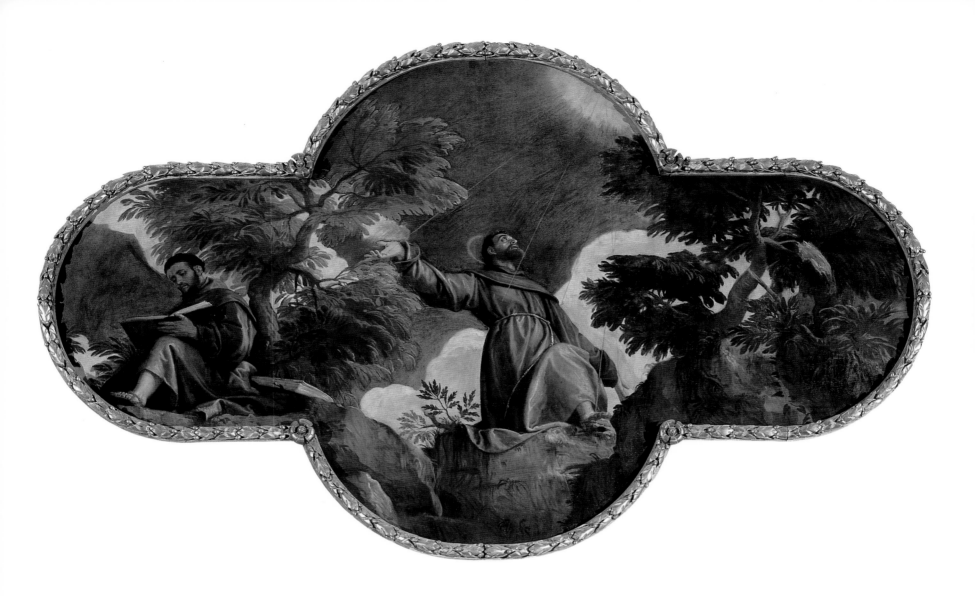

PAOLO CALIARI
CALLED VERONESE   109

Verona, c.1528—Venice, 1588
Saint Francis in Ecstasy
Oil on quatrefoil canvas, 172 x 102" (cat. no. 833)
Last restored 1986.

Like the painting that follows, *Saint Francis in Ecstasy* came from the ceiling of the Franciscan Church of San Nicolò della Lattuga, or dei Frari, on whose adornment Veronese and his colleagues lavished great effort. Just as the *Saint Sebastian* became the crowning achievement of the artist's youth, this project evolved as the glory of his mature years. Beginning at the organ, it included, besides the *Saint Francis*, an eccentrically

formatted *Adoration of the Magi* at the center, and, at the corners, the *Four Evangelists*, together with *Saint Nicholas Acclaimed Bishop of Myra* near the high altar. After the suppression of the Franciscans in 1806, the Order's church reverted to the State, which later tore it down and placed the pictures in storage before allowing them to depart for various destinations. The *Adoration of the Magi* and the *Four Evangelists* now grace the ceiling of the rebuilt Rosary Chapel at the Church of Santi Giovanni e Paolo. The painting seen here went to the Vienna Academy in 1838, and entered the Gallerie only as war reparation in 1919.

Probably the best-preserved section of the mutilated cycle, *Saint Francis in Ecstasy* has always seemed unquestionably to be from the master's own hand. Reflectography confirms a discontinuity in the pigment, revealing minor

pentimenti related to the attitude of the Saint's arm.

The painting exemplifies the new role of landscape in Veronese's last period. Tree foliage, Mannerist in conception, rises into the Saint's own space, while Brother Leo stands aside, immersed in some sacred text. Like *Saint Nicholas*, this picture illustrates the changing taste of the artist at the turn of the 1580s, when his palette progressively darkened and his illusionism grew taut. A faint disquiet pervades these airy, open spaces, with little ripples passing across the figures' timeless beauty.

Sansovino, writing in 1581, makes no mention of the ceiling, yet he cannot have overlooked a work of such importance. Thus, the church probably received its pictorial cycle between that date and the building's consecration on September 17, 1582.

PAOLO CALIARI
CALLED VERONESE   110

Verona, c.1528—Venice, 1588
Saint Nicholas Acclaimed Bishop of Mira
Oil on canvas, diameter 79" (cat. no. 661)
Last restored 1986

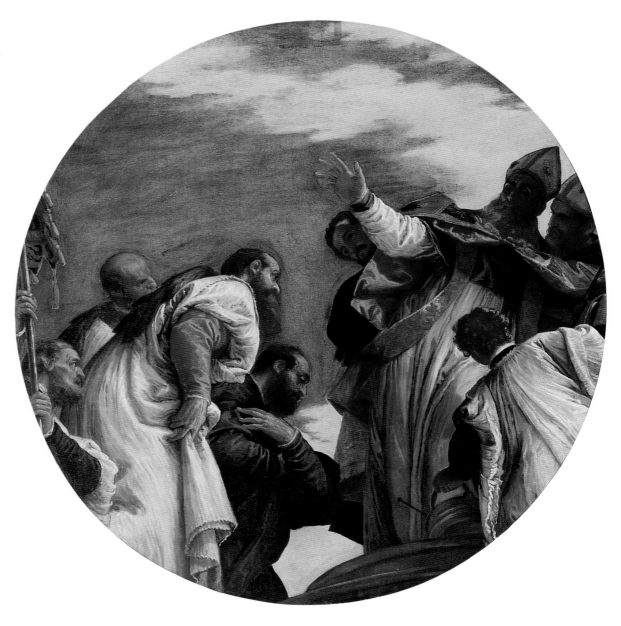

Originally a pendant to Veronese's *Saint Francis in Ecstasy*, executed for the ceiling of San Nicolò della Latuga and endowed with the same lobed format, this picture, by 1815, "had sustained grave damage," according to Edwards, who suggested that its shape be modified for installation in a chamber of the Appeals Court. In 1817, however, the Gallerie got the painting and, after some trimming, inserted it into the central space of the first hall's 15th-century ceiling, in place of a *Madonna della Misericordia* wood-carved in high relief. Here it remained until the end of the 19th century, before being exhibited in one of the galleries.

Radical mutilation also caused a drastic change in the very nature of the painting. The original dimensions, like those of the *Saint Francis*, are known from various 17th- and 18th-century drawings, including one preserved at the Tayler Museum in Haarlem, as well as from a copy now in the hands of Robert Nolan in Nice. The sky in particular is irreversibly different from what Veronese painted.

Reflectographic examination confirms the generally good condition of the figures, while also disclosing a minor *pentimento* on the steps of the unseen church.

Veronese drew on Jacobus de Voragine's *Legenda Aurea*, in which a prophetic dream reveals that the new Bishop of Mira would be the first man to set foot in the Cathedral on a particular day.

As in his earlier treatment of the subject—a painting executed (1561-62) for the Mantuan Church of San Benedetto Po and now in London's National Gallery—Veronese conflated the two-part narrative—acknowledgment and consecration—in a single episode, whose brilliant illusionism alone should be sufficient to render the present attribution beyond doubt, despite the cavilings of certain 20th-century critics unprepared to take account of the picture's troubled history.

Verona, c.1528—Venice, 1588
Assumption
Oil on canvas, 119 x 186" (cat. no. 541)
Last restored 1988

Along with an *Annunciation* and a *Visitation*, this big canvas once embellished the refectory ceiling in the now-destroyed San Giacomo Monastery on the Giudecca. Sources such as Boschini (1664) describe it as surrounded by "adornments of arbors, statues, patterns, and figures that bind together the aforesaid paintings." On the wall of the same room hung a *Feast in the House of Levi*—lent to Verona in 1910 and now in its City Hall—that certainly came from the master's studio and probably from the hand of Benedetto. The entire group of paintings, catalogued by Edwards in 1812 among works earmarked for the Gallerie, arrived there only in 1818-20, thanks to transport problems. Edwards had wished to assemble them all in one room, but only the *Assumption* went on display, in 1834. The *Annunciation* and the *Visitation*, originally oval, were recut as rectangles, probably in 1882, at the time of their transfer to the Church of Zan Degolà. Today they form part of the Gallerie reserve. Also in reserve are some 130 feet of the frieze that once accompanied these pictures. At some unknown date, the frieze lost five heads, representing young men and women, three of them donated to the Premier's office and lost. The other two have been returned to their proper places in a 43-foot section of the frieze restored in 1988.

If this pictorial ensemble derived from a joint effort, as sources indicate, Veronese himself is certainly responsible for the overall conception, which, with its linking arbors, is clearly Mannerist and much indebted to the schools of Correggio and Parmigianino. The baluster motif would reappear in the *Feast in the House of Levi* (ill. no. 104).

Severely damaged by an early, unskilled effort at restoration and long ignored by commentators, the large *Assumption* underwent cleaning in 1988 and now discloses Veronese's characteristic hand far more clearly than once seemed possible.

Some fragments evince a level of achievement not previously suspected, especially in the central passage depicting God the Father with Angels, as well as in the organ and cello-playing angels. X-rays also have brought revelations. This is a late work, not mentioned by Sansovino in his 1581 description of Venice, which makes it assignable to the period between that commentary and the artist's death in 1588.

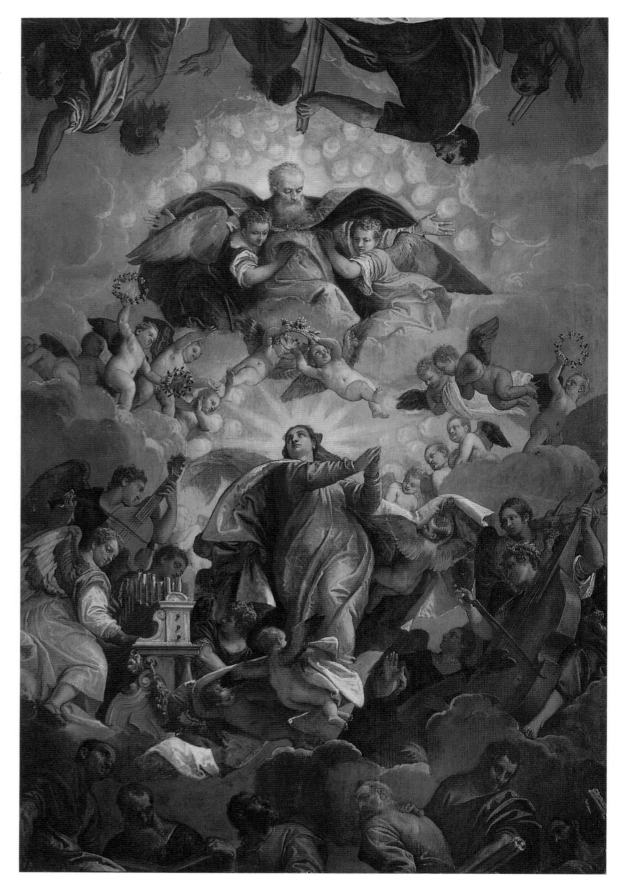

Venice, c.1550-1628
The Crucifixion of Saint Peter
Oil on canvas, 67 x 53" (cat. no. 660)

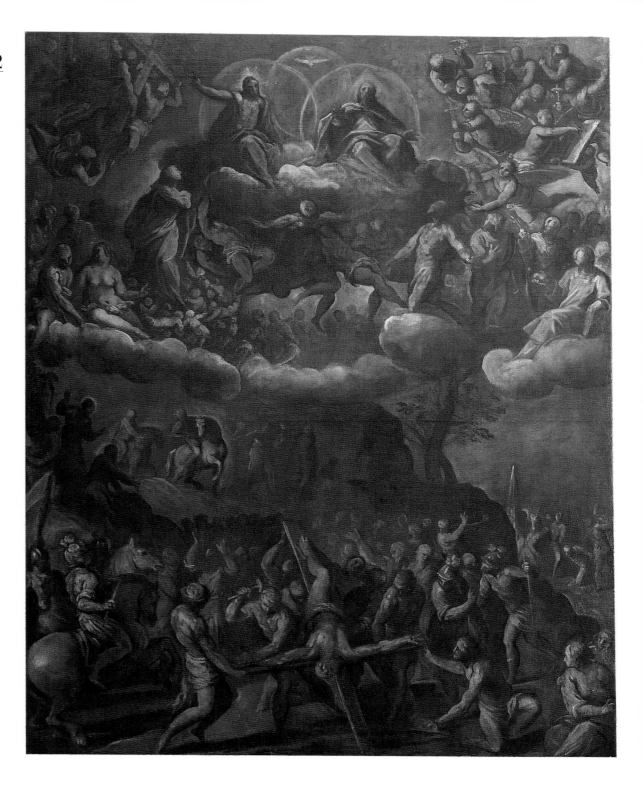

This painting, presented to the Gallerie by Mr. M. Guggenheim in 1901, is probably a *modelletto*—a relatively small, full-color proposal—for a ceiling, which, however, is not mentioned by contemporary commentators and may never have been executed.

For the upper zone—where the Trinity and the Virgin appear surrounded by angels bearing the symbols of the Passion hovering above the blessed, among them Adam and Eve—the artist repeated a signed composition now in a Roman private collection as well as a preparatory drawing dated 1614 and now in the Royal Library, Windsor (no. 68090).

In the lower zone, the Crucifixion of Saint Peter recalls Michelangelo's fresco in the Pauline Chapel at the Vatican. Datable around 1614, the painting exemplifies Palma Giovane's eclecticism, his gift, that is, for intelligent recycling of the achievements of those great 16th-century Venetians—Titian, Veronese, and, most of all, Tintoretto.

DOMENICO FETTI   113

Rome, 1588/89—Venice, 1623
David
Oil on canvas, 70 x 51" (cat. no. 669)
Last restored 1961

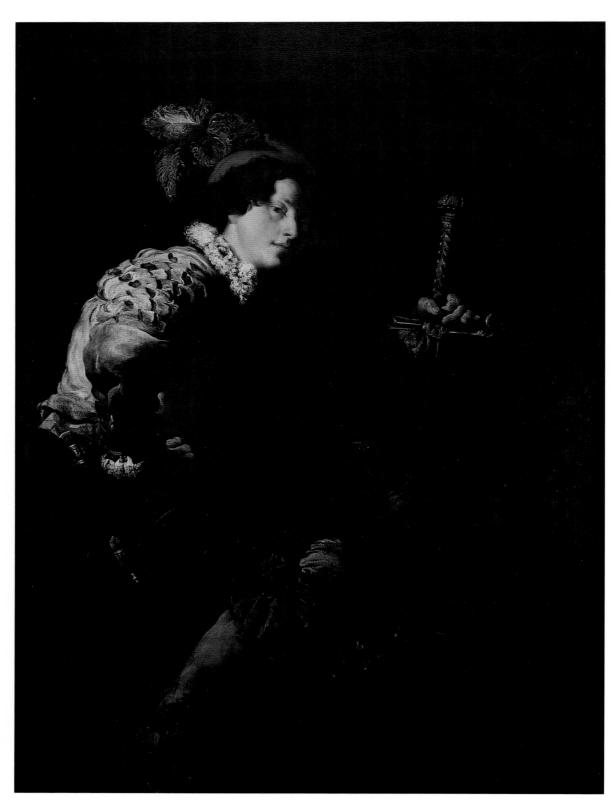

An 1838 gift from Girolamo Contarini (a descendant of Giorgio Contarini dagli Scrigni, who had been Fetti's patron), this painting is one of several versions that Fetti made on the subject of the victorious David holding the head of a vanquished Goliath. Others may be found in Dresden (Gemäldegalerie) and Moscow (Pushkin Museum). The canvas seen here belongs to a group painted during 1616-19 in Mantua, where Fetti studied the works of Rubens and various 16th-century Venetian masterpieces. Prior to this sojourn, the artist

had been in Rome frequenting the circle of Caravaggio, an experience reflected in his choice of theme and his way of treating it, as well as in his violent contrasts of light and dark, albeit with a total absence of naturalistic detail. Still, his mastery of luminary effects and his almost tactile feeling for the oil medium have their source in Venetian figure painting.

A shaft of light from outside the composition falls obliquely across the shoulders of the young David, picking out the frothy ruffles of

his shirt, the delicacy of his collar, and the plumed red cap, while also skimming along the intricate metal inlay of his sword. The head of Goliath, immersed in shadow, can scarcely be made out.

As ripe with character as a portrait, David symbolizes youth and all its qualities: overweening pride, strength, utter confidence, and ostentatious self-assertion through rich attire, here described with loving care. The Landesmuseum Joanneum, Alte Galerie, in Graz owns a workshop copy.

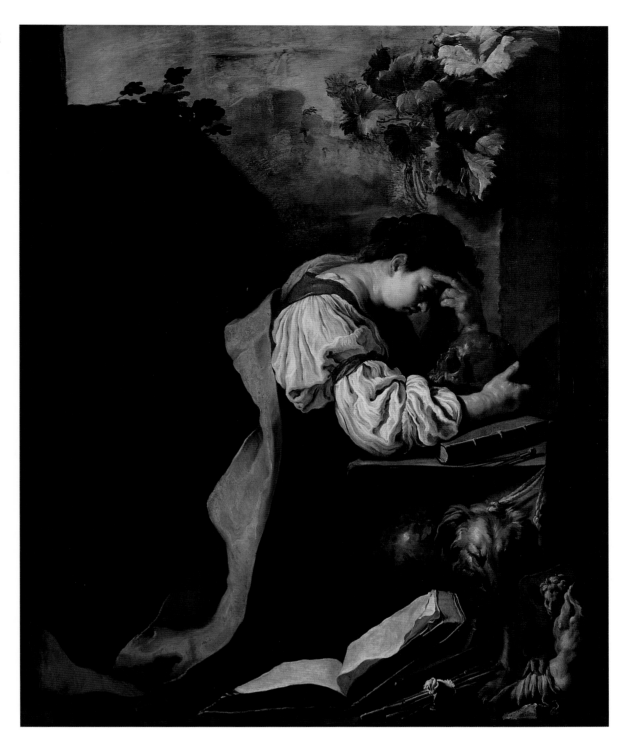

Like the previous work, this important painting was received in 1838 from Girolamo Contarini, a descendent of Giorgio Contarini dagli Scrigni, who was Fetti's patron in Venice. On the globe near the ear of the dog, one can read MED, and more faintly the letters AML on the book.

There are numerous copies of this work and a replica in the Louvre, wrongly considered in the past as the prototype of the Venetian version. The later can, on the other hand, be dated to 1618 during the artist's Mantuan period, and is of superior quality. This work of complex symbolism was inspired by several iconographic sources- above all the pose of the praying figure with head in hand. Among possible sources is a bas relief, known as "Germania capta" under the statue of Rome in the Capitoline Museum, familiar to the artist perhaps through drawings or engravings. Unless, of course, he was inspired by compositions of a similar theme by Dürer, Corregio and Rubens. From Dürer's famous 1514 engraving representing Melancholy (Melanconia 1), Fetti has assumed several allegorical attributes, endowing them with the ultimate significance of a Vanitas. The presence of a skull could also inspire an interpretation of the subject as the penitent Magdalen, the title given this picture in the past.

In common with the Dürer engraving is the dog, attached to a rope, a probable allusion to fidelity, and the compass and globe, symbols of intellectual faculties and the rationality attached to a melancholic temperament. Besides these, there are other symbols of knowledge, the astrolabe and books, and of the arts; paint brushes, an easel, and small statue. Thus, melancholy has become linked to a meditation upon vanity, and the fragility of human existence when confronted with the immortality of art and science.

In the allegorical Meditation, just as in Fetti's devotional works, we witness a process whereby transcendental meaning would disappear through its translation into essentially humanist terms.

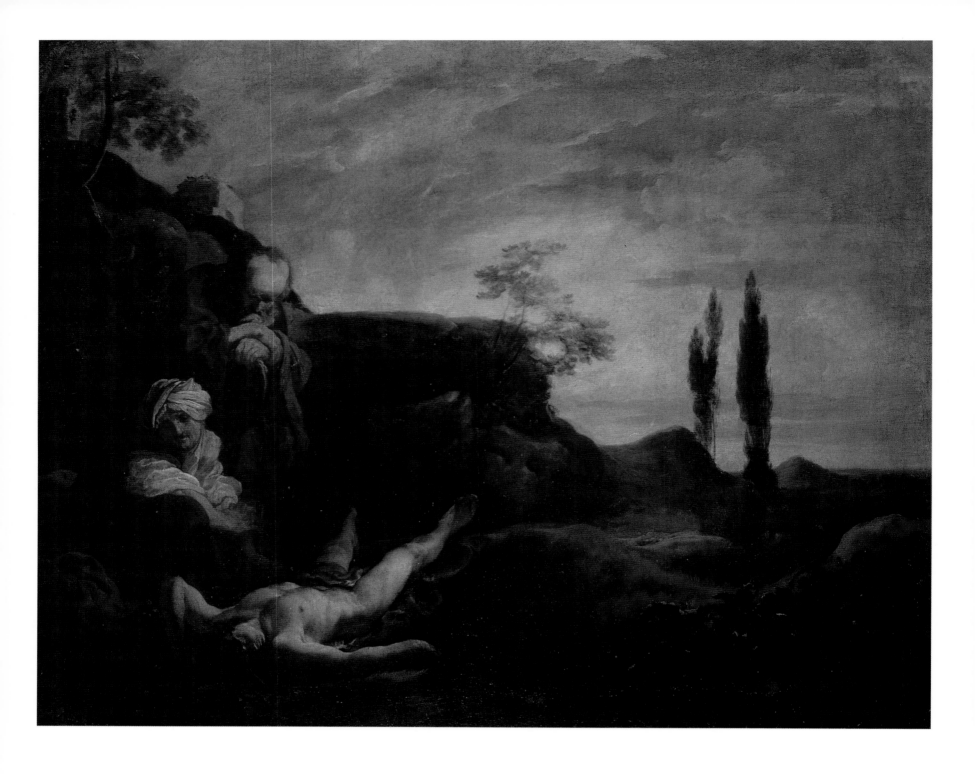

JOHANN LISS 115

Oldenburg-im-Holstein, 1597—Venice, c.1629
Abel Mourned by Adam and Eve
Oil on canvas, 27 x 36" (cat. no. 913)
Last restored 1959

Acquired from the Giovanelli collection in 1932, along with its companion piece, the *Sacrifice of Isaac* (see below), this work was seen in Liss' studio and recorded as there by Sandrart while in Venice during 1628-29. Pietro Monaco cites the owners in his engraving of the Liss picture: "the noble house of Giovanelli at S. Agostino." *Abel Mourned by Adam and Eve* is one of the last works by a painter who, along with Strozzi and Fetti, contributed much to the renewal of Venetian art.

It all but reprises, in vertical format, the slightly earlier version in the Capparoni collection in Rome. The dramatic impact is softened by the artist's fluid, lyrical handling, clearly evident in the freedom and breadth of the crepuscular landscape.

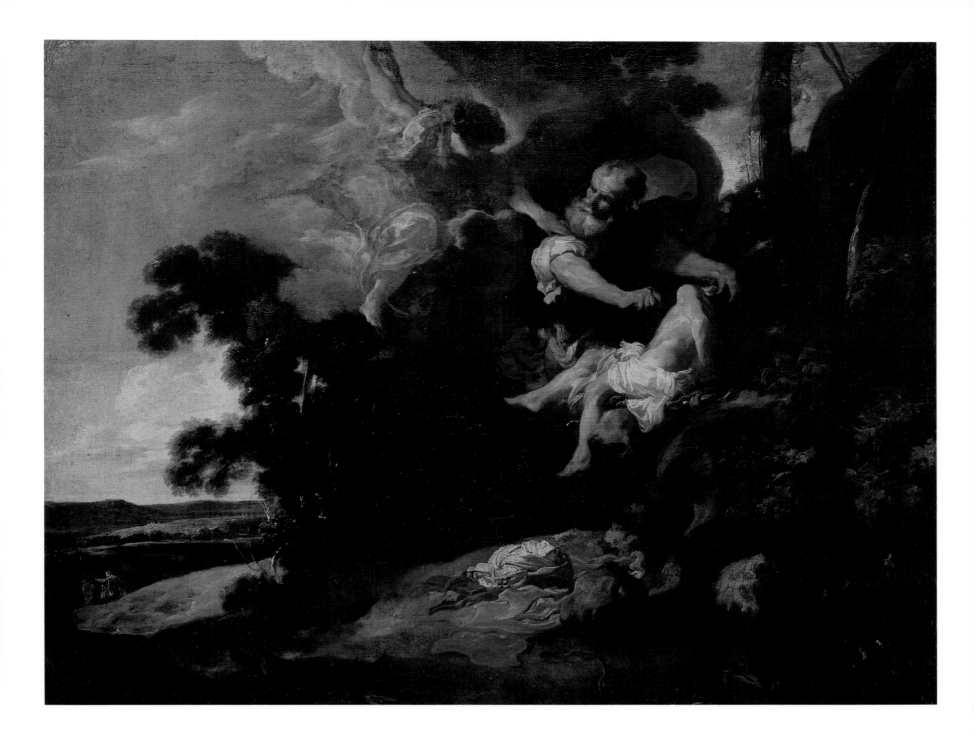

JOHANN LISS   116

Oldenburg-im-Holstein, 1597—Venice, c.1629
Sacrifice of Isaac
Oil on canvas, 26 x 34" (cat. no. 914)
Last restored 1959

Like the preceding work, to which it is a pendant, the *Sacrifice of Isaac* can be dated to the artist's Venetian sojourn in 1628-29. Liss addressed the subject in other paintings and in different ways, the best of which belong to the Uffizi (Florence) and the Bredins Museum (The Hague). In this version especially, with its horizontal format, the narrative drama is tempered by the lyrical painterliness of the sweeping landscape.

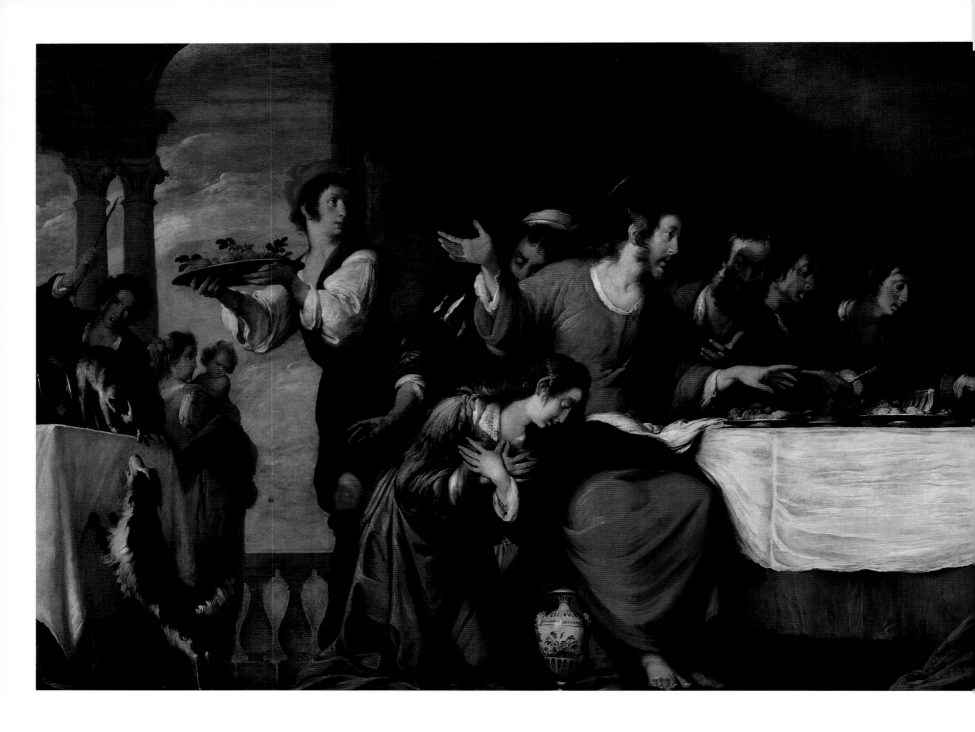

BERNARDO STROZZI   117

Genoa, 1581—Venice, 1644
Feast in the House of Simon
Oil on canvas, 109 x 296" (cat. no. 777)
Last restored 1981

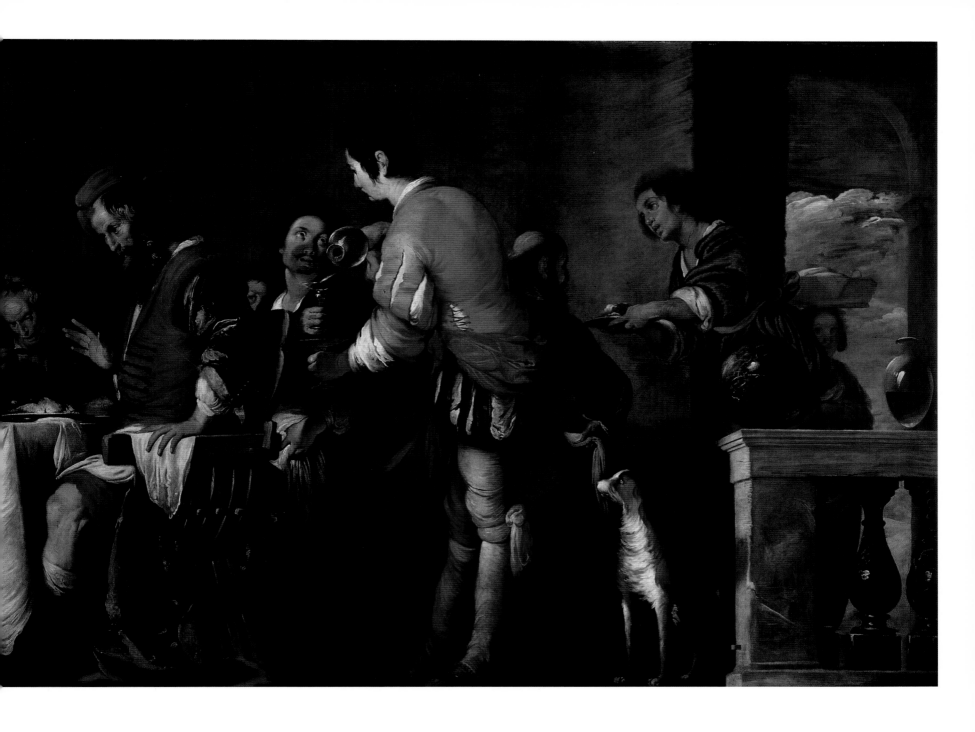

Acquired in 1911 from the Vicenzan lawyer Paolo Sartori, this is one of many interpretations that Strozzi painted of the same subject, and it can be dated towards the end of his Genoese period in the late 1630s. The canvas may have hung in the chapel of the Palazzo Gorleri in Genoa. The latest restoration, which removed considerable repainting from the background, has not only revealed the shaft of light falling behind the table; it also confirms that the entire work comes from the artist's own hand.

In this large and elaborate composition, reminiscent of Paolo Veronese's banquet scenes, Strozzi once again shows himself a master of color, inspired no less by the Lombards Cerano and Procaccini than by Rubens, after whose example he transposes the innovations of Caravaggio into a Baroque key.

Genoa, 1581—Venice, 1644
Portrait of a Procurator
Oil on canvas, 91 x 59" (cat. no. 1358)

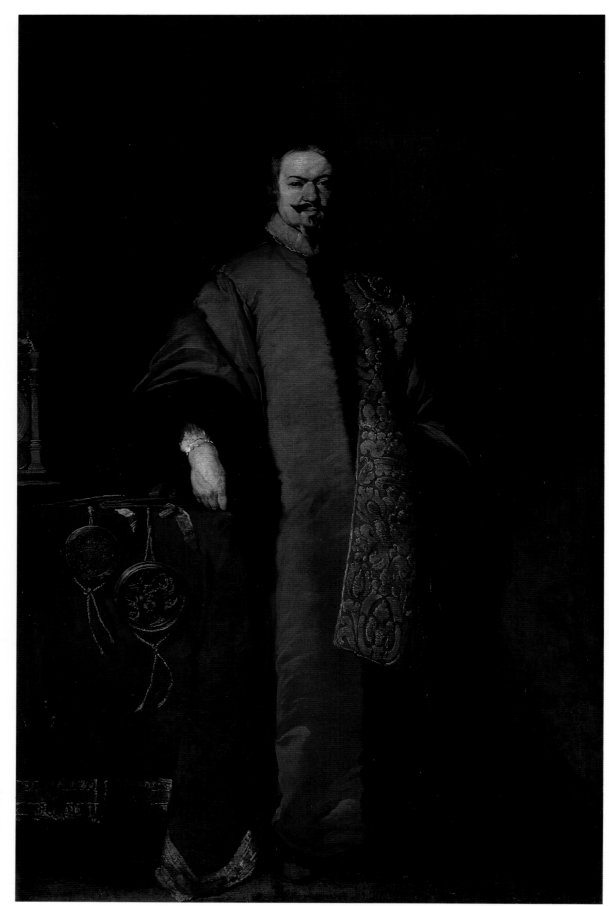

From the Grimani family, who owned it until 1894, this painting passed in 1914 to Charles Newton-Robinson, before its acquisition in 1942 by the Curtis family for their collection in the Palazzo Barbaro. Purchased by the Gallerie in 1981, the picture is one of the finest of the official portraits from Strozzi's Venetian visit in late 1630 and early 1631, when, along with Fetti and Liss, the artist brought profound changes to the city's artistic life. Some have identified the sitter as Giovanni Grimani, son of Procurator Antonio, at the time of his appointment in 1636 as a Knight and Ambassador-in-Ordinary to Vienna. But whoever he may be, the subject exudes pride and a keen sense of his own status. This kind of official likeness would become a model for Venice's great portrait painters, from Sebastiano Bombelli to Ghislandi and from Alessandro Longhi to Giambattista Tiepolo himself.

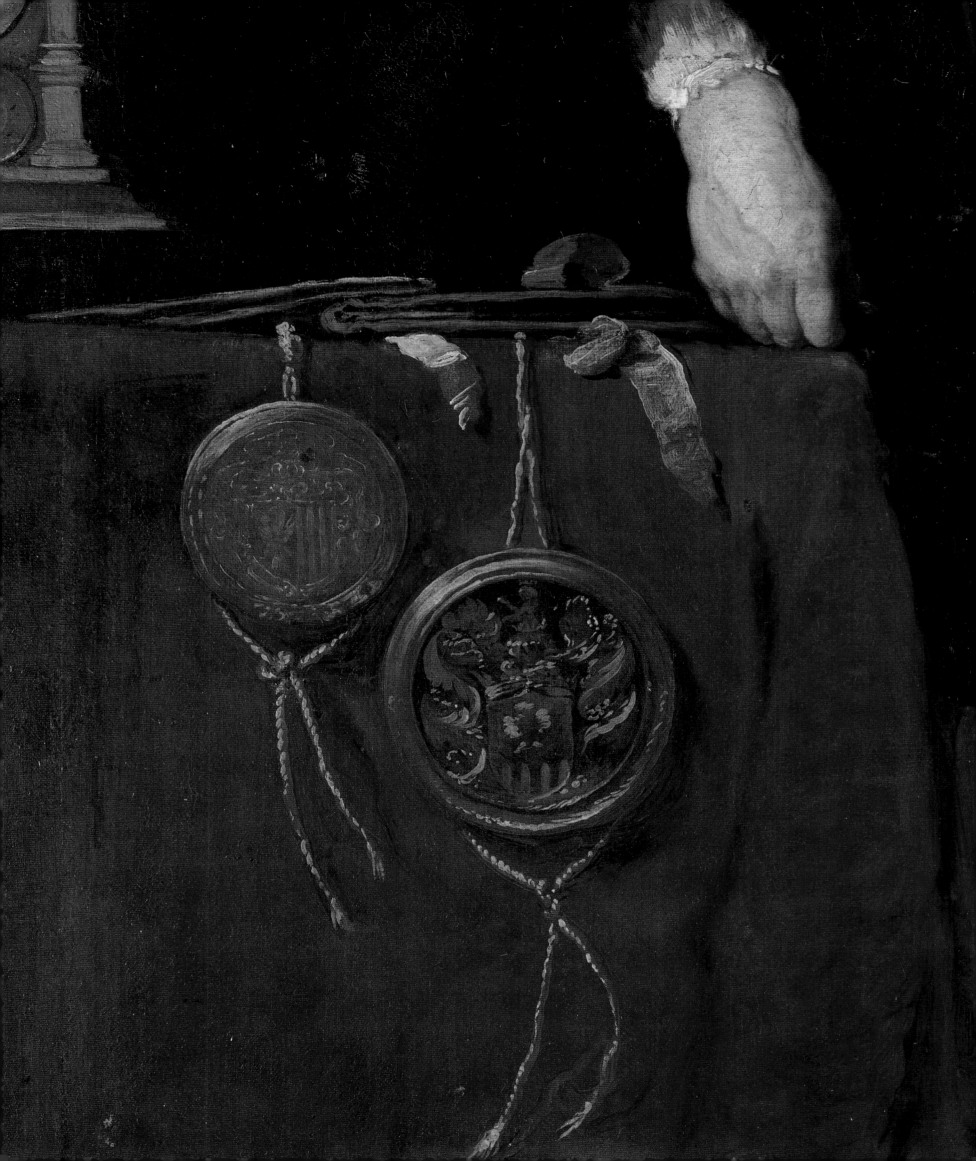

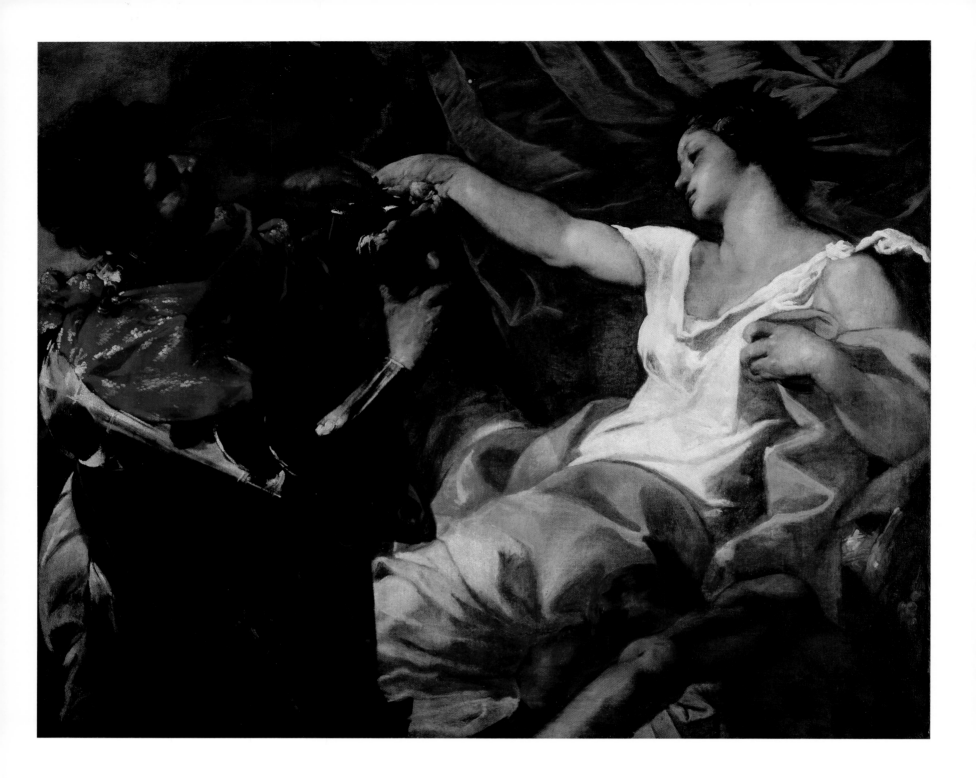

FRANCESCO MAFFEI   119

Vicenza, 1605—Padua, 1660
Mythological Scene
Oil on canvas, 52 x 64" (cat. no 1341)
Last restored 1968

By virtue of their affinities with works in Trento and in the Accademia dei Lincei in Rome, this painting and its companion piece (ill. no. 120) appear to date from the 1650s. They were in Budapest until the beginning of the 20th century, after which the Gallerie acquired them in 1968 from Katherine L. Gonusz of Miami Beach, Florida. The pictures exemplify residual Mannerism surviving in the fully Baroque form that characterizes so much of this artist's style, the consequence of his training in Vicenza.

Although the story is not clear, the figures in the foreground may allude to the amours of Venus and Mars, while the dark figure in the background could be Mercury, with Vulcan as the ominous grotesque seen under Venus' garments. Structured along divergent diagonals, the composition evinces a powerful sense of theater. The fluid brushwork and the alternation of "shot," velvety colors (as in the whites and pinks of Venus' garments or the red and gold of Mars' cloak) with cooler hues (like those of the armor) reveal how thoroughly Maffei had mastered the innovative painterliness of Fetti, Liss, and Strozzi.

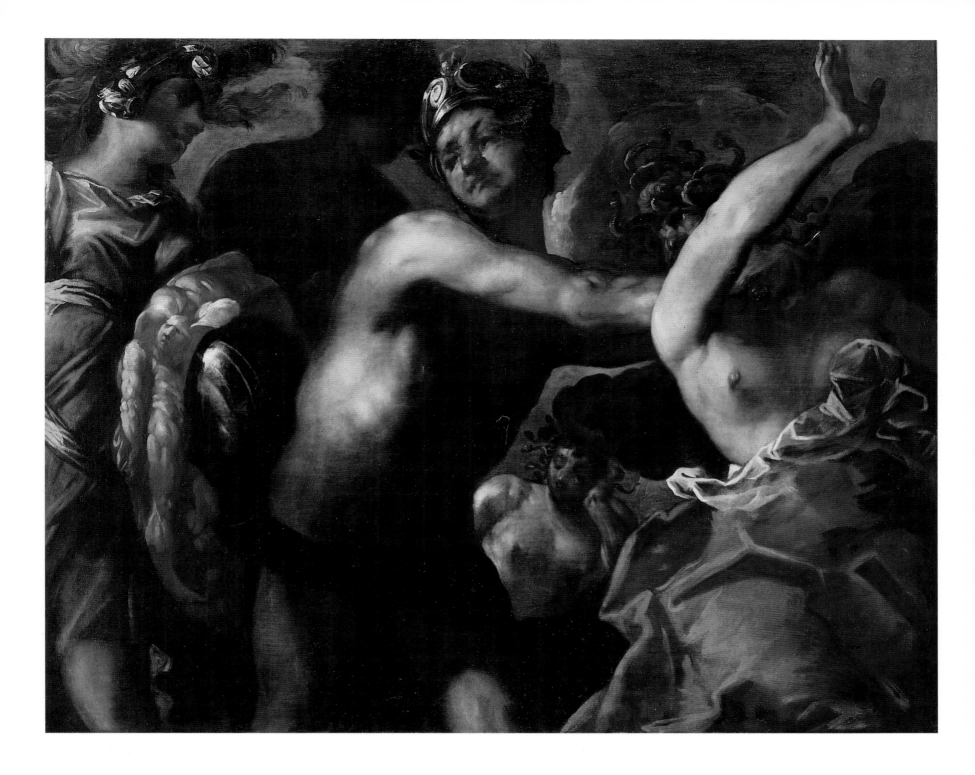

FRANCESCO MAFFEI   120

Vicenza, 1605—Padua, 1660
Perseus Beheading Medusa
Oil on canvas, 52 x 64" (cat. no 1340)
Last restored 1968

In this fine example of his free, whimsical imagination, Maffei staged the sanguinary episode with a flamboyant theatricality of attitude and gesture still charged with Mannerist power, while simultaneously rendering his imagery in rich, materially sensuous color, and so full-bodied as to seem compressed within the space of a rectangular field.

Florence, 1611—Venice, 1678
The Annunciation
Oil on canvas, 62 x 45" (cat. no. 1329)
Last restored 1959

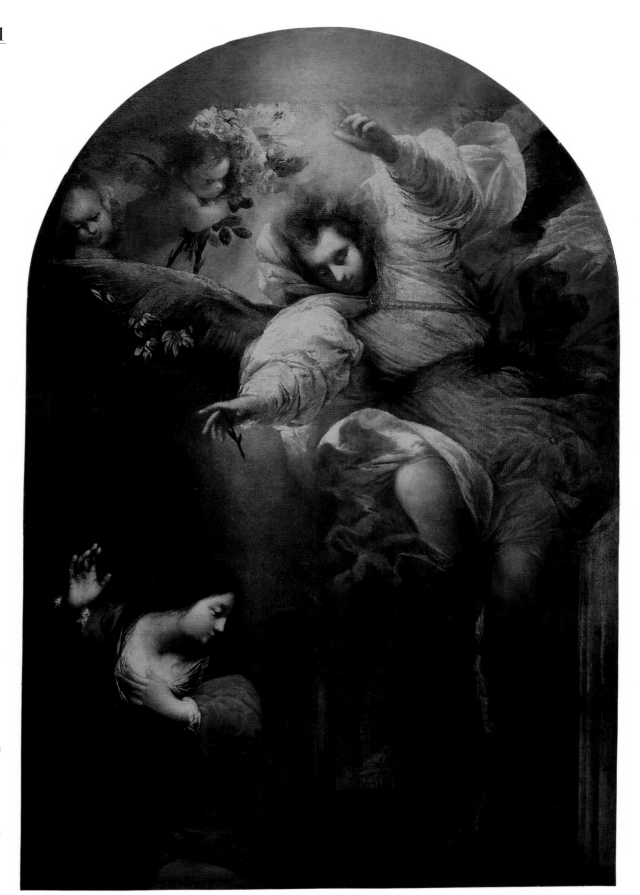

Mentioned at the beginning of the 19th century as in the Church of Santa Caterina, by then State-owned, this painting arrived at the Gallerie only in 1945. It may be the work that Boschini (1664) located in the Church of San Luca, possibly rejected by those who commissioned it in the late 1640s as too innovative. And indeed the canvas does repudiate the conventional iconography of the period. As a result of the latest restoration, the picture has recovered its rounded-headed format, which had been arbitrarily reduced to a rectangle, a process that also sacrificed a strip along the lower edge. Now, we have a better sense of what the original work was like.

The great angel, radiant with diffused light, suddenly appears in a whirlwind of flying hair and drapery, high above the foreground figure of Mary, who leans forward in a way that highlights her womanhood, at the same time that it risked violating the canons of contemporary good taste. Even while evoking such Tuscan masters as Furini and the Matteo Rosselli circle, thus reminding us of the artist's early training, the painterly warmth and delicacy of the palette seen here suggest how profoundly Mazzoni had been influenced by his Venetian experience.

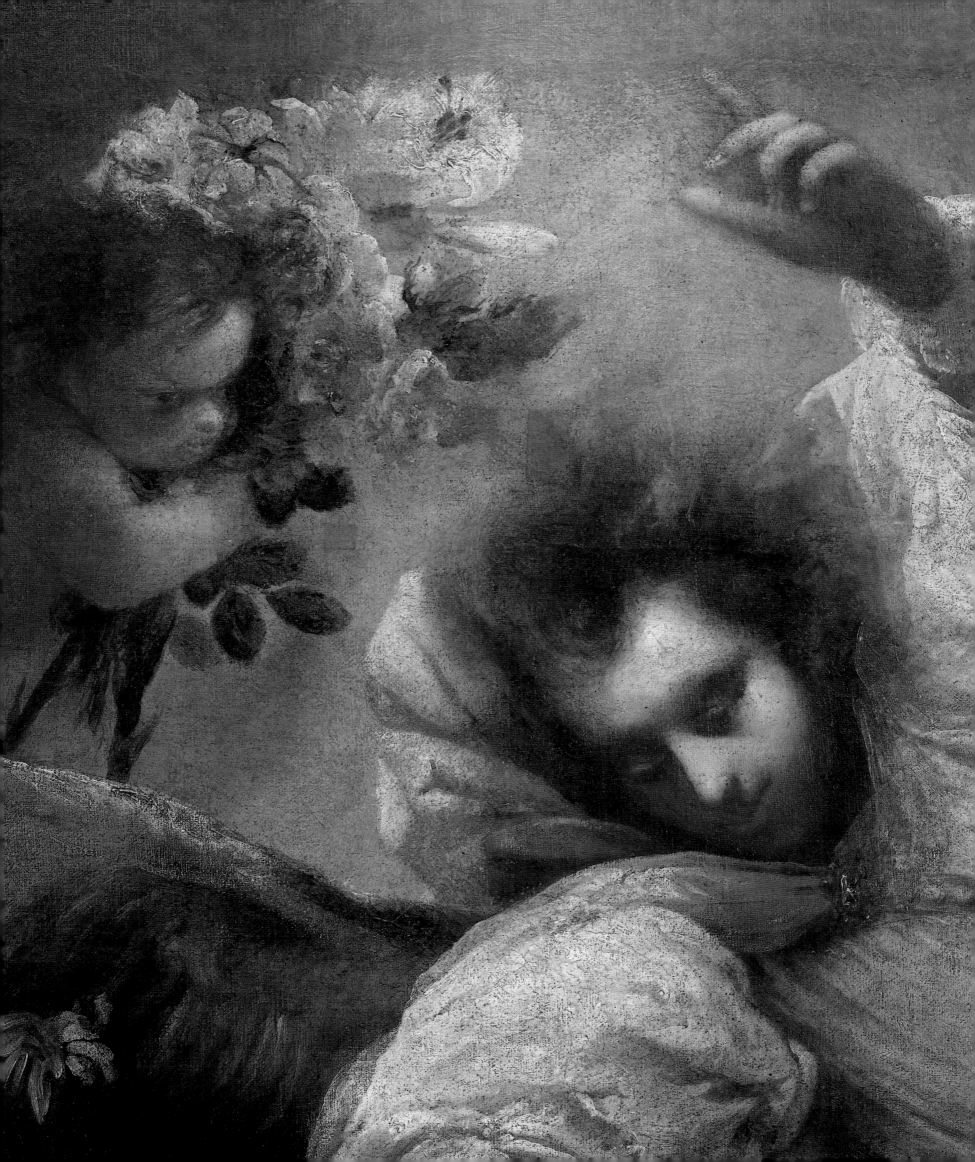

Naples, 1634-1705
The Crucifixion of Saint Peter
Oil on canvas, 78 x 103" (cat. no. 751)
Last restored 1984

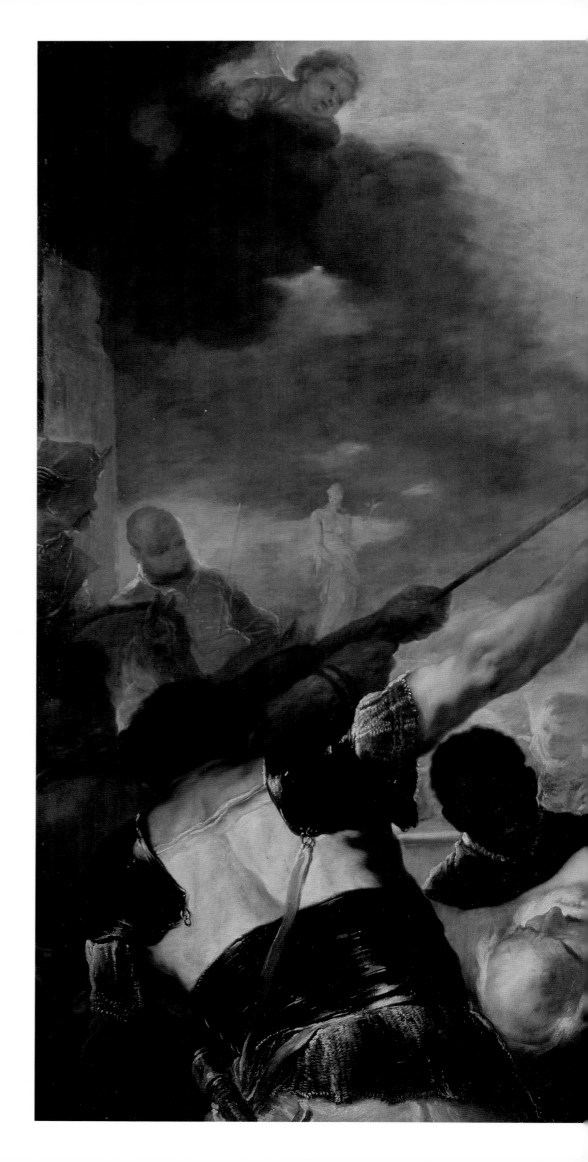

Although considered apocryphal, a signature
appears in the lower left zone of this painting:
L. GIORDANO F. 1962. The Gallerie acquired
Giordano's *Crucifixion of Saint Peter* in 1910
through the agency of Venice's *Ufficio
esportazione*, or "Office of Export Control."

At a younger moment in his career, Giordano
had also addressed the same subject in a
version now in the Church of Saint François
Xavier. Meanwhile, the work seen here has
generally been assigned to the late 1650s.
Since the last restoration, however, it seems
clear that whatever the influence from Ribera
on the earlier painting, this eventually
dissipated in Giordano's own vaporous
luminosity and vibrant, painterly way of
generating forms and composition. To achieve
such effects, he had absorbed and
reinterpreted the Roman experience of Pietro
da Cortona, Caravaggism, and, in a highly
personal synthesis, the art of the great
Venetians—Titian, Veronese, and Tintoretto—
as well as Rubens, all of which suggests that
Giordano painted the *Crucifixion of Saint
Peter* at a date much later than formerly
thought. Paintings like this one would prove
crucial for the dissemination of the Rococo
throughout Italy and Europe.

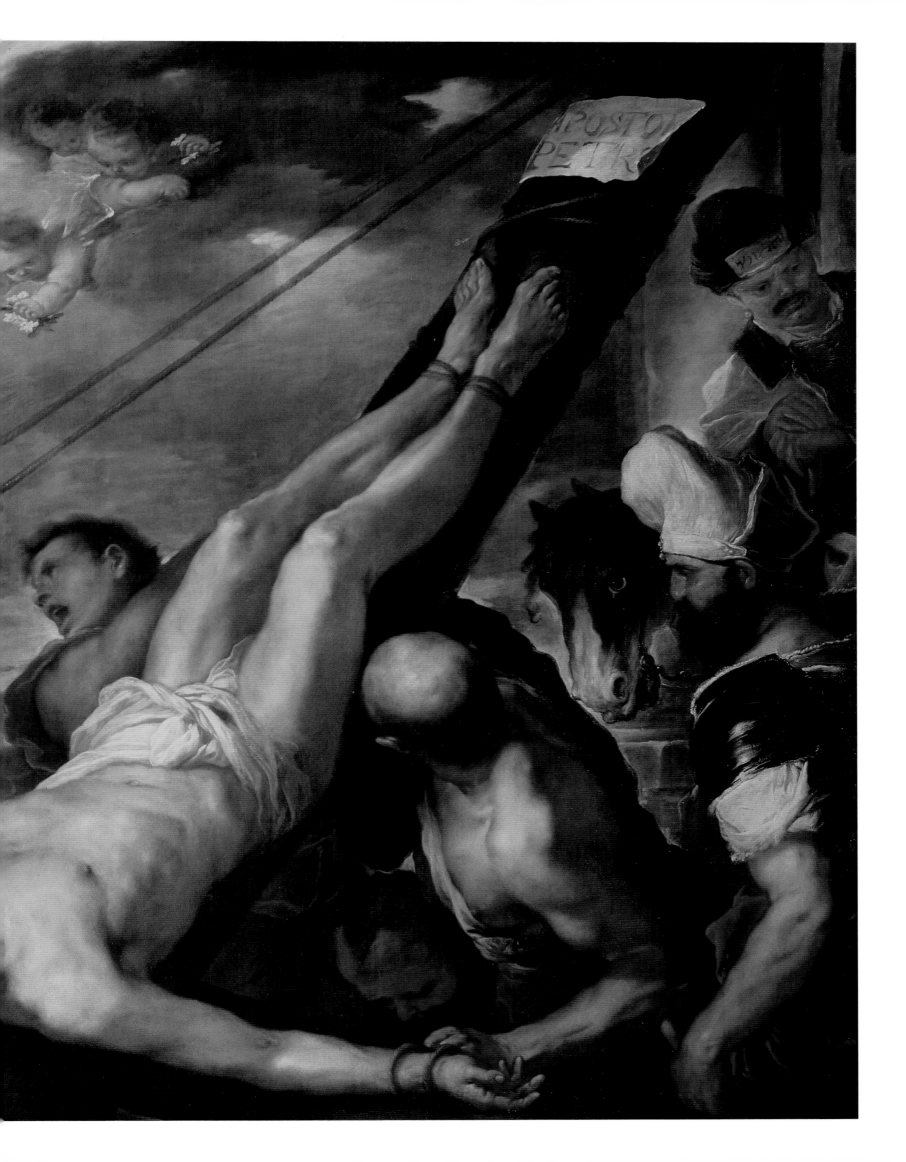

Bergamo, 1655-1743
Portrait of Count Giovanni Battista Vailetti
Oil on canvas, 90 x 55" (cat. no. 778)

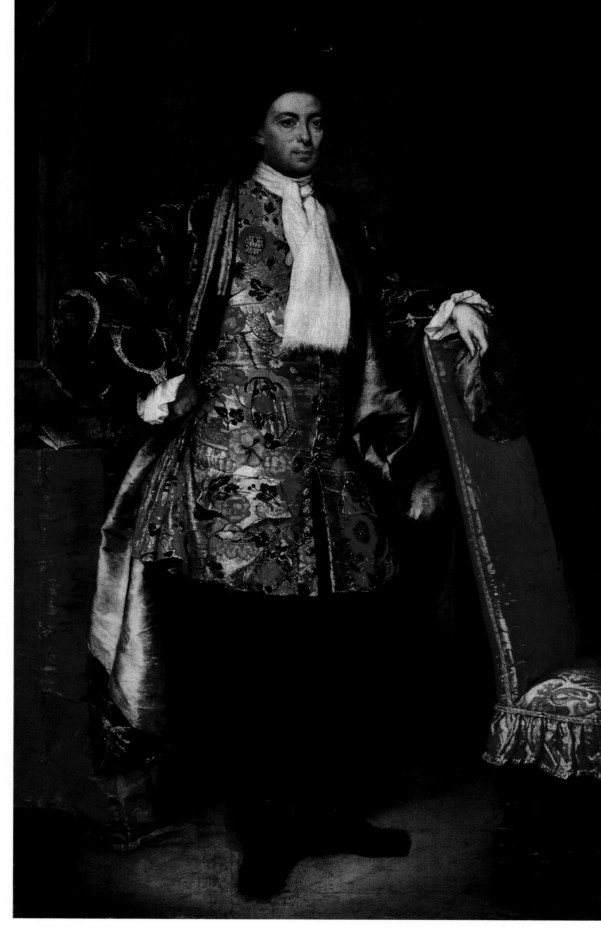

Acquired in 1912 from A. Olivotti, through the Office of Export Control in Florence, this painting once belonged to Countess Rosa Piatti Lochis, whose family had owned it since, at least, the mid-19th century. The portrait, which dates from around 1710, has been rightly described as a "still life of precious fabrics." Perhaps because of his Lombard origins, Ghislandi worked very much against the grain of the formal, frivolous qualities characteristic of international trends in contemporary portraiture. He shows us Count Vailetti in the intimacy of his study, splendidly but elegantly clad, the image manifestly realistic in intention, despite its idealization, and as rigorously rendered as a medieval illumination.

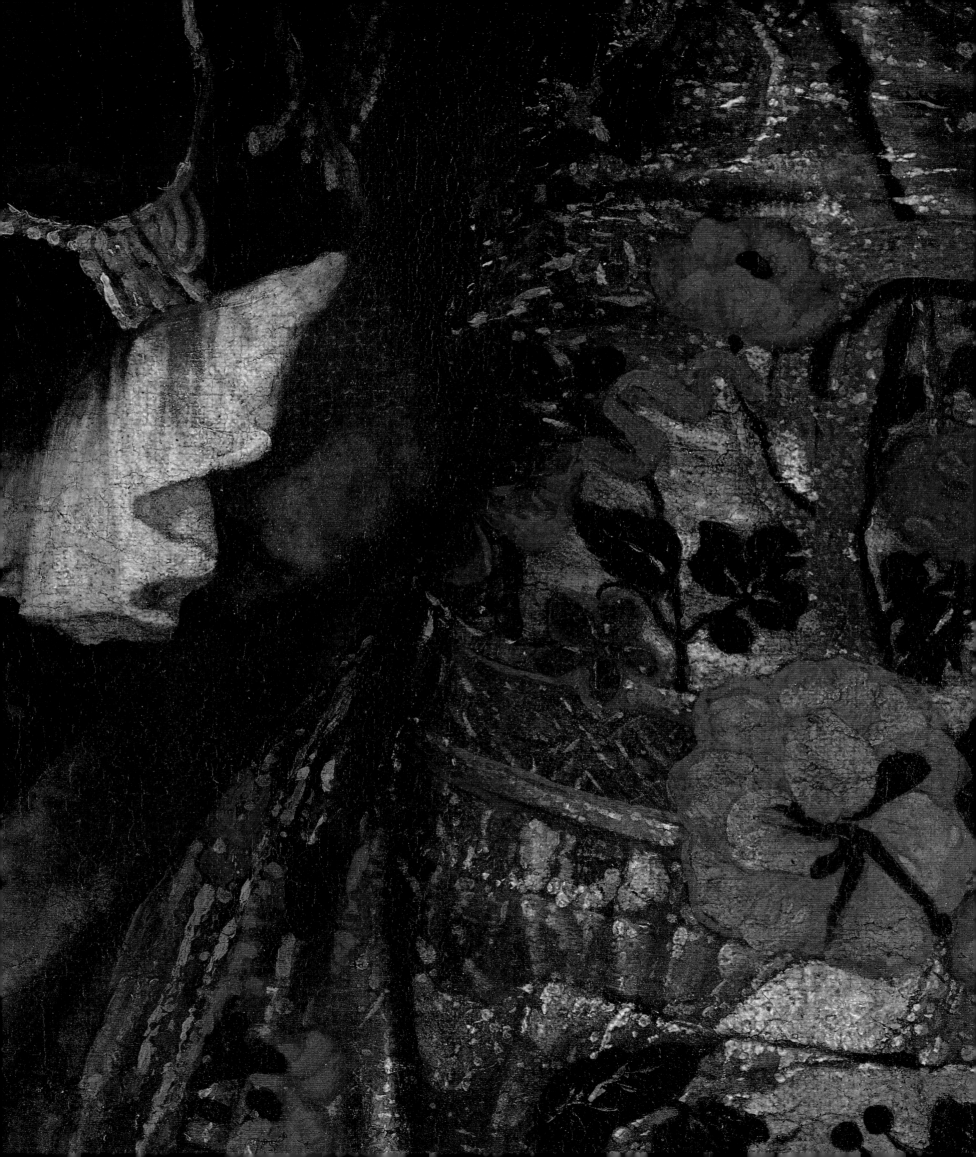

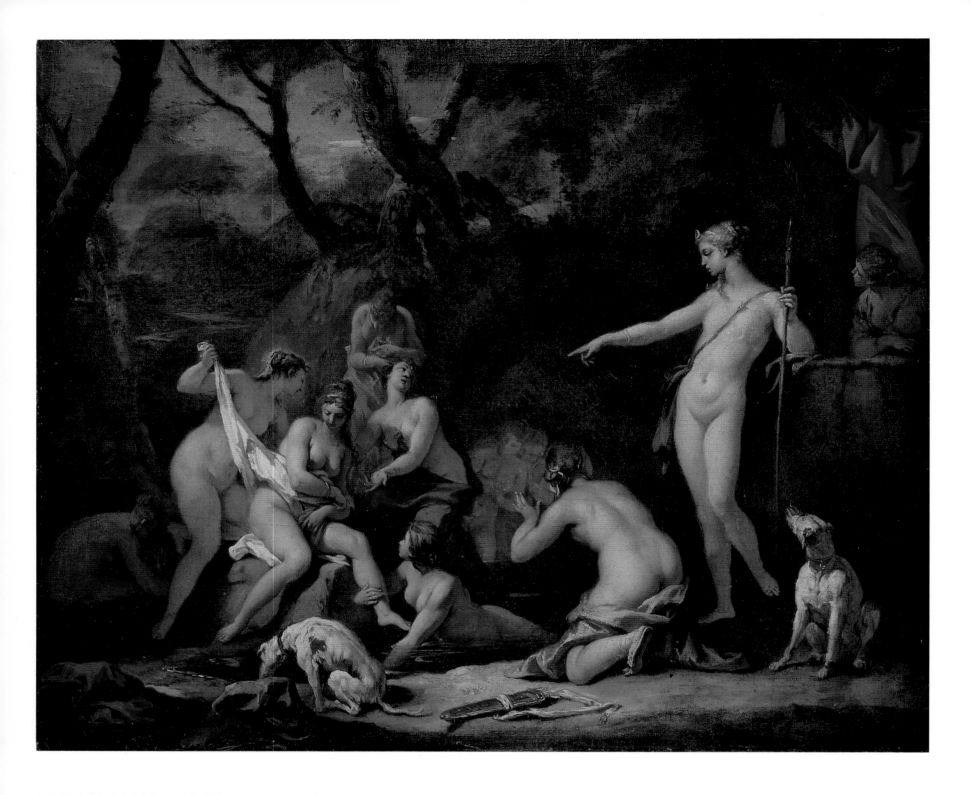

SEBASTIANO RICCI   124

Belluno, 1659—Venice, 1734
Diana and Callisto
Oil on canvas, 30 x 25" (cat. no. 1383)

From a private collection in London, Sebastiano's *Diana and Callisto* entered the Contini Bonacossi collection in Florence, whence Hermann Goering acquired the painting in 1941 and shipped it to Germany. After Rodolfo Siviero recovered the work in

1948, it remained at the Pitti in Florence until 1988, when the Gallerie finally took possession, as the *Consiglio Superiore* had intended from the start.

The painting narrates a passage from Ovid's *Metamorphoses* (442-453) in which Diana, surrounded by nymphs, accuses Callisto of being pregnant with a son by Jove. Because of its stylistic closeness to Sebastiano's Burlington House cycle, particularly *Diana and Her Nymphs Bathing*, the painting reproduced here would seem to have come from the artist's London period (1712-16). No full preparatory drawing is known for the work, but compositional studies can be detected in a drawing now at the Royal Library, Windsor

(no. 7188). And these seem even more apt when considered in relation to the grisaille medallion in the Pitti (1707-08) and a sheet with female figures in the Gallerie (R.96).

The palette has a neo-Veronesian flavor, while the landscape in the background accords quite clearly with similar exercises by Marco Ricci. Nor is the painting without a touch of influence from France, whose painting Sebastiano could have encountered during his brief sojourn in Paris while traveling home from London. However, all these diverse implications resolve themselves in the artist's luminary refinement, in his masterful equilibrium, and in the emotional undercurrent subtly charging the entire scene.

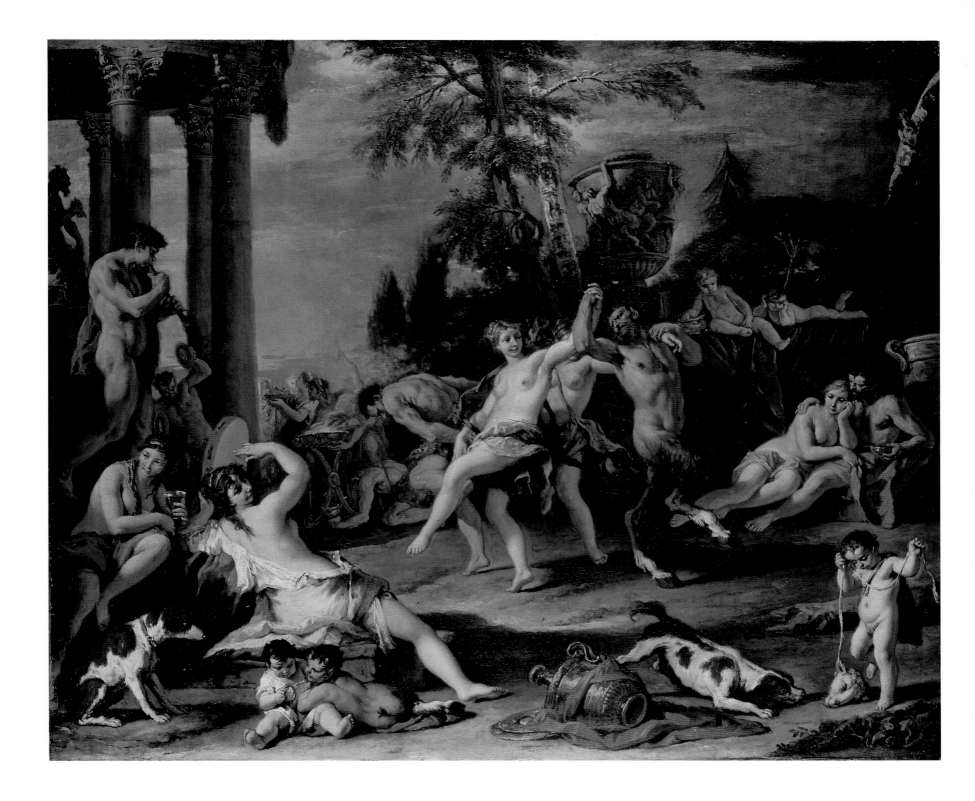

SEBASTIANO RICCI   125

Belluno, 1659—Venice, 1734
Bacchanal in Honor of Pan
Oil on canvas, 33 x 40" (cat. no. 1384)

From the Detsy collection, Sebastiano's *Bacchanal in Honor of Pan* found its way, in 1884, to the Voss collection in Wiesbaden and then to the Barsanti collection in Rome. Illegally exported to Linz for the museum that Hitler had begun to form, the painting was recovered in 1954 and deposited at the Pitti until 1988, when the Gallerie gained possession of it.

There are several preparatory studies in the Royal Library, Windsor (nos. 7171, 7177), and a sketch for the dancers in the Gallerie (R.46).

However, the Royal Library's drawing of the entire composition (no. 7170) looks more like a copy of the finished picture preparatory to an engraving.

The Watteau-like touches make the painting datable around 1716, after Sebastiano had passed through France while returning from London. Now he could treat the mythological fable with an unusually felicitous palette and a typically joyous Rococo grace, while also bringing great conviction to a scene of almost panicked abandon to music and dance.

GIOVAN ANTONIO PELLEGRINI 127

Venice, 1675-1741
Allegory of Painting
Oil on canvas, 57 x 53" (cat. no. 1319)
Last restored 1959

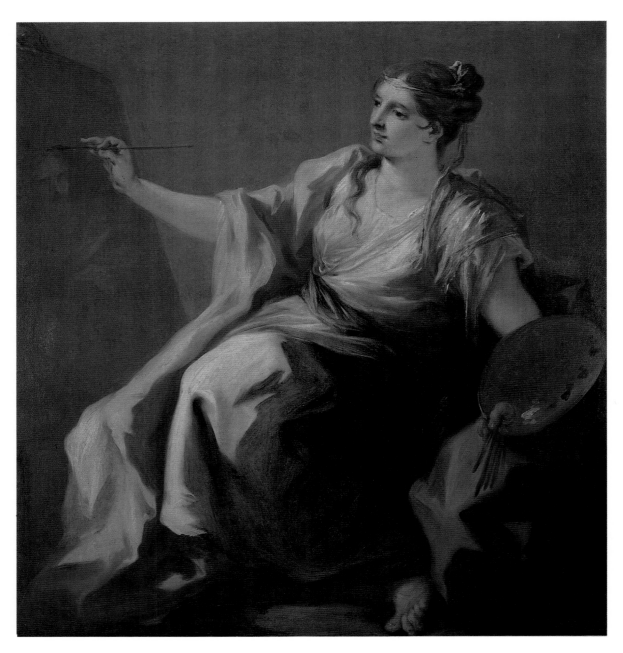

The Gallerie acquired this personified *Allegory of Painting* in 1959 from Count Alvise Giustiniani, along with its pendant *Sculpture* (ill. no. 128).

The two pictures, dating from the late 1720s, typify the aesthetic personality of an artist who gave the international Rococo one of its leading exponents. Thus, while Pellegrini's figures remain solidly sculpturesque and firmly planted in deep space, his forms have nonetheless begun to dissolve into a liquid, vaporous colorism, a quality that today is unfortunately obscured by filtering varnish. Even so, enough delicate pastel comes through to remind us of the artist's sister-in-law Rosalba Carriera, who in turn owed much to Pellegrini for the airy grace and elegant subtlety of her pastels, qualities that made Carriera one of the most commissioned portraitists in 18th-century Europe.

GIOVAN ANTONIO PELLEGRINI 128

Venice, 1675-1741
Allegory of Sculpture
Oil on canvas, 57 x 53" (cat. no. 1320)
Last restored 1959

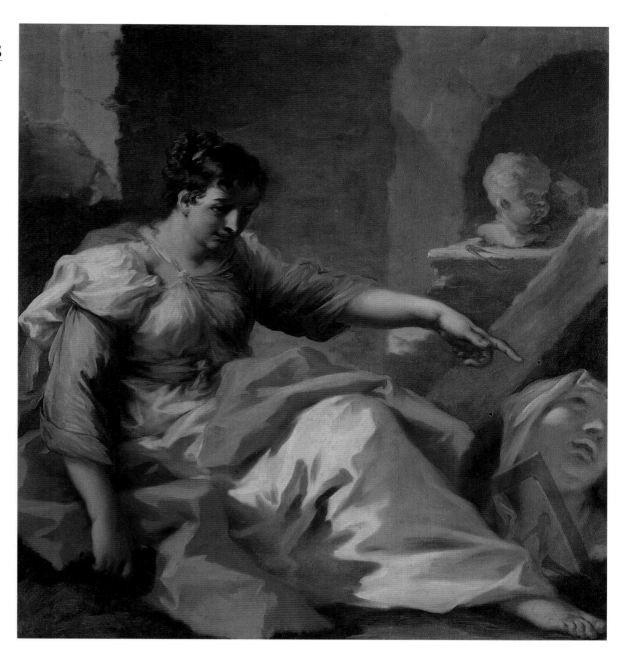

Like the pendant entitled *Allegory of Painting* (ill. no. 127), the personified *Sculpture* exemplifies the refined painterliness cultivated by Pellegrini.

The female subject, posed diagonally in space and constructed with buttery, light-filled impasto, points an elegant, attenuated finger towards her attributes: compasses, square, chisel, a block of marble waiting to be roughed out, and several finished busts.

While all this makes Pellegrini a close aesthetic cousin of Sebastiano Ricci, who undoubtedly exercised a powerful influence over the younger artist, the latter achieved a profoundly independent identity through not only the vaporous luminosity of his touch but also the fluidity of his brush, qualities that helped to make "his painting one of 18th-century Europe's most felicitous and serene artistic expressions."

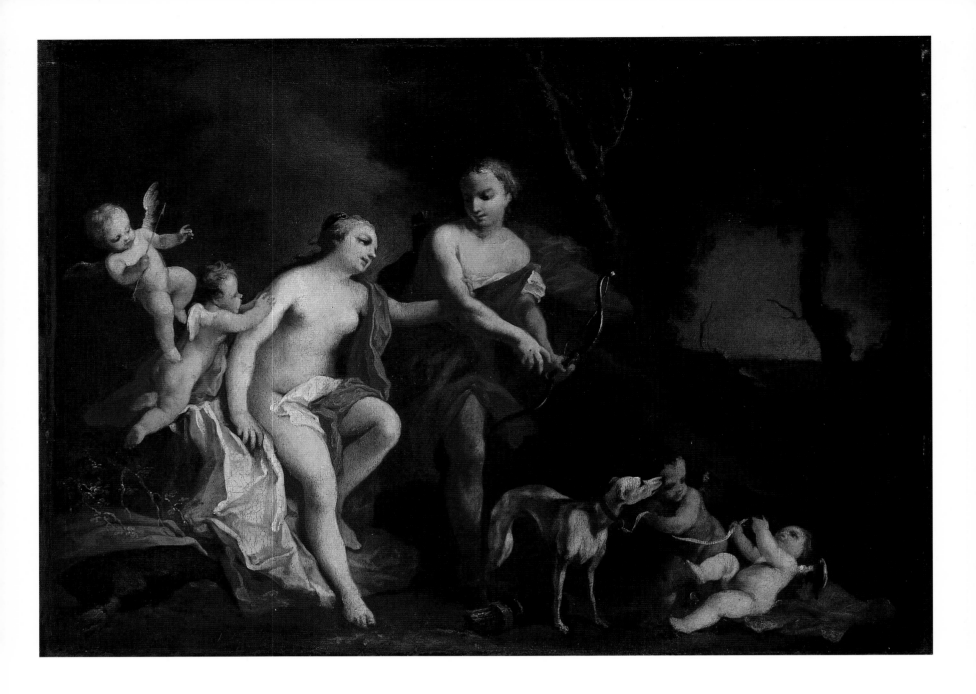

JACOPO AMIGONI 129

Naples, 1682—Madrid, 1752
Venus and Adonis
Oil on canvas, 22 x 30" (cat. no. 743)
Last restored 1962

The Gallerie acquired this work in 1910 from the Milanese dealer Antonio Grandi. Amigoni, a master of Continental Rococo, avoided large-scale compositions, sacred or secular, in favor of minor mythologies on which he could lavish his airy grace, subtle delicacy, and playful way with pastel colors.

Here, the scene concerns the love of Venus and Adonis at the point of the latter's departure, a subject so dear to the artist that he rendered it several times.

Compared with the other versions, such as that in a Venetian private collection or another in the Staatsgalerie of Schleisseim, the painting seen here is notable for the intense luminosity of its figures set against a dark background, all of which recalls late-17th-century Neapolitan landscape painting as well as the seductive interpretations of Marco Ricci.

A pendant *Bacchus and Ariadne* is in a private collection in Zurich.

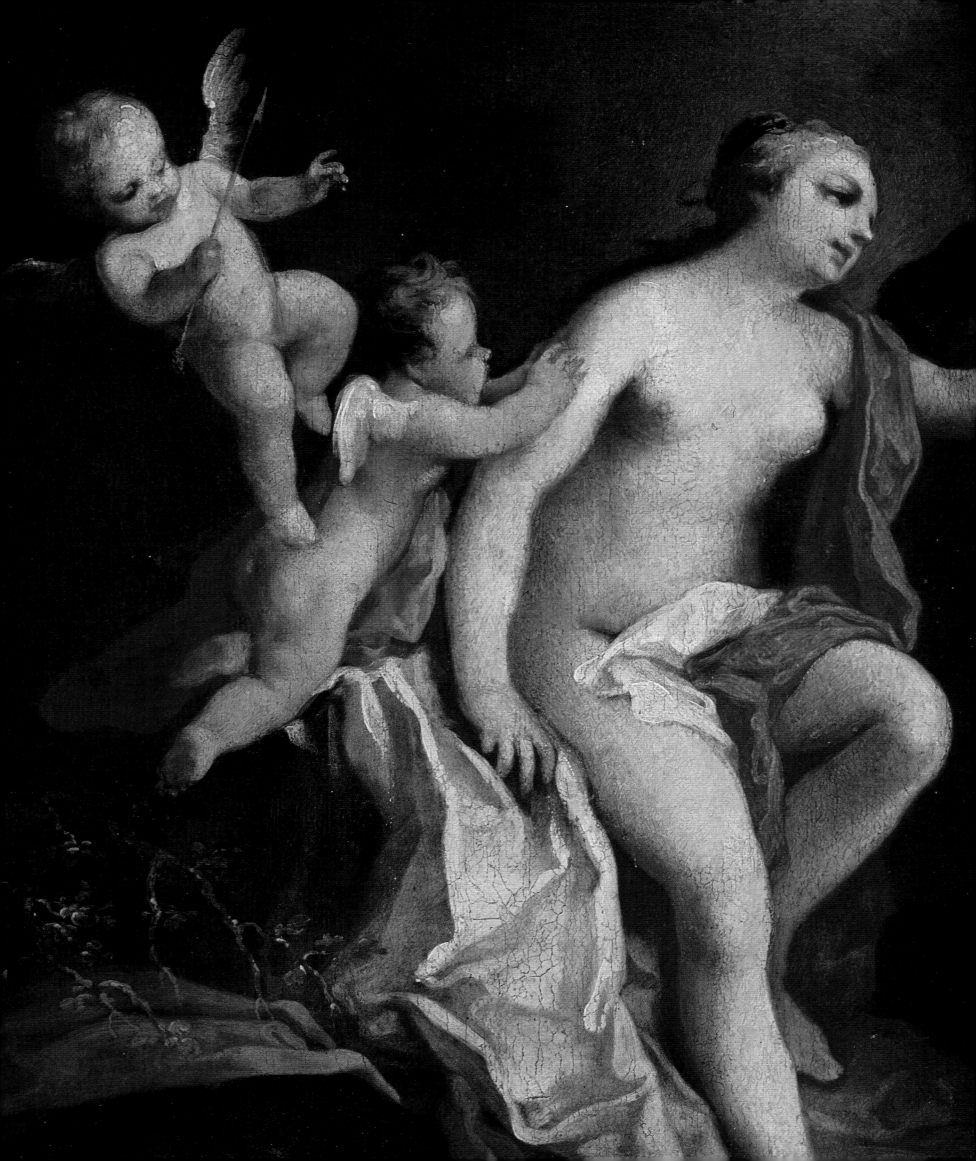

Venice, 1675-1758
Portrait of a Little Girl with a Ciambella
Pastel on blue paper, 14 x 11" (cat. no. 444)
Last restored 1986 (special conservation)

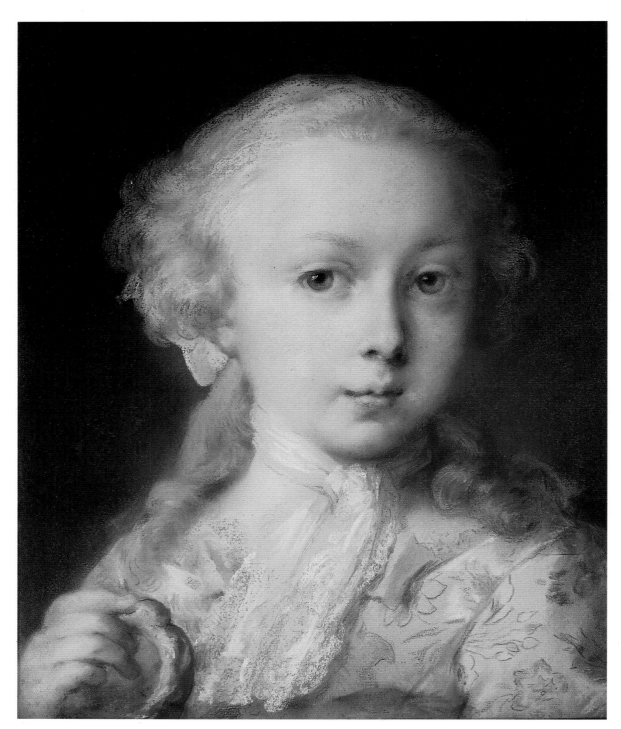

One of a group of ten pastels, six of them undoubtedly autographic, that came to the Gallerie in 1888 at the death of Vincenzo Omoboni Astori, by the terms of the donor's bequest made in 1876. The group consists mainly of portraits of French members of Astori's maternal family, the Le Blonds, who held various diplomatic appointments in Venice and Milan.

Astori's will speaks simply of "my ten pastel pictures by Rosalba," but Cecchini, secretary of the Accademia, while drawing up an inventory, dated February 22, 1878, preparatory to taking possession of the portraits, provided more information about the sitters and their place in the Le Blond family. The girl in the present pastel and the boy in the next one were the children of "Mr. Le Blond, maternal grandfather of the testator, Consul-General of France in Milan." Rosalba noted in her diary for May 13, 1725: "I began a portrait of the daughter of the French Ambassador," and on July 22 she added: "received from the French Ambassador a snuff box with ten zecchini." This was probably in payment for the work seen here, an inferior version of which is owned by the Museo Glauco Lombardi in Parma.

Cunningly adept with pastels, which she had specially prepared for her in Rome by an English friend, Christian Cole, Rosalba built up the picture in successive layers of soft color, virtually without underdrawing, as reflectographic analysis seems to confirm. The blue support lends her images an especially luminous tonality. The cool palette and pliant technique responded admirably to the delicate grace of the Le Blond child, enabling the artist to work with consummate sensitivity in describing the subject's elaborate costume, the red bow in her hair, her lace collar, and the *bussolà* (doughnut), a typical Venetian sweetmeat, clutched in the small hand.

ROSALBA CARRIERA 131

Venice, 1675-1758
Portrait of a Boy
Pastel on blue paper, 14 x 11" (cat. no. 445)
Last restored 1991 (special conservation)

Also part of the Astori legacy of 1888, this portrait must have constituted a pendant to the preceding one, since the two images share not only size and style but also composition. Still, Cecchini alone speaks expressly of the Le Blond children's portraits, whereas Rosalba makes no mention of this one in her diary, though she does refer generally to portraits of other family members. Besides payments recorded for the portraits of the Consul and his wife, there is one of 50 zecchini disbursed by the Consul to the painter on January 24, 1727, which, however unexplained, was obviously in satisfaction of work done. It seems probable, then, that the boy's portrait was executed at about the same time as his sister's, in 1726-27, and finished in the latter year.

In this picture too, the melting chromatic impasto brings out, with serene immediacy, the gentle, limpid image of the child in all his immaculate elegance.

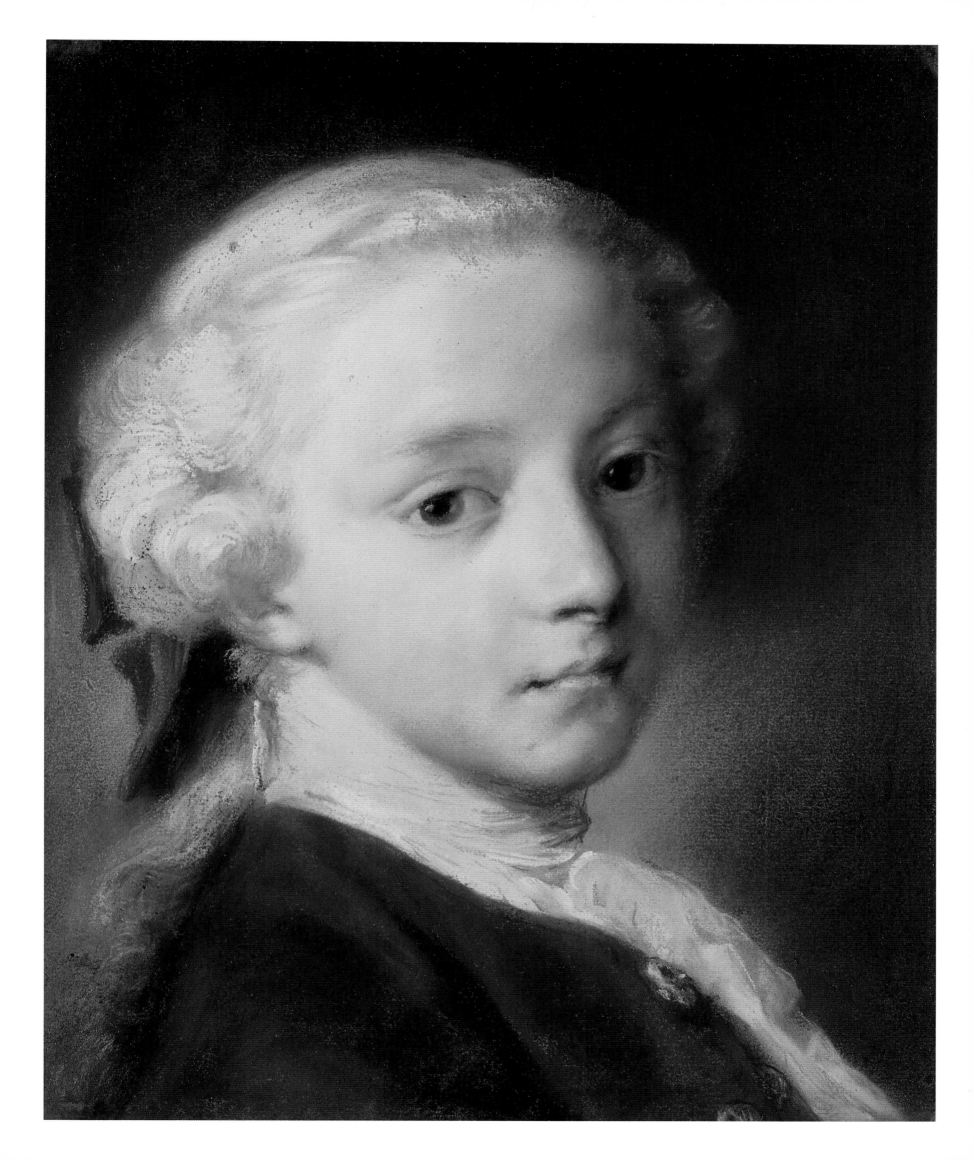

Venice, 1675-1758
Portrait of the French Consul Le Blond
Pastel on blue paper, 23 x 22" (cat. no. 490)
Last restored 1986 (special conservation)

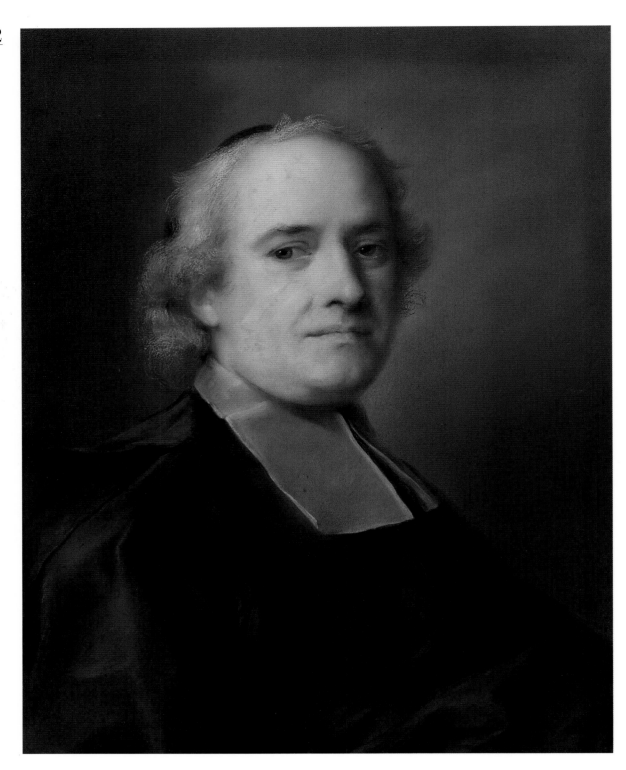

Also among the pastels bequeathed to the Gallerie in 1888 by Vincenzo Omoboni Astori (see ill. no. 130), the subject of this portrait, according to the inventory drawn up in 1878 by Cecchini, secretary of the Accademia, is "Mr. Le Blond, maternal grandfather of the testator, French Consul-General in Milan."

Of the three Le Blond brothers, one, a priest, served as secretary to Cardinal Polignac (see ill. no. 133), another filled the office of French Consul-General in Milan, and the third

performed similar duties in Venice, where he commissioned the portrait seen here. On April 19, 1727, Rosalba wrote in her diary: "Began the Consul's portrait." This must refer to one of the Le Blonds, presumably the diplomat *en poste* in Venice, inasmuch as on April 19, 1727, the artist added that she had received from the French Consul "60 zecchini for the Cardinal" and "16 for himself." A date around 1727 is supported by stylistic consistency with the children's portraits (see ill.

nos. 130, 131) and with those of Sebastiano and Marco Ricci (Staatliche Kunsthalle, Karlsruhe). The work does justice to the sitter's good nature even as it shrewdly takes account of his status, all of which translates into pastel the exemplary portraiture of Bombelli and Cassana, while the sureness of Rosalba's touch and the palette, with its soft, smoky blues, grays, and browns, yield a realism that, even though purified, comes still closer to the truth.

Venice, 1675-1758
Portrait of Cardinal Melchior de Polignac
Pastel on blue paper, 23 x 18" (cat. no. 485)
Last restored 1986 (special conservation)

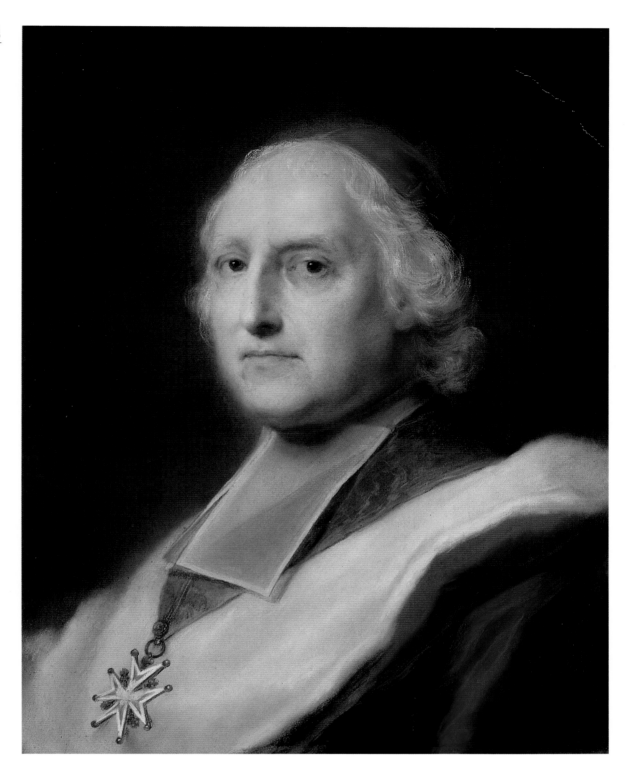

This portrait too came to the Gallerie in 1888 as part of the Astori bequest (see ill. no. 130), which Cecchini inventoried in 1878 and made this relevant note: "Prelate, half-length, Knight of the Holy Spirit, in a red skull cap, a friend of the testator's great-uncle." Later the subject was identified as Cardinal Melchior de Polignac, for a number of years the envoy to Rome from the King of France. During this time *abbé* Denis Le Blond served him as assistant. While in Paris, Carriera was visited by Le Blond and Polignac on more than one occasion, and the latter commissioned several works from the Venetian artist, sometimes paying her through Le Blond.

This portrait was probably executed in 1732, when Polignac was on his way back to Paris after his posting to Rome. In a letter to Rosalba of July 23, 1729, Denis Le Blond told her that the Cardinal intended to "pass through Venice for the express purpose of having his [portrait] from your own hand." In 1732, Felicita Sartori, Rosalba's pupil, worked on the portrait of a Cardinal, probably Polignac, indicating that the artist's workshop had indeed been involved with this commission. Finally, the Parisian collector Jean de Julienne cites a precise date for the portrait, February 14, 1732, in a letter written to the artist: "I have seen the portrait of Msr. the Cardinal de Polignac which you sent . . . ." Thus, after commencing the portrait in 1732,

Carriera finished and dispatched it to the sitter two years later. At the death of the Cardinal, the portrait evidently passed to Denis Le Blond, his collaborator, and from him to the Astori. With its stylistic closeness to Hyacinthe Rigaud's 1715 portrait of Polignac, now in the Louvre, the work under review reflects Carriera's interest in contemporary French portraiture. The fine head and concentrated expression evince strength but also pride, which not even the soft, impastoed color can mollify. One of the very best psychological likenesses made in the 1730s, the picture takes Carriera—the most cosmopolitan of Venetian portrait painters—"to the very threshold of the Enlightenment."

Venice, 1675-1758
Portrait of an Old Lady
Pastel on blue paper, 20 x 16" (cat. no. 489)
Last restored 1986 (special conservation)

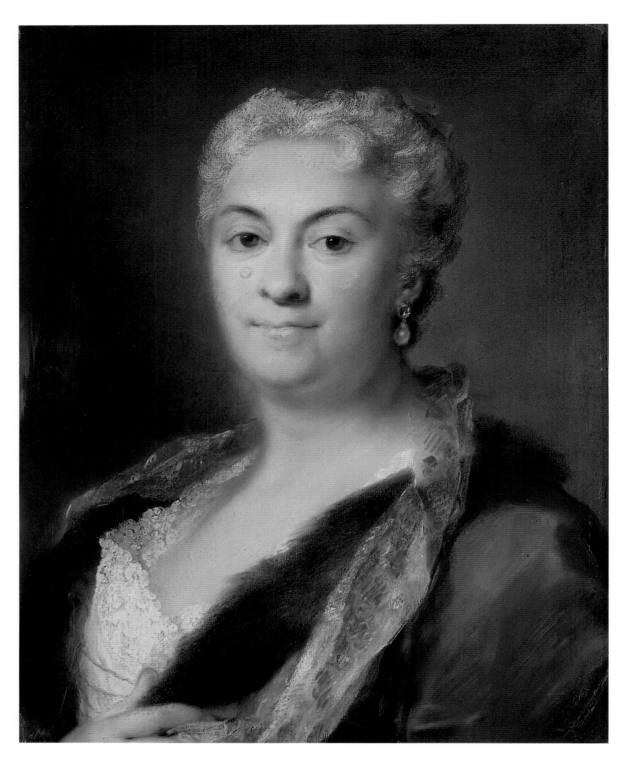

The Gallerie acquired this picture in 1816 through a bequest from Girolamo Molin, whose catalogue characterized the work thus: "Portrait of a Matron with a Wart on Her Cheek." It was long, and erroneously, thought to be a self-portrait. Moreover, the attempt to identify the sitter as Anna Carlotta Gauthier de Loiserelle, wife of the painter Jacques Aved (1702-66), could not be sustained in the light of her known portraits. The work seems to be datable in the mid-1730s by virtue of its closeness to Carriera's portrait of Elisabetta Algarotti Dandolo in the Colloredo Mels collection, Santa Maria la Longa, Udine. Indeed, both pictures evince a cool objectivity on the part of the artist, who succeeded in translating an aristocratic status-consciousness into a kind of serene dignity.

Venice, 1675-1758
Self-Portrait
Pastel on blue paper, 12 x 10" (cat. no. 907)
Last restored 1986 (special conservation)

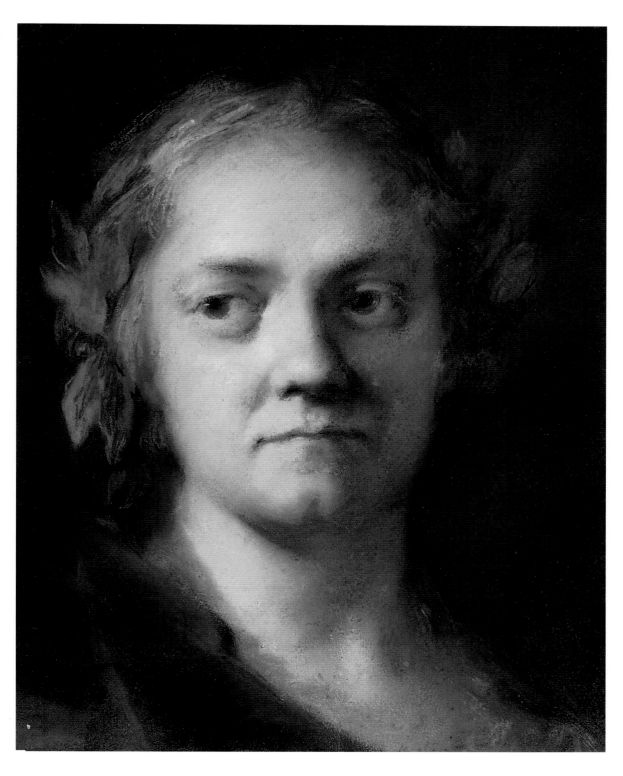

At one time in the collection of the sculptor Dal Zoto, the painting was acquired in 1927 by the so-called Naya, exercising its right of pre-emption. The picture has been securely identified as the self-portrait that, according to Zanetti (1771), Carriera completed a few years before she suffered "a total scrambling of her wits." When asked about the wreath on her head, she replied "that it was the wreath of tragedy, and that Rosalba would end tragically."

The supposed self-portrait once at the Ca' Rezzonico (now lost), formerly regarded as the one cited by Zanetti, has nothing to do with Rosalba, whose features are unequivocally different. On the other hand, it may have portrayed the poetess Luisa Bergalli.

While the work reproduced here resembles the self-portrait in the Royal Collections at Windsor, the features have altered and come to look painfully tired. Stylistic and documentary evidence make it possible to date the picture around 1746. On August 23, 1749, the artist wrote to P.J. Mariette that she had been without sight for three years but had recovered. Then, on January 11, 1851, she wrote him that the blindness was now total and irreversible. As in other late works, Carriera portrayed herself with a solidified grasp of plastic form, as well as with a psychological insight that foreshadowed the drama of her mental and physical decline.

In the inventory of the Manin collection, compiled by P. Edwards and G.M. Sasso on December 6, 1799, we find, among various pictures by Carriera and her circle, entry number 27, "a self-portrait crowned with laurel," which may well be the work now in the Gallerie.

Vienna, 1699—Venice, 1760
Herminia and Vaprino Meet over the Wounded
Body of Tancred
Oil on canvas, 100 x 104" (cat. no. 1387)
Last restored 1970

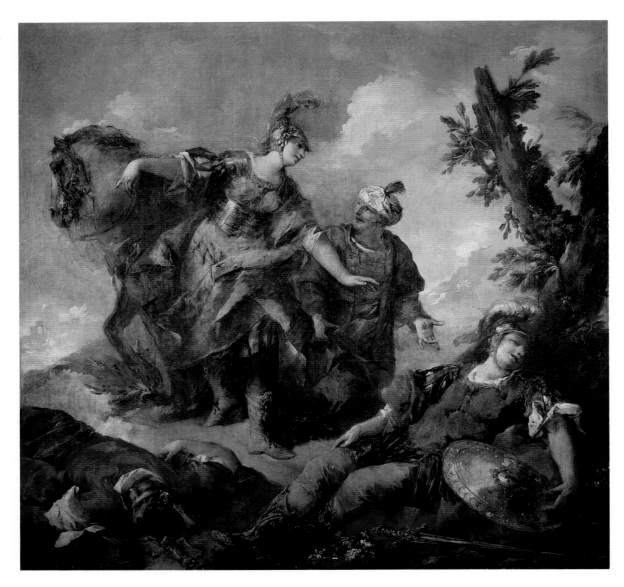

This work probably formed part of a cycle of paintings that originally hung in a villa at Este, a series inspired by Tasso's *Gerusalemme Liberata* in the Albrizzi edition of 1745 with engravings by Giovan Battista Piazzetta. As we know from a letter written by J.C. Goethe and dated February 23, 1740, the cycle took years of effort to complete.

The surviving pictures are *Sophronia Offers Her Life to the Saracen King to Save the Christians* (Ferens Art Gallery, Kingston-Upon-Hull), *Duel between Argante and Tancred* (Museum of Fine Arts, Copenhagen), *Herminia among the Shepherds* and *Carlo and Ubaldo Withstand the Enchantments of Armida* (National Gallery, Washington, D.C.), *Godefroi de Bouillon Summons the Christian*

Princes and *Tancred near the Enchanted Wood with Nymphs* (Neville Orgel, London), and, finally, *Tancred Baptizes Clorinda* (Museum of Fine Arts, Montreal). Around 1829-30, the Earl of Bantry purchased the entire cycle for his house in County Cork.

In 1956, one of his descendants sold *Herminia and Vaprino* to a Dublin dealer, who in turn sold it to the London collector Geoffrey Merton. In 1971, it turned up at Agnew's. Thereafter, by some unknown route, the painting came to figure among those art works recovered during and following the war by Rodolfo Siviero.

In 1988, the Italian government assigned it to the Gallerie.

Herminia and Vaprino narrates Canto XIX of

the *Gerusalemme*, in a manner closely related to Piazzetta's drawing in Turin's Royal Library and the engraving based on it. However, this went no further than the iconography, since Gian Antonio rendered the subject—a fashionable one at the time—with fresh, painterly colorism, sparkling brushwork, and a taste for dramatic composition marked by typical Rococo musicality and grace.

This painting, like the entire cycle, can be dated around 1750-55, when the artist was at the height of his mature powers. Despite an old attribution to Francesco Guardi, *Herminia and Vaprino* is now regarded as entirely from the hand of Gian Antonio, by virtue of its stylistic consistency and its uncompromising quality.

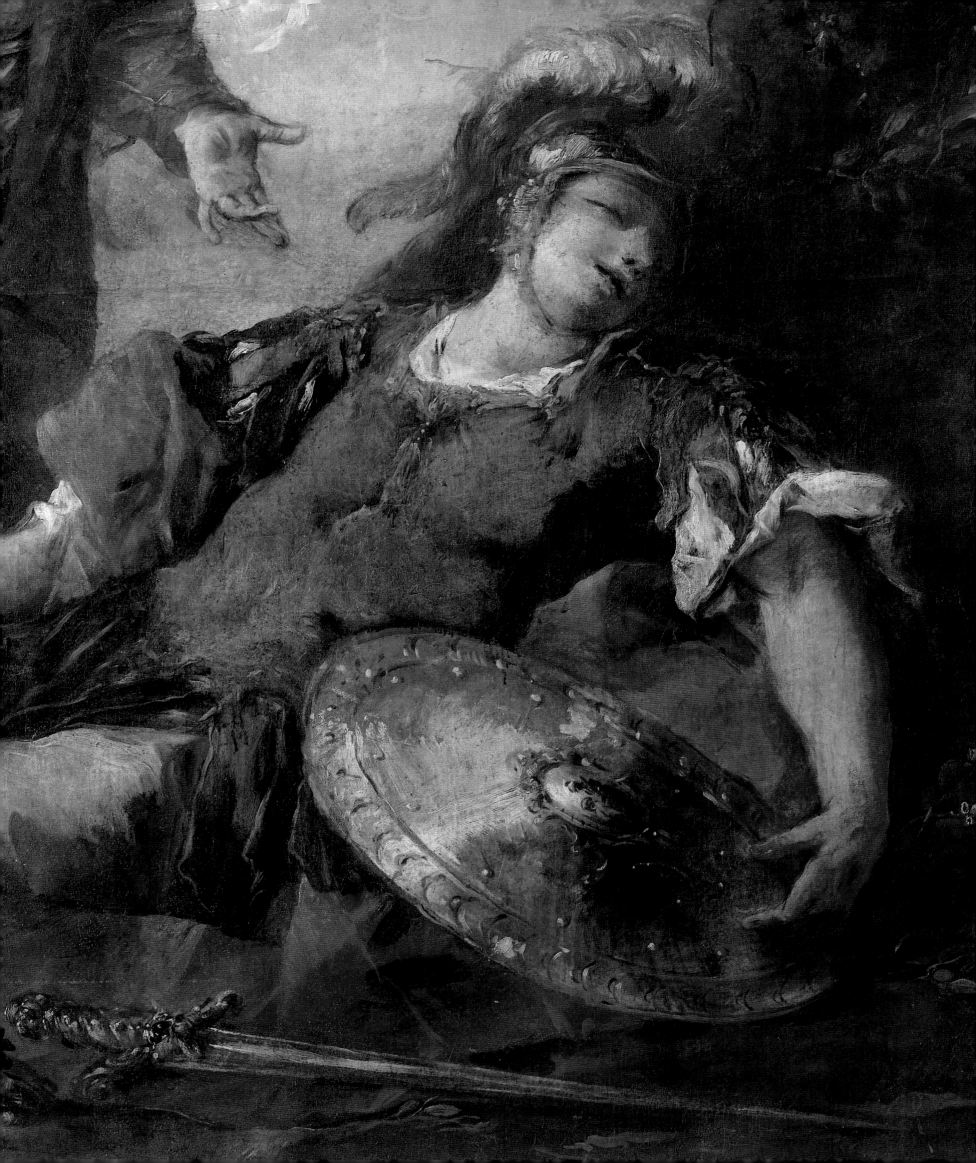

GIAMBATTISTA PIAZZETTA 137

Venice, 1683-1754
Christ Crucified between the Two Thieves
Oil on canvas, 30 x 25" (cat. no. 162)

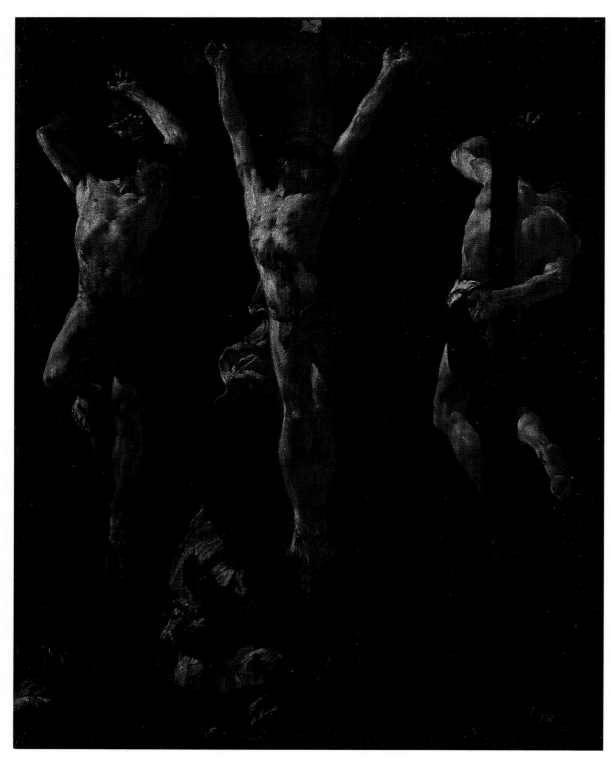

Acquired from the antiquarian Sebastiano Candiani in 1905 and datable to 1710, this canvas counts among the artist's earliest works, realized before he had completely mastered the technique of preparing the support with red ocher and oil.

Too much of the latter undermined the adhesiveness of the paint surface, which has flaked off and exposed the ocher ground, now turned a brownish color. Based on a composition by Rubens, the work evinces stunning virtuosity in the handling of the three nude bodies, their torsioned attitudes the fruit of long and close anatomical study.

The iconography of Christ with his arms stretched upwards is rare in Venetian art, although a precedent exists in a *Crucifixion* by Langetti.

However, Piazzetta addressed the theme in several different works, another one of which the Gallerie also own (cat. no. 809).

GIAMBATTISTA PIAZZETTA   138

Venice, 1683-1754
The Fortune-teller
Oil on canvas, 6 x 46" (cat. no. 483)
Last restored 1983

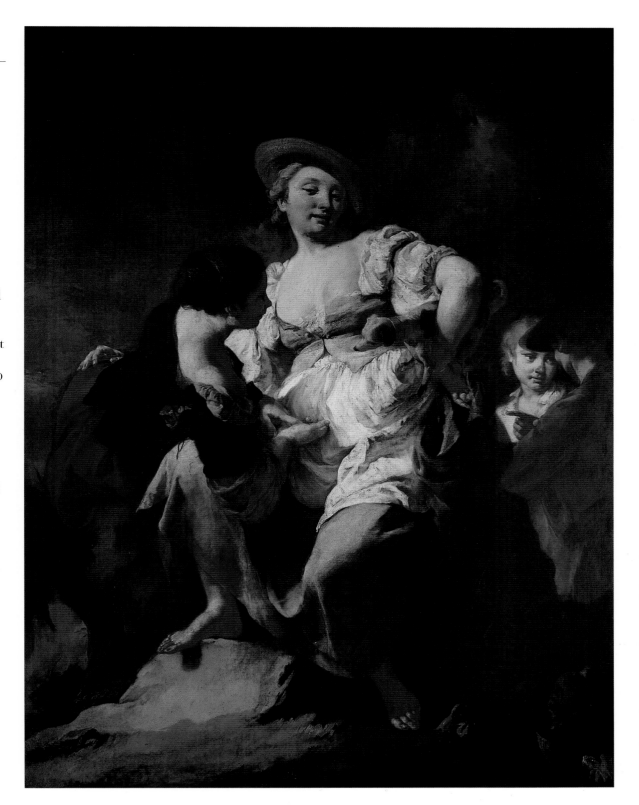

Acquired by the Gallerie in 1887 from the dealer Ehrenfreund, "who claimed that he had bought it in Siena." Until the original canvas was removed during restoration in 1956 (but conserved apart), it bore an 18th-century sheet with this inscription: ISCRITTIONE SEPOLCRALE DEL FAMOSO PITTOR PIAZZETTA AUTORE DI QUESTO QUADRO FATTOLI FARE A VENEZIA IL 1740; E PAGATO ZECCHINI QUINDICI ("The epitaph of the famous painter Piazzetta who painted this picture in Venice in 1740; he was paid fifteen zecchini"). Thereafter came the epitaph itself. The date of 1740 is generally accepted for the painting seen here, but a fee of fifteen zecchini seems derisory, given that in these same years Marshal Schulenburg paid the artist 110 zecchini apiece for two commmissioned pictures, *Pastoral Scene* at the Chicago Art Institute and *Idyll on the Shore* at the Wallraf-Richartz-Museum in Cologne. All three paintings contributed to that incandescent moment of clear, luminous colorism which contemporaries extolled for its *lume solivo*, or "sunniness." Although universally known as the *Fortune-teller*, owing to the pose of the woman on the left, who appears to offer the other figure the proper hand for reading, the title does not really suit. It is a genre or pastoral scene in which, as recently suggested, the young woman thrown into such striking relief by the wash of light over her may be taken for an allegory of corrupt Venice, as bedizened and beckoning as a prostitute. Or the painting may have to do with the *éducation sentimentale* of the two young men at right, or of one of them and the bare-shouldered young woman on the left. Still, the true fascination of the painting arises from its elusive grace, from the sensual flood of sunlight coursing through it, and from the extraordinary, harmonious palette of muted greens, pale pink, and browns.

However rustic her attire, this fortune-teller evinces a serenely sophisticated manner that makes her a true sister of those resplendent women with whom Giambattista Tiepolo would populate the walls of villas and palazzi all over the Veneto.

Venice, 1681-1747
Judith and Holofernes
Oil on canvas, 22 x 42" (cat. no. 1345)

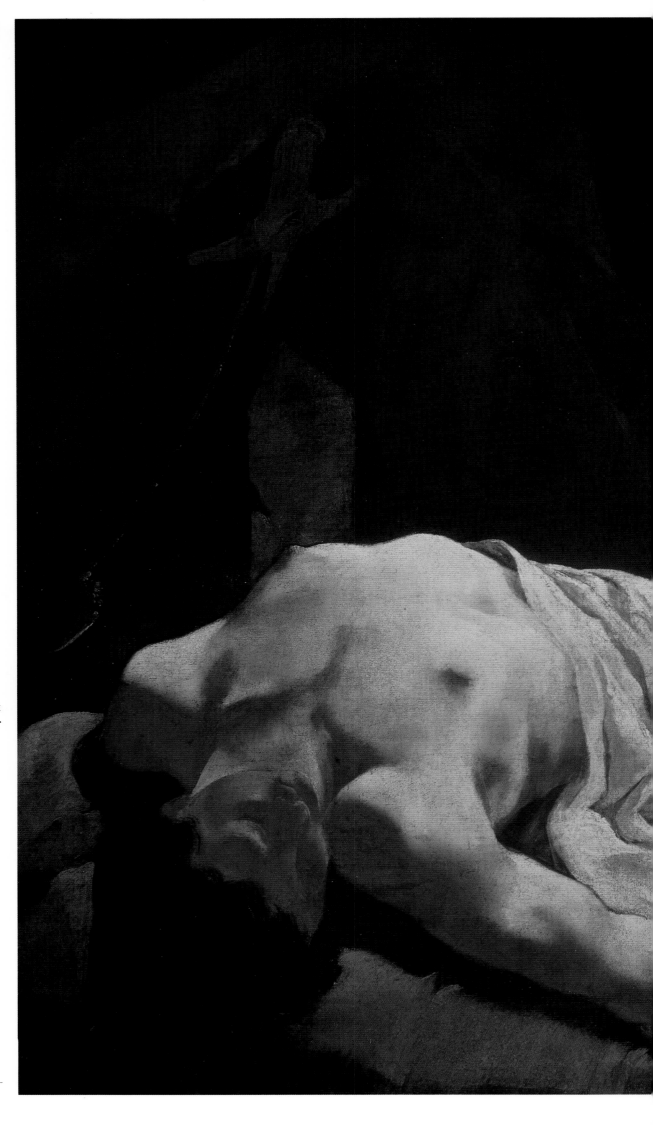

Acquired by the Gallerie in 1976, through the Office of Export in Milan, the picture seen here is generally associated with Lama's *Crucifixion* in the Venetian Church of Saint Vidal. However, it seems closer to Giambattista Piazzetta's *Susanna and the Elders* in the Uffizi, a painting with the same stongly contrasted chiaroscuro and the same dramatic content. The artist, perhaps the most independent of Piazzetta's pupils, is notable for the vigorously plastic draftsmanship that underlies the whole of her oeuvre. The Gallerie also own a "nude study" by Piazzetta (cat. no. D-303) upon which his pupil based the supine body of Holofernes. Pitteri engraved the same study for a vignette in his *Beatae Mariae Virginis Officium*, published in 1740, which makes the source anterior to this date. It also means that Lama's canvas should be more or less contemporary with the Piazzetta drawing and thus datable in the decade 1730-40. In contrast to the numerous Piazzettesque versions of the subject, Lama depicted the Biblical heroine in a prayerful moment, while the wide composition benefits from the artist's impressive virtuosity—"the incredibly skilled calculation with which the staging of the scene and the play of light have been woven together."

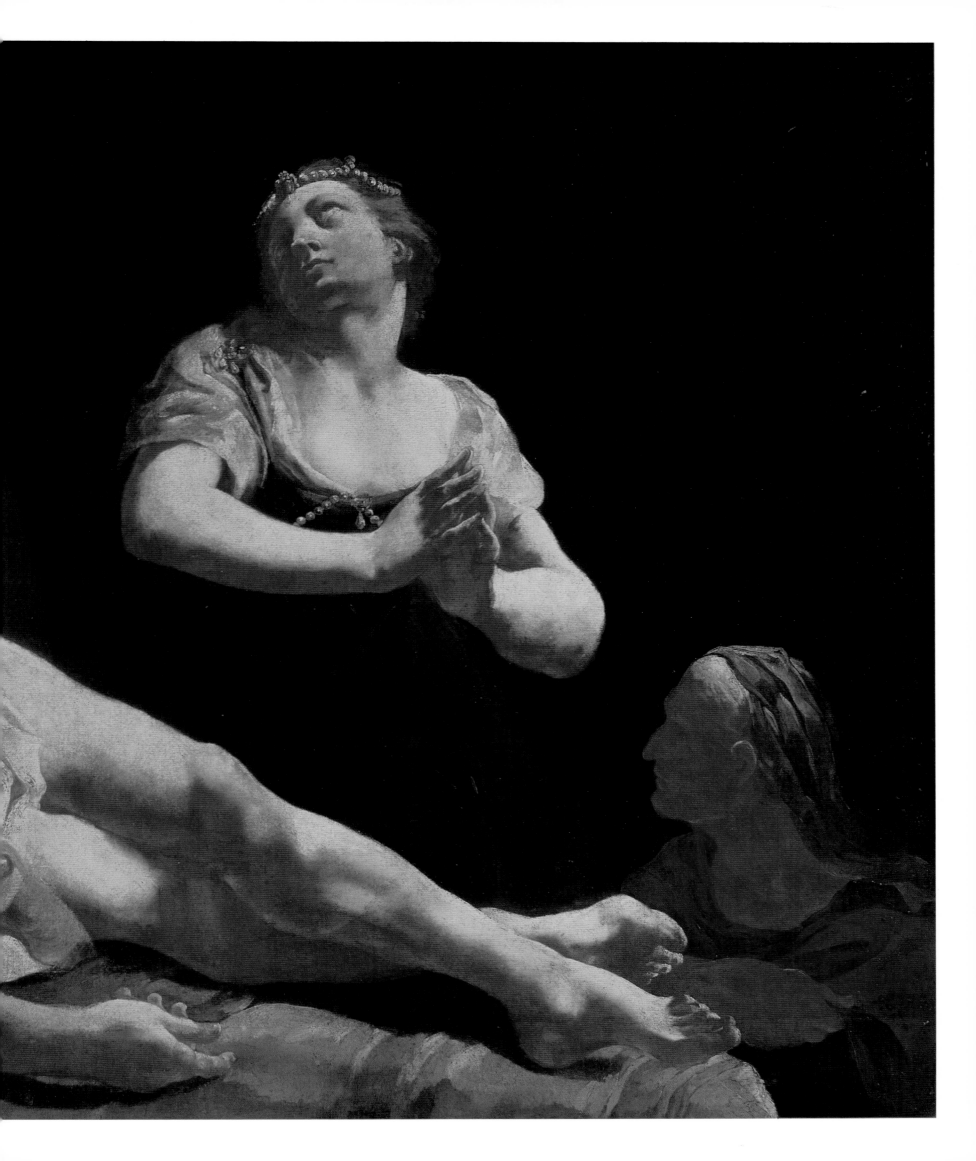

Venice, 1687-1767
The Penitent Magdalene
Oil on canvas, 19 x 15" (cat. no. 707)

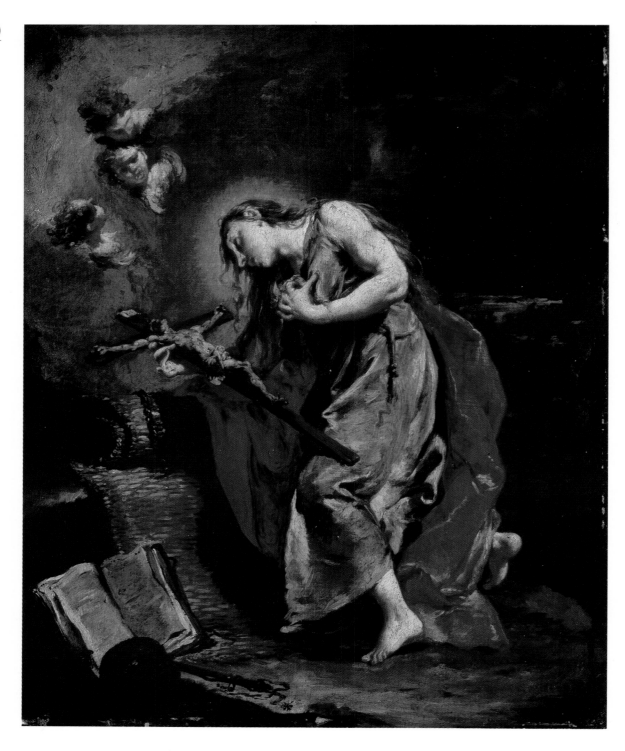

This painting arrived at the Gallerie in 1903 as a gift from Wilhelm Bode, who had acquired it in Venice from the painter G. Zennaro. It served as the working model for the artist's painting in the Church of Santa Maria Maddalene dei Padri Cappuccini in Parma, now the home of that city's National Gallery.

The subject is the closing scene in the life of the Saint, after she had renounced her worldly goods and retired to a hermitage. Pittoni portrays the Magdalene with Rococo sentiment

in all its refinement, showing her at the mouth of a cave, in adoration before the Crucifix, and surrounded by emblems of penitence and meditation. Compared to the finished product, this little canvas exemplifies how the free, melting painterliness and sparkling luminosity of an initial effort can be frozen and more or less polished away in the final, larger composition, even while retaining important formal qualities. An engraving by Pietro Monaco so enlarges upon the detail in the

landscape at left that it simply documents the existence of another version of the model painting, which has been found in the Venetian collection of Giovanni Boschi. Marco would reproduce several Pittonesque inventions in the third edition of his engravings, published in 1789 by Teodoro Viero, with the year 1740 cited as the date of the Boschi picture, which therefore provides a *terminus ad quem* for the work seen here, as well as for the related altarpiece.

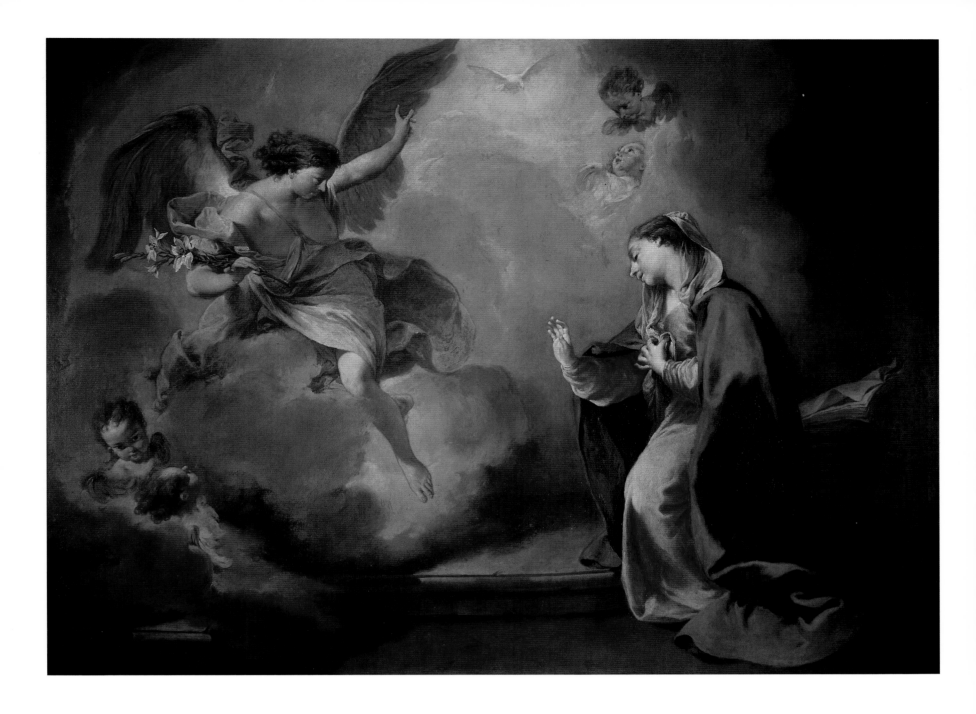

GIAMBATTISTA PITTONI 141

Venice, 1687-1767
The Annunciation
Oil on canvas, 61 x 82" (cat. no. 438)
Last restored 1961

Pittoni painted this picture for the very building in which the Accademia found itself briefly established at San Marco near the Fonteghetto della Farina. Thirty years after its exhibition at the Ascension Day Fair in 1777, Pietro Edwards claimed the painting for the Gallerie, then, in 1807, being formed.

Since the Accademia had chosen to place itself under the protection of not only the Virgin Annunciate but also Saints Mark and Luke, patrons of painters, and the *Quatro Santi Coronati* ("Four Crowned Martyrs"), patrons of sculpture (because, as early Christians, the four sculptors had, according to legend, chosen martyrdom rather than comply with Emperor Diocletian's order to carve a statue of the god Aesculapius), pictures of all these holinesses must have adorned the *stanza dello studio*. Originally, Giambattista Tiepolo was to have done the *Virgin of the Annunciation* and Pittoni both *Saint Mark* and *Saint Luke*. As things worked out, Pittoni undertook the *Annunciation*, delivering it on June 14 of the following year (1757). Meanwhile, Giuseppe Angeli executed the *Saint Mark* and Antonio Marinetti (*il Chiozzoto*) the *Saint Luke*, both of which

paintings are now in a reserve near the Monte Rua Hermitage.

The composition, by contrast with the artist's earlier treatments of the same theme, now in Cracow and Feltre, breaks no new ground, repeating as it does the angel from the Lecco altarpiece, while lifting many details of the Virgin from the London *Nativity* and the Parma *Magdalene*, as well as from the prototype just seen (ill. no. 140). As the product of tried and true precedent, the work becomes a demonstration of the artist's technique, especially the softness of the painterly touch, the Rococo languor of the figures, and the grace that borders on affectation. Three preparatory drawings exist, for the heads of the *putti* above the Virgin, at the Fondazione Cini.

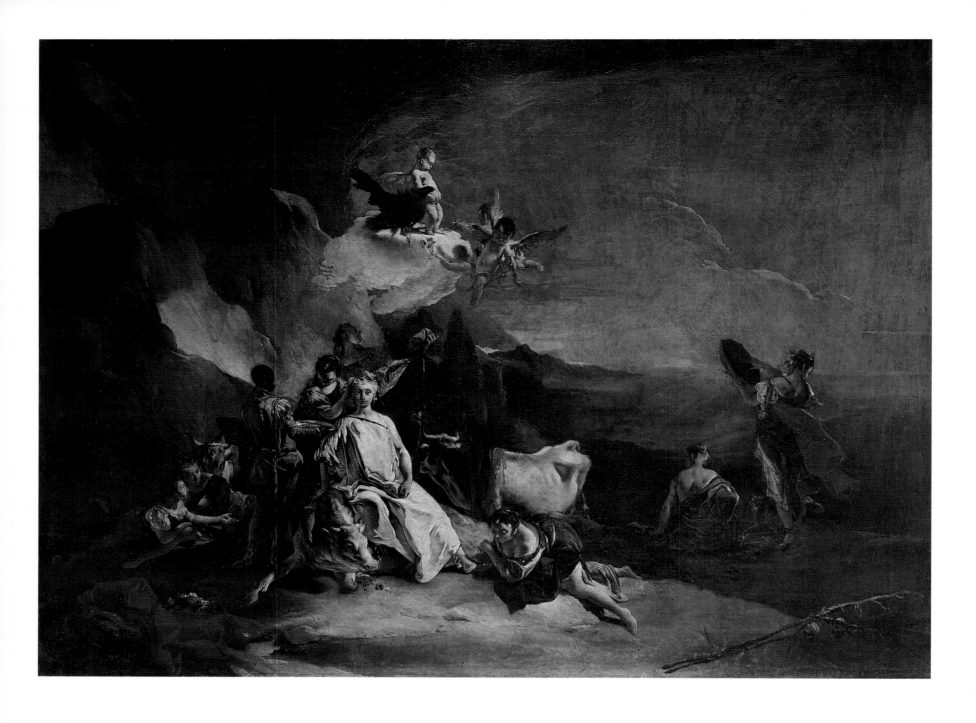

GIAMBATTISTA TIEPOLO 142

Venice, 1696—Madrid, 1770
The Rape of Europa
Oil on canvas, 40 x 54" (cat. no. 712)

The Gallerie acquired Giambattista's *Rape of Europa*, along with the artist's *Apollo and Marsyas* (see ill. no. 143), in 1907 from Countess Capponi, in Belluno, through the antiquarians Piccoli and Barozzi. In 1898, meanwhile, Count Francesco Agosti, also of Belluno, had sold to the State two other mythological paintings with the same dimensions, *Diana and Actaeon* and *Diana and Callisto* (cat. nos. 435, 440). It seems possible that all three works had been part of the same series.

Datable, like the following picture, in the mid-1720s, this painting adheres faithfully to a passage in Ovid's *Metamorphoses*, but with an ironic note that subtly undermines a theme dear to 18th-century poets, a theme already well known to Venetians through Paolo Veronese's famous pictorial version now in the *anticollegio* at the Palazzo Ducale, bequeathed to the Republic by the heirs of Bertucci Contarini.

On an enchanted seashore, a modest and solemn Europa (in whom some have recognized the artist's young wife Cecilia Guardi) sits upon a bull—really Jove in disguise—calmly allowing her ladies, assisted by a black page, to continue her toilette. The eagle in the clouds alerts us to the presence of Jove, while several impudent *putti* frolic all about.

Here Tiepolo edges towards the visual language of Sebastiano Ricci, away from the "tenebrous" influence of Piazzetta.

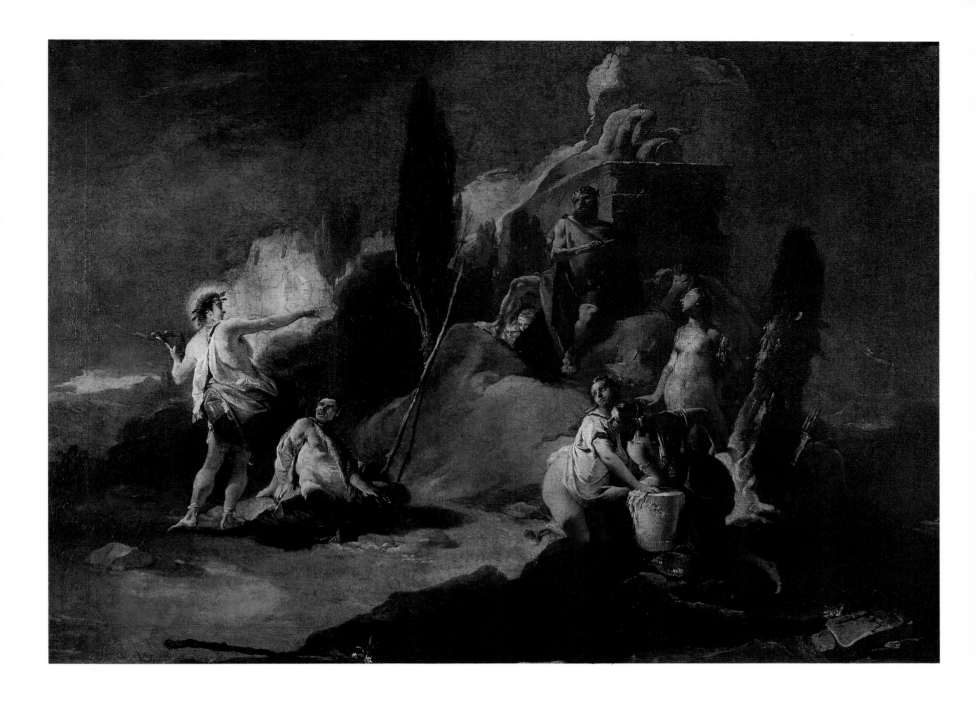

GIAMBATTISTA TIEPOLO 143

Venice, 1696—Madrid, 1770
Apollo and Marsyas
Oil on canvas, 40 x 54" (cat. no. 711)

This painting, like the preceding one (ill. no. 142), scrupulously follows the chosen passage in Ovid's *Metamorphoses* (VI:382-400). The satyr Marsyas, so the story goes, finds the flute invented by Athena and challenges the lyre-playing Apollo to a contest.

After winning, Apollo condemns Marsyas to be flayed alive. The poor victim lies at right in bleeding tatters while fauns, nymphs, and even Jove weep for him, their tears soaking the ground until they promise to become a running stream.

The highly contrasted chiaroscuro of earlier pictures has now been supplanted by a refined impasto of soft, luminous color, in a well-articulated treatment of space that approaches the manner of Sebastiano Ricci. The free handling of the scene foreshadows the powerful touches of theatricality that would characterize the artist's more mature work.

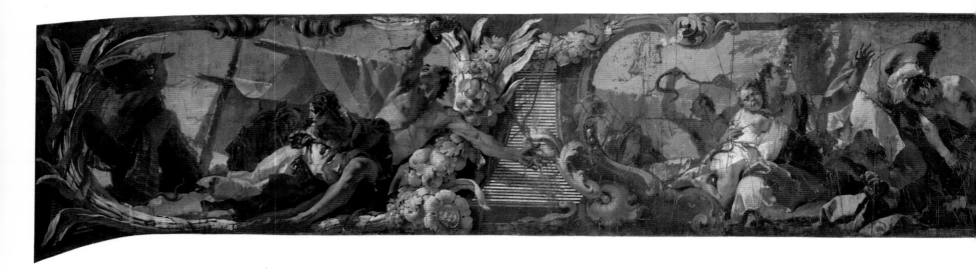

GIAMBATTISTA TIEPOLO 144

Venice, 1696—Madrid, 1770
The Plague of Serpents
Canvas, 66 x 542" (cat. no. 343)
Last restored 1893

Giambattista's *Plague of Serpents* was commissioned for the Church of Santi Cosma e Damiano on the Giudecca, where Zanetti (1771) mentions it "below the choir." After the church had been secularized in 1810, the painting, now State property, was placed in reserve but finally released in 1839 to the Church of Santa Maria e Liberale in Castelfranco. Here, perhaps because of its unusual dimensions, it remained unrolled, until it was assigned in 1893 to the Gallerie.

Although not cited by Zanetti in his revision of Boschini's *Descrizione* (1733), the painting does figure in the 1736 edition of Fra Pacifico's *Cronica Veneta*. Zanetti's omission would not appear so important, given that scholars tend to date the work, at the latest, in the early 1730s. In 1728, Santi Cosma e Damiano acquired, among other things, large canvases by Sebastiano Ricci and Giambattista Pittoni, which, together with its Angelo Trevisani and its 17th-century paintings, gave the church one of the most comprehensive Biblical cycles in Venice. The episode concerns the bronze serpent that God commanded Moses to erect in

the desert (Numbers 21:4). Anyone who set eyes on it was cured of the deadly bite of those venomous snakes which God had sent to punish the children of Israel for their impatience and lack of faith. The subject had interested Giambattista since his youth, as we know from the many drawings that antedate the painting seen here.

Along an extended frieze, whose grandiose and inventive composition remains intact despite damage caused by rolled-up storage, Giambattista lets the Biblical story unfold in three episodes, all presented with extraordinary dramatic power and sovereign color and contained within a mock-stucco frame. The sheer quality of the painting has discouraged any attempt to repair the lacunae, which in any event do not compromise the work's legibility. What may well be a preparatory study, once in the Drey collection in Munich and then sold at auction (Sotheby's, May 25, 1969), has now disappeared. A copy without the subdivisions, signed by Cesare Ligari and dated 1740, is in Milan's Pinacoteca Ambrosiana.

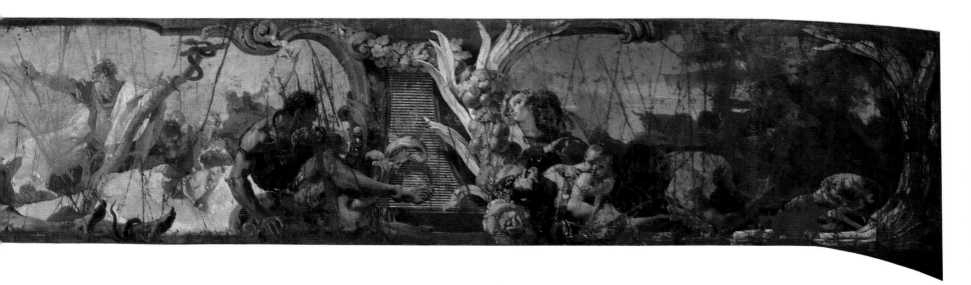

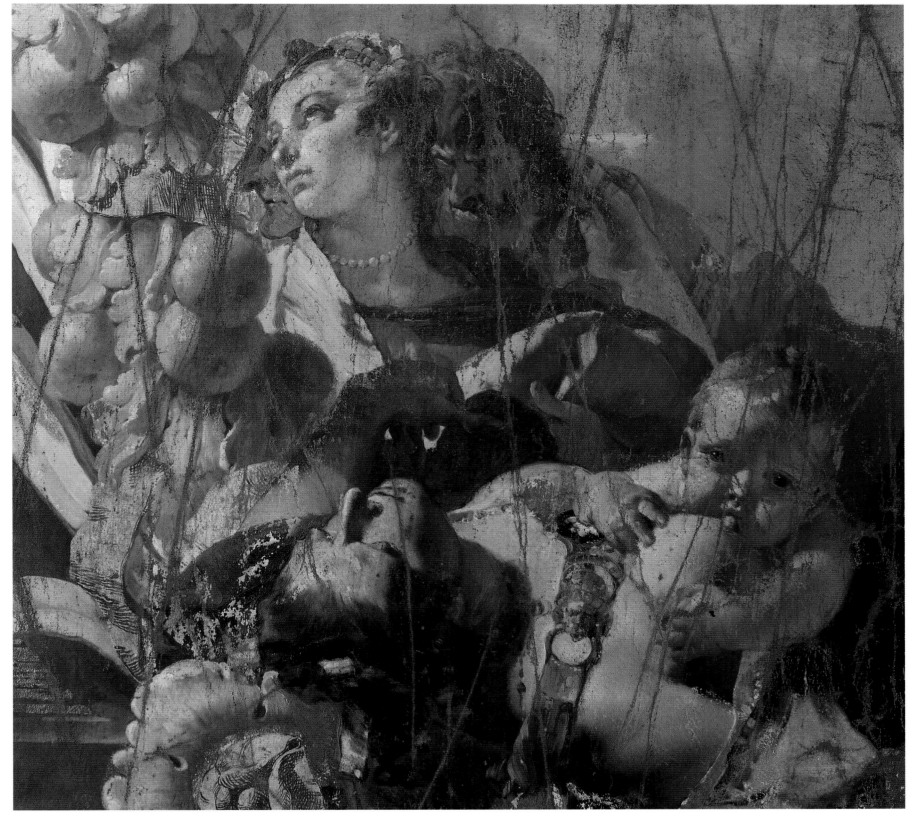

Venice, 1696—Madrid, 1770
The Holy Family Appearing in a Vision to San Gaetano
Oil on canvas, (cat. no. 481)

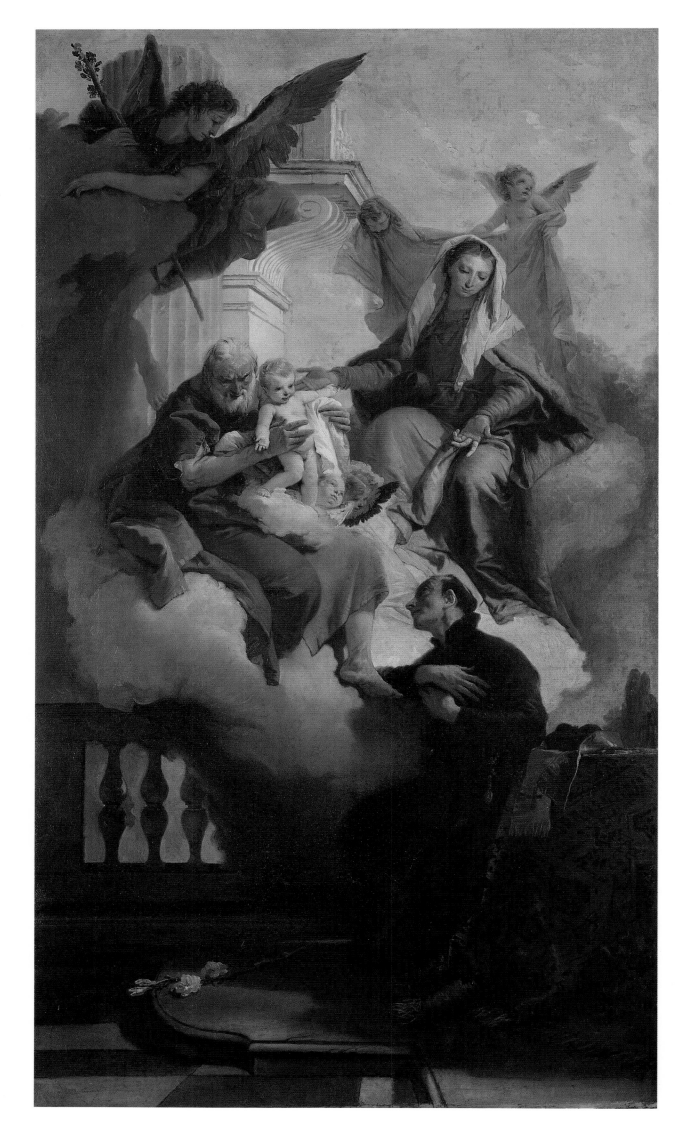

Painted for the altar of the little chapel in Venice's Palazzo Labia, this picture came to the Gallerie in June 1887 from the religious Königsberg Foundation in Vienna, at that time the owner of the Labia. It dates from 1735-36 and corresponds almost certainly to the altarpiece ascribed to Tiepolo in an inventory of Labia paintings taken in 1749. Giambattista probably found his subject in a pamphlet on the Saint's life issued in 1726 by *padre* Gaetano Maria Magenis, who describes in detail the dream in which the Virgin appeared to the Saint and handed him the Child Jesus.

A novel conception of the traditional "Sacred Conversation," the scene occurs outside a building, in a rising series of diagonals that endow the picture with an illusory space far greater than its limited dimensions might seem to allow. In the foreground, by contrast, hovers the dark, austere figure of Saint Gaetano, immersed in a diffuse and uncertain light.

The painting may resemble some of Piazzetta's altarpieces from the same period, particularly the one of San Vidal, but its closest affinity is with Giambattista's own sketch entitled *The Virgin and Child Appearing to a Group of Saints* now in the National Gallery, London.

Venice, 1696—Madrid, 1770
The Transport of the Holy House of Loreto
Oil on canvas, 50 x 34" (cat. no. 91)

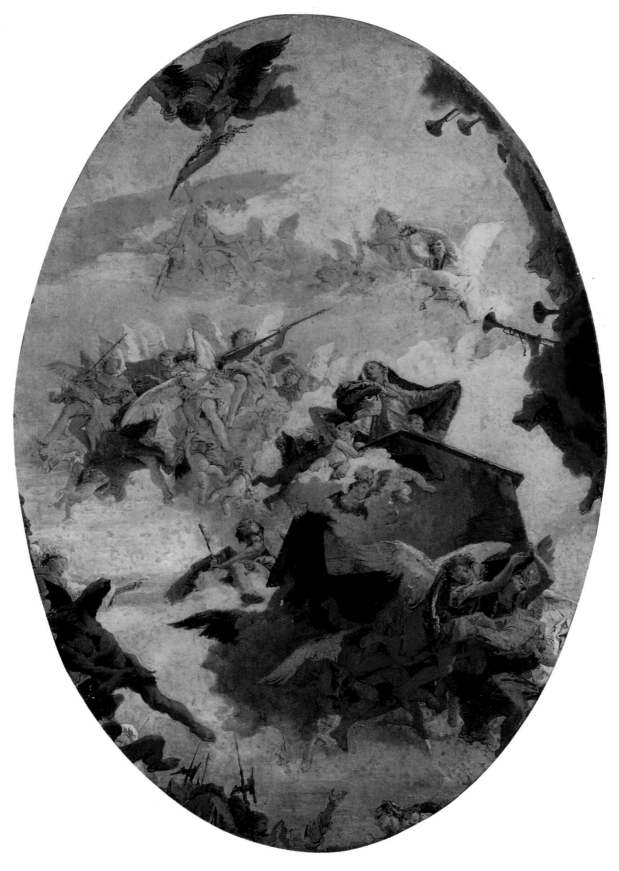

Acquired in 1930 from the heirs of the sculptor Dal Zotto, who had discovered it in a private oratory at Crespano, this painting of about 1743 is a color model for the ceiling fresco that Giambattista painted in the Church of Santa Maria di Nazareth, called *degli Scalzi*, a structure almost entirely destroyed by Austrian artillery on the night of October 28, 1915.

On September 13, 1743, Tiepolo committed himself to the enormous undertaking. In preparation for it, he did another sketch, slightly different but closer to the finished work, which was in the Rosebery Collection, London, and is now on loan to the National Gallery from the British Rail Pension Fund. Both sketches relate to an early conception limited to a central oval, but gradually the artist managed to claim the whole of the vault's surface (see ill. nos. 148, 149) for an ampler, freer composition whose main groups would, after all, emerge from the preparatory studies. Even in the limited dimensions of the work reproduced here, Giambattista demonstrated consummate skill at expanding the pictorial space illusionistically, while also employing his gift for impastoed color to create evanescent images of angels, nebulous clouds, and the splendid Virgin. Now the solid volumes of a few years earlier have yielded to bodies structured of the most refined, painterly colorism.

The Pierpont Morgan Library in New York owns what may be a very quick sketch for this study, and the Princeton Art Museum a preliminary study for the figure of Mary.

Venice, 1696—Madrid, 1770
Pendentive with a Page Looking Over a Balcony
Detached fresco, 160 x 79" (cat. no. 836)
Last restored 1916-17

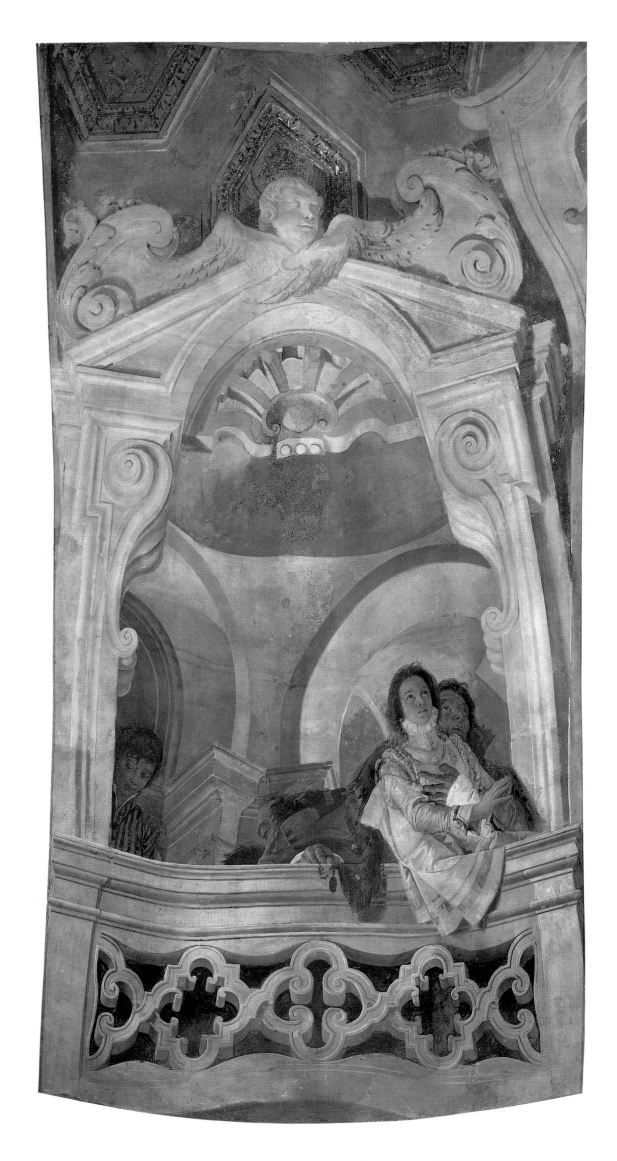

Commissioned by the Discalced Carmelites for the ceiling of the Church of Santa Maria di Nazareth, this fragment formed part of the last great religious cycle that Giambattista executed in fresco. The church and its decorative program were shattered by an Austrian bombardment during the night of October 28, 1915.

Giambattista signed the contract on September 13, 1743, and on the following October 10 Girolamo Mengozzi Colonna began painting the sham architectural framework. Giambattista had prepared two oval *bozzetti* or models in oil on canvas (see ill. no. 146) but revised the project several times until he had extended the *Transport of the Holy House of Loreto* to the entire vault. The artist received payments between April 14 and November 23, 1745, presumably the period during which he realized the work, and certainly before Mengozzi did his *quadrature* or trompe-l'oeil corners.

To fill the four curved corners, Giambattista designed balconies that Mengozzi no doubt painted before the master added the figures of a few faithful as astonished witnesses to the miracle, all attired in 16th-century costume. Among the vestiges of peripheral decoration recovered after the disaster were the four pendentives; the one reproduced here and another to be seen next were assigned to the Gallerie in 1919. The other two, three grisaille canvases, and a decorative fragment, all restored in the 1960s, are conserved in the laboratory of San Gregorio or on loan at the Palazzo Ducale.

The devout figures, prayerfully intent before an extraordinary event, along with a third, rather distracted individual, filled the left-hand corner of the entrance wall. With the vivid counterpoint of their clothing against the pale surfaces of the sham architecture, they recall the art of Paolo Veronese.

The Hermitage in Leningrad owns a drawing of the page (no. 35301).

GIAMBATTISTA TIEPOLO 148

Venice, 1696—Madrid, 1770
*Pendentive with Praying Figures Peering Down
from a Loggia*
Detached fresco, 160 x 74" (cat. no. 837)
Last restored 1916-17

Originally, this fresco filled the corner to the
left of the sanctuary (see also ill. nos. 146,
147). As in the works just observed, the
worshipers, who attend the miracle in a quasi-
rapt state, have been realized in colors of
extraordinary luminosity set against the clear
forms of the painted architecture.

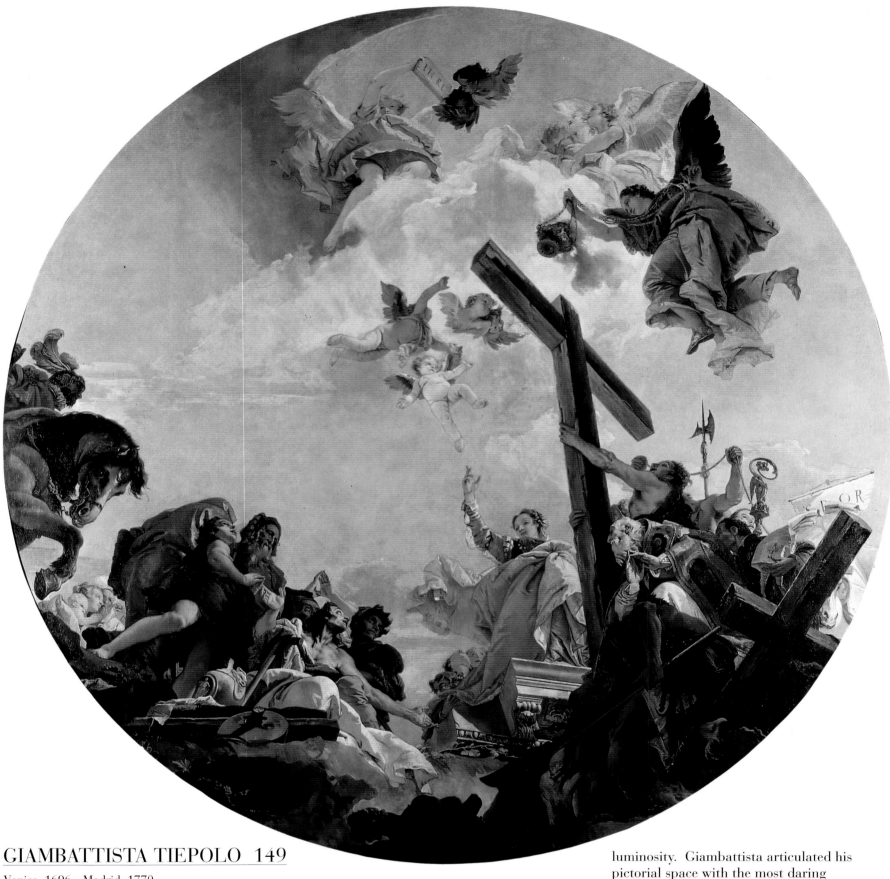

GIAMBATTISTA TIEPOLO 149

Venice, 1696—Madrid, 1770
Exaltation of the Holy Cross with Saint Helen
Oil on canvas, 195" in diameter (cat. no. 462)
Last restored 1982

Originally, this painting formed part of the ceiling decorations at the Capuchin church in Castello, destroyed to make way for the Napoleonic gardens. Surrounding Giambattista's work was sham architecture painted by Girolamo Mengozzi Colonna.

With the Napoleonic secularization, the painting became public property, allowing Pietro Edwards to include it among the first works to enter the Gallerie, even though it did not go on display until after the middle of the 19th centeury. The latest restoration re-endowed the large painting with a chromatic impasto of extraordinary refinement and luminosity. Giambattista articulated his pictorial space with the most daring illusionism, a quality that today cannot be fully appreciated owing to the loss of the original architectural setting. The painting was presumably commissioned during the tenure of Francesco Antonio Correr as Patriarch of Venice (1734-41), a Capuchin who may have favored the church of his own order. The Gallerie also own a compositional sketch for the work (cat. no. 789).

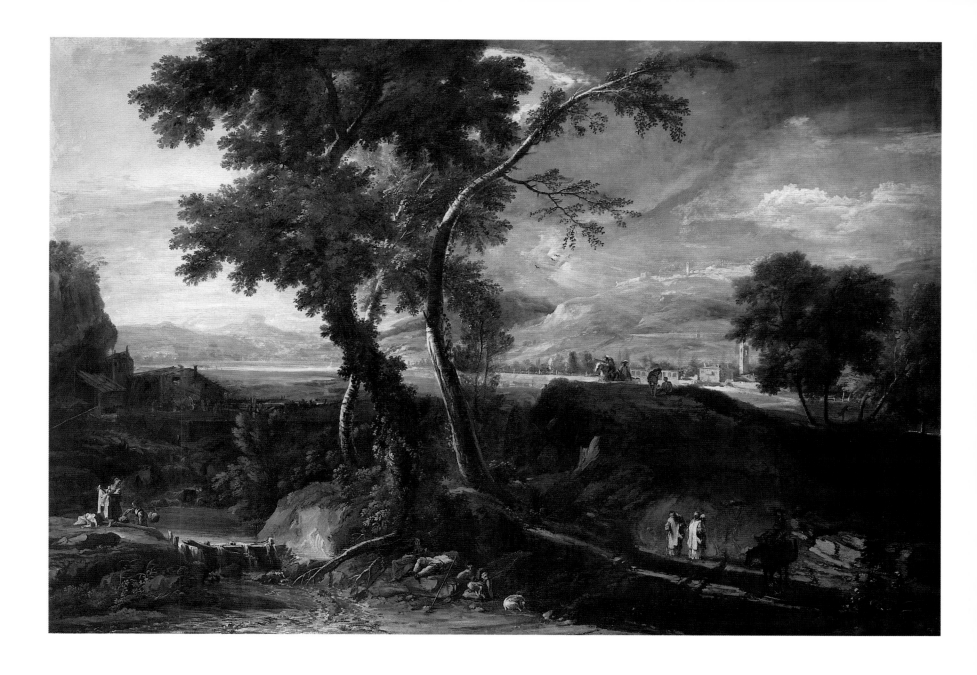

MARCO RICCI 150

Belluno, 1676—Venice, 1730
*Landscape with Stream, Monks, and
Laundresses*
Oil on canvas, 54 x 79" (cat. no. 457)
Last restored 1963

This painting and the next one, *Landscape
with Horses and Drinking Trough* (ill. no.
151), have been recorded as once in the
Galleria Corniani degli Algarotti in Treviso,
whence they passed by inheritance to Countess
Perazzolo.

Finally, the Gallerie acquired them in 1878
from Count Zanetti of Venice. Marco Ricci,
nephew of the celebrated Sebastiano, had a
predilection for shadowy, rolling landscapes,
wide valleys with rushing streams, great trees

under luminous skies, and ruins evoked in a
proto-Romantic manner that would be
exemplified not only by Zais and Zuccarelli
but also by Canaletto and Marieschi.

Datable, like its pendant, to about 1720, the
painting seen here is considered the
masterwork of the artist's mature years. In it
Marco assimilated Titian's drawings and
Domenico Campagnolo's engravings quite
harmoniously with real or imagined features of
his native Piave Valley.

Belluno, 1676—Venice, 1730
Landscape with Horses and Drinking Trough
Oil on canvas, 54 x 79" (cat. no. 457)
Last restored 1963

Like the painting just seen (ill. no. 150),
Landscape with Horses and Drinking Trough
is a masterpiece of the artist's maturity, a work
distinguished by compositional breadth and
originality as well as by close attention to both
color and light, resulting in extraordinary,
atmospheric effects, none of which would be
lost on the young Canaletto. The provenance
is the same as that of the preceding work by
Marco.

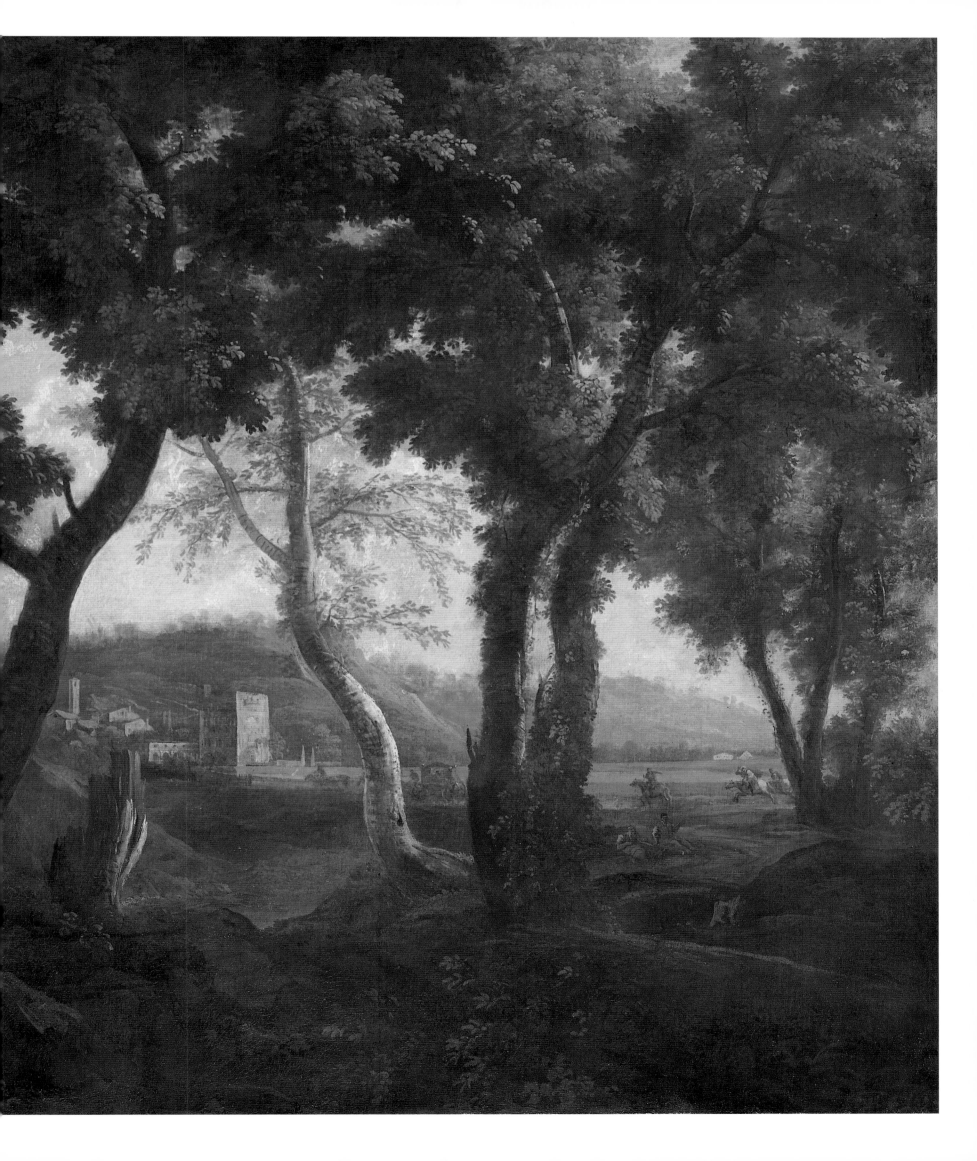

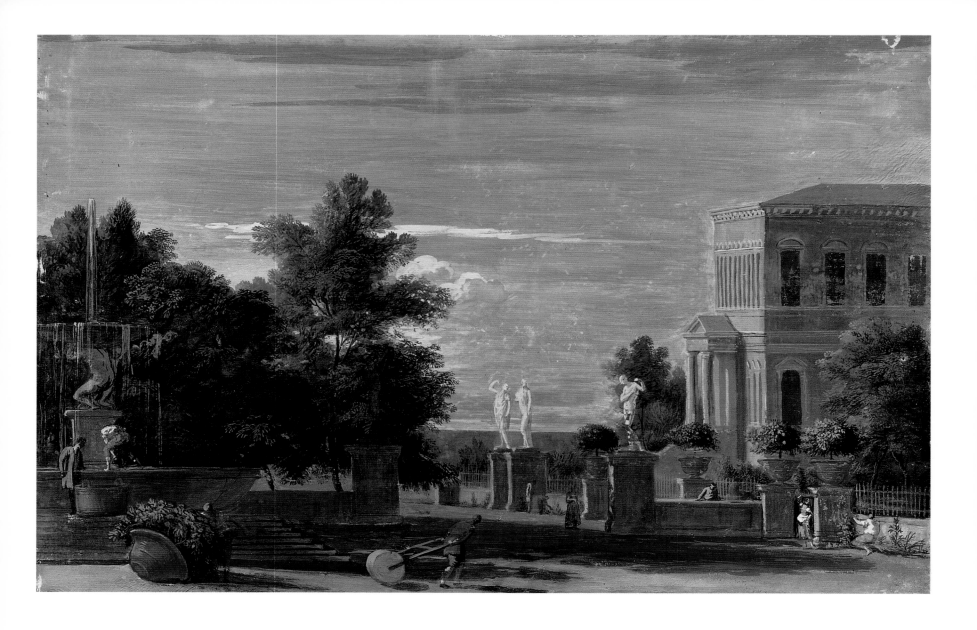

MARCO RICCI 152

Belluno, 1676—Venice, 1730
Villa in a Park Setting
Tempera on kidskin, 14 x 18" (cat. no. 1307)

From its former home in the Palazzo Reale, *Villa in a Park Setting* and its pendant (ill. no. 153) were assigned to Venice's Gallerie in 1956. Where they originally hung is not known; however, Pietro Edwards notes that at San Giorgio Maggiore he took possession of two "tempera" landscapes "in the manner" of Marco Ricci. Given the medium involved, the picture must date from artist's last decade, when, according to Zanetti (1771), Ricci employed this technique. The unusual kidskin support, though one familiar to miniaturists and other medieval artists, made it possible for Marco to obtain a special kind of luminary and atmospheric effect. In the painting seen here he mingled fantastic invention with lucidly observed reality, for a scene dominated by a Veneto villa, generally Palladian but carefully described, and alive with busy gardeners who, at the return of Spring, draw water, bring huge vases out-of-doors, and roll the earth. At the Ashmolean Museum, Oxford, there is a drawing in which the nucleus of all these elements can be found (no. 1059).

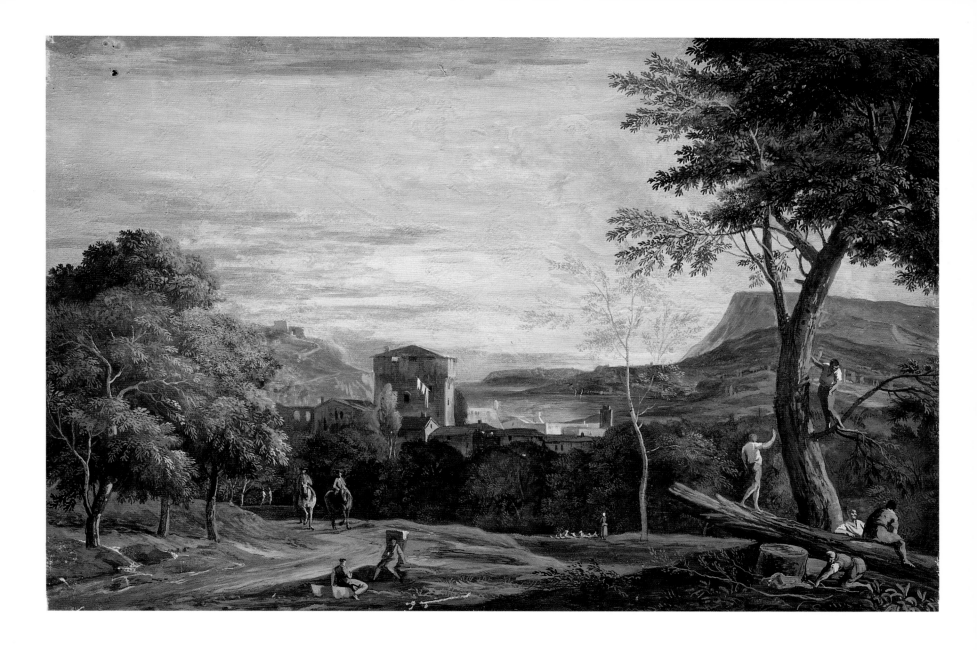

MARCO RICCI   153

Belluno, 1676—Venice, 1730
Landscape with Woodcutters and Two Horsemen
Tempera on kidskin, 12 x 18" (cat. no. 1308)

In this landscape, a pendant to the one just seen (ill. no. 152), we find similar events and the same Titianesque echoes, especially in the lateral, framing trees and the tall tower at center, skillfully translated into a limpid Veneto landscape inspired by the valleys of Belluno. On the left the woodcutters at their humble toil are so treated as to become objects of rapt fascination. There was a copy of *Landscape with Woodcutters and Two Horsemen* in the Alessandro Morandotti collection in Rome in 1963, sold at auction on October 29 of the following year at the Finarte in Milan.

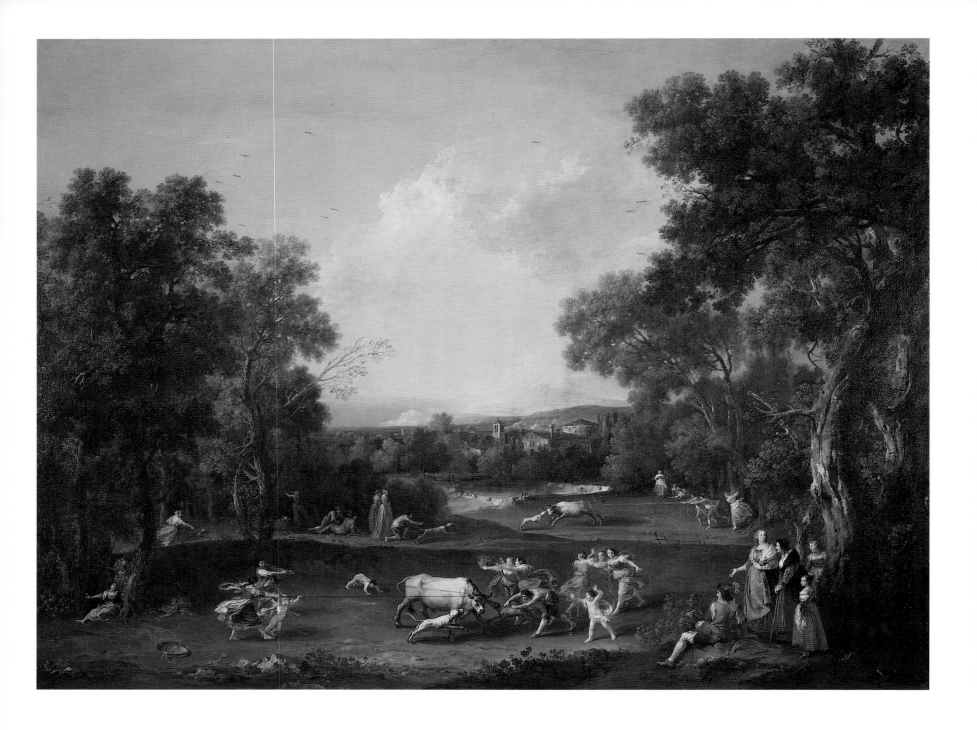

FRANCESCO ZUCCARELLI   154

Pitigliano, 1702—Florence, 1778
Chasing the Bull
Oil on canvas, 46 x 60" (cat. no. 869)
Last restored 1948

With secularization, which made it public property, Zuccarelli's *Chasing the Bull* was removed from its original home in the Benedictine Monastery of San Giorgio Maggiore and hung in the Palazzo Reale, whence it was assigned to the Gallerie in 1949. Justifiably, the painting has been considered a youthful work, executed shortly after the artist's arrival in Venice around 1732, as would seem to be evinced by the Tuscan and even Flemish elements still present in *Chasing the Bull*.

Thereafter, the artistic climate of Venice, especially that generated by the landscape painting of Marco Ricci and Zais, had a profound effect on Zuccarelli, who would then evolve into the most international of Venetian landscapists, thanks as well to the patronage of the British Consul Smith and the interest of Francesco Algarotti.

Chasing the Bull radiates a serene, idyllic view of nature, not least because the artist transformed a cruel sport into a kind of bucolic minuet.

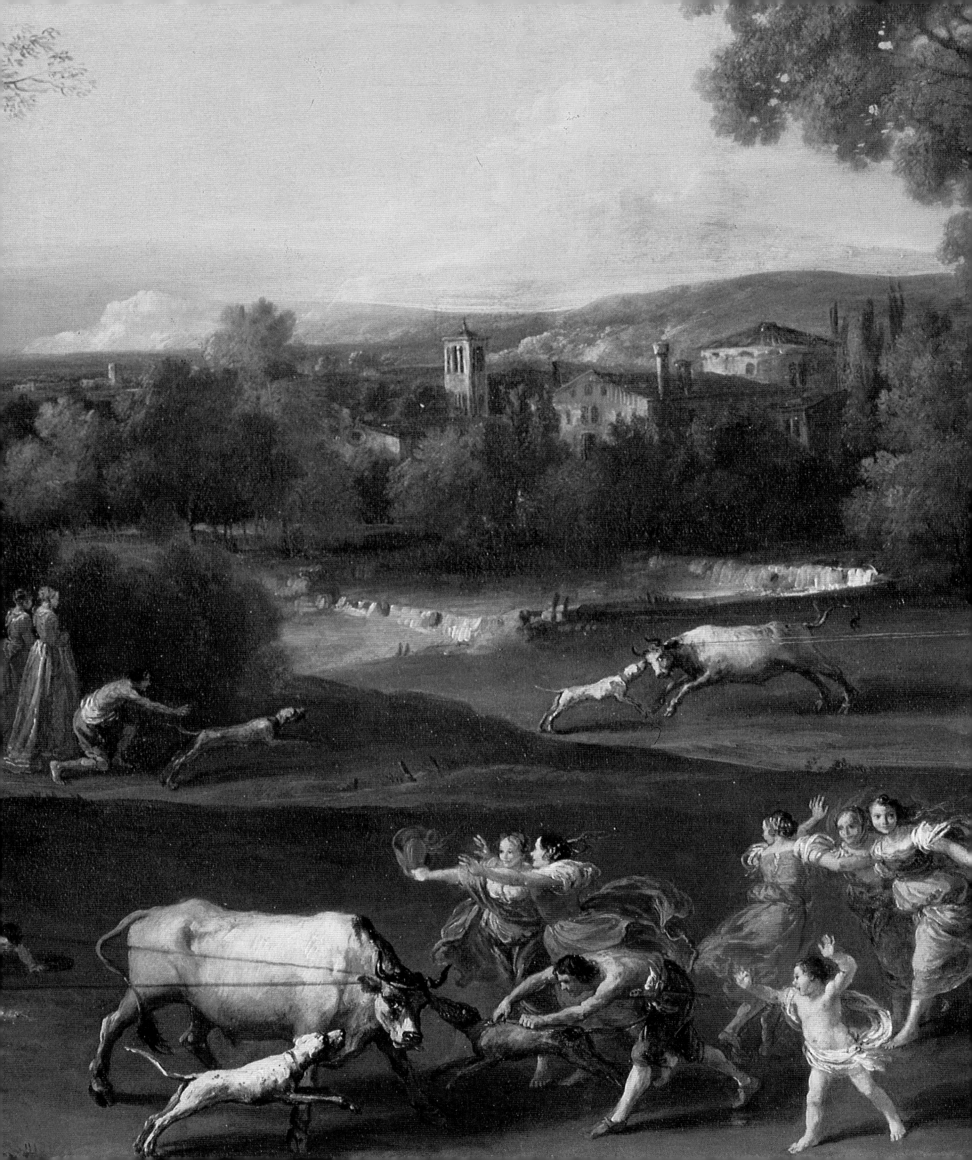

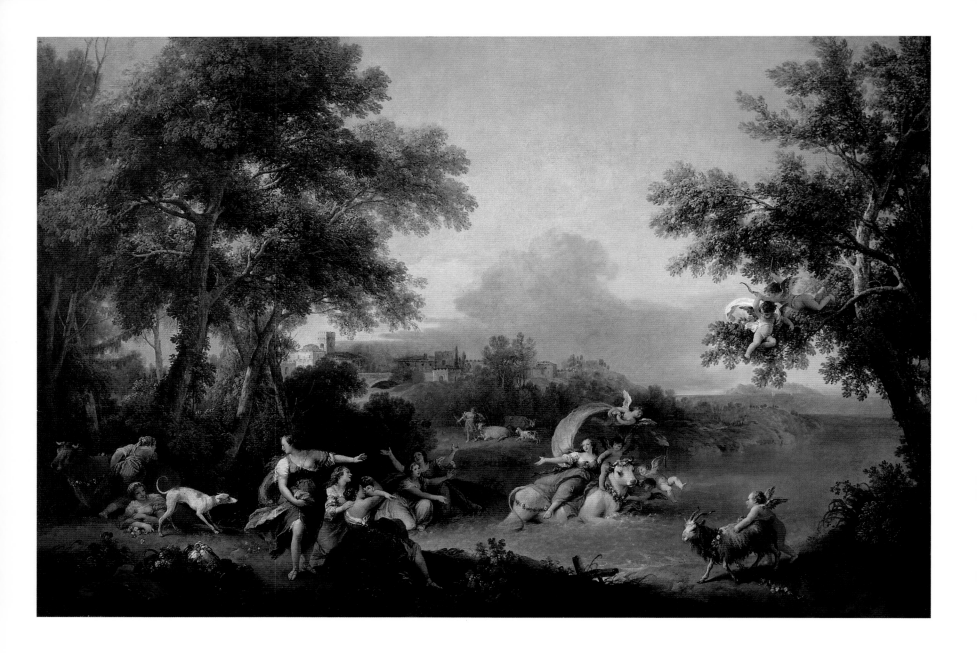

FRANCESCO ZUCCARELLI   155

Pitigliano, 1702—Florence, 1778
The Rape of Europa
Oil on canvas, 57 x 83" (cat. no. 858)
Last restored 1982

The artist inscribed his signature on the dog's collar at lower left: ZUCARELI. Like both the preceding picture and the one to follow, the *Rape of Europa* forms part of a set (including six other, smaller pictures) that Zuccarelli painted for the Pisani, who kept them in their villa at Stra until the end of the 18th century. When the Napoleonic government bought the villa in 1807, the paintings did not count in the transaction. Those by Zuccarelli became public property through a different, extremely intricate series of negotiations, which ended with the art works hung in the Palazzo Reale, whence they came to the Gallerie only in 1923.

The *Rape of Europa* is accepted as the artist's masterpiece, which even the administration of Teodoro Matteini acknowledged when its agent valued the work at 150 zecchini as opposed to 50 for the *Bacchanal*.

Both of these pictures can be dated in the 1740s, given their affinities with the *Bacchanal* in the Werner Predeval collection, which is signed and dated 1744. In the work seen here, Europa's abduction unfolds against an idyllic landscape, the drama played out, in a gossamer range of blues, pale pinks, and soft greens, with something like the rhythm and grace of a Metastasio melodrama.

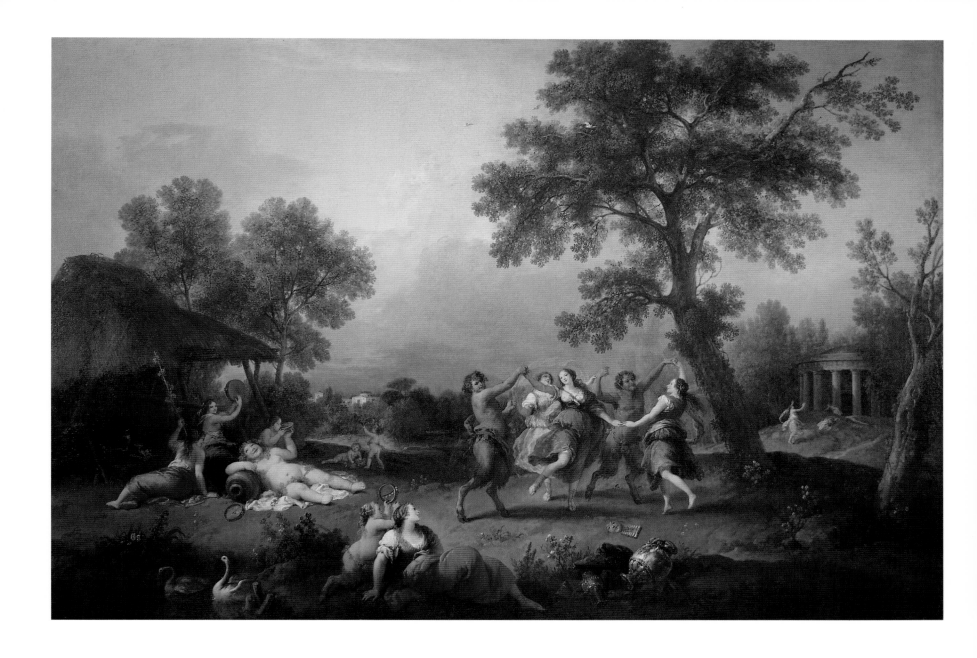

FRANCESCO ZUCCARELLI

156

Pitigliano, 1702—Florence, 1778
Bacchanal
Oil on canvas, 57 x 83" (cat. no. 859)
Last restored 1982

The presence of Pietro da Cortona can be felt throughout the canvas, with its gentle, idealized bucolic scene in the foreground and its glimpse a of small Classical temple in the distance, its interlace of gaily dancing nymphs and fauns. In the shade of a rustic cottage on the left, a besotted Bacchus slumbers on an empty wineskin.

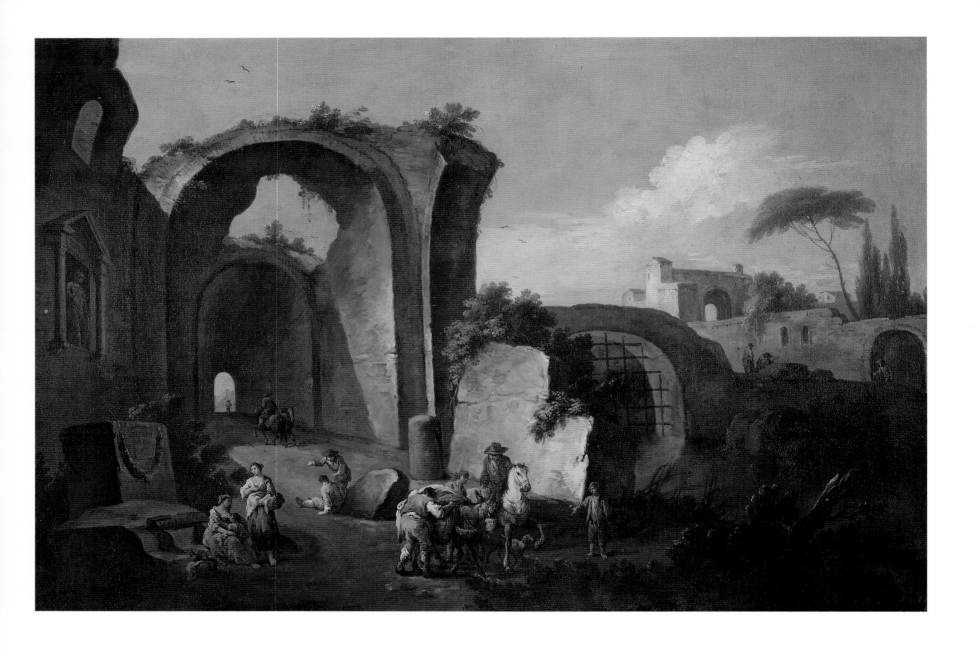

GIUSEPPE ZAIS   157

Forno di Canale, 1709—Treviso, 1784
Ruins of a Vaulted Building
Oil on canvas, 39 x 59" (cat. no. 846)
Last restored 1984

The artist inscribed his signature on the marble stele at left: JOSEPH-ZAISE-F. From the Palazzo Reale, where it once hung, *Ruins of a Vaulted Building* came to the Gallerie in 1923, along with its pendant, the next painting to be seen here (ill. no. 158). Both date from the later 1730s and were both destined for the Monastery of San Giorgio Maggiore. Clearly influenced by the landscape art of Marco Ricci, Zais translated this legacy into a more arabesque language of brilliant, vivacious painterliness.

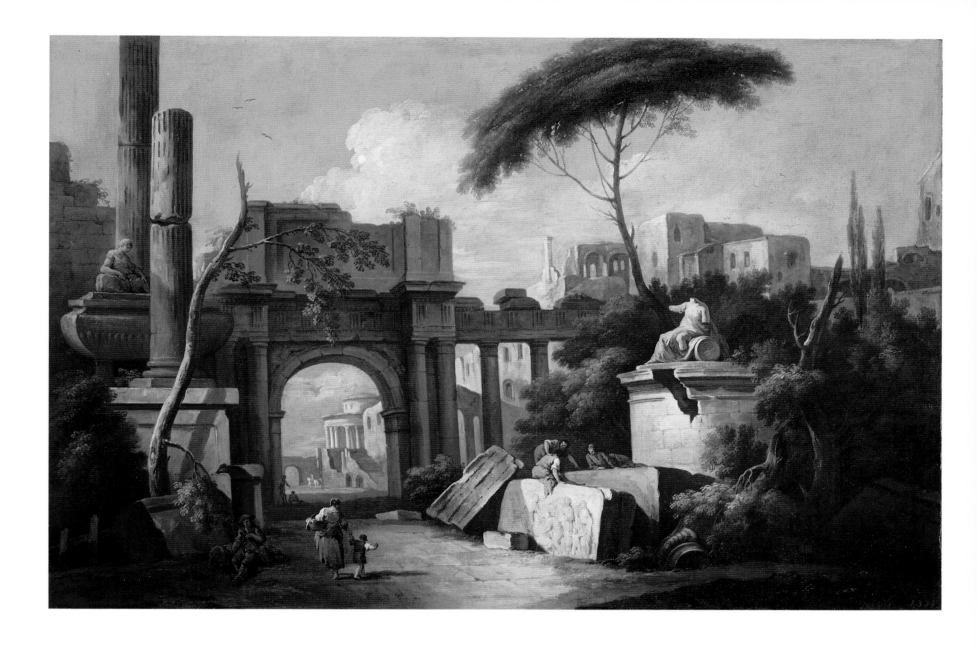

GIUSEPPE ZAIS   158

Forno di Canale, 1709—Treviso, 1784
Antique Ruins with Monumental Arch and Columns
Oil on canvas, 36 x 79" (cat. no. 847)
Last restored 1984

Perhaps even more than in the preceding canvas (ill. no. 157), *Antique Ruins with Monumental Arch and Columns* betrays the influence of Marco Ricci, especially his taste for the vestigial remains of Classical antiquity. A private collector in Paris owns a Zais drawing with variations on the figures and composition seen here, no doubt representing a preparatory study.

Forno di Canale, 1709—Treviso, 1784
The Swing
Oil on canvas, 39 x 59" (cat. no. 1309)
Last restored 1957

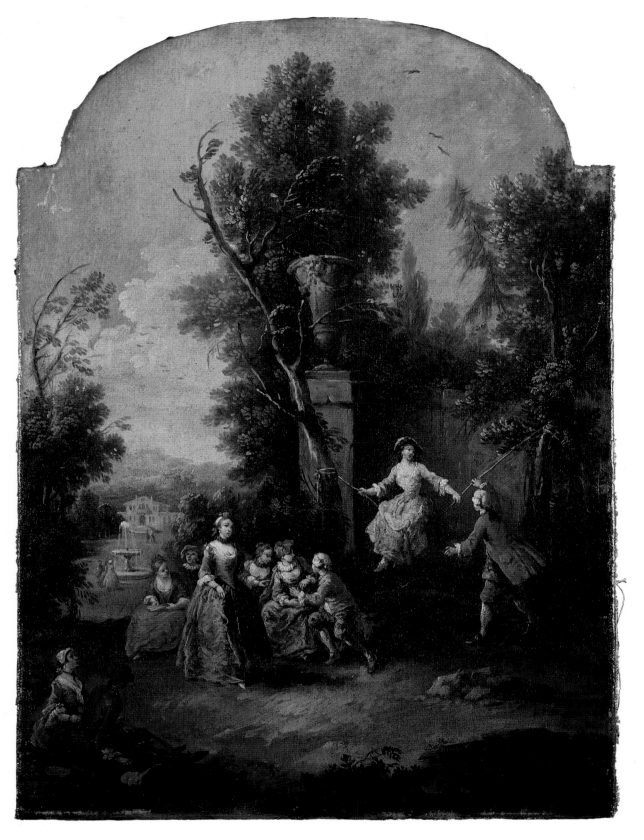

This painting too came to the Gallerie in 1957 from the Palazzo Reale, along with three others in a series depicting country-house diversions (*Open-Air Concert*, *Pierrot with Couples*, and *Trysts near a Fountain*). Where the pictures first hung is not known. For this small canvas as for the others, Zais had evidently succumbed to the *fêtes galantes* of contemporary French painting, more perhaps through engravings and printed illustrations than through knowledge of the originals.

Into the delicious *Swing*, for example, Zais appropriated from Watteau's so-called *Venetian Ball* (engraved in 1732 by Laurent Cars and now in Edinburgh's National Gallery) the central group and the two figures in the foreground, even if reversed, as well as the tall plinth supporting a large vase.

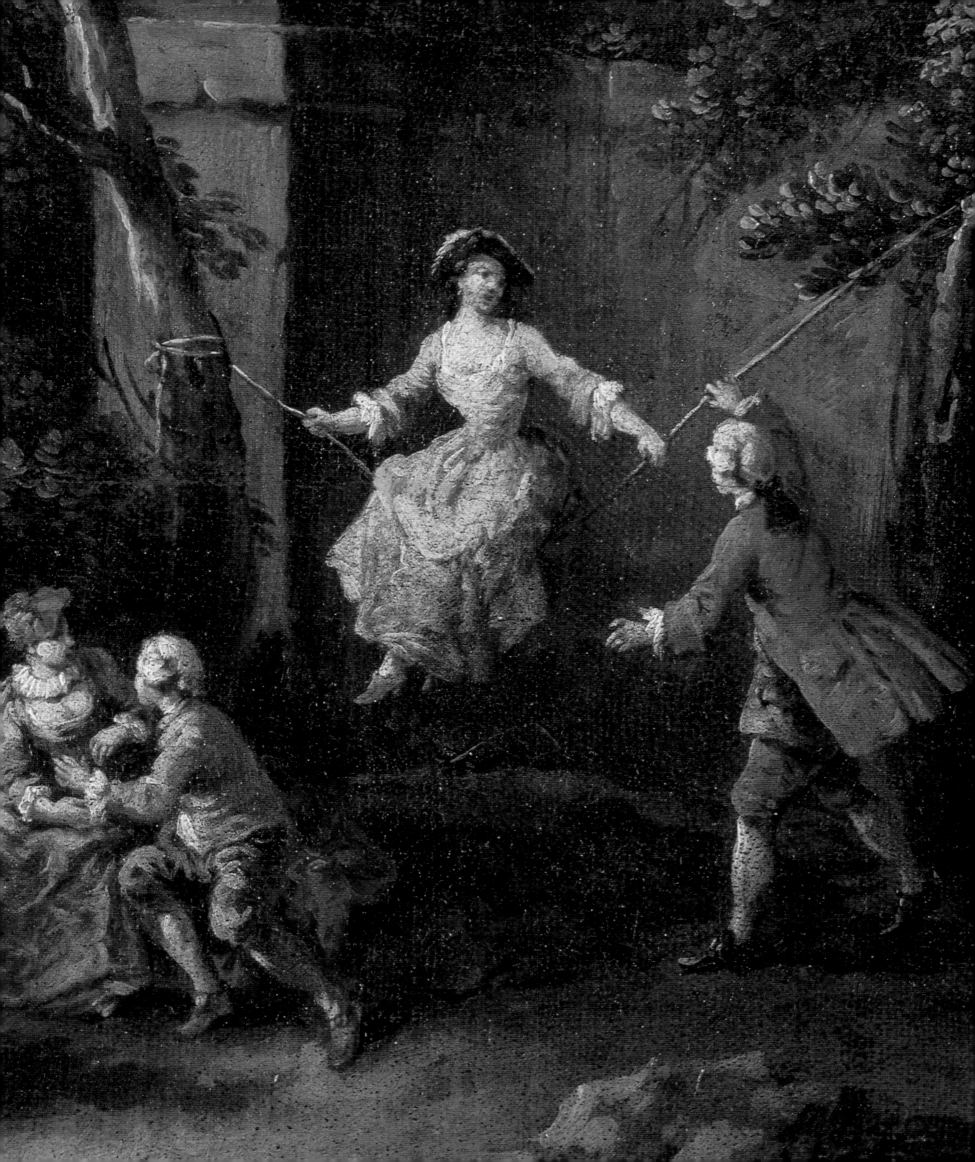

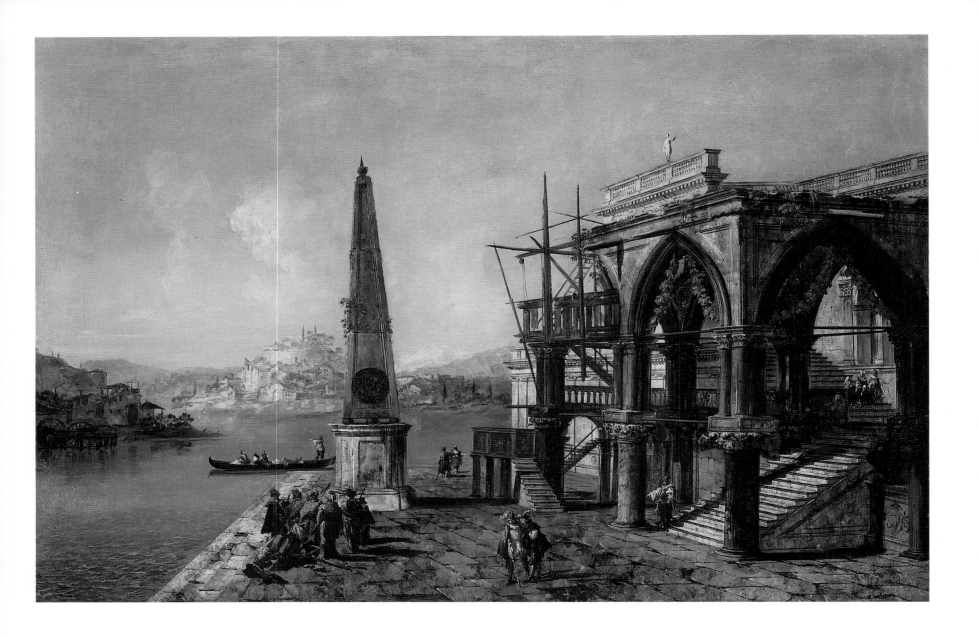

MICHELE MARIESCHI   160

Venice, 1710-44
Capriccio with Gothic Building and Obelisk
Oil on canvas, 22 x 33" (cat. no. 728)
Last restored 1962

Like the next work, acquired in 1903 from Countess Elena Prine di Breganze, in this fantastic, very original scene, the artist has combined a Gothic portal under restoration, an obelisk that becomes a sort of focal point for the entire composition, old windmills reflected in a sheet of water at the left, and a distant hillside landscape. The painting exists in several versions, one of which, privately owned in Milan, may very well have been made by the artist himself, while the others are workshop versions, like the enlarged copy in Milan's Museo del Castello Sforzesco.

Throughout a brief artistic career, Marieschi specialized in landscape, both imaginary and real. After 1741, he became famous for his twenty-one engraved views of Venice, all much sought after by travelers making the Grand Tour.

The work seen here corresponds closely to the Stuttgart Staatsgalerie's *Capriccio with Equestrian Statues and Obelisk*, sharing not only the obelisk placed near the focal point but also a feeling for composition and color. Equally evident in both canvases is their sparkling, tightly flecked brushwork. The two paintings derive from the artist's last period, probably after 1741.

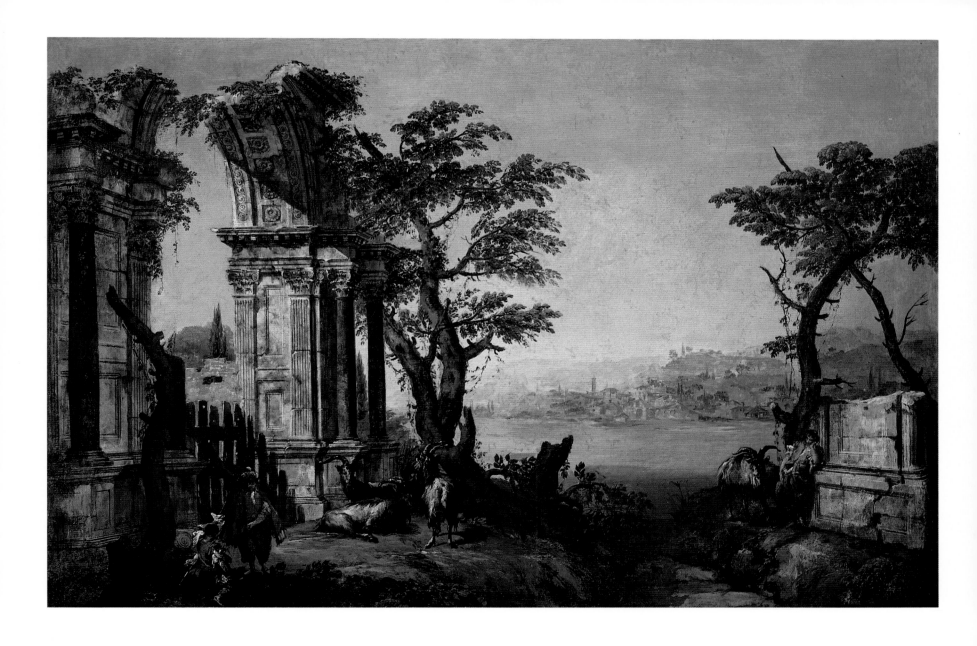

MICHELE MARIESCHI   161

Venice, 1710-44
Capriccio with Classical Arch and Goats
Oil on canvas, 22 x 33" (cat. no. 727)
Last restored 1962

A pendant to the preceding work and, like it, acquired from Countess Contessa Elena Prine di Breganze. One of the artist's happiest capriccios, this picture combines the painterly fluency of Marco Ricci with the flashing sketchiness of Giannantonio Guardi and the chromatic freshness of Zuccarelli.

The distant, barely hinted landscape, the ruined arch, the foliage built up with deft,

vivacious strokes, the scintillating luminosity— all mark the work as characteristic of the artist at the zenith of his short career, allowing us to date it, along with the preceding canvas, around 1741.

The painting seen here may be compared with the privately owned *Caprice with Farmhouses and Goats* (Pescara) from the same period.

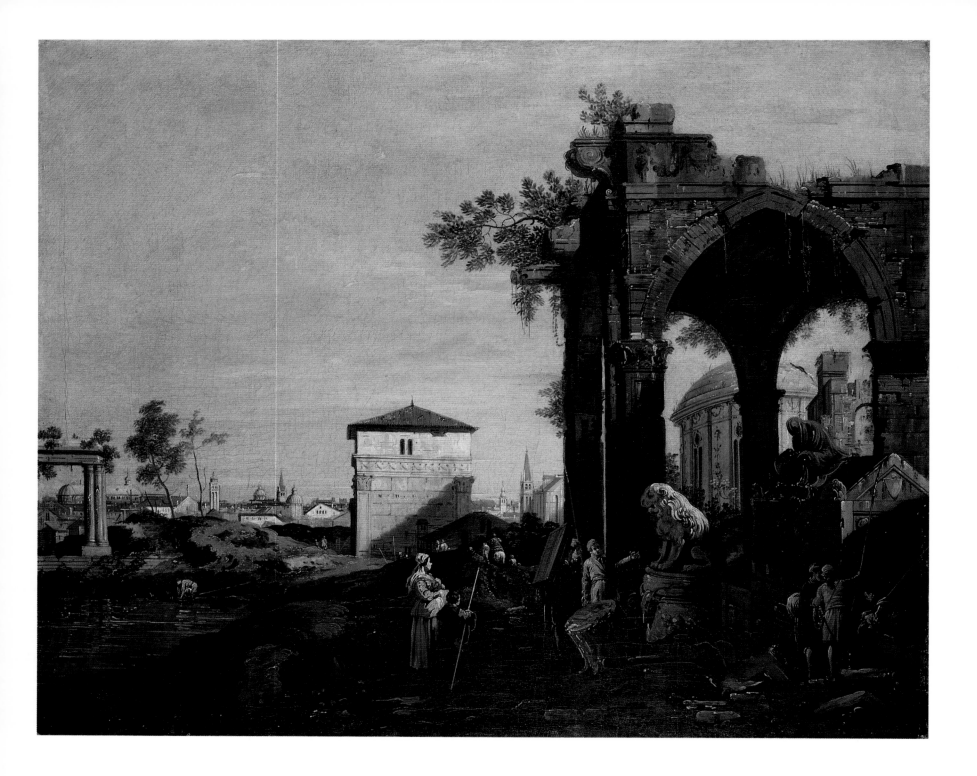

ANTONIO CANAL
CALLED CANALETTO   162

Venice, 1697-1768
Capriccio with Ruins and the Porta Portello in Padua
Oil on canvas, 25 x 31" (cat. no. 1385)

From the Contini collection in Rome, the painting passed to the Contini-Bonacossi of Florence, from whom Reichsmarschall Goering acquired it in 1941. It was returned to the Italian government in 1948, and assigned to the Gallerie in 1988.

Of the Paduan buildings depicted, the only one that cannot be mistaken is the Porta Portello, which, with its corners buttressed by Ionic pilasters, also figures in a Canaletto drawing at Windsor Castle.

The structure with the imposing roof in the left background could be either the Salone in Padua or Palladio's Basilica in Vicenza.

This *capriccio* enjoyed great popularity, as we know from the many and variant versions of it, some twenty-two of them attributable to the circles of Canaletto and Bellotto. As for the original, it would seem to be in the Hamburg Kunsthalle, according to most authorities.

Recent critical opinion, in general, considers the version seen here to be by Canaletto himself, and indeed the work's painterly qualities, together with the purity of its light and color, are characteristic of the master's own work in the 1760s.

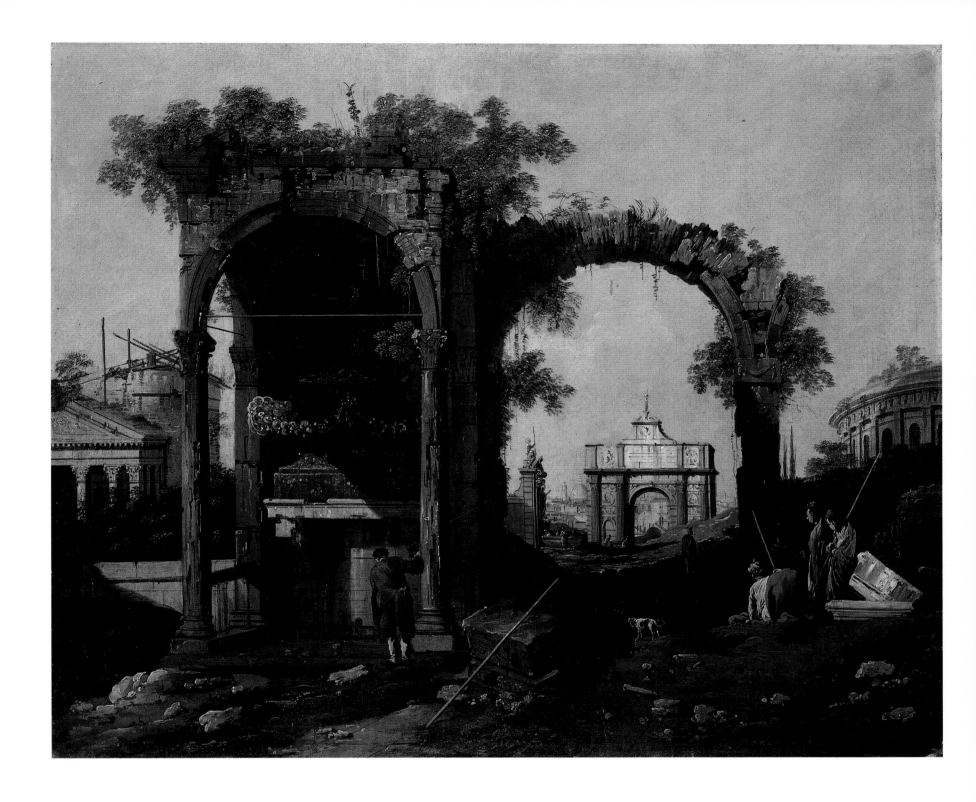

ANTONIO CANAL
CALLED CANALETTO   163

Venice, 1697-1768
Capriccio with Ruins and Classical Buildings
Oil on canvas, 25 x 30" (cat. no. 1386)

This *capriccio* reached the Gallerie in 1988 by the same route as the foregoing work, to which it was originally a pendant. The buildings shown all appear to be imaginary even where they allude to real ones, such as the ruined arch, which seems to echo the Porta di San Giovanni in Padua, or the dome rising above the city's skyline, which, on the whole, evokes Venice more than Rome.

Among the sixteen known variants of the work seen here, the one in Milan's Poldi-Pezzoli Museum is generally thought to be the prototype. However, the present canvas does not suffer by comparison, thanks to the greater luminosity of its color and the limpid incisiveness of the master's descriptive touch.

ANTONIO CANAL
CALLED CANALETTO 164

Venice, 1697-1768
Perspective View with Portico
Oil on canvas, 52 x 37" (cat. no. 463)
Last restored 1985

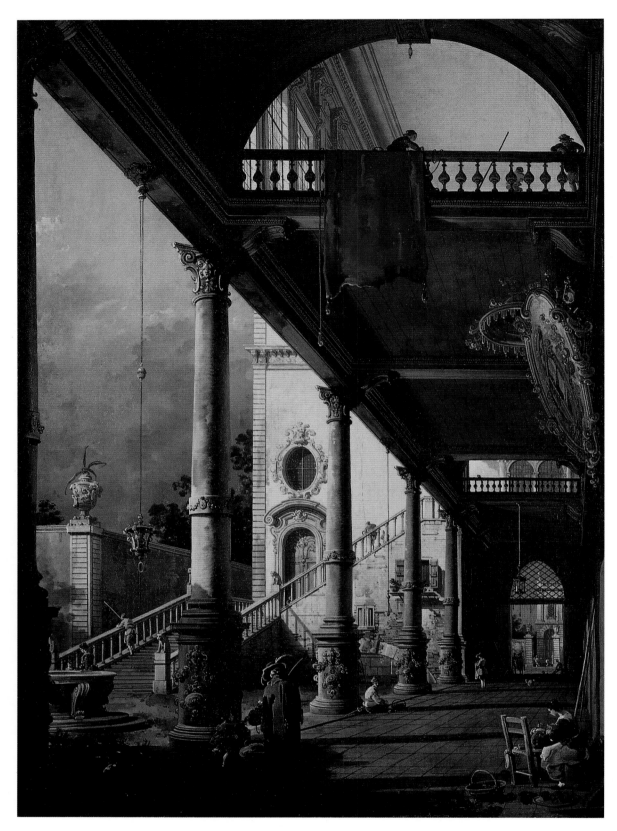

Although rejected by the first round of voting, on September 11, 1763, Canaletto was finally elected to the Accademia di Scultura e Pittura as "Professor of Architectural Perspective."

Two years later Canaletto executed this *pièce de réception*, signing as well as dating the picture, as we know from a fragmentary inscription at the lower right—"ANTON . . .1765"—and presenting it to the Accademia in accordance with custom. After the artist's death, the work was exhibited in the Piazza San Marco during the Ascension Day Fair of 1777. It remained in the old Accademia at Fonteghetto della Farina until April 26, 1807, at which time Pietro Edwards removed it to the new Carità complex.

The subject—the entrance to a Venetian palazzo, complete with courtyard, grand staircase, and gallery—certainly gave the artist a vehicle for displaying his skill in perspective. Even so, an extaordinary chromatic luminosity also brings great impact to the architectural imagery, in which every last detail has been rendered with such analytical precision as to seem a quasi-record of reality.

Among the various copies (one in the Ca' Rezzonico), those belonging to London's National Loan Collection Trust and to the Staatliches Schloss of Dobris, Czechoslovakia, are probably autographic.

A preliminary watercolor sketch can be found in the Albertini collection in Rome, while an early study for the composition is recognizable in a folio with other architectural sketches owned by the Museo Correr.

In the artist's own hand, the folio has been inscribed *per la Cademia* ("for the Accademia").

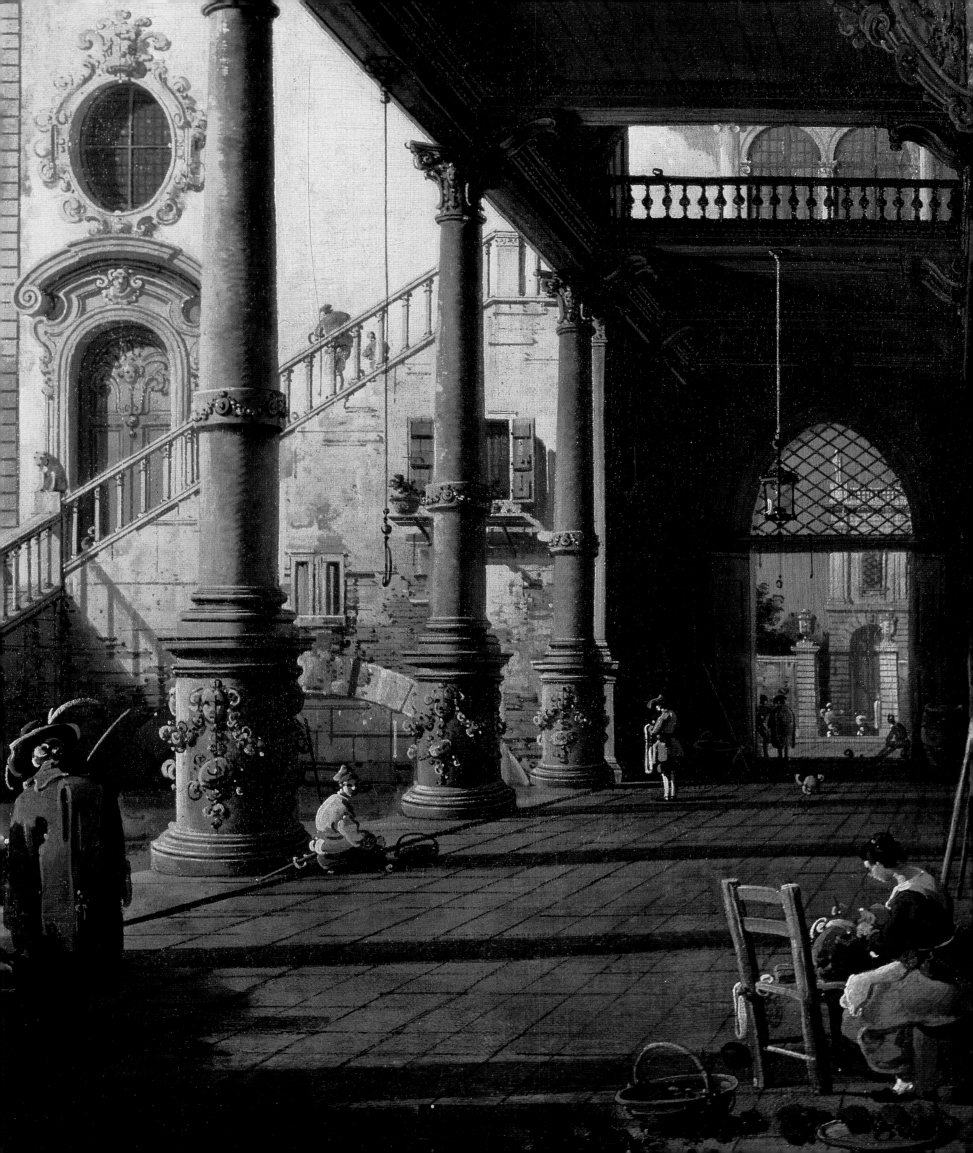

ANTONIO VISENTINI 165

Venice, 1688-1782
Perspective View with Students of Architecture
Oil on canvas, 53 x 37" (cat. no. 465)
Last restored 1986

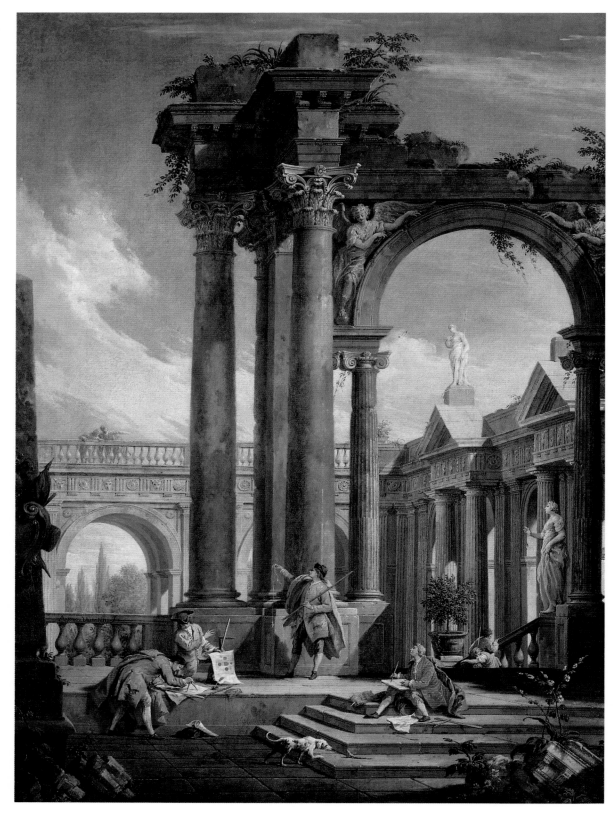

Visentini signed this painting on the parapet of the balustrade at left: ANTONIO VISENTINI F. Elected an academician on February 13, 1756, among the first artists thus admitted, Visentini served as acting professor of architectural perspective from 1761 to 1767, when the agent for "Reformers of the Padua Workshop" gave the position to the scenographer Francesco Costa. On the latter's retirement in 1772, Visentini recovered his old position and remained at the Accademia until 1778.

The subject clearly relates to the artist's course material, which in turn favored the rationalistic principles of *padre* Lodoli, principles by then firmly established and available to Visentini through the circle of his friend and protector Consul Smith. The picture must have been painted after 1771, the publication year of Zanetti's *Pittura veneziana*, which made no mention of the work seen here, and before 1777, when this was exhibited at the Ascension Day Fair in Piazza San Marco. Rather than the stereotypical *capriccio* with its ruins, Visentini assembled four young students in contemporary dress, who, with the tools of their trade (plumb line, compass, and square), are engaged in scrupulously measuring and copying some dilapidated antique monument. Next to the draftsman making notes on the steps rests a book entitled *Palladio*.

This is an authentic piece of architectural scenography, complete with echoes of Veronese and Palladio skillfully coupled in the background, as well as with hints of Pannini in the foreground arch with its winged Victories. In 1779, the painting was engraved by Wagner.

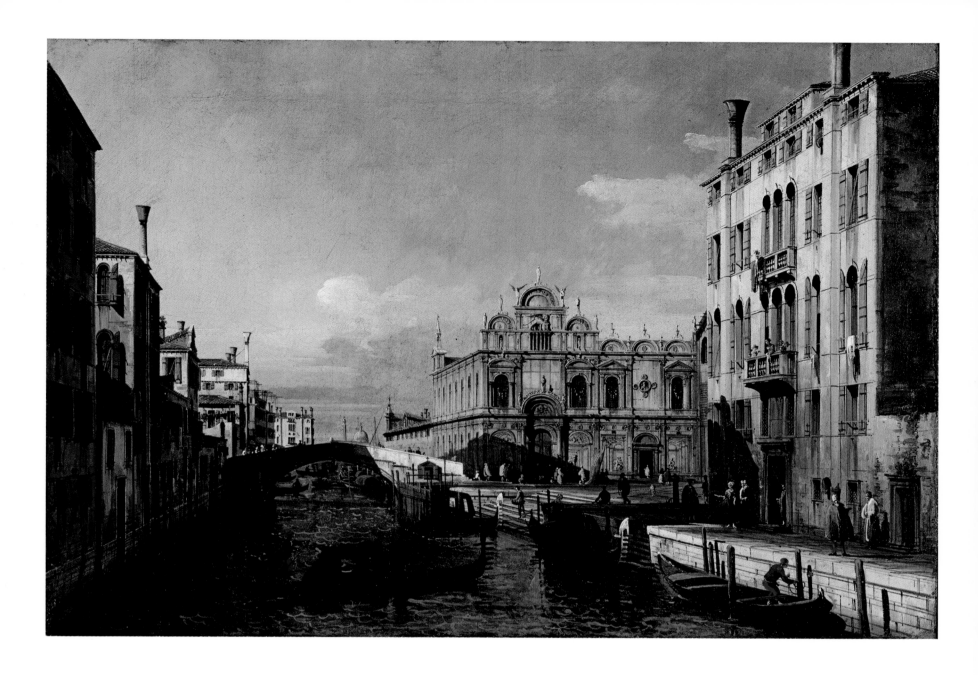

BERNARDO BELLOTTO   166

Venice, 1721—Warsaw, 1780
The Rio dei Mendicanti and the Scuola di San Marco
Oil on canvas, 17 x 28" (cat. no. 494)
Last restored 1990

Acquired in 1856 by the Gallerie as a Canaletto from the Vendramin collection, this *veduta* is probably the very one that Ruskin had in mind when he disagreed with the Venetian master while painting the same view. Nineteenth-century guidebooks repeated the attribution to Canaletto, then briefly, at the turn of the century, corrected it in favor of Bellotto, before reasserting the traditional authorship. After the restoration of 1958, and still more following the recent cleaning, the majority of expert opinion has given the picture to Bellotto. Actually, the painting would seem to be a work from the years the young artist spent in the workshop of his uncle Antonio Canal, better known as Canaletto. Even at this early date, Bellotto proved himself sufficiently well grounded in Canalettesque principles to depart from them towards greater naturalism and concretion, more firmly grasped details, and a very particular sense of

light, cooler and sharper yet also shimmering with the roseate tones that come just before sundown.

There is a larger version of the subject at the Museum of Fine Arts in Springfield (no. 3603), the work for which Bellotto probably did the preparatory drawing signed and dated December 8, 1740, and now in the Hessisches Landesmuseum at Darmstadt (AE22180). The painting seen here may be dated the same year. The view it presents is from what is now the Ponte delle Erbe, along the Rio dei Mendicanti towards the north. On the right we see the 17th-century Dandolo Palazzetto, with its tall chimneys, which hides the Colleoni monument and the façade of Santi Giovanni e Paolo, only a corner of which is visible, the façade of the Scuola di San Marco, and, in front of it, the campanile and dome of San Michele, represented as if viewed through a telephoto lens.

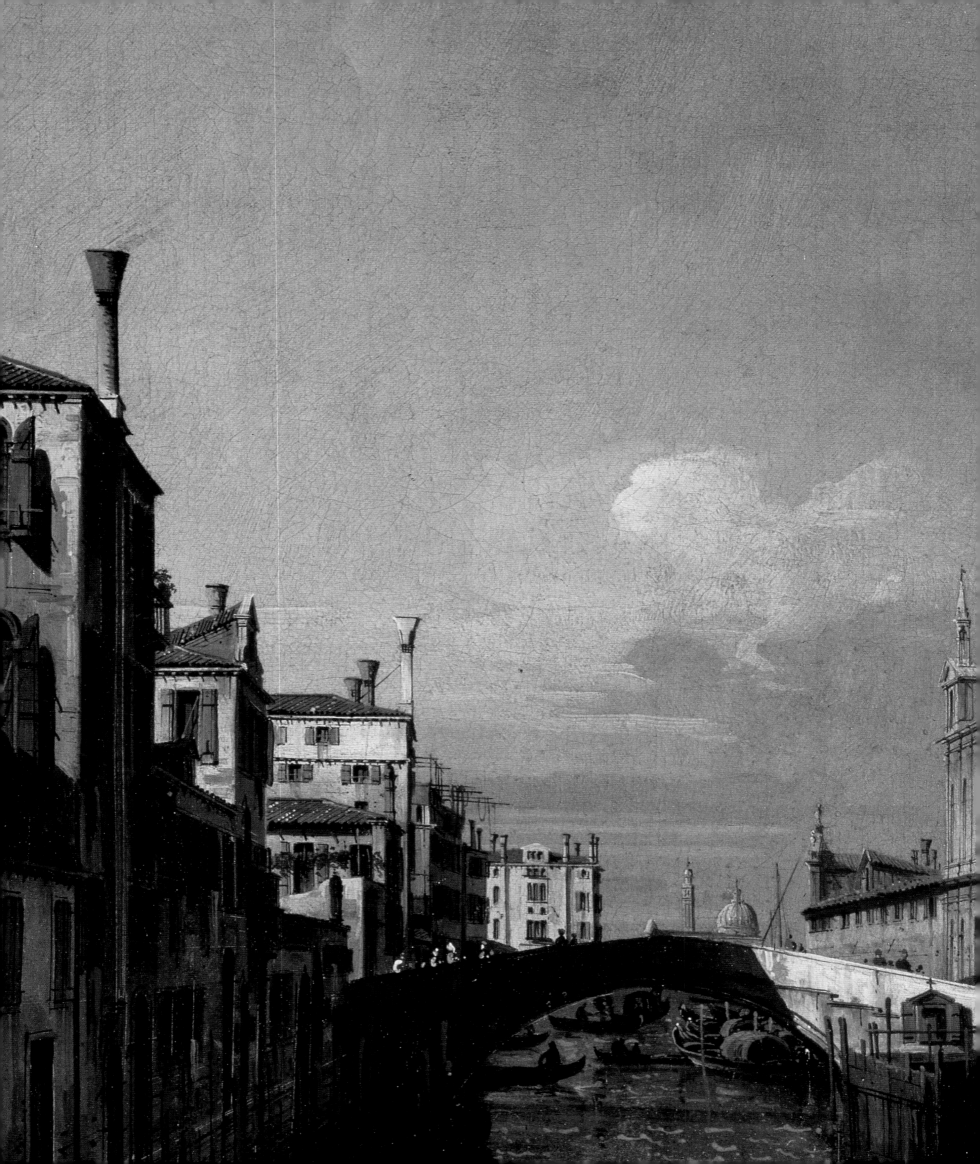

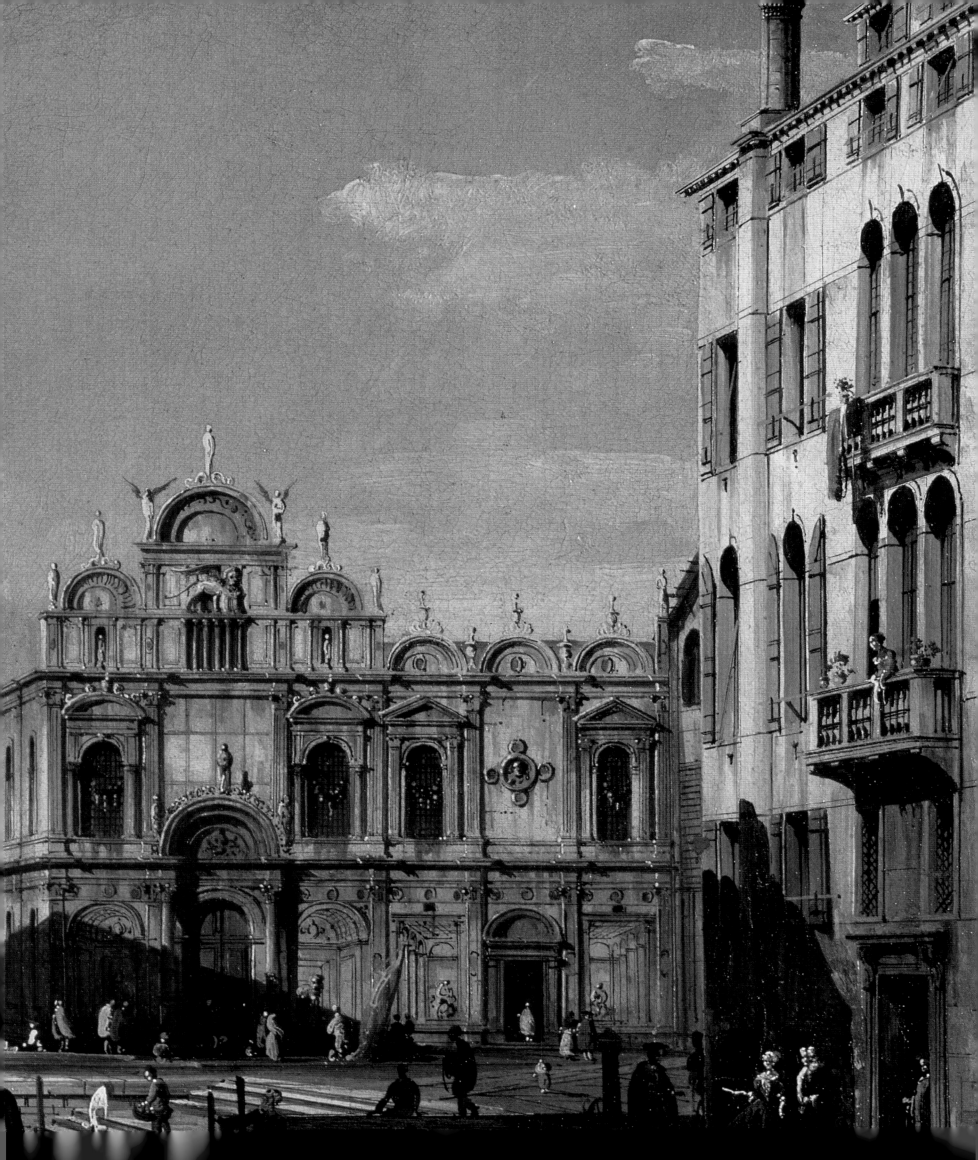

Venice, 1702-85
The Concert
Oil on Canvas, 24 x 19" (cat. no. 466)
Last restored 1955

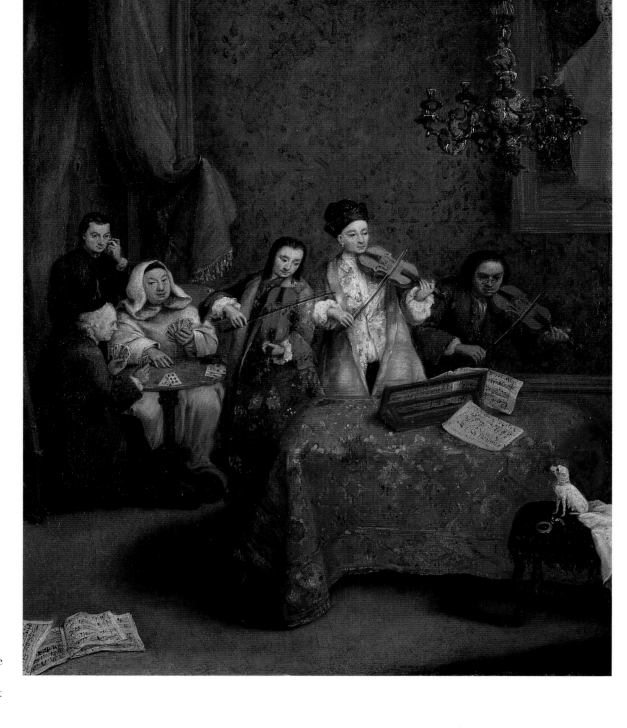

Girolamo Contarini presented this painting to the Gallerie in 1838, along with five other Longhis (see also ill. nos. 168-170). Signature and date both appear on the back of the canvas: "Petrus Longhi 1741." A bench-mark work in the course of his development, *The Concert* shows Longhi moving away from history painting to "conversation pieces" in the English or French manner, which the artist probably knew from engravings and prints of Hogarth as well as from French pictorial art in the tradition of Watteau. Such work may have come to his attention through the Frenchman Joseph Flipart, who lived in Venice from 1737 to 1750 and on a number of occasions made engravings after Longhi's pictures.

Despite the small format, the artist gives a lucid account of the scene's refined atmosphere, describing it in minute detail and with surpassing grace, not to mention the sly contrast between the intense concentration of the performing musicians and the distracted indifference of the cardplayers.

PIETRO LONGHI 168

Venice, 1702-85
The Dancing Lesson
Oil on canvas, 24 x 20" (cat. no. 465)
Last restored 1955

This work counted among the gifts made to the Gallerie by Girolamo Contarini in 1838 (see ill. no. 167). Whatever its relationship to a painting with the same subject in Munich's Alte Pinakothek, attributed to Giuseppe Maria Crespi as well as to Giannantonio Guardi, *The Dancing Lesson* reveals Longhi in all the originality of his very distinctive way with light and color. The Museo Correr in Venice owns a sheet of studies among which there is a partial drawing for the dancing couple, together with no less than four sketches for the dancing master's hands, all of which attest to an ever-more exact search for "truth" prior to giving the picture its definitive state.

The Dancing Lesson, with its airy grace and refined description of costumes and setting, enjoyed great favor among contemporary artists, as well as further afield, thanks to its dissemination through the engravings of Flipart and Hayd.

Like *The Concert*, the present painting may be dated in the early 1740s.

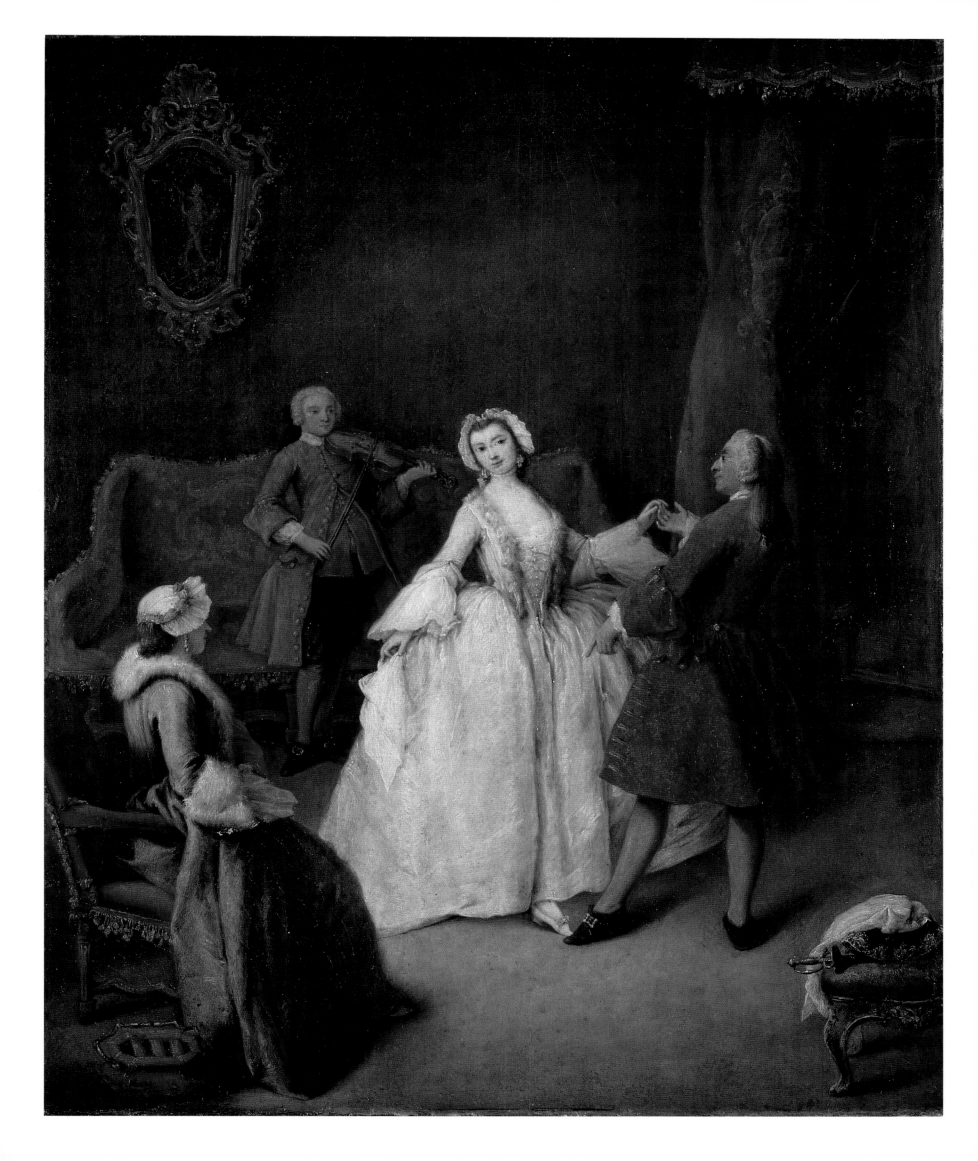

Venice, 1702-85
The Fortune-teller
Oil on canvas, 24 x 20" (cat. no. 468)
Last restored 1955

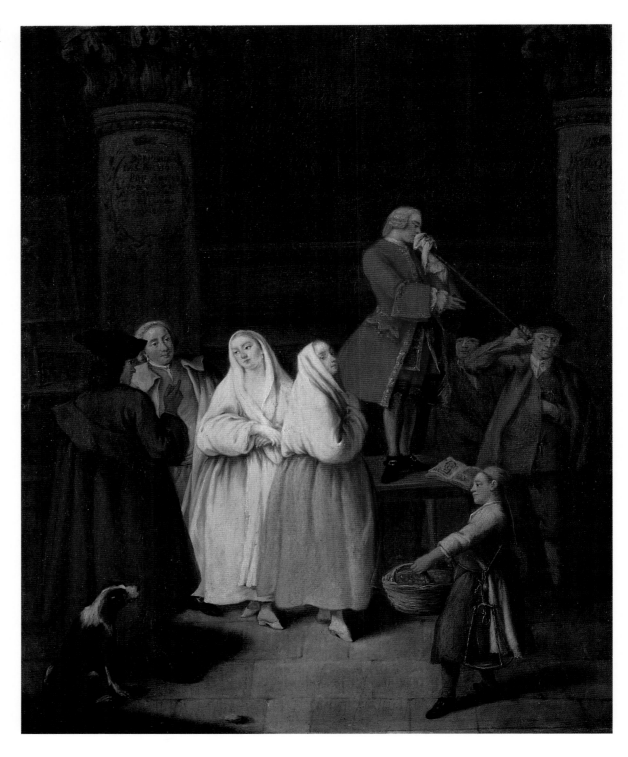

This canvas, also given to the Gallerie in 1838 by Girolamo Contarini (see ill. nos. 167, 168), was signed on the back by the artist. And here too, Longhi adopted a popular theme, this one set outdoors, on the portico of the Palazzo Ducale, and used the scene as an occasion for displaying his characteristically limpid colorism, as well as his good eye for attitude and detail.

The Museo Correr in Venice owns two preparatory studies (nos. 492 and 6058), one for the gentleman standing behind the two "commoners," and the other for the honey-seller's scales.

A near cousin of Longhi's *Tooth-drawer* in the Brera, this painting, like the one in Milan, can be dated towards the end of the 1740s.

Venice, 1702-85
The Pharmacist
Oil on canvas, 24 x 19" (cat. no. 467)
Last restored 1955

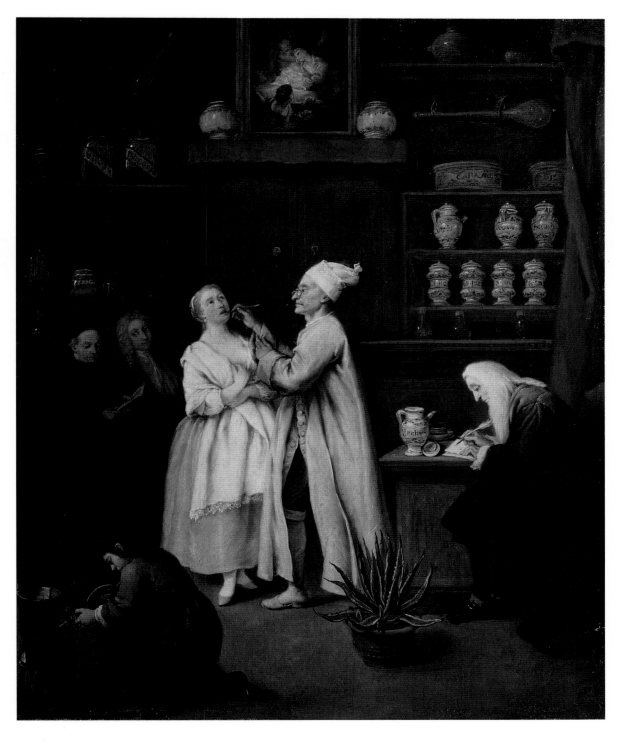

Once again, Longhi signed on the back a work given in 1838 to the Gallerie by Girolamo Contarini (see ill. nos. 167-169). *The Pharmacist* may be the best known, or at least the most widely disseminated, of the artist's works. The interior is rendered in such minute detail that one can identify the picture framed on the back wall as Antonio Balestra's *Nativity*, which exists today in a Venetian private collection. The painting reproduced here is a remarkable evocation of an 18th-century *bottega*, a scene of shelves lined with herb jars, a young woman being treated for a toothache, an old clerk making up prescriptions, a boy tending the flame under some decoction, other patients waiting their turn, a splendid agave plant in the foreground. Here, French influence has been harmoniously assimilated with a wide palette of exceptional limpidity, all in the service of lucidly observed figures and environment.

Longhi's *Pharmacist* belongs to the same period as his *Rhinoceros* in the Ca' Rezzonico, which bears the date 1751.

Venice, 1733-1813
The Family of the Procurator Luigi Pisani
Oil on canvas, 100 x 134" (cat. no. 1355)
Last restored 1959

On the world map the artist's name appears in script: LONGHJ. The original signature, now fragmentary, has been inscribed along the upper edge of the page of the book in the lower right: ALESSANDRO ABATE. Nearby one also finds an apocryphal inscription: OPUS PIETRO LONGI.

This huge canvas, together with a pendant, was executed under commission from the Pisani of Santo Stefano, who wanted a group portrait of the entire family. While one of the two pictures, only a fragment of which survives at the Museo Civico of Belluno, portrayed the family of Ermolao Alvise I Andrea Pisani, the painting seen here portrays Doge Alvise Pisani (1664-1741), his son the Procurator Luigi Pisani (1701-67), the latter's wife Paolina Gambara, and their children, Ermolao I Alvise, Elena, Ermolao II Carlo, and Elisabetta. The two persons in the background on the right are probably other Pisani sons—Ermolao IV Giovanni Francesco (1703-81) and Ermolao II Francesco (1693-1732)—while the elderly, black-clad gentleman offering a *bussolà* to the little Pisani may be *abate* Giovanni Gregorietti. The surrounding allegorical figures no doubt symbolize the many family virtues, and this family's ancestral house at Stra appears quite clearly in the right background. The painting would pass by inheritance to Bentivoglio d'Aragona and thence to Nani Mocenigo, from whom the Gallerie acquired it in 1979.

Alessandro Longhi projected on a grand scale the little scenes of Venetian life painted by his father Pietro, while also investing them with a psychological insight that transforms this painting into one of European portraiture's most memorable documents.

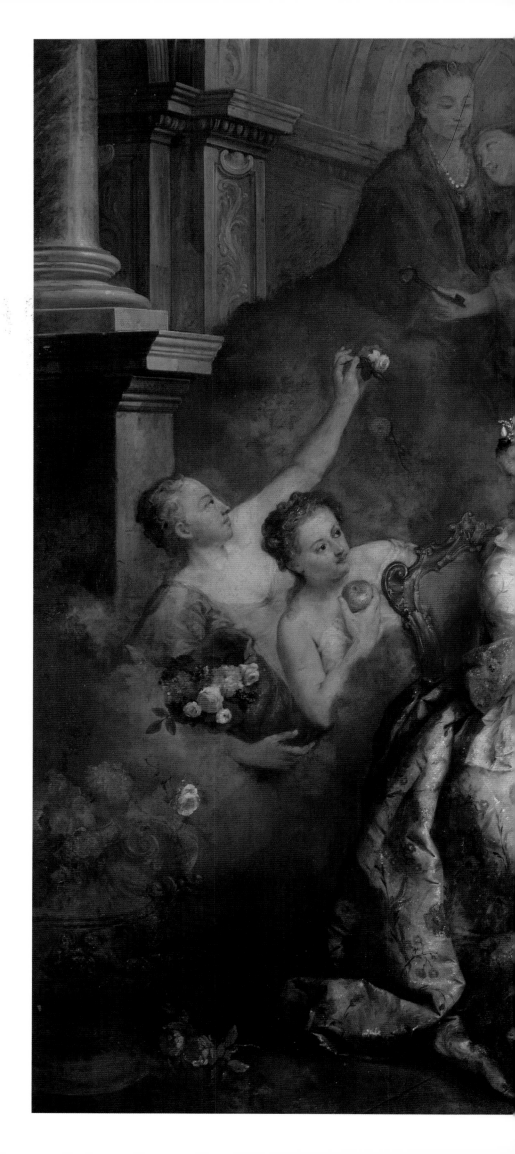

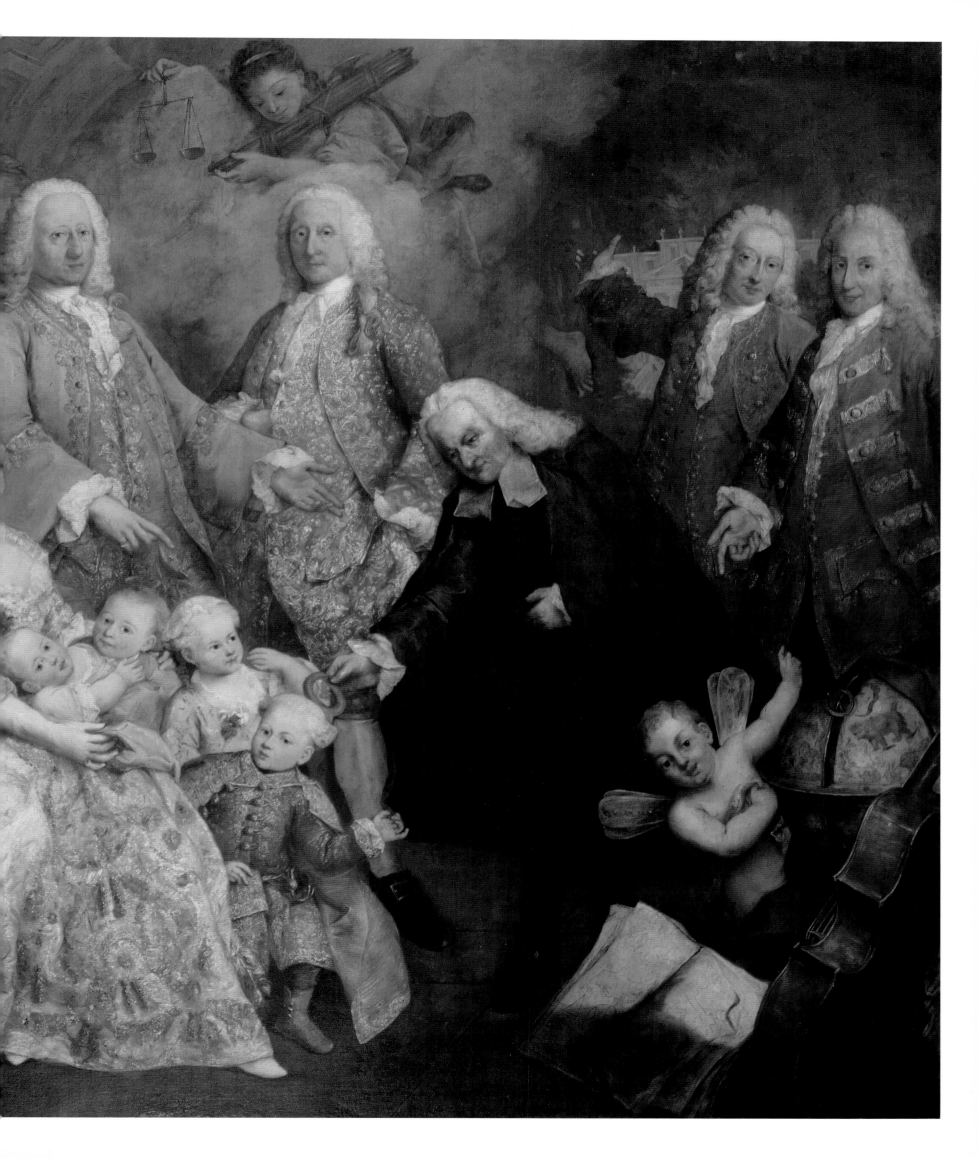

ALESSANDRO LONGHI   172

Venice, 1733-1813
Painting and Merit
Oil on canvas, 51 x 37" (cat. no. 493)
Last restored 1958

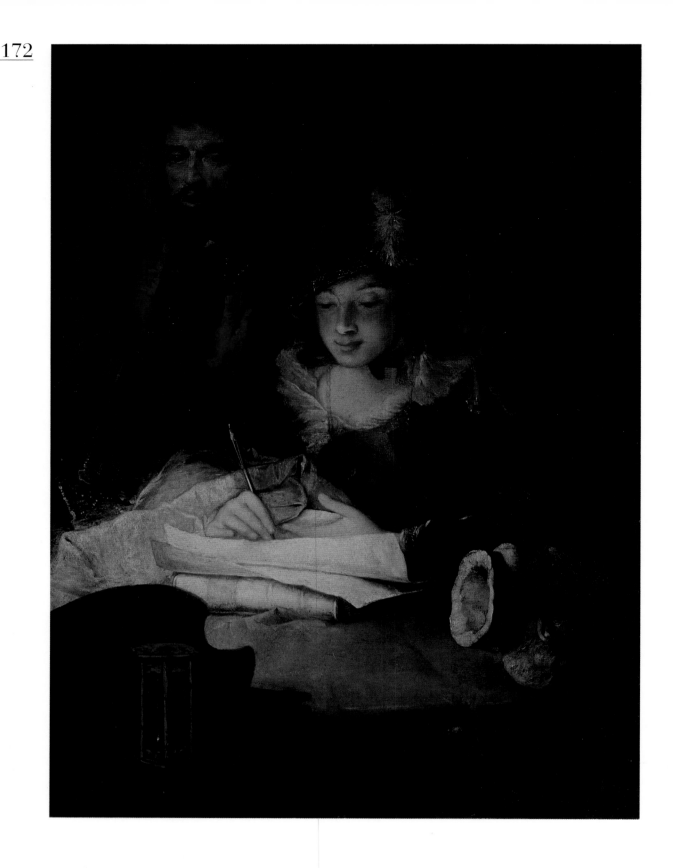

This was the *pièce de réception* presented by Alessandro to the Accademia, from which it comes. On the spine of the book held by the male figure we can read the artist's signature: ALESSANDRO / LONGHI / PINX.

At lower left, on the binding of the book under the water clock, we again find "Alessandro Longhi," this time written in an old script. The title of this personified allegory has been deduced from the one given on the engraving of the same subject, based on the work seen here and dedicated to John Udny, British Consul in Venice in 1761 and again in 1773-75.

The engraving shows more detail in the upper zone, as well as the portrait of a man in the right background, which cannot be distinguished in the original, owing to an excess of repainting. Alessandro was elected to the Accademia in 1759, and since his name does not appear on the list of members requested, by a resolution of November 14, 1762 (repeating one made on May 17 of the preceding year), to submit their delinquent pieces on the required subject, it seems likely that he executed *Painting and Merit* in 1761, the first year of Udny's consulship.

Venice, 1733-1813
Portrait of Carlo Lodoli
Oil on canvas, 79 x 37" (cat. no. 908)
Last restored 1958-59

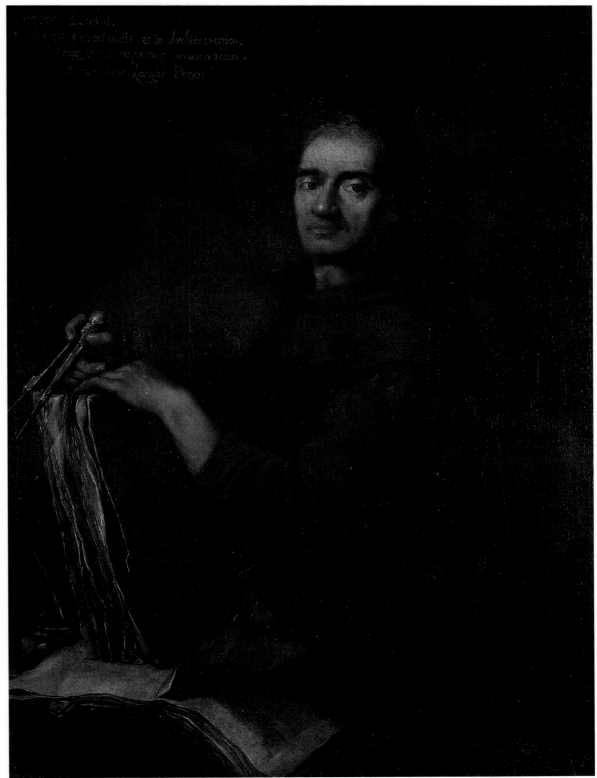

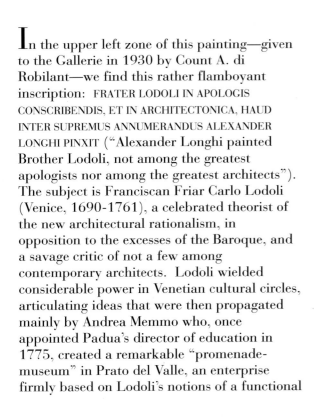

In the upper left zone of this painting—given to the Gallerie in 1930 by Count A. di Robilant—we find this rather flamboyant inscription: FRATER LODOLI IN APOLOGIS CONSCRIBENDIS, ET IN ARCHITECTONICA, HAUD INTER SUPREMUS ANNUMERANDUS ALEXANDER LONGHI PINXIT ("Alexander Longhi painted Brother Lodoli, not among the greatest apologists nor among the greatest architects"). The subject is Franciscan Friar Carlo Lodoli (Venice, 1690-1761), a celebrated theorist of the new architectural rationalism, in opposition to the excesses of the Baroque, and a savage critic of not a few among contemporary architects. Lodoli wielded considerable power in Venetian cultural circles, articulating ideas that were then propagated mainly by Andrea Memmo who, once appointed Padua's director of education in 1775, created a remarkable "promenade-museum" in Prato del Valle, an enterprise firmly based on Lodoli's notions of a functional architecture. Ascerbic in the extreme, Lodoli made numerous enemies, with the result that, in 1761, the year the Friar died, Pietro Longhi painted *Monks, Canons, and Friars of Venice* (Pinacoteca Querini Stampalia) that includes a mordantly malicious caricature of Lodoli.

As we have seen, even the inscription on Longhi's portrait offers the subject a back-handed tribute. Thus, it seems difficult to accept the hypothesis that the unknown client was Memmo himself, whose daughter Lucia married a Mocenigo of the San Samuele branch. It was her heirs, the Robilants, in whose palazzo on the Grand Canal the painting hung.

In any case, the portrait seen here is not the same as the one reproduced by Pietro Vitali and characterized by Memmo, in 1788, as a work by Alessandro Longhi for Pietro Moschi. The engraving shows an oval format with the bust of the Friar viewed from the front. It would therefore seem that Longhi painted more than a single portrait of the controversial Lodoli. It is not easy to date such an incisive and psychologically acute image, but the painting surely must be posthumous.

Venice, 1727-1804
The Three Angels Appearing to Abraham
Oil on canvas, 80 x 112" (cat. no. 834)
Last restored 1960

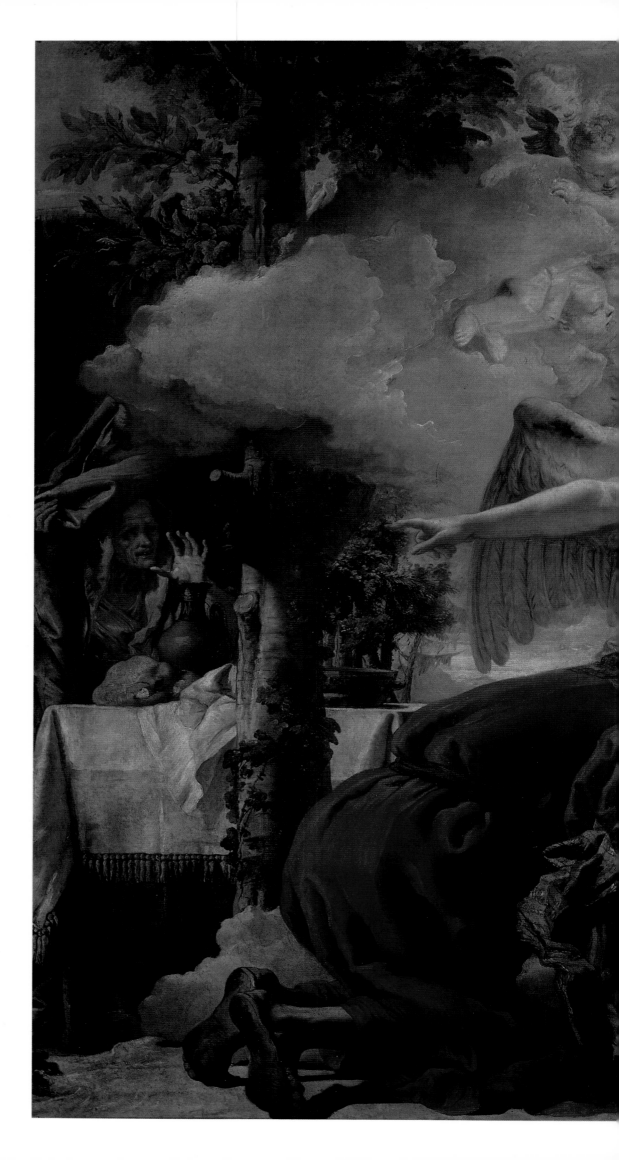

Executed for the *sala dell'albergo* of the Scuola della Carità, also known as "the new chancellery," the painting remained in place after secularization and passed with the building to the Accademia. Between 1817 and 1924 it was on long-term loan, first to the Oratorio di Gesù e Maria and then to the Church of San Cassiano.

The painting seen here was the last commissioned by the confraternity to complete the decoration of a hall built in 1764. Between 1768 and 1770 the program brought to the Scuola's walls Giambettino Cignaroli's *Death of Rachel*, Lorenzo Gramiccia's *Elias and the Angel*, and Guistino Menescardi's *Moses Rescued from the River*. Meanwhile, Jacopo Marieschi painted *Divine Wisdom* and *The Theological Virtues* for the ceiling. One further painting was done by Pietro Gradizzi; indeed, he did it twice but never succeeded in giving satisfaction. As a result, the Scuola organized a competition and invited artists to submit sketches to an academic committee in Rome that included Anton Raphael Mengs. Giandomenico Tiepolo won by unaminous consent.

On March 8, 1773, the artist signed a contract committing himself to complete the work "which is to depict the appearance of the three angels to the patriarch Abraham, and his adoration of them, within one year more or less, in consideration whereof there have been paid to me . . . 116 zecchini."

The work repeats, albeit in reverse, a 1742 drawing by Giambattista Tiepolo now in Berlin (Staatliche Museen, M. 38). The group of angels also recalls Giambattista's painting on the same theme in the Prado, while the figure of Abraham was inspired by a painting in the Luna-Villahermosa collection in Madrid. The Museo Correr owns three of Giandomenico's preliminary studies, for Abraham's hands, for an arm, and for a foot (nos. D 92, 97, 98 v.) On May 16, 1967, the Musée Galliéra in Paris sold a watercolor drawing of the whole, perhaps a study for the competition. On June 25, 1970, Sotheby's sold it again, this time at auction. The chalky smoothness of the palette and the chill purity of the drawing already reflect the advent of Neoclassicism, and it is no coincidence that the painting itself found unconditional favor with Mengs.

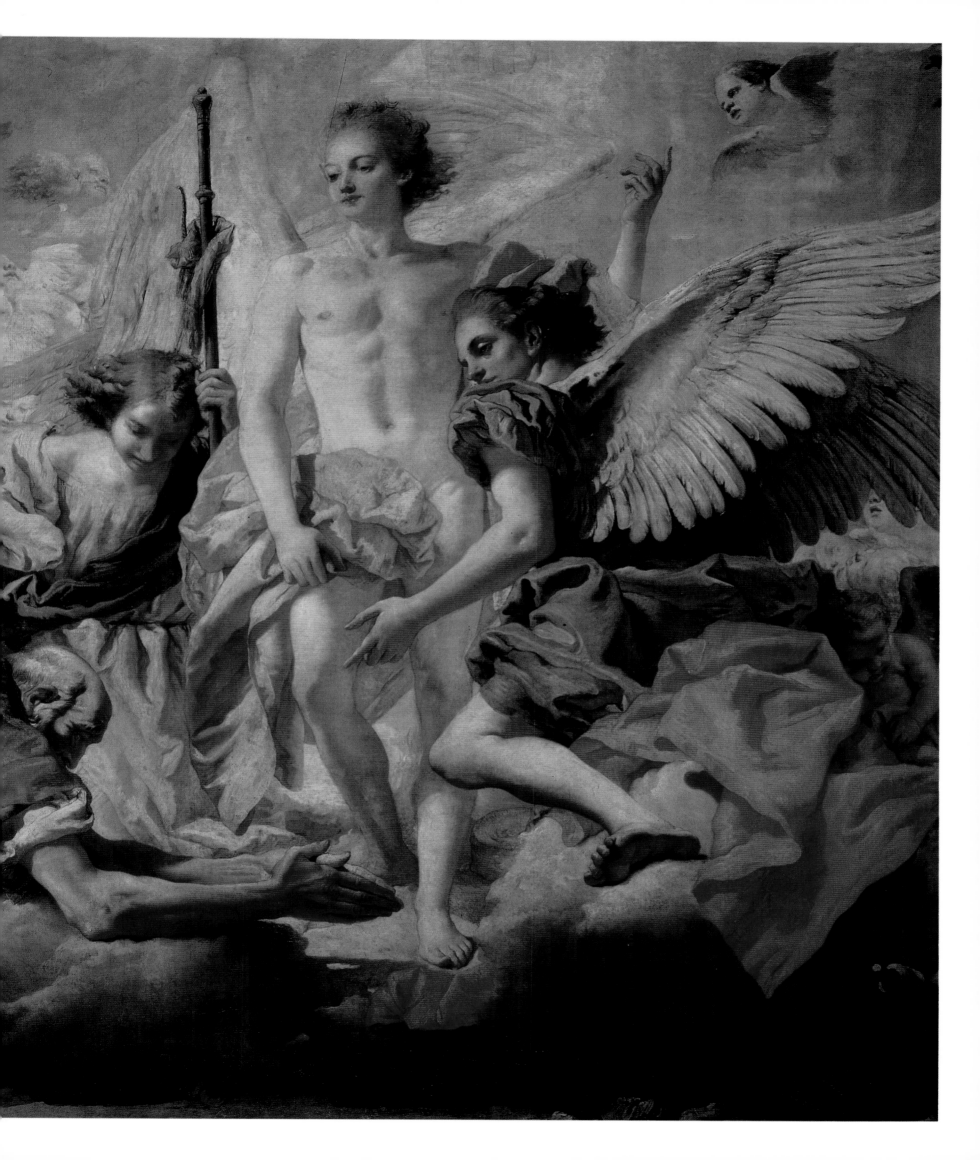

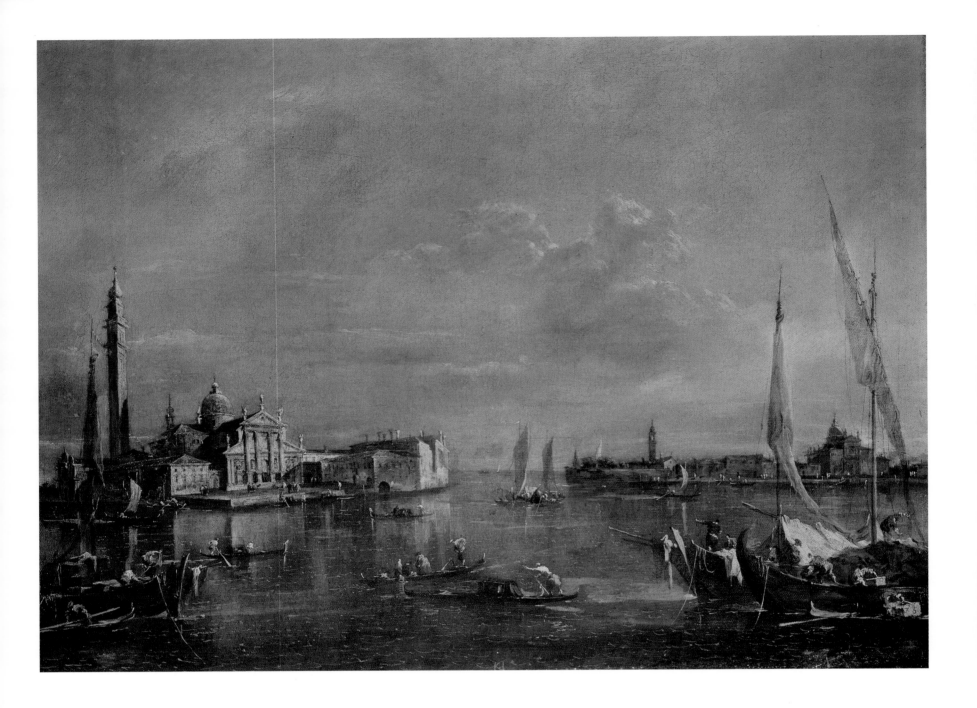

FRANCESCO GUARDI   175

Venice, 1712-93
Saint Mark's Basin with San Giorgio and the Giudecca
Oil on canvas, 29 x 39" (cat. no. 709)

In the collection of M.A. Fèbre until 1882, the painting came to the Gallerie in 1903 as a gift from Prince Johann of Liechtenstein. On a chest aboard the boat in the lower right foreground appear the initials F.G.

In this painting the artist took up one of his favorite and most frequently repeated subjects. The scene encompasses, on the left, the island of San Giorgio Maggiore and, at right, the Giudecca, the latter complete with its now-destroyed Church of San Giovanni Battista, several Camaldolite monks, and the church *delle Zitelle* ("of the Spinsters").

This particular *veduta*—probably part of a series of three, the other two being the *Church of the Salute with the Punta della Dogana* (Liechtenstein Collection, Vaduz) and the *Piazza San Marco* (whereabouts unknown)—recalls one in London's Wallace Collection. Behind both pictures, and others similar to them, may very well lie a signed drawing in the Wallraf collection in London.

The flaking colors have always made the painting seem a late work, but it could not have been executed later than 1774, the year in which the old onion-domed campanile on San Giorgio Island—still present in Guardi's *veduta*—suddenly collapsed.

Despite a rather poor state of preservation, the picture, with its labile, allusive imagery, continues to radiate a magical, expressive power.

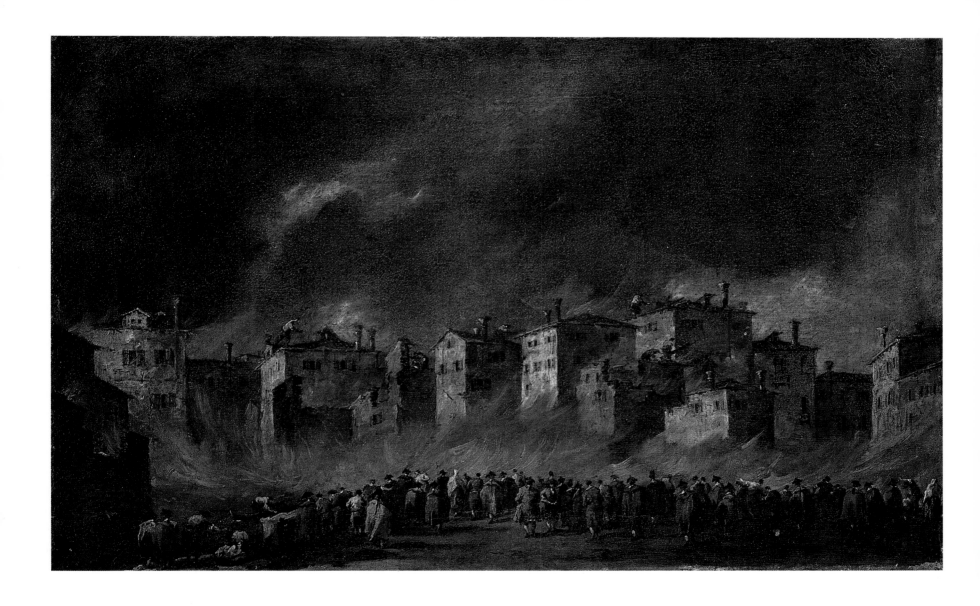

FRANCESCO GUARDI　176

Venice, 1712-93
Fire at the Oil Deposit at San Marcuola
Oil on canvas, 16 x 24" (cat. no. 1344)

Having passed from the Lazzari collection in Padua to the Mazzarino-Brambilla collection in Milan, the picture came up for auction at the Finarte on November 9, 1971, after which the Gallerie acquired it on February 5, 1972.

The painting depicts a contemporary event in Venetian history—the dramatic fire that broke out at the oil-storage facilites in the Ghetto on November 28, 1789. As noted in the *Gazzetta Urbana* of December 5, 1789, the catastrophic damage left 60 houses and 15 shops destroyed and 150 families homeless, prompting the Council of Ten to initiate an immediate inquiry into the cause.

Among the documentary works painted by Guardi—*Ascension of the Balloon, Festivities in Celebration of Pope Pius VI's Visit to Venice, Festival for the Arrival of the Northern Counts*—the one seen here is undoubtedly the masterpiece of the artist's late maturity, its intense expressionism typical of his finest landscapes devoted to the Lagoon. The directness and dynamism of the rendering suggest an eye-witness account, as do several drawings, the most exactly relevant of which belongs to the Metropolitan Museum in New York. The drawing in the Museo Correr, with the apocryphal (and erroneous) annotation "Fire at S. Marcuola in the year 1789, October 28," was probably completed by Canaletto's son Giacomo. Moreover, it appears to be less a preparatory work than a variation on an analogous theme found in a painting now owned by Munich's Alte Pinakothek. In this depiction, the fire had reached its last phase, with the surrounding houses already destroyed, the smoke thicker and darker, the flames redder as well as less furious, and the watchers already in darkness.

BIBLIOGRAPHY

BALLARIN, A. "Una nuova prospettiva su Giorgione: la ritrattistica degli anni 1500-1503," *Giorgione*, Acts of the International Congress of Studies, Cast lfranco, Veneto (TV), 1978.

BARCHAM, W.L. "Giambattista Tiepolo's Ceilings for S. Maria di Názareth in Venice: Legend, Traditions, and Devotions," *Art Bulletin* 61, 1979.

—. *The Religious Paintings of Giambattista Tiepolo*, New York, 1989.

BERNASCONI, J.G. "The Dating of the Cycle of the Miracles of the Cross from the Scuola di San Giovanni Evangelista, *Arte Veneta* XXXV, 1981.

BORLA, S. "Paolo Veneziano e il fratello Marco," *Arte Veneta* XXIV, 1970.

BOSCHINI, M. *La carta del navegar pittoresco*, Venice, 1660.

—. *Le miniere della pittura*, Venice, 1664, 1674.

BOSKOVITS, M. "Ferrarese Painting about 1450: Some New Arguments," *Burlington Magazine* CXX, 903, 1978.

BOTERO, A. *L'opera completa di Carlo Crivelli*, Milan, 1975.

BURCKHARDT, J. *Der Cicerone*, Basel, 1855; Florence, 1952.

CHRISTIANSEN, K. "Venetian Painting of the Early Quattrocento," *Apollo* CXXV, 301, March 1987.

—. *Gentile da Fabriano*, London, 1982.

CIERIVIA, C. "Allegorie morali dalla bottega belliniana," in *Giorgione e la cultura veneta tra '400 e '500*, Acts of the Congress of Studies, Rome, 1981.

CIOCI, F. *La Tempesta interpretata dieci anni dopo*, with a preface by P. Zampetti, Florence, 1991.

CIOLINO, C. "Antonello da Saliba," in *Antonello da Messina*, exh. cat., Rome, 1981.

COCKE, R. *Veronese Drawings*, Oxford, 1984.

CONTI, A. *Storia del restauro*, Milan, n.d.

DANIELS, J. *L'Opera completa di Sebastiano Ricci*, Milan, 1976.

D'ARCAIS, F. "Le tavole con le storie di San Benedetto, un problema ancora aperto," *Arte Veneta* XXX, 1976.

DE MARCHI, A. "Per un riesame della pittura tardogotica a Venezia: Nicolò del Paradiso e il suo contesto adriatico," *Bollettino d'Arte* 44-45, 1987.

DEGENHART, A., and P. SCHMITT. *Corpus der italienischen Zeichnungen 1300-1450, II, Teil, Venedig*, Berlin, 1980.

DOLCE, L. *Dialogo della pittura intitolato L'Aretino*, Venice, 1557.

Dopo Mantegna: Arte a Padova e nel territorio nei secoli XV e XVI, Milan, 1976.

EISLER, C. *The Genius of Jacopo Bellini*, New York, 1989.

FERRARINO, L. *Tiziano e la corte di Spagna nei documenti dell'Archivio General di Simancas*, Madrid, 1975.

FINARTE. *Vendita pubblica all'asta di quadri antichi*, Milan, Oct 29, 1964.

FOGOLARI, C. "L'Accademia veneziana di pittura e scultura del Settecento," *L'Arte* XVI, 1913.

FORTINI-BROWN, P. *Venetian Narrative Paintings in the Age of Carpaccio*, New Haven and London, 1988.

FRA' PACIFICO (D. PIETRO ANTONIO PACIFICO). *Cronica veneta sacra e profana o sia un compendio di tutte le cose più illustri ed antiche della città di Venezia*, Venice, 1736.

FURLAN, C. *Il Pordenone*, exh. cat., 1984.

GAMULIN, G. "Contributi alla pittura del Quattrocento," *Arte Veneta* XXXVII, 1983.

The Genius of Venice: 1500-1600, Royal Academy of Arts, London, 1983.

Giambattista Piazzetta, il suo tempo, la sua scuola, exh. cat., Padua, 1983.

Giorgione a Venezia, exh. cat., Milan, 1978.

GIOSEFFI, D. "Giorgione e la pittura tonale," in *Giorgione*, Acts of the International Congress of Studies, Castelfranco Veneto (TV), 1978.

Giovanni Girolamo Savoldo, exh. cat., Milan, 1990.

GOFFEN, R. *Giovanni Bellini*, Milan, 1990.

HASKELL, F. *Patrons and Painters*, London, 1963.

HIRST, M. *Sebastiano del Piombo*, Oxford, 1981.

HUMPHREY, P. *Cima da Conegliano*, Cambridge, 1983.

HUSE, N. *Studien zu Giovanni Bellini*, Berlin and New York, 1972.

—, and W. WOLTERS. *Venezia: L'arte del Rinascimento*, Venice, 1989.

HUTER, C. "Jacobello del Fiore, Giambono, and the St. Benedict Panels," *Arte Veneta* XXXII, 1978.

Johann Liss, exh. cat., Augsburg, 1975.

KNOX, G. *Giambattista and Domenico Tiepolo: A Study and Catalogue Raisonné of the Chalk Drawings*, Oxford, 1980.

LEVEY, M. *Giambattista Tiepolo: His Life and His Art*, New Haven, 1986.

LIGHTBROWN, R. *Mantegna*, Oxford, 1986.

LINKS, J.G. "Verona, Castelvecchio Museum Bernardo Bellotto," *Burlington Magazine* CXXXII, Sept 1990.

—. *Canaletto*, Oxford, 1976.

LIVAN, L. *Notizie d'arte tratte dai notatori e dagli annali del N.H. Pietro Gradenigo*, Venice, 1942.

LONGHI, R. *Viatico per cinque secoli di pittura veneziana*, Florence, 1946.

LORENZI, G.B. *Monumenti per servire alla Storia del Palazzo Ducale di Venezia ovvero serie di atti pubblici dal 1253 al 1797*, Venice, 1868.

LUCCO, M. *Sebastiano del Piombo*, Milan, 1980.

—. "Il Giudizio di Salomone di Sebastiano del Piombo a Kingston Lacey," *Eidos* 1, 1987.

LUDWIG, G. "Bonifazio de' Pitati da Verona, eine archivalische Untersuchung," *Jahrbuch der Königlischen Preussischen Kunstsammlungen* XXII, 1901-02.

MAGAGNATO, L. *Da Altichiero a Pisanello*, exh. cat., Venice, 1958.

MALAMANI, V. *Rosalba Carriera*, Bergamo, 1910.

MARINI, G. "Bernardo Bellotto," in *Verona e le città europee*, exh. cat., ed. by S. Marinelli, Verona, 1940.

MARIUZ, A. *Giandomenico Tiepolo*, Venice and Milan, n.d., but after 1971.

—. *L'opera completa del Piazzetta*, with foreword by R. Pallucchini, Milan, 1982.

MARTINI, E. *La Pittura veneziana del Settecento*, Venice, 1964.

MARTINIONI, G. *Venetia Città . . . descritta dal Sansovino*, Venice, 1663.

MASON RINALDI, S. "Contributi d'archivio per la decorazione pittorica della Scuola di San Giovanni Evangelista," *Arte Veneta* XXXII, 1978.

MENEGAZZI, L. *Cima da Conegliano*, Treviso, 1981.

MEYER ZUR CAPELLEN, J. "La figura del San Lorenzo Giustiniani di Jacopo Bellini," *Centro Tedesco di Studi Veneziani, Quaderno n.19*, Venice, 1981.

—. *Gentile Bellini*, Stuttgart, 1985.

MICHIEL, M.A. *Notizia d'opera di disegno pubblicata e illustrata da D. Jacopo Morelli (1541-1543c.)*, 2nd ed., ed. by G. Frizzoni, Bologna, 1884.

MODIGLIANI, E. *La collezione di Luigi Albertini*, Rome, 1942.

MOLAJOLI, R. *L'opera completa di Cosmè Tura e i grandi pittori ferraresi del suo tempo*, Milan, 1974.

MORASSI, A. *Guardi*, Venice, 1973.

MORTARI, L. *Bernardo Strozzi*, Rome, 1966.

MOSCHINI, G.A. *Guida per la città di Venezia all'amico di belle arti*, Venice, 1815.

MOSCHINI MARCONI, S. *Gallerie dell'Accademia di Venezia: Opere d'arte dei secoli XIV e XV*, Rome, 1955.

—. *Gallerie dell'Accademia di Venezia: Opere d'arte del secolo XVI*, Rome, 1962.

—. *Gallerie dell'Accademia di Venezia: Opere d'arte dei secoli XVII, XVIII e XIX*, Rome, 1970.

MURARO, M. *Paolo da Venezia*, Milan, 1969.

Napols il el barroc Mediterrain, exh. cat., Barcelona, 1990.

NEPI SCIRÈ, G. "Andrea da Murano, Polittico," in *Venezia e la peste*, 1348-1797, exh. cat., Venice.

—. "Il pittore trevigiano Pier Maria Pennacchi," in *Lorenzo Lotto*, Acts of the International Congress of Studies for the 5th Centenary of the Artist's Birth, Venice, 1980.

—. *Canaletto: Dipinti, disegni et incisioni*, ed. by A. Bettagno, exh. cat., Venice, 1982.

—. "Il restauro del *Convito in casa di Levi* di Paolo Veronese," *Quaderni della Soprintendenza ai Beni Artistici e Storici di Venezia* 11, 1984.

—. "Il restauro della *Presentazione di Maria al tempio* di Tiziano," *Bollettino d'arte studi veneziani*, supplement no. 5, Rome, 1984.

—, and G. Valcanover. *Gallerie dell'Accademia*, Milan, 1985.

—. "Il Ritratto di gentiluomo nel suo studio di Lorenzo Lotto," in *Venezia restaurata 1966-1986*, Milan, 1986.

—. "Restauri alle Gallerie dell'Accademia,"

Quaderni della Soprintendenza ai Beni Artistici e Storici di Venezia 13, 1987.

—. "Il *Convito in casa di Levi* di Paolo Veronese: Restauri," *Quaderni della Soprintendenza ai Beni Artistici e Storici di Venezia* 15, 1988.

—, ed. *Gallerie dell'Accademia: Nuove acquisizioni*, Venice, 1988.

—. "Recenti restauri di Paolo Veronese alle Gallerie dell'Accademia," *Venezia Arti* 15, 1989.

—, ed. *Veneziansko slikarstvo XVIII veka* (*La pittura veneziana del Settecento: Cultura e società*), Belgarde, 1990.

L'Opera ritrovata: Omaggio a Rodolfo Siviero, exh. cat., Florence, 1984.

PALLUCCHINI, R. "Nuovi Ricci e Canaletto alle Gallerie di Venezia," *Arte Veneta III*, 1949.

—. *La pittura veneziana del Settecento*, Venice and Rome, 1960.

—. *I Vivarini*, Venice, 1962.

—. *La pittura veneziana del Trecento*, Venice, 1964.

—. *L'opera completa di Giambattista Tiepolo*, Milan, 1968.

—. *La pittura veneziana del Seicento*, Milan, 1981.

—. *Bassano*, Bologna, 1982.

—, and P. Rossi. *Tintoretto: Le opere sacre e profane*, Milan, 1982.

PANAZZA, G. *Girolamo Romanino*, exh. cat., Brescia, 1965.

PAOLETTI, P. *Catalogo delle Gallerie di Venezia*, Venice, 1903.

PAOLUCCI, A. *Piero della Francesca*, Florence, 1990.

PAVANELLO, C. *Venezia nell'età del Canova 1780-1830*, pp. 18, 30, 36, 37. Venice, 1978.

PEDROCCO, R. "Scuola di Sant'Orsola," in *Le Scuole di Venezia*, ed. by T. Pignatti, Milan, 1981.

Per la storia del Manierismo a Venezia da Tiziano a El Greco: 1540-1590, with intro. by R. Pallucchini, Milan, 1981.

PIGNATTI, T. *Pietro Longhi*, Venice, 1968.

—. *L'opera completa di Giovanni Bellini detto Giambellino*, Milan, 1969.

—. *L'opera completa di Pietro Longhi*, Milan, 1974.

—. *Paolo Veronese*, Venice, 1976.

—. *Giorgione*, Venice, 1978.

—. *Venezia: Mille anni d'arte*, Venice, 1989.

PILO, G.M. (with essay by R. Pallucchini). *Marco Ricci*, exh. cat., Venice, 1963.

La pittura in Italia: il Quattrocento, Milan, 1987.

La pittura nel Veneto: il Quattrocento, Milan, 1989.

PUPPI, L. "Riflessioni su temi e problemi nella ritrattistica del Lotto," in *Lorenzo Lotto*, Acts of the International Congress of Studies for the 5th Centenary of the Artist's Birth, Venice, 1981.

RIDOLFI, C. *Le meraviglie dell'arte*, Venice, 1648, ed. by von Hadeln, Berlin, 1914-24.

RIZZI, A. *Sebastiano Ricci*, 1989.

"Riflettografia computerizzata infrarosso," *Quaderni della Soprintendenza ai Beni Artistici e Storici dei Venezia* 6, 1984.

ROBERTSON, G. *Giovanni Bellini*, Oxford, 1968.

ROSAND, D. *Painting in Cinquecento Venice:*

Titian, Veronese, Tintoretto, New Haven and London, 1985.

ROSSI, P. *Jacopo Tintoretto: I ritratti*, Venice, 1973.

ROTHLISBERGER, M. "Studi su Jacopo Bellini," *Saggi e memorie di Storia dell'Arte*, 1959.

RYLANDS, P. *Palma il Vecchio: L'opera completa*, Milan, 1988.

SABELLICO, M.A. *De situ Urbis Venetae*, Brescia(?), c.1490.

SAFARIK, E.A. *Fetti*, Milan, 1990.

SANDRART, J. *Teutsche Academie der Bau-, Bildhauer- und Malerkust*, Nuremberg, 1675.

SANI, B. *Rosalba Carriera: Lettere, diari, frammenti*, Florence, 1985.

—. *Rosalba Carriera*, Chieri (TO), 1988.

SANSOVINO, R. *Venetia città nobilissima e singolare descritta in XIII libri*, Venice, 1581.

SANUDO, M. *I diari (1496-1533)*, ed. by R. Fulin, F. Stefani, and L. Barozzi, 59 vols., Venice, 1879-1902.

SANUDO, M., IL GIOVANE. *De origine, situ et magistratibus urbis Venetae ovvero La Città di Venezia (1493-1530)*, ed. by A. Caracciolo Aricò, Milan, 1980.

SAVIO, L.S. "Restauri alle Gallerie dell'Accademia," *Quaderni della Soprintendenza Artistici e Storici di Venezia* 13, 1987.

SCHULZ, J. "Veronese's Ceilings at San Nicolò ai Frari," *Burlington Magazine* 694, 1961.

—. *Venetian Painted Ceilings of the Renaissance*, Berkeley and Los Angeles, 1968.

SCHWEIKHART, G. "Giorgione e Bellini," in *Giorgione e l'umanesimo veneziano*, Florence, 1981.

El Seteciento veneciano: Aspectos de la pintura veneciana del siglo XVIII, exh. cat., Saragossa, 1990.

SIMONETTI, S. "Profilo di Bonifacio de' Pitati," *Saggi e memorie di Storia dell'Arte* 15, 1986.

SIMONETTO, L. "Lo Pseudo Boccaccino fra Milano e Venezia: Certezze e dubbi di una cronologia," *Arte Lombarda* 84-85, 1988.

SINDING-LARSEN, S. *Christ in the Council Hall: Studies in the Religious Iconography of the Venetian Republic*, with a contribution by A. Kuhn (Institutum Romanum Norvegiae Acta ad archaeologiam et artium historiam pertinentia V), Rome, 1974.

SPEZZANI, P. "La *Presentazaione di Maria al Tempio* di Tiziano ai raggi X," *Bollettino d'arte studi veneziani*, supplement no. 5, Rome, 1984.

STEDMAN SHEARD, W. "Bramante e il Lombardo: Ipotesi su una connessione," in *Venezia e Milano*, Milan, 1984.

STEER, J. *Alvise Vivarini: His Art and Influence*, Cambridge, 1982.

SUCCI, D. *Da Carlevarijs al Tiepolo: incisori veneti e friulani del Settecento*, Venice, 1983.

—, ed. *Canaletto e Visentini a Londra*, exh. cat., Cittadella (PD), 1986.

—, ed. *Marieschi tra Canaletto e Guardi*, exh. cat., Turin, 1989.

Titian: Prince of Painters, exh. cat., Washington, D.C., and Munich, 1990.

TOLEDANO, R. *Michele Marieschi: L'opera completa*, Milan, 1988.

VALCONOVER, F. "Aggiunte al catalogo di Antonio Vivarini," *Paragone* 123, 1960.

—. *Restauri nel Veneto*, vol. 1, Venice, 1966.

—. "Gli *Eremiti* di Giovanni Girolamo Savoldo alle Gallerie dell'Accademia," in *Atti del Convegno su Girolamo*, Brescia, 1984.

—. "Le *Storie di Sant'Orsola* di Vittore Carpaccio dopo il recente restauro," *Atti dell'Istituto Vento di Scienze, Lettere e Arti*, Venice CXLIV, 1985-86.

—. "Zur Restaurierung von Gemälden Jacopo Tintorettos in Venedig," in *Die Bamberg Himmelfahrt Maria*, Munich, 1988.

VASARI, G. *Le vite de' più eccellenti architetti, pittori et scultori italiani*, from the types of Lorenzo Torrenti, Florence, 1550, Turin, 1986.

—. *Le vite de' più eccellenti architetti, pittori et scultori italiani*, Florence, 1568, ed. by G. Milanesi, 1878-85.

Venedig: Malerei des 18. Jahrhunderts, Munich, 1987.

Venezia e Bisanzio, exh. cat., Venice, 1974.

VERCI, G.B. *Notizie de' pittori di Bassano*, Venice, 1775.

WAAGEN, G. *Art Treasures in Great Britain*, London, 1857.

ZANETTI, A.M. *Descrizione di tutte le plubbliche pitture*, Venice, 1733.

—. *Della pittura veneziana . . . .*, Venice, 1771.

ZANOTTO, F. *Pinacoteca della I.R. Accademia Veneta delle Belle Arti*, 2 vols., Venice, 1833-34.

ZAVA BOCCAZZI, R. *Pittoni, l'opera completa*, Venice, 1979.

ZERI, F., ed. *La pittura in Italia: Il Quattrocento*, Milan, 1987.